Socialising the Child
in Late Medieval England
c. 1400–1600

YORK MEDIEVAL PRESS

York Medieval Press is published by the University of York's Centre for Medieval Studies in association with Boydell & Brewer Limited. Our objective is the promotion of innovative scholarship and fresh criticism on medieval culture. We have a special commitment to interdisciplinary study, in line with the Centre's belief that the future of Medieval Studies lies in those areas in which its major constituent disciplines at once inform and challenge each other.

Editorial Board (2018)

Professor Peter Biller (Dept of History): General Editor
Dr T. Ayers (Dept of History of Art)
Dr Henry Bainton (Dept of English and Related Literature)
Dr J. W. Binns (Dept of English and Related Literature)
Dr K. P. Clarke (Dept of English and Related Literature)
Dr K. F. Giles (Dept of Archaeology)
Dr Holly James-Maddocks (Dept of English and Related Literature)
Professor W. M. Ormrod (Dept of History)
Professor Sarah Rees-Jones (Dept of History): Director, Centre for Medieval Studies
Dr L. J. Sackville (Dept of History)
Dr Hanna Vorholt (Dept of History of Art)
Professor J. G. Wogan-Browne (English Faculty, Fordham University)

Consultant on Manuscript Publications:

Professor Linne Mooney (Department of English and Related Literature)

All enquiries of an editorial kind, including suggestions for monographs and essay collections, should be addressed to: The Academic Editor, York Medieval Press, University of York, Centre for Medieval Studies, The King's Manor, York, YO1 7EP (E-mail: gmg501@york.ac.uk).

Details of other York Medieval Press volumes are available from Boydell & Brewer Ltd.

Socialising the Child
in Late Medieval England
c. 1400–1600

Merridee L. Bailey

YORK MEDIEVAL PRESS

© Merridee L. Bailey 2012

All rights reserved. Except as permitted under current legislation no part of this work may be photocopied, stored in a retrieval system, published, performed in public, adapted, broadcast, transmitted, recorded or reproduced in any form or by any means, without the prior permission of the copyright owner

The right of Merridee L. Bailey to be identified as the author of this work has been asserted in accordance with sections 77 and 78 of the Copyright, Designs and Patents Act 1998

First published 2012
Paperback edition 2018

A York Medieval Press publication
in association with The Boydell Press
an imprint of Boydell & Brewer Ltd
PO Box 9, Woodbridge, Suffolk IP12 3DF, UK
and of Boydell & Brewer Inc.
668 Mt Hope Avenue, Rochester, NY 14620–2731, USA
website: www.boydellandbrewer.com
and with the
Centre for Medieval Studies, University of York

ISBN 978–1–903153–42–0 hardback
ISBN 978–1–903153–76–5 paperback

A CIP catalogue record for this book is available
from the British Library

The publisher has no responsibility for the continued existence or accuracy of URLs for external or third-party internet websites referred to in this book, and does not guarantee that any content on such websites is, or will remain, accurate or appropriate

CONTENTS

Acknowledgements	vii
Abbreviations	viii
Transcription conventions	ix
Introduction	1
1. Courtesy Poems	11
2. Readers	43
3. Virtue and Vice	79
4. Sixteenth-Century Books	127
5. The School	159
Conclusion	194
Appendix A: English Vernacular Courtesy Poems	203
Appendix B: Incunabula	221
Appendix C: Sixteenth-Century Books	226
Appendix D: Educational Sources	235
Bibliography	243
Index	265

ACKNOWLEDGEMENTS

As one would expect, this book has benefited from the advice and help of a number of people. The first acknowledgment must be to John Tillotson who supervised my doctoral thesis. Stephanie Tarbin and Robert Barnes have also provided invaluable assistance over many years. Thanks must also go to the Research School of Social Sciences in the College of Arts and Social Sciences at the Australian National University where this book was completed. I am also very grateful to the Vice-Chancellor's publication subsidy for a grant towards this book.

While at the Australian National University I benefited enormously from the collegiate atmosphere amongst medieval historians, past and present. Of these, enormous thanks go to Tania Colwell, Julie Hotchin, Libby Keen, Val Spear and Dianne Tillotson for thought-provoking conversations about the medieval world.

In conducting research for this book in both Australia and the United Kingdom, I have been fortunate to have benefited from a Scouloudi Foundation Historical Award which allowed me to carry out research at the British Library where much of this material is located. A grant from The Bibliographical Society also allowed me to study incunabula at Cambridge University Library. Staff at the Bodleian Library were exceptionally helpful, particularly Greg Colley and Dr B. C. Barker-Benfield who assisted with locating obscure manuscripts and early printed books, and discussing various dating issues with me.

Sincere thanks go to Tony Edwards who encouraged me to publish, and to colleagues who read drafts of this book, including Juanita Feros Ruys. In particular, I wish to express my gratitude to Jeremy Goldberg and Helen Jewell for their support, encouragement and enormously helpful comments over many years. I have been indebted to Peter Biller, Jocelyn Wogan-Browne, and Caroline Palmer at York Medieval Press and Boydell for the care and attention they have given to this book. I would also like to mention the late Beryl Rawson and also Christopher Allmand, Philippa Maddern and Elizabeth Archibald for their kindness, support and encouragement. Finally, I thank my family for their help and support.

ABBREVIATIONS

BL	British Library
Bodl.	Bodleian Library
CUL	Cambridge University Library
DNB	*Oxford Dictionary of National Biography*, Oxford University Press at www.oxforddnb.com
EEMM	*Early English Meals and Manners*, ed. F. J. Furnivall, EETS OS 32 (London, 1868)
EETS	Early English Text Society
ES	Extra Series
OS	Original Series
SS	Supplementary Series
Furnivall & Rickert	*The Babees Book, Medieval Manners for the Young*, ed. F. J. F Furnivall and E. Rickert (New York, 1913)
Instructions, d'Evelyn	*Peter Idley's Instructions to his Son*, ed. C. d'Evelyn (Boston, 1935)
Leach, *Edu Chtr*	*Educational Charters and Documents 598–1909*, ed. A. F. Leach (Cambridge, 1911)
LMA	London Metropolitan Archives
Mustanoja	*The Good Wife Taught Her Daughter; The Good Wyfe Wold a Pylgremage; The Thewis of Gud Women*, ed. T. F. Mustanoja (Helsinki, 1948)
OED	*Oxford English Dictionary* at www.oed.com
QEA	*Queene Elizabethes achademy (by Sir Humphrey Gilbert). A booke of precedence; the ordering of a funerall, &c, Varying versions of The good wife, The wise man, &c.; Maxims, Lydgate's Order of fools. A poem on heraldry, Occleve on lord's men, &c. / ed. by F. J. Furnivall, with essays on early Italian and German books of courtesy, by W. M. Rossetti & E. Oswald*, ed. F. J. Furnivall, EETS ES 8 (London, 1869)
SPAM	*Stans puer ad mensam*
TNA	The National Archives

TRANSCRIPTION CONVENTIONS

In transcribing texts, 3 has been typed as 'y'; þ as 'th'; and, ß as 's'. However, in *How the Good Wife Taught her Daughter*, 3 more often stands for 'th' or 'gh' (and may be the result of occasional corruptions in the manuscript from þ).

In Caxton's editions, the final flourish on some words (signalling 'e') has been left off.

Expanded letters appear in square brackets.

INTRODUCTION

'Nature is an effectual thynge, but educacion more effectual.'[1]

This book addresses the socialising roles of the late medieval household and the school. It asks how childhood was imagined by medieval writers and educators and then presented to contemporary child and adult readers. Although several studies have examined medieval childhood, there has been no systematic attempt to place the socialisation of children in late medieval and early modern England into the broader context of society, politics and religion. Childhood represents more than a chronological age or physical form; it is a time of instruction and learning, when relationships and abilities are developed and identity is created. As Erasmus advised, nature is effectual, but 'educacion more effectual'. This book investigates the manner in which late medieval English society looked to children as the standard bearers of good conduct and behaviour, charging socialisation with broader social and political meaning. Each chapter analyses a particular genre of literature that conveys a sense of childhood and children. In doing so, it addresses both chronological as well as thematic shifts in the socialising process, building a picture of childhood over 200 years from the end of medieval England to the early modern period.

I have deliberately chosen the time-frame this book covers in order to encompass both the late medieval and early modern periods. The idea of a boundary between the late medieval and the early modern still remains pervasive, despite a growing interest over the last several decades in collapsing such boundaries[2] and using sources that seem to be both medieval and early modern. These boundaries, although variable and permeable in reality, have tended to lead to an arbitrary and often false marking out of territory. This book contributes to the challenge to relax, or at least traverse, the supposed margins between these periods and to introduce more subtlety to our understanding of childhood in England over the late medieval and early modern

---

1   R. Sherry, *A treatise of schemes [and] tropes very profytable for the better vnderstanding of good authors, gathered out of the best grammarians [and] oratours by Rychard Sherry Londoner. Whervnto is added a declamacion, that chyldren euen strapt fro[m] their infancie should be wel and gently broughte vp in learnynge. Written fyrst in Latin by the most excellent and famous clearke, Erasmus of Roterodame* (London, 1550), Bvii^v.
2   Judith Bennett discusses perceptions of 'the medieval' and 'the early-modern' in J. M. Bennett, 'Medieval Women, Modern Women: Across the Great Divide', in *Culture and History, 1350–1600: Essays on English Communities, Identities and Writing*, ed. D. Aers (Detroit, 1992), pp. 147–75.

periods. Indeed, throughout this book conflicting and sometimes contradictory attitudes to childhood are illuminated. Contradictory attitudes are not to be rejected, but rather celebrated as a way of understanding the richness and colour of late medieval and early modern childhood and the flexibility of attitudes to the socialising process.[3]

In this book, socialisation is defined as the social norms, ideologies and customs presented to young people as they moved from infancy to *pueritia*, then into adolescence and eventually, adulthood. These life stages correspond to the medieval ages of man borrowed from the classical world which divide life-cycles into at least three, and as many as twelve, stages. Shulamith Shahar's 1990 *Childhood in the Middle Ages* was one of the first books to convincingly use medieval classifications to demonstrate the physical and mental characteristics of medieval childhood.[4] Nicholas Orme's discussion of the 'ages of man' observes that only the Latin *infantia* (infancy) and *adolescentia* (adolescence) have remained in common usage.[5] Of these ages, it is *pueritia* (delineating the stage after infancy and before adolescence) and *adolescentia* which best represent the children discussed throughout this book. In many of the cases identified in this study, courtesy literature is profoundly relevant to children and young people between the ages of seven and twenty. These texts engage with the development of formative behaviour and teach crucial lessons about society, lessons best learnt when young. *How the Wise Man Taught his Son* specifically refers to a youth of fifteen years. In other poems youthful characters are described with the words 'babee', 'child', 'children', 'young', 'young man' or 'son'. Often the complexity of rules, the types of manners described and the variety and skill of the activities suggest an appropriate age.

Households and families are the basic units of western society. Recognition of the late medieval household as an emotional and functional site, reflecting and shaping the interests of the nation, allows us to explore childhood inside a specific locale, subject to the pressures of an increasingly volatile political and religious environment.[6] Exploring these households takes us into the world of late medieval social mobility, religious change, mercantile practices and elite-bourgeois diversity. Children and young people were participants in these worlds. The manner in which they were socialised says a great deal about English identity and culture: an observation made in the fifteenth century by a Venetian traveller to England who remarked on the

---

[3] For childhood in other periods and geographical areas see B. Rawson, *Children and Childhood in Roman Italy* (Oxford, 2003); S. Crawford, *Childhood in Anglo-Saxon England* (Stroud, 1999); and J. A. Schultz, *The Knowledge of Childhood in the German Middle Ages, 1100–1350* (Philadelphia, 1995).

[4] S. Shahar, *Childhood in the Middle Ages* (London, 1990), pp. 21–31.

[5] N. Orme, *Medieval Children* (New Haven, 2001), pp. 6–7.

[6] S. D. Amussen, 'Punishment, Discipline, and Power: The Social Meanings of Violence in Early Modern England', *Journal of British Studies* 34 (1995), 1–34.

Introduction

means by which the English, unlike other Europeans, commonly sent their children out of the natal home to be trained.[7]

These households saw to the needs of children according to the social and economic pressures they encountered. Social status necessarily influences the nature of the socialising process. Literary evidence, principally gathered from courtesy poems, reflects the extent to which a household's socialising responsibilities reproduced the broader social characteristics of its class: the elite household demonstrates a different set of interests from that of a bourgeois household; the elite's interest in courtesy and observable behaviour is different from the interests of merchants. Such disparity, however, does not give a total picture of the properties of this literature or the nature of medieval hierarchy. The degrees of separation between elite and bourgeois reading material, the manner and reason of changing literary ideals across social classes and the subtle gradations in socialising norms at different moments in history address more directly the issues of social identity and mobility in late medieval England. These changes are not evaluated as reflecting boundaries between the medieval and early modern but rather serve to demonstrate permeability over a 200-year period as ideas about childhood, courtesy and morality formed in cyclical ways.

The approach used throughout this book is to look at the preoccupations of intellectuals, writers and parents in order to understand the manner in which childhood was recognised. Extensive use is made of courtesy poems, didactic tracts and instructional manuals from the fifteenth and sixteenth centuries to gauge apprehensions and philosophies of childhood. Contemporary manuscripts and printed books offer diverse perspectives on the dynamics of childhood and of how children were perceived. Running throughout this book is the theme of literary texts in their broader context, particularly the means by which family organisation, household formation and educational practices affected, and were affected by, literary ideals. This book draws heavily on normative portrayals of childhood, which do not cover pragmatic concerns with misbehaving children, indifferent parents or economic realities. Anna Dronzek has reminded us that the ideal of didactic literature is a useful way of uncovering what has been privileged in medieval philosophy.[8]

England was not a monoglot linguistic culture. We now know the extent to which the Anglo-Norman language thrived in England after the Norman Conquest and it appears that written and spoken French was used by a greater

---

[7] See *Women in England c. 1275–1525: Documentary Sources*, translated and edited by P. J. P. Goldberg (Manchester, 1995), pp. 87–8.

[8] A. Dronzek, 'Gendered Theories of Education in Fifteenth-Century Conduct Books', in *Medieval Conduct*, ed. K. Ashley and R. L. A. Clark (Minneapolis, 2001), pp. 135 59 (p. 136).

range of people than previously supposed.⁹ French language indicators have been discovered in Latin estate accounts, in municipal accounts of bridge building in regional areas and in medical treatises.¹⁰ It also appears that non-aristocratic professionals were comfortable speaking French well into the fourteenth and fifteenth centuries. Work on French–English bilingualism, and trilingualism when one includes Latin, provides a useful context to the development of courtesy material in the fifteenth century, whether it is in the English vernacular or otherwise. The long-standing tradition of *corteisie* in French material circulating in England since the twelfth century provides a longer history to the *courtesy* of the English vernacular literature. Such linguistic history offers a starting point for the study of English vernacular texts and particularly the manner in which the concept of courtesy was dealt with in the fifteenth century in the majority of English language sources.

While French, Latin and English created a rich linguistic society, there are unique relationships between the English vernacular and literature and between the English vernacular and the construction of English nationhood and identity. By the end of the fifteenth century fifty-nine per cent of incunabula were of English vernacular composition, with Latin following at thirty-three per cent and Law French at eight per cent. In comparison, over seventy per cent of European incunabula were in Latin.¹¹ There is no doubt that literature in the English vernacular made texts accessible to a greater class range of readers, even given the use of French at the non-aristocratic level. Early English vernacular printing has been cited as an important determinant of national identity: William Kuskin has shown that English printing was connected to the creation of English national identity in the late fifteenth century.¹² How far this can be extended into the sixteenth century is one of the interests of this study. To that end the decision has been made to include sixteenth-century material of both English and Continental origin.

This book draws on several branches of history and literary criticism. Models of literary transmission are addressed throughout, and I note the

---

⁹ *The Anglo-Norman Language and its Contexts*, ed. R. Ingham (York, 2010), p. 1. *Language and Culture in Medieval Britain: The French of England c. 1100–c. 1500*, ed. J. Wogan-Browne et al. (York, 2009) contains many insightful essays.

¹⁰ R. Ingham, 'Mixing Languages on the Manor', *Medium Aevum* 78 (2009), 80–97; D. Trotter, 'Bridging the Gap: The (Socio)linguistic Evidence of Some Medieval English Bridge Accounts', in *The Anglo-Norman Language and its Contexts*, ed. R. Ingham (York, 2010), pp. 52–62; M. H. Green, 'Salerno on the Thames: The Genesis of Anglo-Norman Medical Literature', in *Language and Culture in Medieval Britain: The French of England c. 1100–c. 1500*, ed. J. Wogan-Browne et al. (York, 2009), pp. 220–31.

¹¹ See *The Cambridge History of the Book in Britain, Vol. III, 1400–1557*, ed. L. Hellinga and J. B. Trapp (Cambridge, 1999), p. 17.

¹² W. Kuskin, '"Onely Imagined": Vernacular Community and the English Press', in *Caxton's Trace: Studies in the History of English Printing*, ed. W. Kuskin (Notre Dame, 2006), pp. 199–240.

work of Linne Mooney on medieval manuscript commissioning, commercial scribes and scribal collaborations.[13] Detailed work by Jeremy Goldberg on poll tax records offers insightful evidence about urban families and servants in the fourteenth century.[14] Fascinating work by C. M. Woolgar on elite households uses household ordinances and accounts to understand the organisation and formation of the noble medieval household in late medieval England.[15] Courtesy literature offers a complementary perspective to this work on service and households, and frames questions about household membership, domestic service and food arrangements with the means by which contemporary writers imagined these spaces as emotional, and not just functional, sites.[16]

Male experiences of childhood are easier to unearth in late medieval England than female experiences, although Kim Phillips's significant study of young women provides insights into adolescent femininity.[17] Contemporary literature discusses male socialisation more frequently than female socialisation, with some notable exceptions: the mid-fourteenth century poem *How the Good Wife Taught her Daughter* and de la Tour Landry's didactic manual written in French and translated into English in 1484 by Caxton formulate theories on the upbringing of young women, and as such are important exemplars of female socialisation. In the next century two conduct books for girls were translated into English from Continental sources: Juan Luis Vives' *De Institutione Foeminae Christianae* was translated by Richard Hyrde, and Giovanni Michele Bruto's *La institutione di vna fanciulla nata nobilmente* by Thomas Salter and William Phiston. Why English authors did not write conduct material for girls and instead drew on conservative Continental examples warrants further investigation and is discussed later. The comparison of different types of sources relevant to each of the sexes creates particular difficulties and risks

---

[13] L. Mooney with L. M. Matheson, 'The Beryn Scribe and his Texts: Evidence for Multiple-Copy Production of Manuscripts in Fifteenth-Century England', *The Library* 7th s. 4 (2003), 347–70. Also L. Mooney, 'John Shirley's Heirs', *Yearbook of English Studies* 33 (2003), 182–98; L. Mooney, 'Professional Scribes?: Identifying English Scribes Who Had a Hand in More Than One Manuscript', in *New Directions in Medieval Manuscript Studies*, ed. D. Pearsall (York, 2000), pp. 131–41.

[14] P. J. P. Goldberg, 'Urban Identity and the Poll Taxes of 1377, 1379, and 1381', *Economic History Review* n.s. 43 (1990), 194–216.

[15] C. M. Woolgar, *Household Accounts from Medieval England*, 2 vols. (Oxford, 1992–3); C. M. Woolgar, *The Great Household in Late Medieval England* (New Haven, 1999). Kate Mertes has also written on this in *The English Noble Household 1250–1600: Good Governance and Politic Rule* (Oxford, 1988).

[16] For studies on food consumption in medieval England see C. M. Woolgar, 'Food and the Middle Ages', *Journal of Medieval History* 36 (2010), 1–19. Also, C. M. Woolgar, 'Fast and Feast: Conspicuous Consumption and the Diet of the Nobility in the Fifteenth Century', in *Revolution and Consumption in Late Medieval England*, ed. M. A. Hicks (Woodbridge, 2001), pp. 7–26.

[17] K. M. Phillips, *Medieval Maidens: Young Women and Gender in England, 1270–1540* (Manchester, 2003).

drawing conclusions that are based on the comparison of dissimilar sources instead of disparity in gender assumptions.[18]

A wide range of sources is available for a study of this type. A conscious decision has been made to focus on a particular genre: that of courtesy material. Latin moral exemplars, such as the fifteenth-century collections lifted from Valerius Maximus's writings, penitential lyrics, romances, printed sermons and pamphlets also resonate with the themes explored throughout this study, principally moral identity, conduct and courtly ideals. However, true courtesy material, by which I mean the collection of poems loosely categorised as dealing with the conduct and manners of young people in noble households, is the most apposite configuration of literature that explores the themes of childhood behaviour, ideals of conduct and manners in late medieval England. Courtesy poems are in fact loosely concerned with a number of subject matters, including serving at the lord's table, ways of eating, how to talk to companions at mealtimes and the household duties of a high-status young servant.[19] Linked to these are religious and educational themes, important in their own right but usually subordinated to distinctively pragmatic lessons. This, along with other linguistic and textual features including shortened length, absence of named characters and narrative story arcs, sets courtesy literature apart from chivalric and romance material.

Chapters 1 and 2 address poems with sustained narratives of varying lengths. Most of these poems appear in a number of manuscripts, and manuscript variations are extensively analysed throughout. Chapter 1 focuses on core elite themes in *Stans puer ad mensam*, *The Babees Book*, *Urbanitatis*, *The Lytylle Childrene's Book* and *the boke of curtasye*. John Russell's *Boke of Nurture* is substantially longer and different in tone, and the task of assessing its elite characteristics is more problematic, but it includes detailed instructions on noble household offices and is used to highlight the applied nature of socialising norms for young people, information absent from other sources. Finally, the poem *How the Wise Man Taught his Son* is used to compare these texts to a contemporary (fictional) dialogue between a father and his son.[20]

---

[18] A. Dronzek, 'Gender Roles and the Marriage Market in Fifteenth-Century England: Ideals and Practices', in *Love, Marriage, and Family Ties in the Later Middle Ages*, ed. I. Davis, M. Müller and S. Rees Jones (Turnhout, 2003), pp. 63–76.

[19] For the Latin tradition of courtesy literature see S. Gieben, 'Robert Grosseteste and Medieval Courtesy Books', *Vivarium* 5 (1967), 47–74.

[20] I have excluded the *ABC of Aristotle*, about which an excellent article has been written by Martha Dana Rust, 'The "ABC of Aristotle"', in *Medieval Literature for Children*, ed. D. Kline (New York, 2003), pp. 63–78. Furnivall transcribed and published numerous courtesy poems in several anthologies, including *Queene Elizabethes achademy* (*QEA*), *Early English Meals and Manners* (*EEMM*) as well as Rickert's edition of *The Babees' Book*, taken from Furnivall's texts (Furnivall & Rickert). This antiquarian work should not be dismissed too readily. It was meticulous and painstaking and care was taken to offer accurate transcripts according to the standards of the time.

Introduction

In Chapter 2, the analysis of these poems is extended to interpolated and variant manuscripts from the fifteenth century. Sylvia Huot has demonstrated that variations in over 200 manuscripts containing the thirteenth-century poem *Romance of the Rose* establish how scribes and readers conceptualised, modified and glossed material as they chose. Courtesy poems are less rarely used to investigate multiple and intrinsically different readings of the courtesy theme. Often they are read in diplomatic editions or antiquarian transcripts where editors have chosen the 'best' version of a poem or else have rewritten the text in modern idiom. It is perhaps because of this literature's relationship to children that its linguistic features are seen as less important, devaluing the study of variant readings. *Stans puer ad mensam* is extensively altered in manuscript Ashmole 61 and illuminates the means by which modifications of the courtesy theme substantially alter assumptions about reading audiences. Chapter 2 also investigates the manner in which certain courtesy poems became increasingly associated with non-elite households, offering alternative statements about socialisation from those discussed in other courtesy texts. Here, *The Lytylle Childrene's Book*, *The Young Children's Book* and Peter Idley's *Instructions to His Son* are investigated for a new and different presence of morality hidden within the courtesy topos. Three courtesy poems for girls – *How the Good Wife Taught her Daughter*, *The Good Wyfe Wold a Pylgremage* and *The Thewis off Gud Women* – highlight how courtesy and morality had a significant relationship with the socialisation of young girls, and comparisons are made to bourgeois and mercantile reading groups.

Since courtesy poems engage with expectations of conduct and behaviour, throughout this book the movement of English vernacular courtesy literature from the elite household and into the gentry, merchant and urban bourgeois household is investigated. This is extended both chronologically and thematically by widening the survey of literature to include printed books composed in the English vernacular, first by evaluating six books from William Caxton's Westminster press and second by analysing a number of the most important instruction manuals from the sixteenth century. These latter sources allow the theme of lay readership to be evaluated, and comparisons can be made to models of reading networks prior to this.

Tracing the means by which technological advances in early printing, such as the increased production of books, greater range of texts, development of elaborate typesets and more detailed title pages, affected the transmission of ideas for non-elite audiences is a particularly important thread that ties together chapters 3 and 4. The speed of change, partly due to books becoming progressively more available, especially in London and its close

---

Anyone wishing to survey extant courtesy texts would be well advised to start here. The courtesy poems examined in chapters 1 and 2 nevertheless represent a considerable proportion of extant texts aimed at both genders. Every effort has been made to view and examine variant manuscripts.

environs, sets out a model for the spread of ideas to non-elite readers. Work on the history of the book has been particularly preoccupied with identifying how and when the transition between manuscript and print took place and the degree to which printing influenced literary and cultural ideas. Adrian Johns and David McKitterick have analysed early printing culture in terms of social context and slow change.[21] This provides a useful context for analysing the nature of change in courtesy and, more generally, instructional literature in the late fifteenth and sixteenth centuries. Attentive discussion of variant print editions of a text, long a staple of manuscript studies, also throws into sharper relief the relationship between texts and reading communities.

Few of these insights into early printing have been applied to the study of children's literature. William Kuskin has argued that Caxton contributed to shaping and defining late fifteenth century literary culture through publishing 'ideologically complex' works. The publication of the Worthies Series has demonstrated by what means three separate books, unified by common themes, shaped literary culture by presenting readers with a cohesive unit of titles to read.[22] It is worthwhile noting that nine per cent of Caxton's known output is relevant to youths; this is a significant group of literature and worth attention. This idea is developed in Chapter 3, where six didactic books relevant to younger people are identified as part of a specific genre or series. Excluded are *Reynard the Fox* and the *Fables of Aesop*, which do not engage with notions of childhood socialisation. Both, however, are useful in demonstrating the extent of Caxton's interests in publishing material relevant to young audiences, even if they do not fall within the instructional/household genre of this study.[23]

Chapter 4 concludes with instructional manuals published in the sixteenth century. Household or parental advice books have been selected as they are the most likely to contain extended references to children. This chapter investigates the means by which socialisation was articulated in response to religious disruption, and comparisons are made with the earlier courtesy literature investigated in chapters 1 and 2. The increasingly prominent role of the household and fatherly authority in the socialisation of children is explored. Male authority is a standard tenet of legal and religious texts, and instructional literature from this period drew heavily on the presupposition of the father's presence in the household.

---

[21] A. Johns, *The Nature of the Book: Print Culture and Knowledge in the Making* (Chicago, 1998). Also, D. McKitterick, *Print, Manuscript, and the Search for Order, 1450–1830* (New York, 2003).

[22] W. Kuskin, 'Caxton's Worthies Series: The Production of Literary Culture', *English Literary History* 66 (1999), 511–51.

[23] Based on Freida Penninger's figures of Caxton's overall publications. F. E. Penninger, *William Caxton* (Boston, 1979), p. 17.

Introduction

The sources used in Chapter 4 correlate to Chilton Powell's seminal work on English domestic conduct books. The intrinsically English nature of this literature has been highlighted, 'although foreign books continued to be translated, the continuation and development of the writing of books concerning domestic affairs may be said to have been almost entirely a native product'.[24] This is tested through the investigation of books which represent the domestic English market; the works of Richard Whitford, Robert Shelford and William Vaughan are all included, as is material translated by Richard Hyrde (from Juan Luis Vives), Thomas Salter and William Phiston (from Giovanni Michele Bruto). Part of this chapter revisits the presence of courtesy in the sixteenth century. Two books published by Hugh Rhodes and Francis Seager are relevant to the earlier fifteenth century courtesy archive. The motif of the household also corresponds to earlier fifteenth century material which related socialisation to household issues and environments.

Chapter 5 goes outside the study of household literature to assess ways in which socialisation was imagined within the school and discussed within contemporary educational sources; these include grammar school statutes, school account books, printed Latin grammars and published educational books. The themes of courteous and moral socialisation are thus transferred out of the domestic household environment and into a formal educational context. Pedagogues expressed concerns with socialisation in terms of religion, obedience, conduct, manners and virtue, and their arguments illuminate the manner in which socialising concerns were dealt with in different locations by different people.[25] This analysis begins with some late fourteenth century sources which establish a longer context for the role of educational institutions in socialising boys, in conjunction with and sometimes exceeding the role of the household. It is the fifteenth century, however, which witnesses the greatest bulk of educational material. This study thus analyses educational upbringing against a context of changing religious practices. Comparisons are drawn with courtesy and moral literature; educational narratives repeat common phrases, concerns and issues located within didactic texts. Socialisation for girls remained more firmly attached to the household, as discussed in chapters 2 and 4.

---

[24] C. Powell, *English Domestic Relations, 1487–1653: A Study of Matrimony and Family Life in Theory and Practice as Revealed by the Literature, Law, and History of the Period* (New York, 1917), p. 101.

[25] On virtue in childhood socialisation see S. Dixon, *The Roman Mother* (London, 1988). Several chapters in *Hoping for Continuity: Childhood, Education and Death in Antiquity and the Middle Ages*, ed. K. Mustakallio, J. Hanska, H-L. Sainio and V. Vuolanto (Rome, 2005) are relevant. See also C. B. Horn and J. W. Martens, *'Let the little children come to me': Childhood and Children in Early Christianity* (Washington, 2009). On virtue generally see M. Linton, *The Politics of Virtue in Enlightenment France* (Basingstoke, 2001).

Studying medieval childhood is, of course, different from studying medieval children.[26] Studying theories of socialisation necessarily privileges the former, focusing as it does on the characteristics of childhood and dominant (and therefore usually adult) perspectives on this time. We come closer to examining medieval children by looking at children's relationships with their peers or the manner in which children engaged with or understood childhood events and activities. The benefit of literature is that it provides a sense of both childhood and children. One author will perhaps emphasise the role of a senior adult servant as a voice of experience and authority while another offers a more nuanced picture of children's activities and play. Such is the case with the influential *Stans puer ad mensam*. While this book therefore recounts childhood socialisation, the interests and preoccupations of children are not ignored.

---

[26] The debate on medieval childhood which began with Philippe Ariès' 1960 *L'enfant et la vie familiale sous l'ancien régime*, translated by Robert Baldick, *Centuries of Childhood* (London, 1962), is now so well-known and well-trodden a path that it need not be much discussed here beyond noting in briefest terms the general outline of claims that followed. Several historians in the 1970s took up the argument of childhood either being invisible or a time of abuse, notably in *The History of Childhood*, ed. L. deMause (New York, 1974); L. Stone, *The Family, Sex and Marriage in England 1500–1800* (London, 1977) and E. Shorter, *The Making of the Modern Family* (London, 1976). A second wave of historians during the 1990s and early 2000s were more willing to credit childhood as a time of nurture, with unique characteristics and distinctiveness, including Linda A. Pollock, Shulamith Shahar, Barbara Hanawalt and more recently Nicholas Orme. See L. A. Pollock, *Forgotten Children: Parent–Child Relations from 1500–1900* (Cambridge, 1983); L. A. Pollock, *A Lasting Relationship: Parents and Children Over Three Centuries* (London, 1986); Shahar, *Childhood in the Middle Ages*; B. A. Hanawalt, *The Ties That Bound: Peasant Families in Medieval England* (New York, 1986); B. A. Hanawalt, *Growing Up in Medieval London: The Experience of Childhood in History* (New York, 1993). Orme's early work on education (relevant to many issues in historical childhood) is extensive. A key later work which specifically addresses childhood is *Medieval Children*. Any reader who is interested in the historiography of historical childhood should read P. J. P. Goldberg, F. Riddy and M. Tyler, 'Introduction: After Ariès', in *Youth in the Middle Ages*, ed. P. J. P. Goldberg and F. Riddy (York, 2004), pp. 1–10 as well as Pollock, *Forgotten Children*, pp. 1–67; C. Heywood, *A History of Childhood: Children and Childhood in the West from Medieval to Modern Times* (Cambridge, 2001), pp. 3–22; and H. Cunningham, 'Histories of Childhood', *American Historical Review* 103 (1998), 1195–1208. For a review of Ariès, see A. Wilson, 'The Infancy of the History of Childhood: An Appraisal of Philippe Ariès', *History and Theory* 19 (1980), 132–53.

CHAPTER ONE

Courtesy Poems

> 'Curteis he was, lowely, and servysable,
> And carf biforn his fader at the table'[1]

A young boy sits alone reading a courtesy poem, or sits with his peers hearing it read aloud by an older male of the household. He reads, or hears, that he must show courtesy if he wishes to be considered a gentleman, possibly that he must even be of royal blood truly to appreciate the lessons he is about to discover in these pages of manuscript. He will walk with his lord in the great hall of an elite household estate, he will show care when he eats and he will not stare or gawp at those he meets in the household.

What did a young boy make of this? According to the poems, he was already a young man occupying a high status position in an elite household, serving the lord in a highly ritualised, personal and, above all, elite role. This may well have been true. The motif of youthful service, and particularly in what manner young boys were to serve courteously in households, reflected the organisational structure of the establishments of the nobility which, in the thirteenth century, could be as much as ninety per cent male.[2] Some of these households did in fact own courtesy books; for instance, the duke of Buckingham's household purchased courtesy books, primers and grammars at the beginning of the sixteenth century for the children.[3] More likely, though, our anonymous boy reading or listening to one of the many courtesy poems found in English vernacular manuscripts was a young son from a gentry family who might have been participating in an intricate and highly politicised child-exchange, common in the medieval period. In the fourteenth century, gentle servants belonging to the social rank above that of

---

[1] These attributes given to the Squire in the *Canterbury Tales* could be drawn straight from the courtesy poems, yet we should keep in mind that Chaucer's Squire was both twenty years of age and had already served in France. *The Works of Geoffrey Chaucer*, ed. F. N. Robinson, 2nd edn (Oxford, 1957), p. 18.

[2] Woolgar, *Great Household*, p. 8. In this book, the term 'nobility' follows Christine Carpenter's definition of the nobility as 'the peerage or men of equivalent standing, even when they were not legally peers'. C. Carpenter, *Locality and Polity: A Study of Warwickshire Landed Society, 1401–1499* (Cambridge, 1992), pp. 35–6.

[3] Mertes, *English Noble Household*, pp. 172–3.

the yeomanry or peasantry made up a significant fraction of the workforce in large households.[4] A high proportion of these gentle servants came from privileged backgrounds, with children from the age of seven placed into households to practise and learn courtesy. Throughout the fourteenth century the status of gentle service rose as a result of its value in advancing the younger sons of gentry families.[5] It is worth noting that the custom of child-exchange was less common in England by the end of the sixteenth century and that there is a noticeable rise in literature that refers to the father and to the small kin-household at this time. Before this, however, elite and gentry families moved into and out of particular classes via deaths, marriages, fostering, child-exchanges, wealth both lost and won, as well as with movements backwards and forwards between urban and rural centres.

How gentry sons were socialised according to elite ideas says a great deal about late medieval class structures and the changes that were taking place in English society as gentry families became increasingly determined to differentiate themselves from the yeomanry and from the wealthy merchants and urban bourgeois, while claiming an affinity to the nobility with whom they shared the characteristics of gentility.[6] Lines between these groups were in a constant state of flux. The boundary between merchants and the gentry was particularly permeable and the fifteenth century sees merchants and gentlemen equated in precedence lists.[7] Conversely, this helps us see how courtesy literature was able to speak to the broadest possible audiences in late medieval England, excluding the peasantry, whose social status and economic realities were obstacles to entering the courteous sphere that could not be easily surmounted. Courtesy literature itself contrasted the behaviours of a chosen social group with those seen as below it. In this way members of the nobility could, and did, distinguish themselves from the gentry, the gentry from the yeomanry, and so on. Courtesy literature was malleable enough to call attention to, and bemoan, inferior social behaviour seen as coming from any, or even all, of these groups.

---

[4] Woolgar, *Great Household*, pp. 20, 37.
[5] Mertes, *English Noble Household*, p. 186.
[6] There were significant differences within the gentry class. On this see M. Keen, *Origins of the English Gentleman: Heraldry, Chivalry and Gentility in Medieval England, c.1300–c.1500* (Stroud, 2002); G. Harriss, *Shaping the Nation, England, 1360–1461* (Oxford, 2005), pp. 137–40.
[7] R. Horrox, 'The Urban Gentry in the Fifteenth Century', in *Towns and Townspeople in the Fifteenth Century*, ed. J. A. F. Thomson (Gloucester, 1988), pp. 22–44 (pp. 32–3). Ambiguities in defining gentry status were acknowledged as problematic even at the time. The importance of public perception of status was particularly important and Keen suggests that it was recognition as being of the gentry class that established status. Keen, *Origins of the English Gentleman*, pp. 103–5.

Courtesy Poems

This chapter considers the nature of the lessons that were taught in courtesy poems and the attitudes towards both intangible and practical attributes, ranging from meekness to good table manners, which had been embodied in figures like the Squire from Chaucer's *Canterbury Tales*. While there was no single courtesy ideology in the late medieval period, poems about behaviour and misbehaviour, serving at the table, eating and talking to others expressed male behavioural traits that were part of a larger socialising system. These were constructed around models of youthful conduct which were conveyed according to distinctions of class and status. While supposedly rigid, they were in fact fluid and shifting. This chapter looks at the manner in which, over two centuries, the canon of courtesy poems demonstrates the presence of particular youthful masculine values, some of which were particular to men and some of which were also presented as ambiguously genderless.

This medieval rhetoric about male youthfulness and socialisation reveals boyhood duties, masculine behaviour and conduct which appealed to a strongly aristocratic identity. While the socialising lessons in courtesy poems play upon the ideologies and concerns of England's aristocracy, for the most part it was families within the gentry and merchant classes which owned the manuscripts in which courtesy poems are found. By buying and copying these texts, gentry and merchant families appropriated elements of behaviour and conduct seen to exist within elite and royal circles, allowing young men from the middle range of the social hierarchy to be praised for their aristocratic courtesy. While demographic household trends are significant, these contemporary authors also wrote about the social household and young people, using language and characteristics that were most important to them. This literature was one of the means through which elite courtesy, social movements and transitions were interpreted and discussed. While these works address the actual practices and internal dynamics of large households in late medieval England, they also relate to the even more complex dynamics between elite society and the socialisation of children from wider class groups.

This chapter considers these issues in more detail as the following seven poems are examined: *Stans puer ad mensam, The Babees Book, Urbanitatis, The Lytylle Childrene's Book, the boke of curtasye*, John Russell's *Boke of Nurture* and *How the Wise Man Taught his Son*. Throughout, attention will be paid to the means by which the youthful characters, mostly anonymously portrayed in the poems, reflect actual socialising experiences, as well as the manner in which the elite household was presented through descriptions of spaces. Equally, the recycling of themes and ideas across courtesy poems suggests not only a chronic shortage of material, but also a desire in gentry and merchant society to retain deeply conservative ideals about young people.

Male socialisation

High status lifestyles were rooted in the realities of inheritance rights, the legal right to rule and furthering family connections linked to the on-going goal of family prosperity.[8] These themes are in fact routinely excluded from courtesy poems. Disinheritance is not referred to in courtesy literature: neither is marriage, which is unusual considering its importance in both high status peer networks and amongst gentry groups. Father–son relationships, along with the idea of promoting and advancing the family name, are also absent. Given the reality of youthful movements into these households it is worth noting that these poems do not take the opportunity to refer explicitly to broader family responsibilities or the father's role in his children's lives. Historians have noticed a lack of direct detail on father–son relationships, but this observation may be a product of their preoccupation with seeing the father–son relationship as an important step in the socialising process. Certainly courtesy poems do not explore this relationship. Two exceptions exist to the 'missing father' rule in courtesy poems: *How the Wise Man Taught his Son* and Peter Idley's *Instructions to his Son*. In addition, two of the three courtesy poems for girls in the *Good Wife* tradition use a parental metaphor, although here it is the mother's voice which is heard.[9] These poems demonstrate a stronger mercantile, or bourgeois, ethic and will be discussed in the following chapter.

Fathers assumed household and parental responsibility for both children and servants and by the late fifteenth century commonly appear in normative accounts as legal and spiritual custodians of male and female household members. The absence of father figures from this literature is most likely a consequence of the emphasis on elite households to where young people moved on leaving their natal homes. Judging by the prevalence of child-exchanges in England in this period, the transfer of young people reinforced family and political networks and provided the affluent classes with access to higher status households.[10] The absence of parental authority does

---

[8] J. R. Lyon, 'Fathers and Sons: Preparing Noble Youths to be Lords in Twelfth-Century Germany', *Journal of Medieval History* 34 (2008), 291–310; W. H. Dunham Jr. and C. T. Wood, 'The Right to Rule in England: Depositions and the Kingdom's Authority, 1327–1485', *American Historical Review* 81 (1976), 738–61; M. Hagger, 'Kinship and Identity in Eleventh-Century Normandy: The Case of Hugh de Grandmesnil, *c.* 1040–1098', *Journal of Medieval History* 32 (2006), 212–30; C. D. Fletcher, 'Narrative and Political Strategies at the Deposition of Richard II', *Journal of Medieval History* 30 (2004), 323–41.

[9] J. F. Ruys, 'Peter Abelard's *Carmen ad Astralabium* and Medieval Parent–Child Didactic Texts: The Evidence for Parent–Child Relationships in the Middle Ages', in *Childhood in the Middle Ages and the Renaissance: The Results of a Paradigm Shift in the History of Mentality*, ed. A. Classen (Berlin, 2005), pp. 203–27.

[10] Child-exchanges have been discussed in anthropological terms. See G. McCracken

not, however, take into account the reality of elite households with their firmly established hierarchies. While fathers were absent from supervising duties, young people were clearly supervised by other adults; these were roles filled by ushers, marshals, stewards, butlers and, of course, the lord. *The boke of curtasye* reminds audiences of this: 'Whille marshall[e] or vssher come fro the dore / And bydde the sitte or to borde the lede'.[11] A number of courtesy poems suggest, however, that even these adult figures were not responsible for the behaviour of young males. Rather than being a mark of neglect, this theme positions socialising lessons more directly onto young people themselves. This is illustrated in lessons where the child or young person appears as the main protagonist of the socialising method. In *Stans puer ad mensam* the child is consistently addressed with the pronoun 'thi', as in 'Ageyne the post let not thi backe a byde' and 'be ryght well ware & this in thi thoght'.[12] This directly appeals to the child or young person as an active and individual participant in the socialising lesson. The regular use of 'thi' also reinforces a sense of inferiority: 'thou' is associated with address to an inferior. On this point Margaret Higonnet suggests that first-person narratives create 'voluntary self-discipline', proposing 'we must speak the poem in our own voices, affixing our own names at the end'.[13] Courtesy poems use a similar notion of self-discipline by promoting children and young people as individuals who are responsible for their own actions. The result is that the self-monitoring of behaviour is a key feature in the socialisation of young boys. Given the emphasis on self-monitoring in the poems, this attitude is worth exploring further as part of the debate on historical concepts of childhood.

Self-responsibility in these poems rests upon two counter-balancing trends. First, the child is a responsible agent of their own socialisation, while, secondly, they are still in need of knowledge. This is well illustrated in many of the opening lines in courtesy poems which emphasise the presence of an experienced adult who possesses knowledge of courtesy: this is often the

---

'The Exchange of Children in Tudor England: An Anthropological Phenomenon in Historical Context', *Journal of Family History* 8 (1983), 303–13. See also P. Fumerton, *Cultural Aesthetics: Renaissance Literature and the Practice of Social Ornament* (Chicago, 1991), pp. 36–44.

[11] London, BL, MS Sloane 1986, fol. 12ᵛ. Adult authority is directly referred to in Caxton's *Book of Curtesye*:

> Be ye husht in chambre scylent in halle
> Herken wel ande gyue goode audience
> Yf vssher or marchal for ony Rumour calle
> Put ye Iauglers to rebuke for silence

Book of Curtesye (Westminster, 1477), 5ᵛ.

[12] London, BL, MS Stowe 982, fol. 10ʳ.

[13] M. R. Higonnet, 'Civility Books, Child Citizens, and Uncivil Antics', *Poetics Today* 13 (1992), 123–40 (p. 132).

voice of the author or narrator. In contrast to this voice, the inexperienced young person is in need of advice. John Russell's the *Boke of Nurture* begins by identifying the experienced adult (Russell) and the inexperienced young man, and this is used as a stage to introduce rules governing behaviour. In the following lines the first-person narrative is used:

> Sonne yf I the teche wylte thou hit lere
> wylte thou be clerke marchaute or artyfycere
> Chamberlayne butteler panter or a kerv (carver)
> ussher sewer ploweman or laborer

The young person directly replies to this offer in the response:

> Off the office of butteler pant[er] and chaberlayne
> Sewer kerv uss[h]er ewer[er] for tayne
> And yema[n] of the seler I fayne
> All thesse to lerne I wolde be rygte fayne

Russell completes this exchange by confirming his intentions: 'Sonne I shalt theche ye with ryght goode wyll'.[14] As a result of this first-person exchange the boy is shown to be a primary figure who can be prevailed upon to undertake learning.

Similar roles are revealed in other poems. The introduction to *Stans puer ad mensam*, in manuscript Ashmole 61, calls attention to youth (inexperience) versus age (experience) in the following way:

> Now chyld take gode hed[e] what th[at] I wyll sey
> My do[c]tryn[e] to th[ee] I p[ur]pos to be gyn[e]
> Herkyn well th[er] to [and] go no awey
> Godd[es] g[ra]ce be w[ith] vs now [and] eu[er] mo[re] Amen[15]

A further account shows by what means age, as opposed to inexperience, reinforces these roles:

> To tech child[er] c[ur]tasy is myn[e] entent
> And th[us] forth my p[ro]ces I p[ur]pos to begy[n]ne ...
> The child th[at] eu[er] think[es] th[at] he wold thryue or the
> My cou[n]cell i[n] th[is] to hy[m] th[at] he take[16]

The similarly conventional opening of *Urbanitatis* identifies the voice of the author or scribe: 'Whoso wyll of nurtur lere / Harken to me & ye shall[e] here'.[17] There are two ways to read this approach. Rather than focusing on

---

[14] London, BL, MS Sloane 1315, fol. 1ᵛ.
[15] Oxford, Bodl., MS Ashmole 61, fol. 17ᵛ.
[16] MS Ashmole 61, fol. 17ᵛ.
[17] London, BL, MS Cotton Caligula A ii, fol. 88ʳ.

how it places the author/narrator in a position above that of the reader or listener, we should look at the way these introductions erect patterns in which the underlying expectation shows that young people were accountable for their own socialisation. The repetition of direct language addressing the child – 'I', 'the' and 'thou' – allows the young readers or listeners to place themselves into the narrative and into the story, as Higonnet suggested. Even when the first-person narrative is absent, which is the case in *The Young Children's Book*, the emphasis on a youthful character is consistent; this alone provides a suitable access point to young audiences. In addition, these poems rarely identify other adult characters or refer to adult behaviour and actions, both of which would take responsibility away from the younger person.

The emphasis on how children and servants should behave before adult intervention became necessary, as well as the light treatment given to the duties of these adults, suggests children had considerable independence. Positioned next to the adult authoritarian environment which existed in reality, the autonomy and responsibility suggested in this literature are worth noting. Adult characters do not dominate socialising lessons and there is no doubt that this reinforces the sense of responsibility and agency in medieval male youthfulness.

A second prominent division in courtesy poems is one that concerns warfare, violence, honour and the role of chivalry. Along with treason, these can be classed as belonging to the political spectrum of high status experiences. Courtesy poems take up only some of these issues, while other supposedly useful knowledge is also absent. The general exclusion of politics may be explained by the target audience being a youthful one; however, this does not explain why the political implications of youthfulness are not engaged with, along the lines of criticisms that beset Richard II.[18] The issue of treason was equally relevant to both elite and middling classes, and young people in courtesy poems are deprived of information about their political duties to England. In this period, the idea of honour was very powerful and in general was a value that made significant inroads amongst gentry groups.[19] Chivalric literature, however, does embrace the narrative trope of young people creating

---

[18] C. Fletcher, 'Manhood and Politics in the Reign of Richard II', *Past and Present* 189 (2005), 3–39.

[19] Jessica Freeman discusses in what ways social status and treason are connected in 'Sorcery at Court and Manor: Margery Jourdemayne, the Witch of Eye Next Westminster', *Journal of Medieval History* 30 (2004), 343–57. Philippa Maddern discusses honour in 'Honour among the Pastons: Gender and Integrity in Fifteenth-Century English Provincial Society', *Journal of Medieval History* 14 (1988), 357–71. Gentry castle building also had a strong symbolic value to a society that went far beyond military functionality. In many ways this ties in with literature that also does not explore military ideas as we might expect. See A. King, 'Fortresses and Fashion Statements: Gentry Castles in Fourteenth-Century Northumberland', *Journal of Medieval History* 33 (2007), 372–97.

an honourable, chivalric, manly identity through their physical actions. Given that the household was such an important setting in chivalric tales, the exclusion of any similar ideas from these poems is worth noting. Adult texts also associated male behaviour with the avoidance of strife, an approach not unlike that in socialising literature for younger people. Less than 0.5 per cent of the twelfth-century *Liber Urbani* by Daniel of Beccles discusses war or soldierly activity, instead referring to restraint.[20] Similarly *mansuetudo* (gentleness of spirit) has been seen as a dominant element in medieval writings.[21] Norbert Elias assumed that increased awareness of others developed only over the course of the sixteenth century and that only at this time did 'the degree of consideration expected of others [become] greater'.[22] The directives in courtesy poems make it seem likely that such considerations were important earlier than this; the recognition of meek behaviour in socialising young people, which is also referred to in adult texts, demonstrates awareness of others, although the motivations that lie behind such behaviour followed patterns of self-interest and opportunism. Nevertheless, these sources attest to a model of behaviour before the sixteenth century in which interaction was based on consideration for others. The socialisation of young people clearly integrated this idea, perhaps because the lessons prioritised outward behaviour, an important part of formative behaviour.

Modern scholarship has generally overlooked the issue of meekness as a key element in youthful socialisation, yet vivid descriptions of meekness in courtesy poems suggest it was an important accomplishment in youthful social customs and norms. Meekness, which literally means gentleness, humility and submission, represented many meanings related to conduct ranging from gentility, hierarchy and observable courtesy to the construction of gendered identity. Meekness is also one of the attributes in which an intangible inner quality is overtly associated with an outward show of behaviour. *Stans puer ad mensam* credits the duties of service with meekness: 'Be quik & redi meke & seruiable / weel awaiti[n]ge to fulfille anoo[n] / What th[at] thi sou[er]eyn co[m]mau[n]dith to be doon.'[23] Such displays of respect towards social superiors reinforce the hierarchical structure of the household; this was particularly important in socialising gentry children for the roles they undertook in elite environments, as well as in strengthening hierarchical constructs more generally.

---

[20] J. Gillingham, 'From *Civilitas* to Civility: Codes of Manners in Medieval and Early Modern England', *Transactions of the Royal Historical Society* 12 (2002), 267–89 (p. 275).
[21] C. S. Jaeger, *The Origins of Courtliness: Civilising Trends and the Formation of Courtly Ideals, 939–1210* (Philadelphia, 1985), pp. 36–40.
[22] N. Elias, *The Civilizing Process: Sociogenetic and Psychogenetic Investigations*, trans. E. Jephcott, rev. edn (Oxford, 2000), p. 69.
[23] London, Lambeth Palace Library, MS 853, p. 153. London, BL, MS Harley 4011 is abbreviated and ends before these stanzas.

Youthful character was not always described as 'meek' and it could be associated with other phrases, including demureness and softness. In *Stans puer ad mensam* the boy is told to 'walke demurely bi streetis in the tou[n] / And take good hede bi wisdom & resou[n]'.[24] Although here meekness is not directly alluded to, it is implied in the use of the comparable term, demureness. Softness is another word with similar meaning. Its apparent relationship to meekness can be detected in certain manuscripts of *Stans puer ad mensam* where 'soft' and 'meek' are used interchangeably. Close comparison between the Lambeth manuscript and other manuscripts demonstrates this. In Lambeth, the young boy is told 'Be *soft* i[n] mesure not hasti but treteable'.[25] In four manuscripts this has been altered to 'Be *meke* in mesure not hasty bot tretable'.[26] Softness and meekness are similar enough for scribes to have easily substituted the two words; both were necessary qualities for servants and subordinates in general. At the same time 'soft' is a genderless description which draws on medieval medical and religious philosophies about the wax-like, fluid softness of young children. This is particularly conducive to customs relevant to infancy, including swaddling, bathing and massage – factors thought to alter physiognomy.[27] It is worth noting that this emphasis on youthful softness continues to be used in later literature and Caxton's translation of the *Book of Good Manners* discusses 'softness' in relation to young children.[28]

These ideas about the meekness of young males are in fact based on contrasting views. The quality's usefulness is blurred by the potential shortcomings of acting meekly towards others. In *the boke of curtasye* a potential problem with meekness warns young men 'Be not to meke but i[n] mene the holde / For ellis a fole thou wyll[e] be tolde'.[29] Overly meek behaviour is associated with pliancy and a lack of judgement, leading to complaints of foolishness. This is overturned later in the poem when the child is instructed 'Onswere hum mekely [and] make hym glose (flattering speech)'.[30] On this occasion, meekness benefits the child because it is a useful contrivance that flatters others. Skill in behaving meekly was desirable in young people but

---

[24] MS Lambeth 853, p. 151. MS Ashmole 61 is different in that neither meekness nor demureness is directly referenced. Yet Rate's version still emphasises decorum and subservience.

[25] MS Lambeth 853, p. 154. My emphasis.

[26] London, BL, MS Harley 2251, fol. 149r. My emphasis. Absent in MS Ashmole 61. MS Harley 4011 is cut short prior to this.

[27] *On the Properties of Things, John Trevisa's translation of Bartholomaeus Anglicus De Proprietatibus Rerum, A Critical Text*, ed. M. Seymour, 3 vols. (Oxford, 1975), I, 298–300. Shahar, *Childhood in the Middle Ages*, pp. 77–120.

[28] J. Legrand, *Here begynneth the table of a book entytled the book of good maners* (Westminster, 1487), fvir.

[29] MS Sloane 1986, fol. 15r.

[30] MS Sloane 1986, fol. 17v.

children did have to be aware that they could potentially be the losers if they were seen as too meek and were consequently exploited. It is worth noting that this latter statement exposes the self-serving quality of meekness. On some occasions self-advancement is put forward in plainer language. This is seen in *Urbanitatis* where meekness is presented as a shrewd goal:

> To th[at] lord thou moste lowte
> W[i]t[h] thy rygth kne let hyt be do
> Thyn owne worschepe th[ou] saue so[31]

As Rosemary Horrox has pointed out, gentle service entailed greater capacity for mutual gain which is missing in the work of lower status servants. Here the 'rewards of service' are alluded to as part of the general benefits accrued by the attentive servant.[32] This hints at the precarious balance between courteousness and self-interest which would become part of the eighteenth and nineteenth centuries' debates over the question of 'etiquette'.[33]

The meekness of women is also described in some courtesy literature. For example, in *How the Wise Man Taught his Son* the father says his son is 'meke & myld',[34] while his future wife should also be 'meke & gode'.[35] It is possible meekness is gender neutral; hence it could appear in descriptions of both men and women. Meekness may also be gender specific, but from the perspective of being highly suited to women; the Knight in the *Canterbury Tales* is described in this way, 'And of his port as meeke as is a mayde', surprising in a figure whose manhood and status were respected.[36] It may be the youthfulness, and hence lack of 'manliness' of young boys that allowed meekness to be attributed to them in the literature. There are also Christian qualities to meekness; Christ himself was the ultimate model of meekness, and as a reflection of religious piety, meekness is entirely appropriate to both genders. The poem by Peter Idley will be perused in a later chapter. However, it is worth noting here that Idley identifies a king's behaviour in a similar way: 'A kyng to be meke and not vengeable'.[37] The association between meekness and its practical value equally makes it a valuable tool in a hierarchical society, as was noted earlier. For young people, the careful demonstration of courtesy and meekness helped to show rational and balanced behaviour. Chaucer's Squire is also introduced as 'lowely, and servysable', and even

---

[31] London, BL, MS Royal 17 A. I, fols. 29r–v.
[32] R. Horrox, 'Service', in *Fifteenth Century Attitudes: Perceptions of Society in Late Medieval England*, ed. R. Horrox (Cambridge, 1994), pp. 61–78 (p. 65).
[33] On etiquette see J. Arditi, *A Genealogy of Manners: Transformations of Social Relations in France and England from the Fourteenth to the Eighteenth Century* (Chicago, 1998).
[34] MS Ashmole 61, fol. 6r.
[35] Cambridge University Library, MS Ff.2.38, fols. 53r–54r.
[36] *Works of Geoffrey Chaucer*, ed. Robinson, p. 18.
[37] Text E, fol. 17v.

though his manliness has been proven by his participation in overseas wars, his identity is still linked to how he demonstrates submissive courtesy and service before others. This does not answer the question of what meekness meant to medieval people, but it does imply young people were prevailed upon to demonstrate their character and nature through multiple attributes. It is also apparent that courtesy texts transmitted sophisticated information about childhood. Far from being simple and trivial, they suggest a clever manipulation of youthful conduct and activities.

Masculinity in the broadest sense of male identity is different from the idea of the way in which young boys became manly or developed robust or vigorous masculinity.[38] These latter two aspects of male identity are noticeably absent from this literature. There was certainly no single all-inclusive concept of masculinity in medieval England, in fact the historiography has been at pains to appropriate the insistence on multiple forms of femininity to the study of men. The absence of manly socialising lessons from a literature about youthful socialisation is significant in large part because it is a core narrative tool in chivalric tales where the male hero travels in order to enhance his manliness while young.[39] In courtesy literature this supposedly useful knowledge is not delivered to young people. While boys and young men were not necessarily expected to develop 'manly' character traits along the lines of aggression, violence and warfare, it is also possible that it is in didactic literature that we come closer to the reality of how manliness was established for many young boys from the gentry and merchant classes.[40]

In terms of the youthful male experiences described in courtesy poems it is apparent that it is the shared experiences that are most prominent. At one level this is suggestive of youthful learning being organised through activities that were shared, or more precisely, open to public scrutiny. The emphasis on behaving well in front of other people and talking appropriately to them is related to the concept of negotiating social relationships in a diplomatic way. This theme is particularly noticeable in rules concerning eating, already mentioned as one of the core elements of courtesy poems. Courtesy poems repeatedly record an interest in the public nature of courtesy, ranging from 'pike not thi nose'[41] to 'pare clene thi nailis thi hondis waische also'[42] and

---

[38] R. M. Karras, *From Boys to Men: Formations of Masculinity in Late Medieval Europe* (Philadelphia, 2003).

[39] Fletcher, 'Manhood and Politics', p. 18.

[40] Sharon Wells has in fact looked at the way in which table manners functioned as a sign of manhood in 'Manners Maketh Man: Living, Dining and Becoming a Man in the Later Middle Ages', in *Rites of Passage: Cultures of Transition in the Fourteenth Century*, ed. N. F. McDonald and W. M. Ormrod (York, 2004), pp. 67–81.

[41] *SPAM*. MS Lambeth 853, p. 151.

[42] *SPAM*. MS Stowe 982, fol. 10ʳ. Similar, but not identical lines are in MS Ashmole 61, fol. 18ʳ: 'Ete th[ou] not mete w[ith] th[i] unwasche honds' and 'luke th[i] honds be clen when th[ou] etys th[i] mete / Pare clene th[i] nayles for aught th[at] may be'.

'kepe clene thi lyppes for fat of flesche or fische'.[43] Implicitly it is acknowledged that behaviour is under constant scrutiny from the ever present critical gaze of 'truly' courteous superiors. The notion of observation and monitoring was one of the means of achieving socialisation in the most important of all elite spaces: the medieval hall.

This emphasis on the hall, variously the 'great hall' or 'main hall', lies in its importance in medieval household rituals and activities; commonly, this was a location where people interacted throughout the day and evening. Indentures, inventories and accounts show the hall was a multi-use space, used both for dining and sleeping throughout the twelfth to fifteenth centuries, although by the fifteenth century this was changing and household accounts increasingly refer to the presence of permanent beds in chambers.[44] The meals held in these halls were the primary occasions when courtesy, as represented within this literature, came into its own. It was thus essential for any young person, and particularly any young man, to know how to behave in this or any other public dining space. The trend towards dining in smaller chambers by the end of the 1500s should be connected to a change in the relevance of courtesy texts. That it is not suggests there was an even deeper need to emulate older traditions through a strong and seemingly inherent conservatism.

The focus on socialisation within internal spaces, primarily the hall, can be accounted for through this conservative ideology, as well as through the strong links that existed between the layout of medieval houses and public activities. For the most part, other domestic environments and tasks associated with socialising young people go unnoticed in courtesy poems. However, in *Stans puer ad mensam* an additional public area is related to the concept of activities that are open to scrutiny. Here, it is the outside environment which imposes additional demands on the young boy:

> Who speketh to the in eny man[ner] of place
> Lomysshyche cast not thi hed adowne
> But w[ith] sadd chere loke hym in the face
> Walke demeverly by stret in the towne and a vertise
> the by wisdom and reson
> Withe Inssolnte laghtins thou do none offence[45]

---

[43] *SPAM*. MS Stowe 982, fol. 10ʳ. In MS Ashmole 61 fol. 18ᵛ, 'Ne wi[th] flesch ne fysshe wi[th] oth[er] mete ne bred'. The use of 'thi', mentioned earlier, can be seen in these phrases also.

[44] Woolgar, *Great Household*, pp. 79–80. The centralising function of the hall is discussed in M. Johnson, *Housing Culture: Traditional Architecture in an English Landscape* (London, 1993), pp. 55–61.

[45] MS Stowe 982, fols. 10ʳ–11ʳ. MS Lambeth 853, p. 151 replaces 'Inssolnte laghtins' with 'bi no wantowne lauginge th[ou] do noo[n] offence'.

The child has a role in the public space of the street as well as in the household, and this conjures the image of public performance: 'Walke demeverly by stret in the towne'. Equally, this passage reinforces the importance of the child's observable gestures as an indicator of good manners: 'Withe Inssolnte laghtins thou do none offence' and 'bi no wantowne lauginge th[ou] do noo[n] offence' emphasise the impact bad behaviour has on others. The capacity for restraint based on consideration for the feelings of others was noted by Norbert Elias as being particularly associated with the aristocracy.[46] *Stans puer ad mensam* widens the standard setting of the interior household to a public environment and connects the basic lessons learnt in the household to other places. The *boke of curtasye* also provides information that could be used when travelling on pilgrimage; more generally, it gives lessons on how to interact with people in new spaces. However, most courtesy texts privilege the elite household, with the emphasis placed firmly on the internal environment. This is all the more noticeable when set against the atypical examples noted here.

Rules on eating are part of the ritual and gesture or communal ritual component of courtesy poems. Rituals were central to high status lifestyles and particularly to the social status of the lord as an adult male. The gestures described in these poems indicate the power relationships that existed between the elite and those serving them, but they equally explore the nature of power relationships between older and younger people. Obviously, the lord was made powerful by having loyal, obsequious servers surrounding him, treating him as the object of ritual gesture. It seems that servers also built up their own power networks by being the main actors in the performance of ritual.[47] When the youthfulness of servers is added to this, it constitutes a new and interesting dimension of the power relationships in households.

Service, as well as the rituals and gestures taking place in large households, relies on hierarchy, and this staging of hierarchy is one of the ways courtesy texts can be compared to actual medieval social practices. Although it may not be stated in each line, hierarchy underpins the socialising lessons in courtesy poems. In these works hierarchy is usually discussed in a very specific way in terms of precedence at the table. For example, in *Stans puer ad mensam* the young person is told 'Sit in that place that thow art assigned to / Press not to high in no maner wise'. This relates on one level to the natural condition of elite households but it is also relevant to the audience of gentry and merchant readers we know owned these texts. Equally these rules overlapped with medieval pedagogy which stressed the need for young people to learn about and obey hierarchical rules.

---

[46] Elias, *Civilizing Process*, pp. 128–9.
[47] K. M. Johnson, 'The Invisible Man: Body and Ritual in a Fifteenth-Century Noble Household', *Journal of Medieval History* 31 (2005), 143–62 (p. 156).

Hierarchy correlates to the supposed characteristics of different class groups, including the notion of gentility amongst high status people. An emphasis on gentility conveys a sense that the particular forms of outward behaviour, some of which have been mentioned, were part of the messages about misbehaviour. Misbehaviour is identified not only by the absence of good behaviour but by sharply worded passages that correlate misbehaviour with the absence of high status. This is evident in the pejorative 'churl', which frequently identifies someone of poor conduct; linguistically, from the thirteenth century this term was also applied to serfs, bondmen, peasants and rustics. There are indications that the Latin *Facetus* poem similarly used 'rusticus' to distinguish boorish behaviour.[48] Both words are clearly accompanied by subjective overtones strongly expressing a sense of disdain. In *Stans puer ad mensam* the boy is told that he will be called a churl if his behaviour fails to meet recognised standards, 'leste th[ou] be callyd els both cherle or gloton'.[49] Spitting is denigrated for its supposed lowly associations, 'For th[a]t is A cherles dede who so doth it'.[50] A positive/negative referral to gentility tellingly shows one of the techniques used. For example, 'lowde for to soupe is agen gentilnes'[51] and later 'Of gentilnese take salt w[i]t[h] thi knyf' directly link a behaviour (eating quietly and using a knife to take salt from a communal dish) to either a positive or a negative statement about class.[52] Such behaviour makes gentility easily recognisable, although given the reality of social mobility in this period, the point that behaviour can be learned is tellingly made.

It is also apparent in *The Babees Book* that the separation of people into gentle and 'other' played a part in how young people were taught to recognise what was important; accusations of poor manners, especially when eating, encourage a young person to realise how their own behaviour reveals their status. In this case, there is a very specific and belittling comment about the manners of field workers:

> Kutte nouht[e] youre mete eke as it were Felde men
> That to theyre mete haue suche an appetyte
> That they ne rekke in what wyse where ne when
> Nor how vngoodly they on theyre mete twyte
> But swete children haue al wey yo[ur] delyte
> In curtesye and in verrey gentylnesse
> And at youre myht[e] eschewe boystousnesse[53]

---

[48] Gillingham, 'From *Civilitas* to Civility', p. 271.
[49] MS Ashmole 61, fol. 18r.
[50] MS Ashmole 61, fol. 18v.
[51] MS Lambeth 853, p. 152. Some lines are reversed in MS Harley 2251, fol. 148r. A similar phrase is used by Rate, scribe of MS Ashmole 61, on fol. 18v.
[52] In MS Lambeth 853, p. 153.
[53] London, BL, MS Harley 5086, fol. 89v.

Poor behaviour is represented in these poems through this use of pejorative language. A common linguistic pattern provides negative examples next to a statement about class: 'Pyke notte thyne errys nothyr thy noscrellys / And thou doo men wylle say thou comyste of karlys'. 'Karlys', elsewhere 'carls', is a linguistic borrowing from the German *kerl* and French *carle*.[54] The author completes *The Babees Book* with a reminder about desired gentle status, followed by a threat of what poor behaviour would do to the child:

> Thenne wylle they sey there aftyr
> That a gentylle man was here
> he that dyspysythe thys techynge
> he ys not worthy with owte lesygne
> Neuyr at a goode mannys tabylle for to sytte
> Nothyr of noo worschippe to wete[55]

Through the creation of these cues, children and young people were part of the dissemination of class ideology, participating in the hierarchical structure of medieval society by learning that social superiority was grounded in outward conduct. This is acknowledged in the *Boke of Nurture* where education in courteous behaviour is shown to lead to eventual employment and economic and social security. This poem will be examined shortly.

Such highly ritualised gestures in these poems give some idea of what life was like, possibly even for the high status young people they are supposedly describing, particularly during the middle part of the day at mealtimes. These rules are, of course, the outward manifestation of a series of comprehensive lessons and ideologies which had to be understood and recognised by all the participants before they could be mastered. The mundane lessons in the poems, such as using knives at dinner time and the correct way to drink from a cup, account for concepts about hierarchy, learning and then putting ritual displays into practice, all couched in the relationships that existed between the lord and young servants. At the level of the elite household this speaks to the role children and young people actually had within the organisation and structure of noble households and to the adult–child and lord–server power relationships that existed. Courtesy poems place children and young people into the adult world of hosting and largesse, and, by implication, into the domestic and highly politicised adult arena. This suggests that social training for young people did take place in these environments and that the customs

---

[54] *The Lytylle Childrene's Book*, London, BL, MS Egerton 1995, fol. 59^r. In Cambridge University Library, MS Ee.4.35, fol. 22^v 'cherleys' is used. Oxford, Balliol College, MS Balliol 354, fol. 142^r also uses 'churles' while the interlinear French translation is 'de villains'. London, BL, MS Additional 8151, fol. 202^r, 'chorlys'. *The Young Children's Book* employs a similar phrase: 'Wype not thi nose nor thi nos thirlys / Than men wyll say thou come of cherlys'. MS Ashmole 61, fol. 21^v.

[55] MS Egerton 1995, fols. 59^v–60^r.

of noble behaviour, particularly the emphasis on high standards of living and dining, were widely known and recognised in relation to both adult and youthful experiences. Given the appropriation of these texts by gentry and merchant readers, such lessons can be understood in relation to the social and economic desires of these groups.

This literature also introduces other ideas about youthfulness and socialisation. The rules about how to eat properly, while a part of the ritual and gesture category, also teach young people about maintaining relationships in general. All of the poems emphasise the manner in which behaviour impacts on neighbours. Could we see this as akin to the rules of diplomacy? We know diplomacy was essential to political alliances between power groups and central to political ambitions.[56] It was also essential to the prosperity of high status families, particularly with marriage alliances reinforcing diplomatic pacts. The practice of diplomacy in a political sense is not touched on in these poems. However, diplomacy as an 'art of peace' or as social mediation is taught. When Catherine de Medici wrote about the 'art of peace' to her son Henry III in 1578–9 she emphasised choosing moderation in all things.[57] The principle of moderation is a model continually emphasised in the poems, in eating, talking, emotions and drinking. Moderation is not necessarily synonymous with diplomacy as it embraces a strongly religious sense of ethics and purity. However, the connection between how to mediate social situations and why this is important in medieval society is present on some levels.

While these poems may only lightly touch on these principles they nevertheless provide a crucial link to key aspects in male experiences such as the importance of diplomacy and gaining and maintaining patronage and alliances. Young people from the middle ranks of society were thus exposed to messages about hierarchy and class. These lessons for young boys in fact establish some of the building blocks of how to create social relationships and social networks that would be of use for later, more sophisticated political and adult careers. Gentry families had good reasons to be interested in courtesy literature. These lessons were also useful self-serving tools for someone to master when acting as a functionary in a household, and we should not forget the value of these instructions to many young people who found they were moving in higher and higher social circles.

---

[56] R. E. Martin, 'Gifts for the Bride: Dowries, Diplomacy, and Marriage Politics in Muscovy', *Journal of Medieval and Early Modern Studies* 38 (2008), 119–45.

[57] D. Crouzet, '"A strong desire to be a mother to all your subjects": A Rhetorical Experiment by Catherine de Medici', *Journal of Medieval and Early Modern Studies* 38 (2008), 103–18 (p. 111).

Virtue and courtesy

What implications do these social norms and customs have in terms of other values which shaped the manner in which young people were brought up? We can extrapolate from these courtesy rules underlying principles which relate to the broader idea of morality. As a simple definition, virtue or morality is separated from courtesy by conformity to moral principles in life and behaviour; it is also a trumping of earthly pleasures, again synonymous with moderation. In the medieval period virtue was a concept compatible with religious principles, particularly charity and piety. Did morality provide a more sophisticated tool to articulate socialisation, responding to theological ideas about man's place and woman's place in the earthly realm? Was there a site of conflict between the ideologies of courtesy and morality or did each of these models keep their own separate identities and traditions alive in literature?

The medieval meaning of courtesy

Was a moral identity important for young boys? Were they taught about moral conduct, ethical behaviour and virtue in these poems? Courtesy poems are often direct and straightforward in their language and teachings, and there is a sense of immediacy and action within the narratives which is attractive to younger readers or aural audiences. Most courtesy poems were written in verse, either in rime-royal stanzas[58] or in rhyming couplets.[59] There is some connection between verse structures and the ability to remember texts, and children and young people may have been directed to learn and remember at least the shorter poems by heart.[60] Equally, what does courtesy mean in the sense identified in these texts? Seemingly straightforward, these questions have implications for the manner in which young people were socialised in the late medieval period. Courteous language in these poems frames actual perceptions of behaviour touching on priorities in common socialising lessons for medieval children. External actions have been argued to demonstrate inner character and Anna Dronzek has suggested that separating conduct from morality in the medieval period is not viable.[61] However, cour-

---

[58] Including *The Babees Book*, Caxton's *Book of Curtesye* and *Stans puer ad mensam* excepting Ashmole 61, which was written in quatrains abab.
[59] Including *The Lytylle Childrene's Book, the boke of curtasye, Urbanitatis* and *The Young Children's Book*.
[60] D. Bornstein, 'Courtesy Books', in *Dictionary of the Middle Ages*, ed. J. R. Strayer, 13 vols. (New York, 1982–9), III, 661.
[61] Dronzek, 'Gendered Theories', p. 137. The moral qualities which tend to be associated with courtesy poems are vividly addressed by Erasmus in *De Civilitate Morum puerilium* but this was not written until 1526. Here the connection between

tesy poems suggest that the connections between courtesy and morality had different layers of meaning that are not revealed by a linear equation between courtesy and morality. In fact, the nature of socialisation for young people developed in response to competition between acting courteously and acting virtuously.

Courtesy is now stripped of many of its older meanings. In its modern usage it is more likely to be a word for politeness, etiquette or manners. It also now appears as a compound term: courtesy car, courtesy call and courtesy title. The medieval concept of courtesy provided space to frame different models of behaviour and conduct that were culturally valuable. England's multilingual society was exposed to courtesy through its long-standing usage in Anglo-Norman romances, saints' lives and legendary historiography. Anglo-Norman texts from the second half of the twelfth century apply courtesy to courtly ideals of politeness and refinement: Thomas of Britain's *Tristan* adopts it for this purpose. Courtesy makes its first appearance in the English vernacular in the thirteenth-century guide for anchoresses, *Ancren riwle*. Here it is related to the anchoresses' gentle behaviour. Staying in the English vernacular, Robert of Gloucester's *Metrical chronicle* (1297) relates courtesy to nobility and goodness. Courtesy also signifies obeisance or respectful gestures to a superior, and this is noticeable in courtesy poems from the fourteenth and fifteenth centuries. From the second half of the twelfth century, courtesy is deployed across didactic material when conduct, behaviour, nobility and service are discussed.

As a socialising value for young people, courtesy is dominated by its link to noble practices, elite lifestyles and observable behaviour. Its qualities are those which young men from elite backgrounds were presumed to display in their actions and, more generally, through their very way of being. This marginalises other groups: how did sons from provincial gentry families, wealthy urban households and the bourgeoisie (a problematic but still handy term) form any kind of relationship with the type of courtesy this literature suggested was essential for young people? Of course, young people had profoundly different prospects when it came to their careers; they lived in households of various sizes and grandeur and learnt how to behave through observation and oral lessons as well as through texts. Also, the merchant classes comprised the wealthiest of England's men of business as well as those lesser figures who existed on the fringes of economic privation. Not all of those in the merchant class would have been able to spend income on manuscripts for their sons, or even have been able to link their lifestyles conceptually to those promoted in courtesy poems.

Medieval fiction is equally useful as an indicator of courtesy values.

---

a noble boy's outer conduct tellingly indicating his inner character and worth is genuinely expressed. It is worth pointing out Erasmus's humanist background. This echoes Elias's analysis of Erasmus: *Civilizing Process*, pp. 47–52.

Wolfram von Eschenbach's *Parzival* and the hero Gawain, for example, are young men whose identities are in part defined through their courtesy. In these fictions, courtesy plays a significant role in helping readers situate unreal characters in real worlds. Typically, courtesy is connected to elite qualities, transforming the impressionable and unformed youthful hero into a fully accomplished courteous and chivalric figure: courtesy is both the goal and the means of achieving social prominence in a society which privileged the courtly ideal of behaviour. Such fictional narratives owe a considerable debt to courtesy poems where a definitive account of courtesy is presented through its niceties, explaining in what ways courtesy is achieved step by step, not in the process of a quest or through the declaration of chivalric love, but in the pragmatic realm of household interaction, table manners and gentle service. In such sources, courtesy is depicted more openly as a practicable system of behaviour or, in other words, as a core socialising philosophy.

The style and manner of courteous behaviour may have developed within monastic life: customaries provide detailed information on domestic offices and the courteous nature of religious offices.[62] Equally, the royal court of tenth-century Europe has strong affiliations with courtesy. Norbert Elias's emphasis on the literary courtesy topos developing out of court life is useful in understanding how closely literary texts were connected to actual court conditions.[63] Upholding this has been Stephen Jaeger, who has identified courtly ethics as modelled on semi-remembered Roman ideologies holding meaning for the Ottonian emperors and the imperial church.[64] These real-life social values, some of which were subsequently embedded in the courtly romances of Europe, found an enduring but not exclusive home within French texts and from this extended outwards as sources were copied and recopied, switching between countries and languages. There is no doubt that England's long-standing practice of trilingualism is a useful indicator of the history of courtesy in England, and as I have indicated above it is now clear that Anglo-French remained central to England's linguistic and cultural landscape into the sixteenth century.[65] The *corteisie* of Anglo-Norman religious, romance and didactic material affected linguistic understandings of courtesy in its English vernacular usage. It also ensured that courtesy was a concept which was widespread and prevalent in English society.

---

[62] J. Nicholls, *The Matter of Courtesy: Medieval Courtesy Books and the Gawain–Poet* (Cambridge, 1985), pp. 22–44.

[63] Elias, *Civilizing Process*, pp. 87, 187–91.

[64] Jaeger focuses on a network of courtesy and courtliness spreading outwards from Germany, a sequence about which Aldo Scaglione has reservations. See Jaeger, *Origins of Courtliness*, pp. 5–6, 269–72; A. Scaglione, *Knights at Court: Courtliness, Chivalry & Courtesy from Ottonian Germany to the Italian Renaissance* (Berkeley, 1991).

[65] *Language and Culture*, ed. Wogan-Browne et al.

Such contemporary linguistic associations are a useful way of understanding the complicated relationship between courtesy in its literary form and courtesy as an idea in socialising young people. Since the beginning of the twentieth century courtesy's function in medieval literature has been the subject of considerable attention. In 1919 F. B. Millett defined medieval courtesy as the 'ornamental' product of morality.[66] In 1935 John Mason defined courtesy as a code of ethics that was relevant to particular class groups, identifying parental advice books as offering practical but not theoretical advice.[67] Millett's and Mason's emphasis on the separation of courtesy from morality is not without qualification and both assume an ongoing connection between medieval courtesy and morality.[68] In contrast to this, an early study of *facetus* literature and courtesy poems by Sister Mary Brentano did not distinguish between courtesy and morality; in fact it celebrated the lack of division between the two, 'indiscriminately casting into their works definite admonitions concerning both morals and manners'.[69] It is worth noting that scholarship on gestures, symbolically and pragmatically analogous to courtesy, also connects outer show to inner ethical conduct, echoing the views of Millett and Mason, as well as Dronzek.[70]

The manner in which the relationship between courtesy and morality can be explored has continued to interest historians and English scholars. Mark Addison Amos has noted that courtesy poems provide 'simple' cause-and-effect statements while other texts develop moral testimony. He also suggests that morality pervades both the language of the texts and its lessons.[71] Jonathan Nicholls comments that morality is generally subordinated in the literature, while maintaining that gestures remain important as indicators of 'inner virtue',[72] and Mark Johnston distinguishes 'ethical literature', including Lati-

---

[66] F. B. Millett, *English Courtesy Literature Before 1557* (Kingston, 1919), p. 1.

[67] J. E. Mason, *Gentlefolk in the Making: Studies in the History of English Courtesy Literature and Related Topics from 1531 to 1774* (Philadelphia, 1935), p. 4.

[68] Deanna Evans suggests that Mason and Millett are indicating a complete separation between courtesy and morality: 'The Babees Book', in *Medieval Literature for Children*, ed. D. Kline (New York, 2003), pp. 79–92 (p. 83).

[69] M. T. Brentano, *Relationship of the Latin Facetus Literature to the Medieval English Courtesy Poems*, Bulletin of the University of Kansas 36, Humanistic Studies 5 (Kansas, 1935), p. 3.

[70] *A Cultural History of Gesture: From Antiquity to the Present Day*, ed. J. Bremmer and H. Roodenburg (London, 1991).

[71] Amos remarks that 'In medieval courtesy literature, the language of morality everywhere links polite behaviour to a moral valuation: as the texts offer advice on personal hygiene, table etiquette, and conversational niceties, they detail the rewards and punishments for these activities in terms of virtue and vice.' M. A. Amos, '"For Manners Make Man", Bourdieu, de Certeau, and the Common Appropriation of Noble Manners in the *Book of Courtesy*', in *Medieval Conduct*, ed. K. Ashley and R. L. A. Clark (Minneapolis, 2001), pp. 23–48 (p. 30).

[72] Nicholls, *Matter of Courtesy*, p. 1, 14.

nate works on moral philosophy and theology, from 'courtesy literature' dealing with table manners, chivalry and courtly love. In 2003, *Medieval Literature for Children* was edited by Daniel Kline to separate works on moral texts from courtesy texts.[73] The relationship between courtesy and morality remains ambiguous.

Morality is imbued with ethical and spiritual connotations while courtesy is less focused on ethical behaviour but also flexible enough to reflect some moral questions; this inherent paradox has resulted in frequent misinterpretations of courtesy literature. This is significant as it is this flexibility which challenges our understanding of the place courtesy literature has in the moral development of children in the medieval period and exactly what role it played in socialising young people. As discussed earlier, these poems display varying socialising agendas, suggestive of a contemporary ambivalence towards outward courtesy and inner morality. The extant courtesy material thus suggests complex variations existed in relation to children's socialisation which could accommodate courteous and moral information; this is particularly visible in poems which cite meekness as a necessary social skill.

The attitude towards religion is worth exploring in terms of the relationship between courtesy and morality. Though courtesy poems primarily represent secular socialising interests, religious values are present in some. This is ultimately unsurprising given the clear connections between this literature and youthful upbringing, which is bound to require some attention to orthodox character formation. Clerical authors such as Robert Grosseteste, in writing the original Latin *Stans puer ad mensam*, attest to a pious interest in youthful socialisation. Tauno Mustanoja and Felicity Riddy both convincingly discuss the clerical origins of the *Good Wife* poems. Some readers could have been led to equate courtesy in these poems with morality; lessons against gluttonous eating are particularly open to signalling religious attitudes while also reflecting the religious context of courtesy. The presence of moral and semi-religious instruction can be credibly established in some poems. However, in most cases the depiction of secular courtesy is protracted while religious material is contracted, suggesting a core grouping of the literature on childhood socialisation remained fixed on the notion of observable, superficial conduct. There is evidence of this type of redaction in the National Library of Scotland's copy of *Urbanitatis* where the usual six-line closing stanza concerning Christ is reduced by four lines.[74] In instances where semi-religious activities are cited, the balance that is struck between advice on courtesy and morality and the extent to which either courteous or moral instruction alters

---

[73] M. D. Johnston, 'The Treatment of Speech in Medieval Ethical and Courtesy Literature', *Rhetorica* 4 (1986), 21–46; *Medieval Literature for Children*, ed. Kline.

[74] M. E. Shaner, 'Instruction and Delight: Medieval Romances as Children's Literature', *Poetics Today* 13 (1992), 5–15 (p. 12).

the prescriptions on socialisation are the most effective ways of determining where and when religious socialisation is being incorporated into the lesson.

One significant example of religious values comes from *The Lytylle Childrene's Book*. It is worth bearing in mind that the opening stanza of this poem treats courtesy as a feature of religion, mediating the audience's interactions with the later, courteous information. The opening stanza provides the first clues to the means by which this is accomplished:

> Ltylle chyldrynne here may ye lere
> asoche curtesy that ys wretyn here
> ffor clerkys that the vii artys con
> Synne that curtesy from hevyn cam
> Whenne gabryelle oure lady grette
> And Elezabethe with mary mette
> Alle vertuys ben closyde in curtesy
> And alle vysye in velony[75]

The direct connection between courteous and religious values draws children's attention to the idea that courtesy is a religious activity. Tellingly, the passage equally reveals the manner in which religious values could be inserted into customary courtesy phrases without changing the overall tone. In fact, the subject matter of a young boy's manners when he eats at his lord's table is retained. This archetypal courtesy theme parallels other poems and retains the same elements of elite socialisation found in other texts. The lessons effectively focus on cleanliness of nails, hands and teeth, breaking bread, eating meat, fish and cheese, not gorging on the food set before you, closing your mouth when eating and not spilling food or throwing bones on the floor. A male child in a high or middle status location would have understood that these were essential rules governing his actions; lessons of this kind also relate his conduct to notions of status.

As already noted, these actions are important in and of themselves. Nevertheless, this idea is developed only after the initial stanza has testified that courtesy developed from religion; the maxim that all courtesy came down to earth from heaven at Christ's coming must have elicited some response from readers. It is conceivable that audiences equated courtesy, and socialisation, with Christian values. Of course, such lessons relate squarely to the religious nature of medieval life at its broadest level. Assumptions about the religious nature of this poem ignore its strong secular character. The connection between courtesy and religion is better seen as a shrewd ploy to impart authority or as a general observance of piety. If the former is the case, then young readers or listeners would find it hard to reject the subsequent behav-

---

[75] MS Egerton 1995, fol. 58ᵛ. In CUL MS Ee.4.35, fol. 22ᵛ the scribe has replaced 'Elezabethe' with 'cortesey' so it reads, 'Whan gabryell owr ladey met / And cortesey w[ith] marey met'.

ioural lessons; if the latter is true, then it does no more than situate these poems into a known context that medieval life was permeated by religion at all levels.

The manner in which virtue existed in courtesy literature can be understood by its placement in the text. *The Lytylle Childrene's Book* states 'Alle vertuys ben closyde in curtesy';[76] Russell's *Boke of Nurture* regards virtue in terms of good living, 'Hyth ys a charitable dede to tech vertu & good lyvy[n]g to kepe a man fro harm';[77] and in probably the most descriptive example, *The Babees Book* states, 'And Facett seyth[e] the Book of curtesye / Vertues to knowe thaym forto haue and vse / Is thing moste heelfull[e] in this worlde trevly'.[78] The value of this lies in revealing in what manner the link between courtesy and virtue was flexible, creating a sense of compatibility between these two concepts and potentially giving courteous acts a deeper moral significance. 'Virtue' adds a layer of meaning to socialisation and furnishes the opportunity for the ensuing codes of behaviour to be relevant both to religious ethics and therefore to inner conduct. References such as these make it possible to associate young people's socialisation with moral values. Yet a closer examination of these examples suggests other interpretations are more likely. 'Virtue' is found close to 'courtesy', separated at most by a few intervening words and lacking any distinct characteristics. Virtue, although used in the literature, is not systematically incorporated into the lessons. Neither does it have a standing on its own terms. What emerges is that these beliefs were not incorporated into the type of socialisation prioritised in courtesy poems for the key reason that it was not necessary for young people to think and reflect on inner character. This is different from the idea that young people were incapable of recognising and taking in virtue. Good behaviour demonstrated your social background and this, when combined with knowing how to behave, was sufficient as a socialising lesson. Courtesy literature accordingly did not register an interest in moral values, nor was it trying to do so, given the genre's background within the court and in elite houses, environments where observable gestures were so highly valued. While courtesy could ideally serve as an indicator of moral continence and ethical behaviour in a socialising sense, the reader or listener of these poems was not drawn to this position via explicit exemplars or systematic moral questions. In courtesy literature, virtue holds a precarious and uncertain position.

There is no way of telling how such ideas were viewed at the time: educated audiences were aware that virtue had clearly defined ethical connotations incorporating notions of chastity and sexual purity. The concept was also associated with the four cardinal virtues of justice, prudence, temperance and fortitude, and with the three theological virtues of faith, hope and

---

[76] MS Egerton 1995, fol. 58ᵛ.
[77] London, BL, MS Sloane 2027, fol. 37ʳ.
[78] MS Harley 5086, fol. 86ʳ.

charity. Contemporary literary texts, including homiletic romances, reveal that ideas about 'virtue' certainly existed and presumably were incorporated in socialising lessons. In a study of moral love songs, Susanna Greer Fein noted that the genre of penitential lyrics such as *The Sinner's Lament* examined virtue and sin allied to religious ideology.[79] It is worth noting that *The Sinner's Lament* can be found in two manuscripts, Advocates 19.3.1 and also Ashmole 61, which also contained courtesy material.

It is possible to identify two themes in the socialisation of young people. First, courtesy poems made no attempt to indicate that moral behaviour was important for young people. Second, moral lessons were fixed in other forms of literature which medieval audiences were familiar with, such as religious and ethical texts. These genres, however, were not specifically addressed to young people, which is why courtesy texts are important sources about socialisation. It is reasonable to speculate that the audiences for courtesy poems were primarily interested in what these narratives could teach about socialisation based on outward courteous rules and behaviour and would turn elsewhere, to less explicitly child-focused texts, for moral guidance.

A 'professional perspective' on socialisation in courtesy poems

The remainder of this chapter looks at the potential problems that could arise for young people later in life when their behaviour did not conform to the lessons set out in courtesy texts. Here, the limits and value of socialisation are set out for contemporary readers to explore from other courtesy narratives. The remainder of this chapter also addresses the manner in which non-elite audiences directly related to this material, given the nature of medieval hierarchies and the exclusion of social groups below the gentry level from this type of status-intense household service. This issue will also be pursued in later chapters.

Two courtesy poems, *the boke of curtasye* and the *Boke of Nurture*, relate to the issues of audience and status by addressing the professional duties of servants. In both of these poems youthful socialisation takes on financial incentives as a consequence of specialised adult tasks. As a result of this, each of the poems forms part of a different tradition which illustrates other avenues for socialisation and, as seen earlier, for the display of courtesy. This is particularly significant in the context of asking for hospitality or when seeking work. The following addresses the manner in which courtesy was shown to be an essential early lesson in socialisation and one that was crucial for professional servants.

As already noted in this chapter, it was common for courtesy poems to use language relevant to elite houses; this was done to emphasise the impor-

---

[79] *Moral Love Songs and Laments*, ed. S. Greer Fein (Kalamazoo, 1998).

tance of the great hall, the eminence of the lord and the scale of hospitality. In *the boke of curtasye* and the *Boke of Nurture* there is a greater engagement with non-elite audiences which is conveyed through the theme of finding employment in one of England's great houses. It is unusual to find different classes alluded to who would be interested in acquiring courtesy but *the boke of curtasye* does this in its opening:

> Whoso wylle of curtasy ler[e]
> Yn this boke he may hit her[e]
> Yf thow be gentylmon yomo[n] or knaue
> The nedis nurture for to haue[80]

This differs sharply from usual statements in opening stanzas and uncouples the direct application of courtesy from elite groups by referring to a range of different audiences; readers are ranked from high to low status. By the late fourteenth century, yeoman is a term used for a superior servant in a royal or noble household or a respectable small landholder under the estate of gentleman. Similarly, 'knave' refers to a boy or male child; more specifically, it denotes a boy employed as a servant or menial. 'Knave' can also be correlated to very young males or, when used in a context relating to service, suggests low status. A range of social ranks, including both the gentlemen who are normally associated with this 'courtesy' and others, like yeomen and grooms, lived in the great households. As Woolgar notes, around a quarter to a fifth of a household might be from gentle rank.[81] Elite lessons would have filtered through the household to affect the manners and conduct of its other members. This accommodates the interests of non-elite groups; however, it is worth noting that there are no further deviations from elite ideologies in Book One of the poem.[82]

Courtesy poems seldom enter into pragmatic discussions about employment. Yet in both of these poems the emphasis on professional service creates separate themes about the reasons for socialisation. It is not unusual to find courtesy described as a self-serving tool. However, Russell develops this into a longer discussion about employment and security in the *Boke of Nurture*. A significant piece of dialogue takes place in the opening section of this poem, drawing attention to this theme. Russell asks the young man to choose a career, in the most direct indication of the ultimate goal of learning manners:

---

[80] MS Sloane 1986, fol. 12ʳ.
[81] Woolgar notes that in 1467 in Sir John Howard's house there were sixteen gentlemen, forty-nine yeoman and twenty-seven grooms: 'Howard's household represented a common balance between the two groups, some twenty-three per cent being of gentle rank.' Woolgar, *Great Household*, p. 20.
[82] See Appendix A for details.

> Sonne yf I the teche wylte thou hit lere
> wylte thou be clerke marchaute or artyfycere
> Chamberlayne butteler panter or a kerv (carver)
> ussher sewer ploweman or laborer

The young man replies to this with:

> Off the office of butteler pant[er] and chaberlayne
> Sewer kerv uss[h]er ewer[er] for tayne
> And yema[n] of the seler I fayne
> All thesse to lerne I wolde be rygte fayne[83]

The acquisition of courtesy is the first step towards gainful employment and becoming an adult. The Harleian manuscript contains a unique line describing this: 'for moche youth[e] in co[n]nyng is baren & full[e] vnable / ther for[e] he th[a]t no good can ne to noon will[e] be agreable / he shall[e] neu[er] y thryve th[er]for[e] take to hym a babul[e]'.[84] This line candidly acknowledges that anyone who will not learn might as well remain a child.

Hospitality

Hospitality in the medieval period was a key social and political activity. It was also ostensibly constructed around the altogether more central activity of charity, one of this period's theological virtues and a Christian obligation. Hospitality, the giving of shelter and food to another, was perceived as a spiritually praiseworthy act: early on the monasteries developed household offices and strategies to provide hospitality to guests. Aside from this charitable aspect, however, the political nature of hospitality is revealing in the elite household context. Aristocratic wealth reached a peak in the thirteenth century with economic stability in aristocratic land and revenues matched by lavish hospitality practices.[85] Great households offered hospitality to individual guests, although the practice of receiving entire households had largely ceased by the fourteenth century.[86] Abstract ideas of honour, friendship and vested interest in salvation, as well as more immediate reciprocity, all encouraged the practice of hospitality, which also appeared as a favoured trope in chivalric literature. There were differences between high and low ranking guests and high and low ranking households. Courtesy poems do not consider tradesmen or workers who ate in the hall where this formed part of their payment. In *the boke of curtasye* hospitality begins with the young man arriving at a house, likely indicating that the poem is relevant to adolescents

---

[83] MS Sloane 1315, fol. 1ᵛ.
[84] MS Harley 4011, fol. 171ʳ. Other manuscripts, 'Thow he nevyr theyne no man shall hym lerne'. See Appendix A for manuscript details.
[85] C. Dyer, *Standards of Living in the Later Middle Ages: Social Change in England, c.1200–1520*, rev. edn (Cambridge, 1998), pp. 27–9.
[86] Woolgar, *Great Household*, p. 21.

or young adults. These roles were mediated according to how well the young man (the receiver) and the lord (the giver) jointly respect the laws of hospitality. Here, for the first time, a text introduces the manner in which courteous socialisation and upbringing prepare young people for this important social situation.

The guest's responsibility to demonstrate correct behaviour is particularly significant in courtesy texts. In these sources, prior knowledge of courtesy and manners is assumed to exist. However, knowing courtesy is not enough; it has to be used with the right emphasis to match the social status of everyone involved. In a practical sense, it was necessary for young people to have learnt this before they could seek hospitality for themselves; this could be done by observation, by verbal instructions or by using texts to learn about such important points. *The boke of curtasye* can be said to represent this latter mode of transmission. Here, hospitality begins with the young man arriving at the house, but it is his actions afterwards which enable him to find a place inside the household.[87]

The result of hospitality in this instance is clear; it has both been given and received correctly. In Chrétien's *Le Chevalier de la Charrette* hospitality is so politically significant that its breakdown occasions violence and discord. Courtesy poems are far less interested in the narrative potential for discord than in the pragmatic securing of honour. It is worth noting that while some courtesy poems are found in manuscripts alongside romance material – for example, in MS Ashmole 61, MS Cotton Caligula A ii and MS Advocates 19.3.1 – other manuscripts show stronger clusters of didactic material, religious texts, chronicles or, as in MS Add. 5467, include the princely guide *Secretum Secretorum*. Less often found beside courtesy poems are chivalric formulas proper. Philippa Hardman and Mary Shaner even see deliberate redaction of chivalric tropes in the romances in Advocates 19.3.1.[88] In the case of courtesy poems, the practice of hospitality is essentially a performance in which the lord is able to enhance his status and publically confirm his generosity, both to his inferiors and to his own superiors. The recurring preoccupation in courtesy poems with public good manners specifically meets needs like these. On this point, Mertes suggests that 'as the household became more central to noble political life it also took on greater symbolic duties: household hospitality, always an important aspect of noble life, took on greater

---

[87] Julie Kerr has categorised the gestures of hospitality according to spatial and chronological phases suggested by the themes of 'the guests' arrival', 'at the threshold' and 'the departure'. J. Kerr '"Welcome the coming and speed the parting guest": Hospitality in Twelfth-Century England', *Journal of Medieval History* 33 (2007), 130–46. See also J. Kerr, 'The Open Door: Hospitality and Honour in Twelfth/Early Thirteenth-Century England', *History* 87 (2002), 322–35 (pp. 324–32).

[88] P. Hardman 'A Medieval "Library *in Parvo*"', *Medium Aevum* 47 (1978), 262–73; Shaner, 'Instruction and Delight', pp. 7–13. See also Appendix A for manuscripts listed above.

significance'.[89] This relationship between household status and hospitality is strongly associated with fifteenth-century courtesy literature. Like the physical accoutrements in these great households, well-observed formalities were critical to a display of status and critical to socialisation.

Finally, another perspective on young people's visibility in public activities is seen in their roles in hosting. An important feature is the practical application of practices and hospitable rules to younger people. While adults had various duties in hosting, youths were functional working members within the household; this was the case both for young people as visitors and young people who were already in a household as servants. The courtesy narrative informed, and was informed by, the contemporary understanding of these practices.

Like Russell's poem, the third book in *the boke of curtasye* returns to the interests of a large household. It is unlike other courtesy poems as a result of extensive passages detailing the function of different household offices and was presumably aimed at those needing to learn specific duties for the various departments within the household; again this makes it relevant to the training of older children and to middling families wishing to acquire the social trappings of older, elite houses. It is difficult to ascribe a casual reader's interests to the list of occupations in *the boke of curtasye*. The work of the receiver of rents is described, as are the duties of bakers, porters, marshals, the clerk of the kitchen, treasurers, almoners and huntsmen.[90] These passages show the structure and organisation of large households and could indicate the progression of professional servants between positions and occupations over time. However, it is difficult to reconcile this level of detail with the interests of most young people. It is possible readers were encouraged to dip into passages at will rather than consecutively read or hear texts in a single sitting. The structure of courtesy poems around common themes, rather than strict narrative passages, may well have suited interrupted readings. It is also tempting to tie the increased sophistication and length of *the boke of curtasye* to an adolescent or young adult readership: the 'child' addressed in this poem is probably not the same young 'child' of *Stans puer ad mensam* or *Urbanitatis* who needed to learn the basics of courtesy in simple ways.

As already noted, there are strong similarities between this poem and Russell's *Boke of Nurture*. The lessons provide evidence about the daily running of a large household, consistent with Russell's appointment as usher to Humphrey, duke of Gloucester in the early to mid-fifteenth century.[91] The level of detail in the poem, which speaks to real household duties, is noticeable in accounts of domestic chores related to the use of linen table-

---

[89] Mertes, *English Noble Household*, p. 187.
[90] Monastic houses had similar offices, including the chamberlain, almoner, kitchener and so forth. Nicholls, *Matter of Courtesy*, pp. 26–7.
[91] MS Harley 4011 is the only manuscript to directly ascribe this work to Russell.

ware. In fact, while household sizes generally decreased in the fourteenth and fifteenth centuries, there was an increasing embellishment of rituals for laying the table and use of tablecloths. From the fourteenth century there was also a heightened use of specialised servants and more formal and elaborate public meals.[92]

It is difficult to judge why young servants received instruction from a text, as workplace activities are best learnt through example and practice. This raises questions about audience; it is possible that both the *Boke of Nurture* and *the boke of curtasye* were styled to reveal elite practices to non-noble patrons wanting to emulate elite customs, or to those suddenly thrust into new environments because of their wealth. At a time of social mobility, conformity to noble practices was a secure way of participating in elite society.[93] Its nature as a learnt process made courtesy acquirable. This diffusion outside elite structure was discussed earlier and will be pursued throughout this book. It is tempting to see courtesy poems as a medium for the dispersal of elite behaviour into households unable to attract servants already trained in elite courtesy practices. If so, poems like these may have shown people the means by which it was possible to transform non-elite houses into elite houses, at least in some ways that could be measured.

There are other similarities between Russell's poem and *the boke of curtasye*. It is obvious that the character in Russell's poem is not a young child, as explained by his having searched for a previous master to learn from:

> Ser y have sowght ferr and ner many a day
> To gete me a master and eche man seethe nay
> By cause I can no good ther for this I pl[ay]
> ffor y am as lewyd as ys a popyngaye[94]

This description also effectively distances him from the elite world: 'lewd' implies belonging to lower orders as well as unskilled and ignorant. This association between learnt manners and stability is a significant one and it is worth noting differences in the manuscripts on this point. Manuscript Royal 17 D. xv suggests 'And said be cause he was nat wele lernede / he wold he were out of this lond exilid'.[95] Manuscript Sloane 2027 shows a correlation between courteous socialisation and future happiness: 'Syr he seyd I wold I

---

[92] Woolgar, *Great Household*, pp. 14, 41, 149–50.
[93] Hanawalt, *Growing Up*, p. 86.
[94] MS Sloane 1315, fols. 1ʳ⁻ᵛ, 'pl[ay]' is probably a scribal error for 'pr[ay]'. MS Harley 4011, fol. 171ʳ instead has:
> In certeyn sir y haue y sought ferr[e] & ner[e] many a wilsom way
> to gete mete a mastir & for y cowd nougt eu[er]y man seid me nay
> y cowd no good ne noon y shewd[e] wher[e] eu[er] y ede day by day
> but wantou[n] & nyce recheles & lewd[e] as Iangelyng[e] as a Iaye

[95] London, BL, MS Royal 17 D. xv, fol. 333ʳ.

were out off thys land wend / Good sone be ware and sey thn nat so in any man[er] wyse / For god forbedyth wanhope that a grete synne ys'.[96] Manuscript Harley 4011 has a particularly affective tone which expands on a sense of despair and futility. This passage is worth quoting in full:

> So god me soceur[e] he said / sir y serue myself & els noon oth[er] man
> is thy gov[er]nuance good y said / son say me iff thow can
> y wold y wer[e] owt of this world / seid he / y ne ne rougt how sone whan
> Sey nought so good son bewar[e] / me thynketh[e] thow menyst amysse
> for god forbedith[e] wanhope for that a horrible synne ys[97]

Such a striking theme differs sharply from other courtesy poems and serves as a dramatic tool for Russell's story – one of the rare instances of a dramatic narrative being employed in a courtesy poem.

As noted earlier, the use of 'I' in this literature fixes socialisation into the young person's own mind. Of this, both the youth and in this case Russell speak in the first person. Russell's influence is derived in part from his automatic authority as the story's author and narrator and in part from the direct insertion of himself into the story. He meets the youth in the woods where they begin their discussion: 'As y [Russell] rose owt of my bed y saw wher[e] walked a semely yong[e] man'.[98] Russell's responses to the youth reinforce his authority, taking the form of offering to teach various occupations before the young man settles on the offices of butler, panter, chamberlain and carver. The significance of locating a theme relating to employment in a courtesy poem was discussed earlier. Yet Russell also allows space for general courtesy rules, a necessary device considering the earlier statement about the young man's ignorance, which is mentioned again later in the poem as an apparently significant point: 'Sympyll condycions off a person that is natt tauhghte / I will the exchewe hem for eu[er] they be nawghte'.[99] The evidence of this and other courtesy poems suggests that a 'set' of basic manners was widely recognised as essential formative behaviour.

Russell makes two important points in his poem. The first concerns by what methods young people are socialised: through a mentor, through learning

---

[96] MS Sloane 2027, fol. 37r.
[97] MS Harley 4011, fol. 171r. MS Sloane 1315 also retains a similar sense of despair. Both lines, 'he wolde he were oute of this londe e[]yly' and 'God for bedyth wanhope a grete syn hyt ys', appear in the Sloane manuscript, fol. 1r. In MS Royal 17 D. xv, fol. 333r the line is given as 'Sonne I said be warre say not so in no wise / god forbiddeth wanhoope agrete syn[n]e it is'. In the poem it is explicitly explained that the young man has searched for a master and continually failed to find one.
[98] MS Harley 4011, fol. 171r.
[99] MS Sloane 2027, fol. 42r.

from observation and through the medium of writing, which Russell himself chooses. The second of Russell's points is new and it focuses on why young people need to learn these lessons. From other courtesy authors it is clear that such skills demonstrate gentle status. Russell, however, makes numerous concessions to pragmatic issues: service in an elite household provides young people with exceptional employment opportunities, securing them a stable position in society. The conspicuous link between courtesy and employment, as well as the frankness and imagination of his narrative, extends courtesy beyond its normal range of interests.

Both poems also outline different stages in socialisation, beginning with basic courteous rules and progressing to more difficult actions. Knowing these rules allowed people, including young servants and those they served, to participate in society, perhaps regardless of initial background. The role of courtesy literature in social mobility and its readership amongst non-elite groups will be developed further to show how gentry and merchant families might be expected to rebel against this and take on other values and ideas in socialising children. The high proportion of extant courtesy poems in the English vernacular, as opposed to Latin or the French vernacular, suggests authors, scribes and readers were ready to appropriate elite ideas into a vernacular tradition for non-Latin-speaking gentry and merchant families. We are, however, witnessing a wider trend towards writing literature in English, as Chaucer attests. A chronic shortage of texts is also suggested by the translation of courtesy poems out of Latin into the English vernacular: *Stans puer ad mensam* was modified by John Lydgate into English and *The Babees Book* is an English vernacular poem based on an older Latin source.[100]

Courtesy poems are the most complete set of sources available from our period that specifically discuss normative behaviour for young people in terms of the household, a form of socialisation which entrenched a theory of high social status as a model of conduct. This significantly decreased in the fifteenth century when female servants and co-habiting married couples were more openly accepted.[101] These poems, however, tell of the underlying ideologies that were part of a boy's upbringing, containing otherwise hidden information about the manner in which youths from the gentry and merchant classes were, in fact, associated with elite activities and behaviour. At a rudimentary level they relate to the involvement of young boys serving and eating in halls and the communal activity of eating and dining, but there is also uncommon insight into the manner in which young people were thought to form relationships with peers and contemporaries and how their behav-

---

[100] According to Nicholls there are five Anglo-Norman courtesy poems and a further eight French courtesy poems, the latter not circulating in England. Nicholls, *Matter of Courtesy*, pp. 186–90.
[101] Woolgar, *Great Household*, p. 36.

iour was expected to conform in an observable and emotional sense to an elite value system.

Tracking where courtesy and morality appear in the literature affords the opportunity to examine what this material meant to audiences and how and why adults and young people approached socialisation. Through these poems, gentry and merchant children and young people were learning and hearing about a rich social world and the possibilities and expectations that set them apart from their less mannered, churlish counterparts. The rules and guidelines in these poems still seem to be dynamic and lively and the language used to describe them even more so. Consistent allusions to children as active participants in their own future and their actions indicate a clear preoccupation of audiences. These courtesy poems were not written for adults to monitor children, but instead gave young people a sense of responsibility and active participation in the direction of their lives.

The promotion of elite environments and lifestyles required these poems to be closely integrated with actual practices, presumably for audiences who were assumed to share the same cultural understandings of behaviour and lifestyles or who could be encouraged to accept how and why these elite lessons were important. The concerns of the upper classes fed into the descriptions of hierarchy, of service to the lord and of courteous behaviour, reflecting not only on the individual but also on the household of which they were a part. *Stans puer ad mensam, The Babees Book, The Lytylle Childrene's Book* and *Urbanitatis* address those matters which had a bearing on living in a lord's household and on being socialised through courtesy and good manners. Returning once more to the qualities of Chaucer's Squire ('curteis ... lowely, and servysable'), for all his flaws, he remains an embodiment of many of the principles of courtesy found in these poems. Any young male reader of *Stans puer ad mensam, Urbanitatis, The Babees Book* and other courtesy texts could only hope that their cleverness in demonstrating these skills and their meek and serviceable character would lead to similar praise.

CHAPTER TWO

Readers

'Thys boke is made fo child[ren] yong'[1]

This chapter provides a comparative examination of the earlier and later courtesy material. In particular, there were continuities and discontinuities between the courtesy poems discussed previously and sixteenth-century material. The changes are viewed in the context of shifting household politics and aristocratic power. By 1500 there were only sixty peers remaining in England, a decline from 200 in c. 1250.[2] At the same time, those who were associated, or were attempting to associate themselves, with the gentry were rapidly increasing in number. In the sixteenth century, the pull towards the Tudor royal court instead of individual elite houses changed the role of the elite household and its social and status-driven meaning.[3] As magnates and lords spent more time at the royal court and at Westminster, the need for on-call household staff lessened. This did not stop the nobility from maintaining large and elaborate seats, nor does it suggest that elite socialisation based on courtesy and manners was no longer of interest to people. It continued to be present in these poems. However, elite socialisation was stable only as long as it related to the elite household and where the concerns of public conduct, hospitality and noble hierarchies remained priorities.

Household staffs and retinues were more likely to be broken up in the sixteenth century, with smaller groups travelling with the lord when he was at the royal court or in London.[4] As discussed in the previous chapter, most courtesy poems tend to date to the period before this, when elite households were politically and socially active. Lawrence Stone's classic model of economic crises within the aristocracy in the late sixteenth century, which led to the loss of social and political power in the mid-seventeenth century, still holds value.[5] Such developments had a pragmatic impact on gentry servant numbers. Consequently, the reduction in the total political power of the

---

[1] MS Ashmole 61, fol. 21ᵛ.
[2] P. J. P. Goldberg, *Medieval England: A Social History 1250–1550* (London, 2004), p. 115.
[3] For a discussion of the decline of the noble household in relation to the king's authority see Mertes, *English Noble Household*, pp. 188–90.
[4] Mertes, *English Noble Household*, p. 190.
[5] L. Stone, *The Crisis of the Aristocracy* (Oxford, 1965).

household and its shrinking role in aiding young people to high status positions shift the value and meaning of courtesy literature. Any movement away from gentle service in the household makes other patronage networks rise in value. Over the sixteenth and seventeenth centuries, previously high status household servants were progressively disconnected from the elite structure of the household, requiring the socialisation of new generations to develop in other ways. The decline in the assumed dominance and supremacy of the nobility and the noble household suggests how and why changing social values and imperatives came to be discussed. The parallel decline in the fostering of children in elite households is also related to this trend.

In this context, elite courtesy lessons are conflated with other agendas more in tune with gentry, bourgeois and merchant preoccupations. As the character of elite service changed, so too did the literature which had been intended to explain the purpose, meaning and value of serving roles to young people. In this chapter competition from gentry and bourgeois consumers (who were anxious to change elements of elite courtesy) and socialisation are examined. Socialisation needed to develop in new ways to meet these changing needs.

Textual variants

Texts must take their audiences into account. Analysing textual variants of fifteenth-century manuscripts allows us to examine the manner in which socialisation was understood in different periods. By looking at audiences – that is, by asking who a particular courtesy manuscript was for – it is possible to understand the interests and approaches of different reading networks and thus what socialisation meant for different groups. It is worth noting at the outset that this literature retained its fundamental concern with the social education of children and young people. My intention in this chapter is to investigate a divergence occurring in the type of household audiences accessing courtesy literature and in what ways lessons for socialisation incorporated qualities other than courtesy. In particular, this chapter investigates by what methods the social norms represented in some manuscripts were responding to bourgeois and mercantile interests.

Understanding gentry and bourgeois concerns helps reconstruct textual transmission and circulation. The work of Sylvia Huot and Kathleen Ashley on manuscript reception and ownership networks is particularly useful in discussing modified courtesy manuscripts in English gentry and urban bourgeois settings and in some instances in what is certainly a family audience network.[6] Reception history reveals how readers were able to approach narra-

---

[6] S. Huot, *The Romance of the Rose and Its Medieval Readers: Interpretation, Reception, Manuscript Transmission* (Cambridge, 1993); K. Ashley, 'The *Miroir des Bonnes*

tives in multiple ways. Merchant, bourgeois and gentry groups were absorbing information about the superiority of elite customs and lifestyles while simultaneously distinguishing themselves in a positive fashion from elite extravagance, outmoded courtesy, falsely courteous behaviour and corrupt (and ailing) elite morality and chivalry. This occurred even as late fifteenth-century London merchants acquired the trappings of chivalric display and became increasingly armigerous. Bourgeois and merchant readers read critically and resisted certain notions of behaviour, a pattern of resistance and questioning seen among female readers of French romances.[7] Margaret Higonnet has more directly observed that 'Manners, as external tokens of propriety and class status, could be mocked even as they were being learned.'[8]

Textual variations and scribal intervention can also suggest where and why material has been reworked to suit domestic settings. Household miscellanies, of the type analysed in this chapter, frequently include a range of textual genres including romances, religious material and courtesy material. The intertextual relationship between the different genres, and indeed between different items in a single genre, provides a way of assessing likely audiences. In an examination of manuscript Edinburgh Advocates 19.3.1 Mary Shaner draws attention to the five categories of additions and emendations that a scribe may have used to embrace a youthful audience: violence, direct speech, an emphasis on domestic and materialistic virtues, simple piety and simple character development.[9] Not all are relevant to courtesy material and it may be more useful to look at specific references to mercantilist practices in some texts to understand the relationship between youthful audience, class and the restructuring of elite narratives.

Household types

The households described in this chapter are understood as being, on the whole, far smaller than noble houses and primarily structured around parents (including step-parents) and children (including step-children) who, along with household servants, co-resided for at least part of the year.[10] The charac-

---

Femmes: Not for Women Only?', in *Medieval Conduct*, ed. K. Ashley and R. L. A. Clark (Minneapolis, 2001), pp. 86–105.

[7] R. L. Krueger, *Women Readers and the Ideology of Gender in old French Verse Romance* (Cambridge, 1993).

[8] Higonnet, 'Civility Books', p. 137. Although this had a very different meaning to middle-ranking bourgeois groups in fifteenth- and sixteenth-century England than the French bourgeois in the nineteenth century who were politically motivated to find differences from the elite.

[9] These categories are based on Hardman, 'A Medieval "Library *in Parvo*"', pp. 262–73; Shaner, 'Instruction and Delight', pp. 5–15.

[10] On affluent households being more likely to retain children than poorer ones see Goldberg, *Medieval England*, p. 20. The classic account of families is D. Herlihy,

teristics of households, whether the small urban unit or the larger elite environments discussed earlier, situate the subsequent ideals about socialisation. Middling landowners or parish gentry, defined as much by shared affinities as by economic interests, probably experienced a higher degree of cultural stability during this period, according to Christine Carpenter. There is some suggestion that a sense of unity and internal cohesion within this middle-ranking stratum partly formed in opposition to restricted elite circles.[11] These groups have ties to this literature.

This chapter looks at the manner in which manuscripts, such as Ashmole 61, were modified to respond to a non-elite environment and by what means their lessons suited children and socialisation, in ways that indicate the prevalence of non-elite ideals. This is followed by an analysis of other variant manuscripts, including Balliol 354 and Harley 541. In addition, two further clusters of texts demonstrate in what manner the elite courtesy narrative could be modified to suit different readerships. The second half of the chapter will focus on the three poems for girls and young women in the *Good Wife* tradition, and comparisons are made between nine extant manuscripts. This chapter concludes with an examination of the gentry and professional advice tract written by Peter Idley for his son.

Bourgeois households and merchant interests

Manuscript Ashmole 61 shows in what manner elite texts could be reshaped for audiences who existed outside the original elite sphere but who were important figures within their own social, and frequently local, networks. Manuscript Ashmole 61 was probably part of the library of a devout merchant or the handbook of a family chaplain. The loose grouping of courtesy material at the start of the manuscript, forming what has been identified as a 'children's corner', is worth noting, although the manuscript contains no discrete codicological divisions.[12] Manuscript Ashmole 61 has been described as a 'one-book library', with the scribe, identified only as Rate, editing his copy-texts to suit a religious and family interest. Lynne Blanchfield's discussion of the manuscript, progressing from 'low-level and relatively unsophisticated "teaching" verses' towards weightier religious and romance texts, provides

---

'The Making of the Medieval Family: Symmetry, Structure, and Sentiment', *Journal of Family History* 8 (1983), 116–30 (p. 117); D. Herlihy, 'The Family and Religious Ideologies in Medieval Europe', *Journal of Family History* 12.1–3 (1987), 3–17.

[11] Carpenter, *Locality and Polity*, pp. 143–4.

[12] On this manuscript see L. S. Blanchfield, 'Rate Revisited: The Compilation of the Narrative Works in MS Ashmole 61', in *Romance Reading on the Book: Essays on Medieval Narrative Presented to Maldwyn Mills*, ed. J. Fellows, R. Field, G. Rogers and J. Weiss (Cardiff, 1996), pp. 208–20.

useful insight into the workings of a 'one-book library'.¹³ The intertextual relationships between romances, religious material and family-based teaching narratives made the manuscript suitable for a household, both as a practical resource and as a recreational one. Malcolm Parkes has observed that similar manuscripts are indicative of a widening interest in 'literary recreation'.¹⁴ The tastes of readers were refined over the fourteenth to early sixteenth centuries, with the manuscripts owned by bourgeois or merchant families showing an interest in recreational literature.¹⁵ There is some suggestion that sophisticated literary tastes developed out of initial contact with purely commercial and administrative material.¹⁶

Rate's personal voice is visible within the manuscript and forms part of what can be identified as his role as a legitimate agent in reworking material: a notion of scribal agency privileged by Huot.¹⁷ His interpolations, glosses and amendments should be considered the products of deliberate and considered choices. The following discussion necessarily focuses on changes to the courtesy material within the manuscript, most particularly within the poems *The Young Children's Book* and *Stans puer ad mensam*, the latter being the subject of F. J. Furnivall's somewhat tetchy comment that 'the poem is so enlarged, by the addition of an Introduction and many new maxims, that it has hardly a claim to the title of Lydgate's short poem'.¹⁸

Issues of age and status provide insight into the appropriateness of this literature for young people. The poem *How the Wise Man Taught his Son* is uncommonly specific on the question of age. In several manuscripts, including Ashmole 61, the son is identified as being a young man of fifteen years: 'Yt was a wyse man had a chyld / Was fully xv wynt[er] of age'.¹⁹ Usefully, the words 'yonge men' are used in the poem and the term is qualified to a chronological age. This is a more comprehensive indicator of age than 'child'. Other texts which refer to 'young men' may likewise have been for readers around fifteen years of age. Significantly, in manuscripts Lambeth 853 and Balliol 354 the age of the son is not stated in terms of years, with Hill writing in the latter, 'A wyse ma[n] had a fayre ma[n] child / he tawght

---

13 Blanchfield, 'Rate Revisited', p. 211.
14 M. B. Parkes, 'The Literacy of the Laity', in *The Mediaeval World*, ed. D. Daiches and A. Thorlby (London, 1973), pp. 555–77 (p. 563).
15 On this see J. Boffey, *Manuscripts of English Courtly Love Lyrics in the Later Middle Ages* (Cambridge, 1985), pp. 125–7; and also, A. F. Marotti, *Manuscript, Print and the English Renaissance Lyric* (Ithaca, 1995), pp. 42–4.
16 Parkes, 'Literacy of the Laity', pp. 557–8, 562–5; C. Sponsler, *Drama and Resistance: Bodies, Goods, and Theatricality in Late Medieval England* (Minneapolis, 1997), p. 54.
17 Huot, *Romance of the Rose*, pp. 2–5.
18 *QEA*, p. xiv.
19 MS Ashmole 61, fol. 6ʳ. CUL MS Ff.2.38, fol. 53ʳ and London, BL, MS Harley 5396, fol. 297ʳ also refer to this: 'A wyse man had a fayre chyld / Was well of xv yere age'.

hy[m] well in te[n]d[er] age'.²⁰ John Trevisa's late fourteenth century translation of Bartholomaeus's encyclopaedic work associated *pueritia*, ending at fourteen years of age, with the phrase 'tender age'.²¹ Hill's phrasing suggests an ambiguous and evocative stage between childhood and adulthood. In manuscript Lambeth 853 the same information is given in slightly different phrasing: 'Ther was a wise man taught his child / while it was yong and tendir of age'.²² Comparable evidence from Chancery petitions shows the use of 'tender age' in cases where young servants claimed they had been taken advantage of when making contracts, suggesting an age of fourteen for boys and twelve for girls. This reflected canonical ages of marriage, at which time young people were assumed to be rational enough to consent to marriage contracts.²³

'Child' is also used in courtesy poems. While it could be gender neutral and refer to both boys and girls, it tends to be employed when discussing young boys, referring to adolescent males in service as well as to young people of aristocratic birth. *Puer* in *Stans puer ad mensam* describes a young child in a pre-adolescent stage of life. It also describes young people from non-noble backgrounds who entered into service in elite households but who did not contribute to the elite hierarchy, instead seeking permanent positions of service.²⁴ Households by the late fifteenth century accepted children at around twelve years of age and occupations varied between high status service to the lord and menial work, making *puer* a suitable, if ambiguous, term to use, as tasks in courtesy poems relating to washing the lord's hands were reserved for high status servants.²⁵ The 'child' used in Rate's version of *Stans puer ad mensam* encompasses economic information which suggests a greater diversity in backgrounds than the terminology might otherwise indicate: 'The child th[at] is c[ur]tas be he pore or ryche / Yt schall hy[m] a vayll[e] th[er]off haue no drede'.²⁶ Both the rich and the poor child were, it seems, to find something of value in this poem.

Another indication of potential audience is found in unique lines on dress,

---

²⁰ MS Balliol 354, fol. 157ʳ.
²¹ Each stage of childhood is connected to 'tenderness'. However, it is only *pueritia* (seven to fourteen) which is labelled with the specific phrase tender age: 'and hath that name *puericia* of *pubertas*, the age of fourtene yere, that is yit a tendir age'. *Properties of Things*, ed. Seymour, I, 291.
²² MS Lambeth 853, p. 186.
²³ R. H. Helmholz, *Marriage Litigation in Medieval England* (London, 1974).
²⁴ On this see S. Trigg, 'Learning to Live', in *Middle English: Oxford Twenty-First Century Approaches to Literature*, ed. P. Strohm (Oxford, 2007), pp. 459–75 (p. 466).
²⁵ On this see P. W. Fleming, 'Household Servants of the Yorkist and Early Tudor Gentry', in *Early Tudor England*, ed. D. Williams (Woodbridge, 1989), pp. 19–36 (p. 25). For associations with working directly with the lord see Woolgar, *Great Household*, p. 41.
²⁶ MS Ashmole 61, fol. 17ᵛ.

incorporated into it a discussion on clothing and identity: 'Kepe wele th[i] sleuys for touchyng off mete / Ne no long[e] sleuys lasyd luke th[at] th[ou] haue'.[27] By inserting this into an elite text Rate can be seen as simultaneously creating multiple cues for his readers. His warning may have been a legitimate caution to gentry readers over the impracticality of some clothing at the table. However, it is worthwhile considering that Rate was prompting bourgeois, merchants and yeomen to remember they were forbidden by sumptuary legislation to wear this manner of clothing. There is evidence that this manuscript was written at a time of growing status consciousness. Shuffelton observes that 'the challenge may have been in recognizing the proper order of a social hierarchy'.[28] It is tempting to suggest that the definitive rules laid down in courtesy poems were of service at this time.

Extensive lacing, which allowed sleeves to be padded with wadding to broaden the overall appearance, was, in fact, popular during Edward IV's reign.[29] 1463 sumptuary legislation prohibited the wearing of padded sleeves for any degree below and including yeoman. There were clear references to children in the legislation and children are cited three times in the 1463 statute (although not at all in the 1483 statute) and twice in the 1533 act. The language employed is a useful measure of contemporary attitudes towards children. In the statute of 1463 children's clothing is based upon inherited rank and governed by the father according to 'his rule or governance'.[30] As already noted in the previous chapter, the language of contemporary courtesy poems was more focused on the responsibilities of children, particularly if they were between seven and fourteen years ('tender age') or fifteen years onwards ('young man'). The formulaic and legalistic nature of the legislation plays a part in accounting for children in this way, limiting the images of childhood responsibility. Courtesy poems, with their imaginative choices, captured a child's responsibilities through different mechanisms.

The young boy from *Stans puer ad mensam* mentioned already in this book is described walking in the street. In Rate's version this is expanded to include a lengthier description of non-household spaces and, although long, it is worth quoting in full:

> And iff thou go w[i]t[h] any man in feld[e] or in towne
> Be wall or by hege by pales or by pale
> To go w[i]t[h] oute hy[m] luke th[o]u be bowne

---

[27] MS Ashmole 61, fol. 19ʳ.
[28] *Codex Ashmole 61: A Compilation of Popular Middle English Verse*, ed. G. Shuffelton (Kalamazoo, 2008), p. 441.
[29] *QEA*, p. 62.
[30] Statutes of the Realm, 3 Edward IV, c.5, 1463, in *Complaint and Reform in England, 1436–1714: Fifty Writings of the Time on Politics, Religion, Society, Economics, Architecture, Science and Education*, ed. W. H. Dunham Jr. and S. Pargellis (New York, 1938), pp. 36, 37.

> And take hy[m] by twyx th[e]e & th[at] same walle
> And if th[ou] mete hy[m] luke th[o]u be sure
> Th[a]t thou go w[i]t[h] oute hy[m] & leue hy[m] nexte th[e] walle
> And iff the schuld enter[e] in at any dore
> Putt befor[e] th[e]e thi bett[er] for ougte th[a]t may befalle[31]

There is scope here to see these variations in location in terms of readership, with merchants, urban bourgeois and even gentle servants dividing their time between urban and country estates during their careers. All may have appreciated guidance on their behaviour outside households. The young reader or listener of *Stans puer ad mensam* in manuscript Ashmole 61 also encountered the dual roles of consuming and serving, and again this played a part in how socialising lessons concerned economic and social positions in the household. In *Stans puer ad mensam* a direct task was set the young servant – to be on hand with water to help his lord wash.[32] This was a high status task and one with which gentle servants were more likely to be entrusted. Rate's opening stanzas presented behaviour and courteous manners as accessible to the rich and poor, with these lessons presumably aimed at a greater number of social groups than are overtly identified in some texts.

In addition to this, another unique courtesy poem found only in the Ashmole manuscript is worth noting for its bourgeois work ethic. *The Young Children's Book* described table manners as well as daily household activities for a young man. Merchant readers would have found actual substantive issues in this poem relating to work, earning money honestly and buying and selling goods. It is certainly suggestive of a non-elite audience and of socialisation in a trade environment in which lessons could no longer focus only on elite courtesy gestures; the text is layered with a strong subtext of ethical and moral lessons. These changes are suggestive of adaptability in the late fifteenth century literature, making this a genre highly suitable for multiple audiences and households. Socialising children according to elite concerns is retained within the 'story', evidenced in rules concerning the manner of eating. The interpolation of stanzas from the well-known contemporary courtesy poem *The Lytylle Childrene's Book* as part of the opening of *The Young Children's Book* indicates a direct borrowing from the established archive of courtesy material. This direct soliciting suggests Rate was familiar with contemporary courtesy literature and knew of its standard tropes. Alterations to the standard patterns are therefore all the more revealing. The poem begins with rising from bed, crossing your breast and head, simple ablutions and attending mass. The first reference to *courtesy*, outside the interpolated stanzas, appears in relation to greeting others courteously.[33] Simple

---

[31] MS Ashmole 61, fol. 19r.
[32] MS Ashmole 61, fol. 19v.
[33] MS Ashmole 61, fol. 20r.

rules for eating breakfast follow on from this, continuing a pattern in which food consumption was integrated into the courtesy theme. However, the high status location of the elite household was replaced with a more general setting. At breakfast, the central guidelines concerned the stomach and diet and incorporated simple religious conventions: 'Blysse thi mouthe or thou it ete / The bett[er] schall[e] be thi dyete / Be for thi mete sey thou thi gr[a]ce / Yt ocupys bot lytell space'.[34] This omitted the elaborate public responses and gestures identified with meals in the elite house, although graces and prayer would have also been said as a matter of course. A different household status may explain why there is little in the way of 'courtesy' in these maxims. Instead, a focus on less elaborate procedures and responses associated with eating encourages an alternative to the usual elite situation. A comment on poor quality meals continues this theme: 'Bot p[ra]yse thi fare w[er] so eu[er] thou be / For[e] be it gode o[r] be it badde / Yn gud worth it muste be had'.[35]

Once breakfast is completed the reader is directed to go about his work, an action relevant to a non-elite audience: 'Than go labo[ur] as thou arte bownde / And be not Idyll[e] in no stounde'.[36] It is worth repeating the extent of the information on work practices in full, not least for the correlation between occupations and Scripture:

> Holy scrypto[ur] th[us] it seyth
> To the that arte of cristen feyth
> Yff[e] thou labo[ur] thou muste ete
> That w[i]t[h] thi hond[es] thou doyst[e] gete
> A byrd[e] hath weng[e]s forto fle
> So man hath armes laboryd to be[37]

This could, of course, be an elaborate metaphor for the work of a lord or superior servant, but the emphasis on physicality – arms, hands, arms labouring, birds wings at work – raises a different set of possibilities and suggests a different type of manual labour. Stephen Knight has shown that terms used for labour in English literature from the fourteenth century 'dehumanized' workers by associating them with land and animals.[38] Here, the wings of birds are one and the same as the arms of workers. Material on a merchant's, shopkeeper's or market seller's occupations is stressed in a later passage and is suggestive of a deeper and more sustained interest in this type of audience:

---

[34] MS Ashmole 61, fol. 20ʳ.
[35] MS Ashmole 61, fols. 20ʳ, 21ʳ.
[36] MS Ashmole 61, fol. 20ʳ. On this see Furnivall & Rickert, p. 183.
[37] MS Ashmole 61, fol. 20ʳ.
[38] S. Knight, 'The Voice of Labour in Fourteenth-Century English Literature', in *The Problem of Labour in Fourteenth-Century England*, ed. J. Bothwell, P. J. P. Goldberg and W. M. Ormrod (York, 2000), pp. 101–22 (pp. 103–4).

> Vse no sueryng [sloth, negligence] noth[er] lying[e]
> Yn thi selling[e] & thi byeng[e]
> For[e] & thou do thou arte to blame
> And at the last thou wyll[e] haue scham[e]
> Gete thi gowd w[i]t[h] trewe[t]h & wy[n]ne
> And kepe the out of dette & sy[n]ne[39]

The emphasis on good reputation and honesty in dealing with other people would almost certainly reflect mercantile activities. Sylvia Thrupp has stressed the importance of moral values to merchants: 'at a pinch, his children could go through life without much knowledge of Latin, but it was essential that they be brought up virtuously'.[40] It is worth noting that Thrupp argued that schools alone could not meet these needs and that moral training was equally a household affair. The issue of whether schools were capable of teaching morality, and indeed prized virtue and social conduct in scholars as highly as they did academic skills, is pursued later in this book. However, it is worthwhile noting here that schools and households shared many similar socialising characteristics. Given that *The Young Children's Book* was addressed to younger readers, these ethical lessons also make this poem highly relevant to another category of young people: apprentices. Apprentices certainly could come from gentry backgrounds, where elite courtesy would already have been an agenda in socialisation. Mercantile careers required another string to be added to socialisation. This emphasis on moral lessons suggested pretension to a moral superiority within merchant and bourgeois groups. It is a trend which takes shape in the connections drawn between mercantile and bourgeois manuscripts and ethical themes.

Further questions about audience are raised with the terms Sir and Dame, which may indicate the household of a knight or baronet (and his wife), although this is complicated by the fact that both titles could refer more generally to any superior: 'To S[er] or dame or th[er] meny / Stand & sytte not furth w[i]t[h] all[e] / Tyll[e] he byde the that rewlys the halle'.[41] However, there is other evidence of a clearer merchant or bourgeois interest operating in the poem. Rate writes about his presumed audience, concluding the poem in the following way:

> This boke is made fo[r] child[er] yong[e]
> At the scowle that byde not long[e]

---

[39] MS Ashmole 61, fol. 20ᵛ.
[40] S. L. Thrupp, *The Merchant Class of Medieval London, 1300–1500* (Chicago, 1948), p. 164. Barbara Hanawalt has also recognised the connections between merchants and moral values in *'Of Good and Ill Repute': Gender and Social Control in Medieval England* (New York, 1998), p. 181. In relation to master–apprentice relationships see P. J. P. Goldberg, 'Masters and Men in Later Medieval England', in *Masculinity in Medieval Europe*, ed. D. M. Hadley (London, 1999), pp. 56–70.
[41] MS Ashmole 61, fol. 20ᵛ.

Readers

> Sone it may be conyd & had
> And make them gode iff thei be bad
> God gyff them gr[a]ce v[er]tous to be
> For[e] than thei may both thryff & the[42]

The theme of a young readership is clear; however, the reference to school is slightly ambiguous and raises questions about literacy, school attendance and class in this period. It may be referring to young children who had only just begun their school years; this would be compatible with the preceding emphasis on young children. Alternatively, it may indicate that Rate was referring to children who only attended school for a short period, leaving after a basic education was acquired.[43] Rate may have been deliberately ambiguous: offering a range of interpretations that family members and readers could privately identify with and find meaning in is a shrewd technique. In a search for literal interpretations we sometimes lose sight of the open contexts authors and scribes may have deliberately intended to create.

It is useful, however, to assess what it might mean if Rate were identifying limited schooling, with educational practices in this period setting a context for the relationship between audience and class-groups. Most available evidence indicates that formal education began at around seven years of age; it is useful therefore to suggest that Rate was writing about children between the ages of seven and ten, and this could even be taken to an age of about twelve. The many ambiguities in age-specific terms in this literature complicate the identification of this poem with a particular age group, and given the level of detailed instructions within the poem, especially the suggestion of mercantile work, it may be appropriate to consider an older age group. This is not incompatible with a still youthful audience when young apprentices are reconsidered. Over the course of the fifteenth century the average age of apprenticeship rose to between sixteen and eighteen in order to accommodate educational training.[44] Schools were also associated with charitable endowments and London guilds in particular increasingly emphasised the need for literate apprentices, to the extent of creating provisions for schooling during the term of an apprenticeship or prior to an apprenticeship commencing.[45] Any encouragement for male children to attend schools subsequently increased the time of childhood and delayed adolescence and adulthood until later in life, a characteristic noted within sixteenth-century

---

[42] MS Ashmole 61, fol. 21ᵛ.
[43] On this see *Codex Ashmole 61*, ed. Shuffelton, p. 445.
[44] Hanawalt, *Growing Up*, pp. 82, 113.
[45] On this see C. M. Barron, 'The Expansion of Education in Fifteenth-Century London', in *The Cloister and the World: Essays in Medieval History in Honour of Barbara Harvey*, ed. J. Blair and B. Golding (Oxford, 1996), pp. 219–45 (pp. 223–4).

London evidence.⁴⁶ That Rate suspected his youthful audience would attend a school but possibly not continue with formal education is compatible with a merchant context where the desire for educated apprentices was increasingly important. It also excludes the nobility and aristocracy who generally eschewed public schooling in favour of private tutoring in the home, at least until the sixteenth century.⁴⁷ It was the gentry, merchant and bourgeois families who increasingly made use of expanding educational opportunities, certainly from the early sixteenth century and probably by the late fifteenth century. Earlier passages also promoted this type of audience through the restructuring of elite courtesy towards mercantile practices.

Finally, it is worth noting that while this is generally considered a courtesy poem, the word 'courtesy' only appears with any degree of frequency in the second half (barring the borrowed opening stanza), at which point the distinctive phrase 'Dame Courtesy' also appears. It is possible Rate worked from another text, appropriating the phrase from a different source – a technique he used in the opening stanza. Since the second half of the poem returns to common courtesy tropes and socialising lessons about behaviour at mealtimes, the fact that these lessons are confined to eating and not to serving would suggest Rate did not intend this to be read by or for young gentle servants. Why advice for career servants was not incorporated is more difficult to judge. Rate could presumably have represented the non-noble child who entered into service as a professional career choice and not to take part in noble networking and fostering, an issue raised in the previous chapter. Instead, the attention given to the interests of younger readers may again be explained by the ownership of the manuscript within a bourgeois family.

The Lytylle Childrene's Book

In order to understand interpolations, intertextual relationships and textual variations of this sort as indicators of audience interests, comparison with other courtesy poems is necessary. The poem *The Lytylle Childrene's Book* was

---

⁴⁶ On the extension of childhood see Hanawalt, *Growing Up*, pp. 112–14. Steve Rappaport discusses the late age men attained adulthood in *Worlds Within Worlds: Structures of Life in Sixteenth Century London* (Cambridge, 1989), pp. 322–9. On this issue Paul Griffiths gives more weight to the independence of young people while still noting that youth was prolonged, *Youth and Authority: Formative Experiences in England, 1560–1640* (Oxford, 1996); P. Griffiths, 'Masterless Young People in Norwich, 1560–1645', in *The Experience of Authority in Early Modern England*, ed. P. Griffiths, A. Fox and S. Hindle (New York, 1996), pp. 146–86.

⁴⁷ N. Orme, *English Schools in the Middle Ages* (London, 1973), pp. 321–2. See also N. Orme, *Education and Society in Medieval and Renaissance England* (London, 1989), p. 175. As Orme explains, aristocratic education in the household was more likely to require training in deportment, courtesy, military exercises, Latin, music and religion and not practical numeracy or even ethical business practices as emphasised here. The mid-fifteenth century does see some noble sons sent to Oxford and Cambridge. Orme, *Education and Society*, p. 15.

examined in the previous chapter. Of the six known manuscripts in which this poem has been found, two are of interest in terms of the manner in which elite imagery was destabilised and modified either by scribes or by owners. These two manuscripts are Richard Hill's household miscellany (manuscript Balliol 354)[48] and manuscript Harley 541. Each of these manuscripts indicates how scribes understood the basic text as malleable and open to interpolation. Manuscript Harley 541 can itself be analysed with reference to two other manuscripts, Stowe 982 and Lansdowne 699.

Manuscript Balliol 354 was owned and written by Richard Hill over three decades between 1503 and 1536 and may have been left to his oldest son John, born in 1518. It was therefore most likely kept within a family environment for at least two generations. The family and business networks described by Hill tie him to a prosperous merchant class, while the manuscript's dual role as a record of family life and repository of recreational texts is intimately demonstrated through numerous manuscript glosses about his children's births and deaths, as well as by his textual choices as owner and scribe.

Hill's choice of material reaches an impressive 354 separate items and reflects the mixture of personal and business interests already mentioned. The intertextual arrangement of material covers Catholic religious tracts, poems, hymns, recipes, proverbs, commercial memoranda on the wool trade, prescriptions, a chronicle of London and miscellaneous items on horse breeding and tree grafting. There is clear evidence that Hill transcribed material from a range of extant sources, including both manuscripts and printed books.[49] Manuscripts associated with bourgeois owners tend to contain material relevant for an entire family, both for their entertainment and education.[50] Hill's personal glosses, as well as his detailed lists of important family events including dates of births and deaths, orientate this manuscript towards a family readership. Equally, his commitment to working on a private family volume is marked by his continuing return to the manuscript over several decades, as new and different material became available to him.

One clear indication that Hill's merchant agenda was connected to this family perspective lies in the extraordinary relationship between mercantile interests and children's material. Immediately preceding *The Lytylle Chil-*

---

[48] For a good discussion of informal and non-commercial manuscript production, particularly commonplace or household miscellanies, see J. Boffey and J. J. Thompson, 'Anthologies and Miscellanies: Production and Choice of Texts', in *Book Production and Publishing in Britain 1375–1475*, ed. J. Griffiths and D. Pearsall (Cambridge, 1989), pp. 279–315 (pp. 292–303).

[49] For a detailed discussion about these sources see H. Collier, 'Richard Hill – A London Compiler', in *The Court and Cultural Diversity*, ed. E. Mullally and J. Thompson (Cambridge, 1997), pp. 319–29. For a discussion of Hill's activities in relation to codicising practices see A. Gillespie, 'Balliol MS 354: Histories of the Book at the End of the Middle Ages', *Poetica* 60 (2003), 47–63.

[50] Parkes, 'Literacy of the Laity', p. 568.

drene's Book is a series of simple English and French phrases emphasising common merchant conversations, including 'good cloth to sell / de bon drapt a vendre'. More clearly still, Hill titles this 'For so myche as it is good For suche as vse m[er]chaundise'.[51] Tables of numbers in English and French are also given; these begin with single numbers (1, 2, 3 ...) and continue into multiple units (50, 100, 1000, 10,000 ...). Arithmetic was not a common feature of this period's educational curriculum which instead focused on humanist learning. As will be noted later in this book, the evidence from school statutes suggests arithmetic was more likely to be a feature of trade learning and apprenticeship. It is worth noting here that Hill also included arithmetic equations and puzzles elsewhere in his manuscript.

The similarities between Hill's textual choices and Caxton's merchant-influenced *Vocabulary in French and English* (1480) are unlikely to be pure coincidence as Hill also transcribed Caxton's *Stans puer ad mensam* of 1476 (an identification which is possible due to a transposed stanza order). Hill also used a Caxton or de Worde printed edition of the *Book of Curtesye* (*Lytyll Iohn*) as a copy text.[52] Hill's interests in French are apparent in the style of *The Lytylle Childrene's Book* in which an interlinear French translation has been provided in the following style:

> Litill children here may ye lerne
> Petitz enfans icy vous pouez apprendre
> Moche curtesie that is here wreten
> Beaucoup de curtoyse qui ecripte ycy ...[53]

Very probably the simple translation is evidence of Hill's own knowledge of French. However, there was a widespread association between French and instructing children, and Hill's translation is in line with the tradition of Walter Bibbesworth's *Traitié* which not only included terms for estate management, but named body parts in French to assist language acquisition in young children; in Hill's manuscript a small column of text on the right of the folio has a similar vocabulary list of English/French words, including 'My face / mon visage', 'My hondes / mes mains'.[54] Hill's interlinear French translation may have been his own work or equally may have been based on

---

[51] MS Balliol 354, fol. 141r.
[52] Hill's *SPAM* and *Book of Curtesye* (*Lytyll Iohn*) are generally identified as either Caxton's editions or later de Worde reprints. See also Collier, 'Richard Hill', pp. 319–29.
[53] MS Balliol 354, fol. 142r.
[54] MS Balliol 354, fol. 142r. This column of text runs along folios 142r–143r. On the way children acquire language skills, see K. K. Jambeck, 'The *Tretiz* of Walter of Bibbesworth', in *Childhood in the Middle Ages and the Renaissance: The Results of a Paradigm Shift in the History of Mentality*, ed. A. Classen (Berlin, 2005), pp. 159–83 (pp. 177–80).

an exemplar such as the *Traitié* which was a dominant model of multilingual glossing from the thirteenth century onwards.[55]

Another manuscript, Harley 541, belonging to the family circle of Sir Thomas Frowyk (c. 1460–1506), a chief justice of the common pleas connected to the mercers,[56] incorporates elements from several texts relevant to children and upbringing. In this manuscript *The Lytylle Childrene's Book* contains lines from the extremely popular *Rules for preserving Health*, better known as Lydgate's *Dietary*, effectively producing a poem that associates food with moderation and safe eating.[57] While this may have been the result of scribal error, it signals a deeper association between elite and bourgeois readership as food and drink in the *Dietary* play an important role in the interests of an urban bourgeois household. At this point it is worth briefly noting that many manuscripts from this period include the *Dietary* along with courtesy poems, including manuscripts Stowe 982, Lambeth 853, Lansdowne 699 and Ashmole 61 (another manuscript with close ties to mercantile audiences already mentioned in this chapter). Equally, given Lydgate's association with *Stans puer ad mensam*, it is possible the two texts were seen by scribes as comparable and of interest to readers.

The popularity of courtesy themes within bourgeois and family-owned manuscripts could be explained by an imitation of elite values. Yet evidence of textual variation and scribal intervention suggests a more dynamic and interactive participation in reading culture and in the transmission of elite courteous ideals. The editorial prowess of Rate and Hill is a guide to the interests of scribes and readers in emending the courtesy genre to suit bourgeois and mercantile ethics and work practices. A similar process of growing bourgeois awareness of inner virtue and conduct developed in Germany.[58] The ownership of courtesy texts within families also subverted narratives that privileged the removal of children from natal homes. At the same time, these households would have contained apprentices, servants and foster children who were equally exposed to the manuscripts, which is suggestive of how audiences could both accept and contest representations of lifestyles, environments and socialisation.

---

[55] S. Crane, 'Social Aspects of Bilingualism in the Thirteenth Century', in *Thirteenth Century England, VI: Proceedings of the Durham Conference 1995*, ed. M. Prestwich, R. H. Britnell and R. Frame (Woodbridge, 1997), pp. 103–15.
[56] Boffey, *Manuscripts of English Courtly Love Lyrics*, pp. 126–7.
[57] MS Harley 541, fol. 209^v. In MS Stowe 982, fol. 11^r this is expanded: 'ete no raw mete take good hed ther to / drynke holsom drynke fede the on light bred'. Sponsler discusses the *Dietary* as a text which fashioned the 'bourgeois consumer'. C. Sponsler, 'Eating Lessons: Lydgate's "Dietary" and Consumer Conflict', in *Medieval Conduct*, ed. K. Ashley and R. L. A. Clark (Minneapolis, 2001), pp. 1–22.
[58] Elias, *Civilizing Process*, pp. 15–28.

The urban bourgeois context in courtesy literature for girls

The previous chapter looked at elite courtesy literature for the social training of young boys and adolescent males, reasoning that while it addressed gentry audiences, it nevertheless paralleled the male-dominated work-forces of elite households. The social upbringing of girls is concealed in this literature by the emphasis on elite male training. Ironically, the higher numbers of women employed in noble households between 1550 and 1600 played their part in reducing the political power and male-dominated patronage networks of this environment.[59] Female interests are portrayed in a separate cluster of texts, with three poems in the *Good Wife* tradition evidence of notions about female socialisation. Here we find prescribed behaviours taking place in smaller urban households, as well as in urban public spaces including the street and the town.[60] Social norms for girls are expressed in terms of appropriate gestures and manners as well as in physical actions that control the body. The type of behaviour that is put forward suggests that there were more levels of meaning outlined for females in comparison with the lessons for boys. Evidence that the literary representations of female relationships were more comprehensive is also apparent; this holds true when comparing the *Good Wife* poems to poems for boys in the merchant and bourgeois cluster. Deeper and more intricate moral and ethical socialisation thus seems to be a priority in these lessons. In the analysis that follows, practical expressions of moral issues will be discussed through the lens of chastity and reputation.

Textual evidence from the three poems

How the Good Wife Taught her Daughter is an example of 'parental ventriloquism' in which a 'mother' tells her 'daughter' how to behave through a series of homilies and instructions replicating the oral tradition of didactic instruction; these are interleaved with the repeated proverbial phrase 'My leue childe' or its variant.[61] The poem, loosely set out around refrains on drinking, household economy, pride and courtship, has been described by Felicity Riddy as an exemplar on domestic culture in which 'The household ideology ... locates the woman as wife and mother within the home; her domesticity is represented as a prime virtue and she herself as the repository and maintainer of bourgeois values.'[62] The poem effectively conveys informa-

---

[59] Mertes, *English Noble Household*, pp. 191–2.
[60] The three poems are separate from each other but there are sufficient similarities to suggest they were part of the same tradition. For a discussion of the poems see Mustanoja.
[61] On the parental voice see Ruys, 'Peter Abelard's *Carmen ad Astralabium*', p. 210. References are to Mustanoja's abbreviations for the texts. See Appendix A of this book for full citations.
[62] F. Riddy, 'Mother Knows Best: Reading Social Change in a Courtesy Text', *Speculum*

tion about supposed female concerns, while textual references to streets and towns place it within an urban bourgeois context. Passages on the daughter's responsibility to discharge her duties in public without falling into boisterous behaviour are associated with the presence of taverns and these dangers are equally suggestive of an urban environment.

Similarly, in *The Good Wyfe Wold a Pylgremage* the mother–daughter formula emphasises the inherent domesticity of female concerns. The desire to incorporate homely truths and personal experiences may very well indicate the emphasis on experience as a technique in the socialisation of girls.[63] It is worth noting that Peter Idley's poem to his son was very much in the vein of experiential writing, as was John Russell's poem, although it is true Russell was not appropriating a parental voice. He did, however, highlight his own experience when he 'talked' to the young man and in his conversations we can see an allusion to parental roles. The differing voices that appear in this literature are worth exploring and while advice to women remains a pivotal part of *The Thewis off Gud Women*, the direct voice of the mother is absent. Most agree that *The Thewis off Gud Women* has a broader appeal, with advice and comments that do not need to be specifically applied to an urban or middling social class.[64] As a result, the text lacks the specific social and class contexts of the other two poems; possibly this allowed a reader to make up their own selection of lessons as they chose, picking and selecting from it at will. The fictional nature of these voices is worthwhile pointing out. Both Mustanoja and Riddy have argued that the poems were in fact written by a male cleric.[65] It is worth noting that the mother–daughter narrative masks this; the authors reinforced the maternal role through the mother's personal phrasing, her tender references to her daughter and the continual play upon the mother's authority and direct voice.

Audience

Despite the image which is promoted in the texts themselves, it is likely that these narratives were not solely read and used by mothers and daughters living in natal family households. Riddy has suggested that these poems were intended to bridge a gap in socialising young females when the rela-

---

71 (1996), 66–86 (p. 68).

[63] Dronzek, 'Gendered Theories', p. 140–2, 151. Ruys sees this type of experience as different from the theoretical experiential writings aimed not at girls but at boys. J. F. Ruys, 'Didactic 'I's and the Voice of Experience in Advice from Medieval and Early-Modern Parents to their Children', in *What Nature Does Not Teach: Didactic Literature in the Medieval and Early-Modern Periods*, ed. J. F. Ruys (Turnhout, 2008), pp. 129–62.

[64] On the influence of sermon literature on this see Mustanoja, pp. 88–92; Phillips, *Medieval Maidens*, pp. 92.

[65] Mustanoja, pp. 89, 126. See also Riddy, 'Mother Knows Best', pp. 70–4 and *Women in England*, ed. Goldberg, pp. 5–8.

tionships between mothers and daughters were interrupted. Useful evidence by Goldberg on urban areas in the late fourteenth and early fifteenth centuries shows that female-led mobility amongst young people was significant, most likely resulting from domestic work opportunities.[66] Poll tax records for the years 1377, 1379 and 1381 demonstrate the high proportion of servants in towns, sometimes as high as twenty per cent to thirty per cent of the population. Equally, one third of households had at least one live-in servant, while significantly smaller were those urban households where dependent children were found.[67] Female servants typically between the ages of twelve and mid-twenties would have embraced the subjects of these poems with their depiction of urban lifestyles and activities, perhaps finding meaning in the themes of measurable, material success.[68] The poems reflect the story of youthful mobility and live-in service, foregrounding the interests of urban communities in maintaining bourgeois work ethics and monitoring the high adolescent population.

However, the reality of mother–daughter relationships deserves, to some degree, to be reinstated into this picture. While there is strong evidence to suggest service and fostering were important contexts for these poems, written texts are not necessarily redundant for mothers and daughters within a household and there is no evidence to suggest that dependent children permanently lived away from their natal homes. For certain periods during the year young women may have returned to their parents, perhaps when contracts had expired and before new periods of service began. It is also possible that these poems circulated orally or in manuscripts within households where mothers and daughters lived side by side for part or all of the year. It is equally probable that additional female servants were to be found in these households. The logic of dual and varied audiences is compelling. Given how problematic it is to determine exactly how audiences used texts, it is therefore useful to read these poems in terms of the relationships they depict, particularly for insight into the relationships associated with urban situations.

Urban girls participated in household economic activities. Messages on this in *How the Good Wife Taught Her Daughter* correspond to what we know of

---

[66] P. J. P. Goldberg, 'Female Labour, Service and Marriage in the Late Medieval Urban North', *Northern History* 22 (1986), 18–38; P. J. P. Goldberg, *Women, Work and Life Cycle in a Medieval Economy: Women in York and Yorkshire, c.1300–1520* (Oxford, 1992), pp. 280–304.

[67] Goldberg, 'Urban Identity', pp. 212–14. Of the later fourteenth and early fifteenth century Goldberg writes, 'comparatively few girls remained within their natal homes by the time they reached their teens and that this was especially true of urban society'. *Women in England*, ed. Goldberg, p. 5.

[68] On this see Riddy, 'Mother Knows Best', p. 69. Maryanne Kowaleski discusses female servants in *Local Markets and Regional Trade in Medieval Exeter* (Cambridge, 1995), pp. 168–9.

the role of urban bourgeois and merchant wives running households, associated with their ability to assume control in the absence of husbands and other male figures.⁶⁹ Texts T, L, N and A depict the girl/wife hiring female servants on 'term day' (a practice of hiring servants at particular times of the year),⁷⁰ while text A is unique in providing additional stanzas on housewifely duties and activities:

> Amend thy hous or thou haue nede
> For better after thou schall spede
> And if that thy need be grete
> And in the country corne be stryte
> Make an hous wife on thy selue
> Thy bred thou bake for hous wyfys helthe
> Amonge thi seruantes if thou stondyn
> Thy werke it schall be soner done
> To helpe them sone thou sterte
> For many handes make lyght werke⁷¹

The social context evoked here, with its emphasis on domestic and economic authority, may have been relevant only to some readers. The challenges of controlling a household, including the hiring of live-in female servants, are less reflective of the interests of young servants themselves. On the other hand, an older readership should not be discounted. Young wives and household mistresses may have felt in need of a learning manual to help them govern their household, with the texts replacing, or augmenting and legitimising, experience. Perhaps it was also husbands who felt the need for their wives to have these manuals.

Character traits

For girls in their mid-twenties marriage was a timely issue. The social freedoms which were part of living in urban areas provided young girls with opportunities for finding marriage partners, while sexual dalliances were not uncommonly noted between servants.⁷² This was a dangerous time for some women; presentments before church courts of women accused of impropriety, pregnancy and immoral conduct are common, while impropriety on the part of both daughters and servants reflected poorly on the moral status of the

---

[69] P. J. P. Goldberg, 'Women's Work, Women's Role, in the Late-Medieval North', in *Profit, Piety and the Professions in Later Medieval England*, ed. M. Hicks (Gloucester, 1990), pp. 34–50 (pp. 45–6).

[70] Text T, fol. 213ʳ. Text L, p. 109. Texts E and H have a more general discussion about servants.

[71] Text A, fol. 8ʳ.

[72] P. J. P. Goldberg, 'Girls Growing Up in Later Medieval England', *History Today* 45 (1995), 25–32 (p. 31). Also *Women in England*, ed. Goldberg, p. 11 for sources that demonstrate this.

household. A girl in *How the Good Wife Taught her Daughter* went to church to ensure she would one day be a suitable marriage partner: 'Doutter yif thou wilt ben a wif and wisliche to wirche/ Loke that thou louie ful wel god and holi chirche'.[73] Religious observance fashioned good character and in these poems was the basis for securing marriage opportunities and future prosperity. Apart from *the boke of curtasye*, courtesy poems do not usually discuss how and why boys should attend church: when they do, they omit this direct link between church attendance and character. In this example, however, the girl's attendance at church is valuable for its evidently womanly, *wifely* duties. As such, the mother's interest in halting potentially harmful behaviour before it was detected by others makes sense. The mother's warnings in the poem also echo the wider community voice, and this idea of community watchfulness and surveillance will be pursued shortly.

As a narrative technique, encouraging good behaviour works best when it can be contrasted with negative behaviour, already mentioned as a practice of poems addressing boys, although it is also the case that the more direct and colourful warnings are, the more likely they are to be appealing to readers. It is almost certain this was the case with didactic literature for girls, conspicuously so in the text of the *Book of the Knight of the Tower*, more of which will be studied in the next chapter. In *How the Good Wife Taught her Daughter* the warnings are pronounced, but only some contain subversive messages that could be read as promoting 'bad' behaviour. For example, 'With riche robes and gerlondes and swich riche thing / Ne cuntrefete no leuedi as thi lord were a king'[74] might very well inspire a girl from the bourgeois class to own and wear the rich robes of a lady, as much a part of Riddy's 'bourgeois ethos' as the mother's domesticity.[75] Elsewhere the poem is more direct with the warnings and the possibilities for encouraging bad behaviour are less obvious; 'Syt not by hym ne stand thou nought / In sych place ther synne mey be wroght'[76] reminds the girl to take care with possible suitors and to consider social customs at this potentially unsafe time without emphasising any potentially exciting experiences. *The Thewis of Gud Women* has similar warnings, sometimes overtly referring to men and sometimes more generally cautious, as in 'Fle ill folk and susspekit place'[77] and 'Fle fra defamyt cumpany / Lyk drawys to lyk ay comonly'.[78]

Familiarity with urban temptations subversively breeds interest in these activities. The mother embodied the voice of the whole community, but in

---

[73] Text E, fols. 48ᵛ–49ʳ. A similar opening stanza appears in all manuscripts.
[74] Text E, fol. 50ᵛ.
[75] On this see Riddy, 'Mother Knows Best', pp. 67–9.
[76] Text A, fol. 7ʳ.
[77] Text C, fol. 49ᵛ. Also in Text J, fol. 164ᵛ.
[78] Text C, fol. 50ᵛ. Also in Text J, fol. 165ᵛ.

her strictures a young reader or listener would have simultaneously absorbed information on different ways of misbehaving, although the emphasis on punishment and correction weighs against this. Nevertheless, misbehaviour is kept alive by the sustained use of negative examples. Readers may have been sophisticated in absorbing, understanding and thinking over these lessons. In their willingness to discuss misbehaviour, the female characters are seen to walk in the streets and speak to men, even though this was heavily proscribed. The girl was also warned against attending wrestling matches, shooting at cock (a popular English pastime) or drinking too much ale in public, a location Goldberg refers to as teeming with male apprentices.[79] The daughter was also warned to stay away from market places when selling her goods: 'Ne go thou not to no merket / To sell thi thrift be wer of itte'.[80] The terms 'burel' and 'borell' (used in Texts E, H, L and T) refer to cheap brown woollen cloth and again indicate a merchant or urban market context. Riddy sees this as a warning against trading without licence or of the danger for women of being seen as a 'huckster', someone who traded goods in the street.[81] Urban households played a part in trade and production, with the poem making visible these networks of trade and related activity. References to market places and selling goods condemn some economic activities while simultaneously suggesting the nature of bourgeois women's work in urban areas, supported in contemporary documents including poll tax records from the late fourteenth century, borough ordinances, wills and guild ordinances testifying to the involvement of women in urban economic activities.[82]

In their desire to establish firm rules for girls to observe, authors of conduct books developed numerous ways of describing acceptable levels of contact between women and public areas, which may hold multiple, unintended, messages as already noted. 'Fra drunkyne folk and tawarne flee'[83] from *The Thewis of Gud Women* echoes the hostile tone of *How the Good Wife Taught her Daughter* and *The Good Wyfe Wold a Pylgremage* towards taverns and drinking ale in large quantities. As Keith Wrightson and David Levine show, the reputation of taverns and alehouses in the early modern period was associated with moral messages: poverty, disorderly conduct and sexual immorality.

---

[79] Goldberg, 'Masters and Men', pp. 64–6.
[80] Text A, fol. 7^v. In Text N 'burel' has become 'Ne go not to market thy barrel to fill'.
[81] Riddy, 'Mother Knows Best', pp. 75–6.
[82] For women's involvement with textile and clothing occupations see Kowaleski, *Local Markets*, p. 153. See also, Goldberg, *Women, Work and Life Cycle*, pp. 118–27. Helen Jewell discusses women in urban areas and their responsiveness and flexibility to recession and changes in trade in *Women in Medieval England* (Manchester, 1996), pp. 84–114. For women in the brewing industry see J. M. Bennett, *Ale, Beer, and Brewsters in England: Women's Work in a Changing World, 1300–1600* (Oxford, 1996). Goldberg also discusses the roles of women in the victualling trades in urban environments in *Women, Work and Life Cycle*, pp. 104–18.
[83] Text C, fol. 51^r. Also in Text J, fol. 166^v.

Tightened control of these spaces was a focused part of the push to promote moral order.[84] Yet in Texts E, T, H, L and N of *How the Good Wife Taught her Daughter*, references to social activities legitimately explore women in private houses or inns:

> And if thou be on eni stede thar god drinke is alofte
> Whether that thou serue or that you sitte softe
> Mesureli tak therof that the falle no blame
> For if thou be ofte drunke it fallet the to schame[85]

Here, shame is associated with female misconduct. Shame, an emotion and state Elias refers to as a key feature in the 'civilizing process', was suggestive of a psychological imperative controlling behaviour, and certainly one that at its core had a moral dimension.[86] Elias's understanding of shame is related to notions of delicacy, repugnance and embarrassment, less so to moral shame and discredit. In this example, however, socialisation and the shame principle are visible, confirming that women's moral behaviour was closely looked at, and that they were condemned for actions and conduct that failed to be mentioned in courtesy poems for boys. As previously discussed, these different internal-external processes are not framed in the literature which described elite courtesy for boys in higher status households.

However, courtesy values per se – that is, identifiable behaviours which were described through directions on controlling the body – are still to be found in these narratives. In Text E the first indication of courtesy appears in stanza three, where courtesy in church is first identified: 'Make thou no iangling with fremde no with sibbe / Lau thou noght to scorn neither olde no yunge / Be of god beringge and of god tunge'.[87] Facial expressions were also discussed as a courtesy trope, with exterior physical actions used to suggest proper conduct: 'Ne laugh thou noght to loude ne gene thou noght to wide / Lage the might & faire mouth make / mi leue child'.[88] In Text A, the physical nature of the act was clearly expressed: 'Change not thi countenans with grete

---

[84] K. Wrightson and D. Levine, *Poverty and Piety in an English Village: Terling, 1525–1700*, rev. edn (Oxford, 1995), pp. 135–8.

[85] Text E, fols. 49v–50r. The most significant alteration occurs in Text A where no location is given indicating public spaces. Instead the line simply notes 'Wher euer thou comme at ale or wyne / Take not to myche & leue be tyme', fol. 7v.

[86] Elias, *Civilizing Process*, pp. x, 114–19.

[87] Text E, fol. 49r. This was a direction retained in all later texts, although Text T omitted the line on not laughing with friends and 'sibbes' (close relations, blood kin) in church. There is a close parallel to this in Caxton's *Book of Curtesye*, addressed to boys, in the lines 'The chirche of prayer / is hous and place / Beware therefore / of clappe or Iangelynge / For in the chirche / it is a ful grete trespaas'. *Book of Curtesye*, 2v.

[88] Text E, fol. 49v. Similarly in Text H. In Text E the proverbial phrases which conclude each stanza have been written in red ink. Throughout this book, Text E's proverbial phrases will be italicised.

laughter'.[89] Text L extended this to include the terms 'soft' and 'mild', terms already noted for their value in describing character: *'But laughe thou softe & myelde / And be not of cheer to wielde / Mi leue child'*.[90] By the time this poem was printed in 1597, explicit gendered language was being used: *'Maydens should laugh softlye / That men here not they bee / My leue dere child'*.[91]

This also addresses the means by which morality was constructed through gestures and actions, in contrast to gestures and actions for boys which were less alert to this. Within the lesson on where a girl was to sit and stand in relation to a man are more layers of meaning relating to feminine propriety and moral behaviour. This manner of providing information on courtesy and socialisation is found in *The Good Wyfe Wold a Pylgremage*. For example, there is a similar warning: 'Sytt not witt no man aloune for oft in trust ys tressoun'.[92] *The Thewis off Gud Women* also warns against women meeting men in town: 'Nocht oys na tratlynge in the toune / Na with na yonge men rouk na roune'.[93] Further evidence on the moral standards expected from girls comes in a passage on women going outside alone:

> Ga nocht alane in hir erand
> Tak child ore maidinge in hir hand
> It is no point of honestee
> A gud woman allane to bee
> In cumpany of mony ane
> And mekill les with ane alane
> It is no point of gud custum
> Fore na man wyll the gud presum[94]

This is an example of the daughter/reader learning that marriage prospects and reputation depended less on personal character, or even attractiveness, than on good conduct and behaviour – in effect on how well they understood the rules governing conduct. There is evidence, however, that good conduct and character were meaningless if they were not seen and observed by others. As David Turner notes, women in early modern England had to both behave well and be seen as behaving well.[95] In taking another female (or child) with

---

[89] Text A, fol. 7r.
[90] Text L, p. 105.
[91] Text N.
[92] Text P, fol. 137r.
[93] Text C, fol. 49r. Also in Text J, fol. 164r. Mustanoja's convention of expanding 'Not' to 'Nocht' has been followed throughout.
[94] Text C, fol. 50v. Text J replaces 'no point of gud custum' with 'Trast weill it is ane euill custum' and 'Fore no man wyll the gud presum' with 'For na folk will t[h]e gud presum', fol. 166r.
[95] D. Turner, 'Conduct and Politeness in the Early Modern Period', in *Defining Gender, 1450–1910, Five Centuries of Advice Literature Online* (Adam Matthew Publications, 2003).

her whenever she left the safety of the house, the girl was not only always in the company of someone familiar but was also provided with a witness in case of any accusations. As the author explained, no good would be thought of someone if behaviour was seen to be improper, although the practicality of this for a female servant is ambiguous as no household mistress would have been willing to lose the labour of an additional household member to accompany a live-in servant on her daily errands.

Going outside, meeting people in town and running errands: there was acknowledgement that for many bourgeois girls, domestic responsibilities and duties would take them outside the household. Unlike upper-class women, these girls could not be sequestered to ensure the safety of their reputation and the burden fell to them to behave well and to learn from experience. However, it may signal the manner in which lower-class girls were seen to be incapable of self-control, needing to be removed from dangerous situations and places, unlike upper-class daughters, such as those in the *Book of the Knight of the Tower*, who were encouraged to deflect potential harm.[96] Equally, however, the practical nature of the *Good Wife* poems and their relative brevity in comparison to de la Tour Landry's book, as well as their general avoidance of highly theoretical concepts or ideas, may yet account for the realistic emphasis on avoiding dangerous spaces (and men) and more generally taking chaperones with you, in place of more learned discussions encouraging self-control. The emphasis on avoiding potentially harmful situations, while still allowing for the fact that bourgeois girls would be active outside the household, was one way to keep girls 'safe' and protected.

Behind the poems is a consistently accusatory tone, elaborated on when observable conduct is raised in relation to one specific activity: unchaperoned interaction with men. The means by which this moral emphasis was expressed across the different manuscripts of *How the Good Wife Taught Her Daughter* is worth exploring. Each stanza concludes with a proverbial phrase, summing up the lesson which has just been given (although frequently the proverbial statements can be read broadly). As a grouping, they serve as a good example of the manner in which moral indicators were raised. These messages could be positive: 'Gode name is golde worthe / My leue childe',[97] 'A good name many folde Ys more worthe then golde',[98] 'Thi good name is to thi freendis / Greet ioie and gladnes',[99] 'For wise men and old / Sayne good name is worth gold'.[100] It was also possible for these pithy statements to be negative: 'For he that

---

[96] On this see Phillips, *Medieval Maidens*, pp. 94–6.
[97] Text H, fol. 218ᵛ.
[98] Text T, fol. 212ʳ.
[99] Text L, p. 109.
[100] Text N. See Appendix A which explains why no page numbers are listed for this text.

cacchith to him an yuel name / It is to him a foule fame',[101] abbreviated in some manuscripts to the even more succinct *'Euil lat euil name'*.[102]

The numerous references to meeting with men raise the issue of whose behaviour needs controlling. It is most obvious in Text H that a girl cannot control how a man acts towards her but she is in a position to control her own response to him. A man's 'foule' behaviour is to be met by a mild and polite response: 'thei he speke foule to the, faire thou him grete'.[103] Didactic literature insisted that all women were to be meek and mild as a matter of course. An inverted comment in Text T extends the warning to a man's sweet response, which was likewise to be treated quickly but politely: 'Thowgh he speke feyre to thee, swyftly thou hym grete'.[104] A man's sweet conversation was no doubt more dangerous than his 'foule' behaviour for many girls.

Meekness was visible in didactic material for girls in particular ways. The girl in *How the Good Wife Taught Her Daughter* is told to behave with meekness towards her husband: 'Mekeli him answere and noght to atterling'.[105] This direct command is absent only in Text T in which meekly is replaced with 'fayre'.[106] As noted earlier, the connection between outer demeanour and inner meekness was established in texts for young people: *Stans puer ad mensam* and *the boke of curtasye* instructed males to exhibit a similarly meek quality in their behaviour. The gendered quality of meekness in fourteenth- and fifteenth-century literature is ambiguous. What is clearer is that it was commonly used as a code for fashioning appropriate behaviours and manners, albeit in ways and environments which were themselves gendered. In this literature, the quality of meekness remains the same; only in the specifics of the ways in which it was demonstrated and to whom do the differences become more apparent. Although the specifics varied, it was often channelled to ensure girls, including upper-class girls, were meek to everyone, and boys to their social superiors. An added stanza in Text A directs the female reader to consider acting meekly to evade domestic violence, with the ability for gentle words to secure peace: 'If that it forteyn thus with the / That he be wroth & angery be / Loke thou mekly ansuer hym ... Ne fayre wordes brake

---

[101] Text L, p. 105. The closest to this is Text N, 'For gif thou haue euill name / It will turne the to grame'. The use of 'he' is at odds with the female characters and interests and is probably a scribal mistake.

[102] From Text E, fol. 49ᵛ and similarly in Texts H and T. Margaret Paston's letter concerning her daughter Margery's contract of marriage with Richard Calle emphasises the importance of a 'good name' and of her kin and friends whom she will disappoint. *Paston Letters: Original Letters Written During the Reign of Henry VI., Edward IV., and Richard III.*, ed. J. Fenn, 2 vols. (London, 1849), II, 28–30.

[103] Text H, fol. 218ʳ.

[104] Text T, fol. 212ʳ.

[105] Text E, fol. 49ʳ.

[106] Text T, fol. 211ᵛ, 'Answere hym fayre and nat as an attrylyng'.

neuer bone'.¹⁰⁷ Text A was, of course, Rate's manuscript (manuscript Ashmole 61). As Shaner notes with Advocates 19.3.1, an editorial voice emphasising violence appealed to families and younger audiences. Of all the manuscripts containing the *Good Wife* poem, this was the most altered in these ways.

How else were visual cues used to define identity and socialisation for girls and young women? In texts for young men, the visual component of behaviour was expressed through courtesy gestures, usually taking place at the table. Similarly, in these three poems gestures play a role in female socialisation, although the manner in which they are dealt with is revealing. An example of this comes from rules on clothing, a topic the patristic writers had paid attention to in their association of female morality with clothing and cosmetics.¹⁰⁸ In *The Thewis of Gud Women* socialisation was discussed through the symbolic meaning of dress. Readers or listeners were made aware that clothing acted as a visible indicator of character and disposition:

> Nocht outragous in hire cleithinge
> Bot plane maner and gudly thing
> Nocht our costlyk na sumptewous
> To mak vthir at hire inwyous
> Na couet nocht cleithing mar deir
> Na be resone suld hir effeir
> And thocht scho be cled honestly¹⁰⁹

The author/scribe of Text J inserted an additional fourteen lines not present in Text C on dress and its consequences:

> And hear honour bettir thing
> And lawar stat lakar cleithing
> For pryd gais no thing be theclais
> Bot be the hert that woman has
> For sum will be sa stoutly cled
> Or thai will crab thar men in bed
> That half the riches that he has
> Sall scant be worth his viffis clas
> Than quhen thai cled ar our statly
> Men will presoyme na gud treuly
> Bot that scho dois it for paramour
> And thus gat said sal hir honour

---

¹⁰⁷ Text A, fol. 7ʳ.
¹⁰⁸ Juvenal wrote about this as did the Church Father Tertullian. On this see *Women Defamed and Women Defended: An Anthology of Medieval Texts*, ed. A. Blamires, with K. Pratt and C. W. Marx (Oxford, 1992), pp. 29–30, 50–8. For medieval examples see pp. 7, 141, 274.
¹⁰⁹ Text C, fol. 49ʳ. Text J, fol. 164ʳ, replaces 'outragous' with 'delicat' and 'honestly' with 'preciously'.

> Tharfor the best thing is I wat
> Is to be cled eftir thair estat[110]

Like courteous behaviour, clothing was a visible and observable feature of identity, coming under the eye of pedagogues, parents and gossiping third-parties. Dress identified inherited class and indicated obedience to hierarchy, as well as more generally a love of worldly goods and material possessions. In discussing this, John Scattergood comments, 'clothing is meaningful as well as practical: it is a gesture, a statement as to how one sees oneself in relation to the rest of the world'.[111] Clothing was also dangerously ambiguous, as explored in Texts E, H, T and A of *How the Good Wife Taught her Daughter*, where it is clothing which alludes to the problematic nature of social mobility: 'Loke thou were no ryche robys / Ne counterfyte thou no ladys'.[112] In using the term 'lady' the author could be referring to the mistress of the household, suggesting this may have been intended for female servants.

Variations on the warning against counterfeiting social status, including the broader theme of envy, are in Texts E, H, L and T. In Text E, 'Be nout to modi no to enuious / For nout that mai bitiden in other man[n]is hous / *Enuious herte him silf fret / Mi leue child*'[113] assures the girl that envy will lead to unhappiness, a loaded message for bourgeois girls and young servants. This sits easily with the following lines: 'if thin neibores wif hauet riche atir / ther fore make you no strif ne bren thou noght so fir / Bote thonke god of the good that he the hatgh igiuen'.[114] Texts H, N and L discuss this from the alternative prospective of the rich wife: 'And if thou be a ryche wiffe be thou nought to harde / Welkome fayre thin neyboures that comen to the towarde / Mete and drynke with fair semblaunte the mor schall be thi mede'.[115] Again, it is Text A in which the most textual variation occurs: 'By syde the if thy neghbores thryve / There fore thou make no stryfe / Bot thanke god of all thi gode / That he send the to thy fode'.[116]

At issue here is not just the nature of individual, discrete socialising lessons for bourgeois girls and young servants but a wider discussion about neighbourly relations and community harmony, or in other words, the

---

110 Text J, fol. 164ᵛ.
111 J. Scattergood, 'Fashion and Morality in the Late Middle Ages', in *England in the Fifteenth Century: Proceedings of the 1986 Harlaxton Symposium*, ed. D. Williams (Woodbridge, 1987), pp. 255–72 (p. 255).
112 Text A, fol. 8ʳ. In Texts E, fol. 50ᵛ; H, fol. 218ᵛ. Text T, fol. 212ᵛ has 'With riche robes and gerlondes and swich riche thing / Ne cuntrefete no leuedi as thi lord were a king'.
113 Text E, fol. 50ᵛ. This stanza does not appear in Text L. In Text N, 'modi' is replaced with 'proud'.
114 Text E, fol. 50ᵛ.
115 Text H, fol. 219ᵛ.
116 Text A, fol. 8ʳ.

weight of social relationships.[117] It is worth briefly noting that Texts C and J of *The Thewis of Gud Women* echo counsel concerning appropriate female company: 'Kep feris of women at are wys / And euir conferme hir to the best / Of women that ar worthyest'.[118] According to conduct authors, it was fundamental that women, more than men, have the ability to form crucial connections within the neighbourhood, with the maintenance of these structures central to female socialisation. The shared cultural experiences taking place between women across vertical and horizontal lines, examined by Sara Mendelson and Patricia Crawford, demonstrate that common female experiences, such as childbirth, childrearing and household duties, had the potential to override class differences. 'Smaller' shared experiences of the type that include verbal networks and material possessions were also particular to women.[119] Tracy Adams has also commented that the contemporary text by Christine de Pizan, *Livre des Trois Vertus* (1405), addressed women from a range of social stations, including elite women (the book was for the young Princess Margaret of Burgundy who was married to the dauphin, Louis de Guyenne) as well as poor women and prostitutes. According to Adams, de Pizan is attempting to 'express a feeling of solidarity, demonstrating that they were all subject to similar constraints as women, even though their situations were very different'.[120]

This capacity to create intensive communities has been noted by Gowing in her study of early modern London women who actively monitored and enforced good conduct and good sexual reputation amongst neighbours.[121] These poems likewise function within the sphere of women determining acceptable behaviour and creating exclusive female networks to monitor and scrutinise youthful conduct and activities, although it is inevitable that this is complicated by the male writers. While there was no single feminine model for young girls to emulate (status, location, age, familial situations and educational levels all complicate this matter), it does seem that for bourgeois girls,

---

[117] On the role of neighbourhoods into the early modern period see N. Tadmor, 'Friends and Neighbours in Early Modern England', in *Love, Friendship and Faith in Europe, 1300–1800*, ed. L. Gowing, M. Hunter and M. Rubin (Basingstoke, 2005), pp. 150–76.

[118] Text C, fol. 50^v. Also in Text J, fol. 166^r.

[119] S. Mendelson and P. Crawford, *Women in Early Modern England, 1550–1720* (Oxford, 1998), pp. 202–55.

[120] T. Adams, 'Medieval Mothers and their Children: The Case of Isabeau of Bavaria in Light of Medieval Conduct Books', in *Childhood in the Middle Ages and the Renaissance: The Results of a Paradigm Shift in the History of Mentality*, ed. A. Classen (Berlin, 2005), pp. 265–89 (p. 270).

[121] L. Gowing, *Domestic Dangers: Women, Words, and Sex in Early Modern London* (Oxford, 1996), pp. 59–110. Also L. Gowing, '"The freedom of the streets": Women and Social Space, 1560–1640', in *Londinopolis: Essays on the Cultural and Social History of Early Modern London*, ed. P. Griffiths and M. S. R. Jenner (Manchester, 2000), pp. 130–53.

socialisation focused heavily on family units and female interactions within the close neighbourhood. Unlike courtesy poems for boys and young men which concentrated on large elite households, these poems for girls focused on the far-reaching female networks which existed between houses in urban areas. While these gender differences may partly come from the comparison of different types of texts, idealised patterns of behaviour are invariably built into the literary genres which are the most popular in a given period (popular being used here in its broadest sense). This also follows when we remember that the girls and boys with access to these poems were probably from the same middling social class.[122]

Courtesy poems, like all conduct literature, were strongly influenced by an awareness of readerships and what it was that socialisation needed to accomplish, particularly when this reflected future occupations and status. In the cluster of male courtesy literature this was relevant to the question of social mobility, with texts used to portray elite lifestyles and household service, either for emulation or legitimisation. In these three poems for girls, social mobility takes place via marriage and access to the wealth of husbands, in a negative sense cited via messages on extravagant clothing. Male courtesy poems tackled the question of social education through the instruction of suitable public behaviour (demonstrated though courteous manners) that would help young men to negotiate social and hierarchical connections and participate in the social world of the household. It was this in turn which directed future preferment and success. Women, at least according to these male writers, were best served by learning about marriage and safeguarding their reputation, while social connections women formed were focused within family units and with neighbouring family units. The voice of the mother suggested both personal authority in these spheres and the authority of the community in emphasising how to behave before and after marriage and equally how to negotiate relationships at various stages of life.[123] Courtesy and socialisation for girls were expressed not just through

---

[122] The complex issue of gender roles in households and urban areas is discussed in P. J. P. Goldberg, 'Household and the Organisation of Labour in Late Medieval Towns: Some English Evidence', in *The Household in Late Medieval Cities: Italy and Northwestern Europe Compared*, ed. M. Carlier and T. Soens (Leuven, 2001), pp. 59–70. Also S. Rees Jones, 'Women's Influence on the Design of Urban Homes', in *Gendering the Master Narrative: Women and Power in the Middle Ages*, ed. M. C. Erler and M. Kowaleski (Ithaca, 2003), pp. 190–211. There is a valuable discussion about the social use of space in York houses in J. Grenville, 'Houses and Households in Late Medieval England: An Archaeological Perspective', in *Medieval Women: Texts and Contexts in Late Medieval Britain, Essays for Felicity Riddy*, ed. J. Wogan-Browne, R. Voaden, A. Diamond, A. Hutchison, C. Meale and L. Johnson (Turnhout, 2000), pp. 309–28.

[123] Dronzek finds similar patterns in the representation of honour (or reputation) for a girl, which was linked to sexual reputation. For boys, reputation was linked to social status. Dronzek, 'Gendered Theories', pp. 147–52.

polite gestures and mannerly acts, important though these were, but through a careful and considered interaction with other people, both male and female, and an ability to negotiate social networks smoothly. Female socialisation and courtesy were wide-ranging and layered, with moral subtexts more easily articulated and given obvious form.

A gentleman's household

This chapter has delved into the manner in which elite narratives could be modified for different social classes. It is worth looking at another branch of didactic literature to see how a poem could differ sharply in the circumstances and context of writing for a young male. This poem is Peter Idley's *Instructions to his Son*. The emphasis on youthful socialisation, primarily found in book one of the poem, leads to interesting comparisons with the texts already examined.

Textual information

Peter Idley's *Instructions* in all probability circulated relatively widely; the text is found in eight surviving manuscripts. Writing between the years 1445 and 1450, Idley originally intended his work to be read across two books, *Liber Primus* and *Liber Secundus*.[124]

Liber Primus and *Liber Secundus* address different topics: *Liber Primus* embraces secular concerns and *Liber Secundus* spiritual instruction. This division, which overtly isolates religious tutoring from secular tutoring, means readers were directed to semi-independent texts. The division is enforced physically in Texts B1 and H which only include *Liber Primus*, and Texts A and B2 which contain only *Liber Secundus*. As a result of this, readers must have approached incomplete texts as complete texts, unaware or indifferent to the existence of a corresponding book. This physical separation does not represent a discrete narrative break, and it is worth noting that secular messages in *Liber Primus* were reinforced through the inclusion of simple religious precepts, some of which will be discussed later.

The life of Peter Idley is unknown, although there are some signs about his identity. Two sixteenth-century glosses made by John Stow in Text H state 'Peter Idle Esquire of Kent' and 'Peter Idle Esquire', and may indicate Idley's background.[125] Changes in social ranks in the late fifteenth century manifested themselves in the gentry or lesser nobility increasingly being

---

[124] Text E is the most complete and will be primarily analysed here. Significant variations will be noted in footnotes. See Appendix A for full citations.

[125] John Stowe was a noted manuscript collector who was surprisingly exact and meticulous in his research on English historical events. B. L. Beer, 'Stow, John (1524/5–1605)', *DNB*.

Readers

composed of knights, esquires and gentlemen.[126] The two sixteenth-century glosses cast Peter Idley into this type of social group, placing him below lords or the peerage and above the yeomanry. Charlotte d'Evelyn has argued that Peter Idley is the same Idley mentioned in Oxfordshire records who gained the position of bailiff for the Honour of Wallingford and of St Valery and Chiltern in 1439. If this was the case, it would have provided Idley with an income of £10 per annum, rising to £27 in 1457–9, at which time the Oxfordshire Idley was recorded with a new title, controller of the king's works.[127] The level of income achieved by Idley supports the opinion that he was part of the lesser gentry. His official position as gentleman falconer and under-keeper of the royal mews and falcons between 1453 and 1456, as well as his later administrative appointment, suggests this Peter Idley would have been familiar with the workings of elite environments.

Nevertheless, this is not an elite courtesy text. That Idley was not writing for children of the nobility is clear both from the social class his son Thomas would have inherited (the poem is addressed to him) and from his recommendation that Thomas make a study of law: 'I conceyve thy witte bothe goode and able / to the lawe therefore, now haue I ment / to set the, if th[ou] wilt be stable'.[128] This unashamedly gentry and professional context explains why the *Instructions* shies away from descriptions of elite courteous behaviour and elite household practices commonly found in courtesy poems proper. While financially secure, the gentry classes lacked the distinction conferred by aristocratic land holdings, what Dyer refers to when he describes a group existing 'on fees and payments for administrative or legal services'.[129]

Idley's poem was not wholly his own creation and his use of other sources is notable; particularly so is his treatment of two popular Latin treatises by Albertanus of Brescia, *Liber Consolationis et Consilii* and *Liber de Amore et Dilectione Dei et Proximi*, which form the basis of *Liber Primus*.[130] As already mentioned, Idley does not draw upon courtesy poems to discuss socialisation, largely disregarding their discussions of table manners, aristocratic culture and hospitality – topics which he rarely notes. While it is certainly true that Idley was not associated with the royal household until the early 1450s, the absence of courteous advice and courtly environments within the text is still worth commenting upon. Instead of highlighting courtesy narratives and discussing socialisation primarily through courteous ideology, *Liber Primus* offered Thomas, and any subsequent readers, counsel on a wide

---

[126] Dyer, *Standards of Living*, p. 15, 20. Also Horrox, 'Urban Gentry', pp. 30–1.
[127] *Instructions*, d'Evelyn, pp. 4–35.
[128] Text E, fol. 3ᵛ.
[129] Dyer, *Standards of Living*, p. 19.
[130] Robert Mannying's *Handlyng Synne* and Lydgate's *The Fall of Princes* (completed between 1438 and 1439) were sources for *Liber Secundus*. For the arrangement of Idley's poem in relation to these sources see *Instructions*, d'Evelyn, pp. 36–57

variety of topics characterised as relating to the secular world and the pitfalls and traps awaiting young men. The advice Idley chose to write ranges over discretion, restraint in dress and expense, the worth of friends and rewarding advisers. This is the advice a fifteenth-century father of the gentry class may have thought suitable for the education of his son in social matters, behaviour and career. What can be said is that Idley's social status anchored his poem to a particular social environment, with the result that he looked at courtesy and morality, in effect the socialisation of his son, in different ways from the authors of those poems ostensibly for the great household.

As Russell's poem indicated, lesser gentry and bourgeois readers employed a variety of techniques to appropriate courtesy texts; in addition to this, however, and perhaps conversely, it was these same groups who also demonstrated an interest in literature and socialisation which described morality and virtue. In general, the lesser gentry, as well as the mercantile networks identified in Hill's manuscript and possibly manuscript Ashmole 61, were more responsive to moral behaviours and ethical work practices than elite groups, with this reflected in the literary texts and socialising themes associated with different manuscripts. As discussed earlier, this was complicated by the often ambiguous distinctions between gentry and nobles, as well as by the blurring of social lines between rankings. Younger sons from the gentry class had to accept that mercantile work and professions in the law could secure them the advancement and security they could not achieve through inheritance or family preferment.

While courtesy was a natural trapping of elite circles, bourgeois, professional and gentry groups still entered into a relationship with courteous conduct and good behaviour. The theme of courtesy in Idley's poem can be identified over five stanzas. Idley portrays courtesy through a discussion about observable manners, specifically relating to the matter of clothing. Idley begins with the most basic precept: that of keeping clothing clean. Text H states that clothing must be 'Kepe hem as honeste & as clenly as ye cane'.[131] The commonplace 'manners makes the man' is also transformed by Idley in support of this point: 'ffor clothyng ofte maketh man'.[132] Idley's qualification of this statement warns his son not to be too over-nice in his clothing, 'But goo not to ouer nyce [and] gay'.[133] Again, the expedient trope of clothing

---

[131] Text H, fol. 23ʳ.
[132] Text E, f. 3ʳ. Similarly in BL MS Add. 57335, fol. 1ᵛ and Text P (Magdalene), fol. 19ᵛ. In Text H, fol. 23ᵛ: 'For maners and clothynge doutelese maketh ma[n]'. In B1, fol. 12ʳ this order was reversed: 'For clothing & good man[er]s makith man'. Horrox offers a different reading of the proverb 'manners maketh man', aligning it with virtue and not birth. Horrox, 'Service', p. 62.
[133] Text E, fol. 3ʳ. Also in BL MS Add. 57335, fol. 1ᵛ and B1, fol. 12ʳ. In Text H, fol. 23ᵛ: 'But goo nott yee as euery nyce gaye'. In Text P (Magdalene), fol. 19ᵛ: 'But medylnot off euery nys gaye'. By 1450, 'nice' was being used to refer to over-fastidiousness.

is used to suggest social roles. As in the *Good Wife* poems, this is tellingly located in manuscripts and texts associated with a gentry and merchant readership. The issue of clothing in relation to the socialisation of young people will be pursued in the following chapter in reference to printed books associated with merchant and bourgeois readers. Outside the household, clothing was the prime example of public show. Equally, as stated within sumptuary legislation, clothing identified the individual by their station while carrying encoded information concerning a person's identity and character; love of finery, aping Continental fashions and, disastrously, over-courtesy and falsity were commonly adopted in support of this. Such was Idley's concern with extravagant dress that he termed it a 'vice', using the same ire when referring to it and to other inappropriate actions such as visiting taverns, ribaldry and swearing. He returned to this theme when he added to his previous comment 'Be not straunge of hatte hoode ne hure'.[134]

In his portrayal of a young man's behaviour, Idley also employs meekness, 'Meke in countenaunce deboneire and mure' appearing in the same stanza as the preceding passage on clothing.[135] Idley shows a theoretical interest in behaviour and socialisation based on his knowledge that these provided an 'outer picture' for others to use in their judgement of you. As he says, 'Therfore do this as I the teche / And gladde of thy companye will be eche a man / And sey of the worship[p]e al th[at] they can'.[136]

Earlier it was noted that religious discussion is incorporated into the first book. One obvious point to make is that religion is used to support secular arguments; religious belief is not in itself a primary concern of *Liber Primus*. The use of religious sentiment to serve secular goals is suggested in a passage on social order: 'ffirst god and thy kyng th[ou] loue and drede / Aboue all thyng th[ou] this p[re]serue'.[137] Second to this is the more personal but equally vital obligation towards parents. Establishing the social order at the start of a text was a fairly standard literary device. Through it, Thomas and other youthful readers were located in a world with which they were already familiar; simultaneously, this also reinforced a sense of hierarchical commitment. A sense of duty towards specific figures (parents, God, monarch) and towards maintaining an inherited station in life is one which has all but disappeared from the overt conditioning children and young people receive today.

---

[134] Text E, fol. 3ᵛ. Also in BL MS Add. 57335, fol. 2ʳ and B1, fol. 12ᵛ. In Text H, fol. 23ᵛ: 'not straunge of thi hode ne of thi hure'. In Text P (Magdalene), fol. 20ʳ: 'Be not stronge of hatred ne off yre'.

[135] Text E, fol. 3ᵛ. Also in BL MS Add. 57335, fol. 2ʳ; B1, fol. 12ᵛ and Text P (Magdalene), fol. 20ʳ. In Text H, fol. 23ᵛ this is 'Meke in countenau[n]ce bono[r] and demure'.

[136] Text E, fol. 3ᵛ. Also in BL MS Add. 57335, fol. 2ʳ; B1, fol. 12ʳ and Text P (Magdalene), fol. 20ʳ. Similarly in Text H, fol. 23ᵛ.

[137] Text E, fol. 1ʳ. Similarly in B1, fol. 10ᵛ. The prologue and lines 1–49 are missing in Text P. BL MS Add. 57335 is also incomplete. Text H lacked the reference to God and simply had '[F]urste that thi kynge thou loue & drede'. Text H, fol. 21ʳ.

Idley's secular emphasis is illuminated in the subsequent passage on the material world. Part of this points to the problems of lewdness, merriness and jollity. What is significant is the absence of religious themes. While these transgressions could have incorporated a religious topic, they are primarily used to paint a picture of worldly problems. Idley is even more aware of material lifestyles when he fails to condemn possessions: 'Richesse in hymsilf y wote is no synne'. He completes the sentiment by stating, 'So w[i]t[h]out goodis temp[or]all may not longe endure'.[138] Idley's practical nature, striving to explain to his son and other youths the world as it existed and the best way of living in it, becomes increasingly explicit:

> W[i]t[h]out goodis temp[or]all th[i]s may not be hadde;
> Also honour, worship, and frendship is past.
> ffor as a ship[e] in the see w[i]t[h]out rother or mast
> Ys ou[er]throw and turned w[i]t[h] waves and flodes,
> So is a man for lak of temp[or]all goodis[139]

For Idley, these lessons were connected to the expectations of the material world and the rules and guidelines which enabled young people to prosper. By reducing the overt religious message of *Liber Primus*, Idley presented a text which was rich in practical, realistic and above all pragmatic examples and models of behaviour suitable for a young man to follow.

Political discussion of English nationality and sovereignty also received some attention. Thomas's socialisation was calculated and gauged both by his personal involvement with friends, his father and his close community and by his involvement in English politics: 'Trust not to moche to thyn owne reason / Dispise not thy feith ne the power of thy kyng / Thow myght happe to stumble and falle into treason / Therfore medle not w[i]t[h] suche man[er] thyng'.[140] In this way, Thomas was taken out of the domestic, and somewhat generic and timeless, household environment and made aware of broader political discussions. This raises a point that will be pursued in the next chapter, where contemporary political culture and concerns with public order, political uncertainties and disruption to the royal succession are shown as breeding interest in moral reform. A heightened desire for moral regulation is linked also with urban bourgeois and merchant classes. What is particularly appealing in Idley's poems is the informal language he uses – for example, 'happe to stumble and falle', as if he were suggesting the ease with which trouble befalls youths. An understanding of youthful misbehaviour

---

[138] Both quotations Text E, fol. 13ʳ. Also in BL MS Add. 57335, fol. 11ᵛ and B1, fol. 20ʳ. In Text H, fol. 35ʳ and Text P (Magdalene), fol. 30ʳ.

[139] Text E. fol. 13ʳ. In Text P (Magdalene), fol. 30ʳ; B1, fol. 20ʳ and BL MS Add. 57335, fol. 11ᵛ. In Text H, fol. 35ʳ.

[140] Text E, fol. 15ʳ. Similarly in BL MS Add. 57335, fol. 14ʳ; B1, fol. 22ʳ; Text P (Magdalene), fol. 32ᵛ; and in Text H, fols. 37ᵛ–38ʳ.

and strife was typical in courtesy works, mostly based on the symbolism of gestures and actions. In elite narratives, presuming to sit in too high a place, showing uncouth or churlish behaviour which overtly placed you outside the privileged group and drawing unnecessary attention to yourself were part of socialisation and identity. Here more wide-ranging behaviours are identified to control and restrain young people's actions and their conduct in a political and social sense. This may suggest Idley was locating his warnings in contemporary political and social contexts. The Hundred Years War, the Wars of the Roses and subsequent national instability were all relevant to Idley. Given the loss of French territories from the 1440s, culminating in the complete loss of all holdings (barring Calais) by 1453, Idley's references to a political context were particularly timely. The ongoing turmoil between the Lancastrians and Yorkists, as well as Richard, duke of York's political manoeuvrings, provided a political and social background to what he was writing; this is true regardless of Idley's adoption of the thirteenth-century tracts by Albertanus.

A connection between Idley's position as a member of the gentry and his reworking of militaristic notions also strikes at the idea of chivalry. Chivalric ideology interested gentry classes in the mid-fifteenth century, moving chivalry further from its traditional knightly context.[141] This interest in chivalry amongst non-aristocratic classes has been noted by Michael Stroud at a time when knighthood came to symbolise less of a chivalric heritage and when neither the king nor the nobility encouraged livery practices.[142] Significantly, merchant and bourgeois classes were embracing the language and ethical practices of chivalry. An echo of the emphasis on ethical conduct and moral behaviour found in courtesy poems associated with merchant and bourgeois readers can be seen in this. The ethical nature of chivalry, what Stroud sees as the transfer of chivalric beliefs to other social groups because of the inherent emphasis on conduct rather than lineage, is a useful idea.[143]

The many levels of meaning within courtesy poems are apparent in the manner in which non-noble readers actively reworked ideals of behaviour, codes of conduct and notions of courtesy. A stronger theme of morality appears in these fifteenth-century courtesy poems and manuscripts, presenting a different picture of the socialising lessons available for young people. The

---

[141] See Keen, *Origins of the English Gentleman*.

[142] M. Stroud, 'Chivalric Terminology in Late Medieval Literature', *Journal of the History of Ideas* 37 (1976), 323–34 (p. 324). For the changing nature of knighthood in the late fifteenth century where it is associated with politics and local leadership rather than military service, see Carpenter, *Locality and Polity*, pp. 85–7.

[143] Stroud, 'Chivalric Terminology', pp. 325–6. For the revival of chivalry in England in the 1460s see R. Barber, 'Chivalry and the *Morte Darthur*', in *A Companion to Malory*, ed. E. Archibald and A. S. G. Edwards (Cambridge, 1996), pp. 19–35 (pp. 30–1).

developing interest in moral behaviour grows out of the parallel merchant and bourgeois context, as well as possibly reflecting the interests of smaller parental households. Family audiences were served by the intertextual nature of household manuscripts, such as manuscripts Ashmole 61 and Balliol 354.

Courtesy literature still retained its conventional attitudes towards courteous behaviour, yet some texts have illustrated the increasing presence of inner qualities as important factors in socialisation. In these texts, often written by and for merchant and gentry readers, a different emphasis is increasingly articulated in which outward manners are aligned with the motif of inner ethics and goodness. Socialisation based on class and courtesy gradually developed to reflect 'truths' about inner value and merit. The poems for girls strongly emphasised true virtue as part of a gendered understanding of behaviour and it is likely that their socialisation and upbringing always appropriated a greater virtuous framework than the socialisation of boys, even across the same period.

No form of literature is static over time. Analysing the changing patterns that develop out of established tropes reveals the manner in which behaviour and virtue changed in the literature and changed in society. The influence of merchant and gentry social groups is important in determining the means by which socialisation and childhood identity were articulated over time.

CHAPTER THREE

Virtue and Vice

'I aduyse euery gentilman or woman hauyng such children desyryng them to be vertuously brought forth to get and haue this book to thende that they may lerne hou they ought to gouerne them vertuously in this present lyf'[1]

The manner in which printed books established new moral and virtuous impulses as part of the rhetoric of upbringing reflects increasing complexity in how courtesy, morality and socialisation were understood in the late fifteenth century. Courtesy manuscripts, while still available and circulating within and around households, were now matched by the London-based distribution of printed books. The extent to which texts from the existing body of English vernacular work were chosen for print and circulated outwards from London's printing trade is evidence that the readership for literature concerned with children's behaviour was changing.

The role of printers in determining reading choices was a development in England's reading culture which was almost entirely new, and from it emerges a different sense of the history of the printed book in relation to scribal activities. William Caxton's productivity at his Westminster workshop extended the reach and breadth of courtesy and instructional literature by manipulating it for the new dynamic printing press. Socialising literature would eventually become an integral part of the printed reading and literary networks in England. Comparing courtesy themes as they appeared in extant manuscripts and those printed by Caxton becomes a way of seeing how early printers developed authority in preserving and altering ideologies in the socialising process.

The transmission and reception of literature concerned with children extends into questions about cultural socialisation, with this literature suggesting a distinctive understanding of moral identity. As such, changing patterns of thought across the manuscript and print corpus are important, with competing ideologies and interests needing to be understood in relation to particular audience networks. These show that audiences were critical readers of texts based on the class to which they belonged.

---

[1] G. la Tour Landry, *Here begynneth the booke which the knyght of the toure made and speketh of many fayre ensamples and thensygnementys and techyng of his daughters* (Westminster, 1484) (hereafter, la Tour Landry, *Knight of the Tower*), Ai^r.

This chapter draws on printed source material, specifically six incunabula produced by Caxton between 1476 and 1487. These books are an undervalued part of Caxton's printing legacy and place children and family reading networks more firmly into the history of childhood and the history of the book. Some of Caxton's books reflected the older courtesy tradition, such as the 1476 *Stans puer ad mensam* and the *Book of Curtesye*. Others crafted wide-ranging arguments concerning good behaviour taken from the moralising and didactic texts which also came out of the manuscript corpus, including *Parvus Cato*, *Caton* and the *Book of Good Manners*, which demonstrate layers of meaning in socialisation when morality and virtuous behaviour are presented in socialising lessons. Finally, the *Book of the Knight of the Tower* reflects many of these themes in relation to a reading audience of girls and young women. Absent from this list are Christine de Pizan's *The Book of Faytes of Arms* and *Morale Proverbes*, since while they explore morality, they do not address children and young people. In addition, the *Fables of Aesop* has been excluded: here, it is existing work on the text's relationship to young people over several centuries which has influenced the decision to exclude it from detailed study.[2]

Vernacular literature played an important role in fostering how socialisation was understood. The first part of this chapter examines the English printing trade and the importance of Caxton's publishing choices. The second part addresses each of these six books in more detail to see how another concept of socialisation was explored and discussed in literature. Caxton's prologues will help to evaluate the different means by which these texts were packaged for readers in the light of pressing social and political events in England, viewed in a context of political disturbances and the conflicts of the Wars of the Roses. While unrest was felt in adult circles, the evidence suggests responses to the same anxieties were present in family reading networks. This chapter also deals with how political anxiety traversed downwards to affect other social groups, including children and families, who are frequently overlooked in studies of social, and particularly political, history. A point regarding terminology: this analysis builds on the work of the preceding chapter addressing the manner in which references to morality and virtue were substituted for other socialising imperatives. As such, the term 'courtesy literature' is increasingly problematic. In order to avoid confusing inaccuracies, this late fifteenth century material will now be identified as instructional or conduct literature except in cases where the term courtesy is particularly appropriate.

---

[2] On this see W. Wooden, *Children's Literature of the English Renaissance, Edited, with an Introduction by Jeanie Watson* (Lexington, 1986).

Printing decisions

Book historians are persistently revisiting the question of the nature of early print's connections to manuscript culture or its disconnect from it.[3] Early print culture, in this light, is loaded with competing claims of conventionality as well as newness.[4] This paradigm is gradually being shifted as other questions are asked concerning the conflicting, multiple and contradictory engagements between and around manuscripts and the printed page.[5]

Asking whether these debates reveal a need to assign Caxton to a single cultural moment, or whether they reflect a deeper confusion over how technological innovations overlap with a change in cultural values, is less useful than seeing the history of early printing in terms of a series of smaller developments and individual choices reflecting successive social, political and cultural practices. The shape of this can be seen more clearly when the focus is shifted to individual aspects of early printing. Caxton's series of courtesy and instructional texts is a means of looking to this broader debate without losing focus on the individuality and specificity of decisions which went into creating and producing books. Caxton's books for young people and families present a cohesive, as well as a conflicting and sometimes contradictory, series of advice volumes. The term 'series' is a deliberate one. Studies on Caxton's Worthies series (*Godeffroy of Boloyne, Le Morte Darthur* and *Charles the Grete*) have shown the manner in which three discrete books can be understood in a unified sense.[6] There are important, indeed there are explicit, connections between these books, and certainly references in *Le Morte Darthur's* prologue to *Godeffroy* are evidence of a sequence of reading choices being deliberately

[3] For early work on Caxton see W. Blades, *The Life and Typography of William Caxton, England's First Printer: With Evidence of his Typographical Connection with Colard Mansion, the Printer at Bruges* (London, 1861–3). Also, *The Prologues and Epilogues of William Caxton*, ed. W. J. B. Crotch, EETS OS 176 (Oxford, 1928); N. F. Blake, *Caxton and his World* (London, 1969); *Caxton's Own Prose*, ed. N. F. Blake (London, 1973); N. F. Blake, *Caxton: England's First Publisher* (London, 1976); N. F. Blake, *William Caxton and English Literary Culture* (London, 1991); G. D. Painter, *William Caxton: A Quincentenary Biography of England's First Printer* (London, 1976); L. Hellinga, *Caxton in Focus: The Beginning of Printing in England* (London, 1982).

[4] The best studies of the relationships between manuscript production and printing are *Manuscripts in the Fifty Years after the Invention of Printing*, ed. J. B. Trapp (London, 1983). Also, D. R. Carlson, *English Humanist Books: Writers and Patrons, Manuscripts and Print, 1475–1525* (Toronto, 1993), pp. 102–22. Elizabeth Eisenstein's work emphasises the fixity of the presses: E. L. Eisenstein, *The Printing Press as an Agent of Change: Communications and Cultural Transformations in Early Modern Europe*, 2 vols. (Cambridge, 1979). Recently, both Adrian Johns and David McKitterick have analysed the culture of printing in terms of slow change. Johns, *Nature of the Book*; McKitterick, *Print, Manuscript, and the Search for Order*.

[5] See particularly William Kuskin's Introduction to *Caxton's Trace*, pp. 1–31.

[6] On this see Kuskin, 'Caxton's Worthies', pp. 511–51.

encouraged. Of Caxton's instructional series, such intertextual signs cannot be found; however, there are other traces, ranging from themes and audience to tone, that allow the idea of an instructional series to gain momentum. Built into this is the assertion that, as Kuskin has argued, bourgeois audiences found it difficult to imagine their community with any coherence. Caxton's literature thus became a means for this middling audience to understand and shape itself, what Kuskin refers to as 'Caxton [articulating] canon, authority, and audience as cogent and interrelated concerns, and thereby [producing] a comprehensive intellectual framework for the physical products rolling off his presses'.[7] This process of unifying an ambiguous and disparate audience is a compelling theme to explore in the reception of an instructional series. Of course, another issue worth exploring is how an imagined series could be given physical weight, and this will be addressed shortly.

First, however, it is necessary to take a slight step back and rethink what we know of a printer's editorial decisions in order to show how material could be rethought and redefined, 'constructed anew' for readers in much the same way that we identify similar motivations in the actions of scribes and readers of manuscripts. In fact, rather than being sensitive only to the manner in which manuscripts were read and created – for example, through the intertextual relationships, bindings, interpolations and glosses which reveal the interests of readers – similar approaches to printed material can, and should, be made. The agency of the scribe should be compared to the agency of the printer. Identifying variant versions of a printed book also calls into question the relationship between printed texts and reading communities.[8] 'Intertext' and anthologised manuscripts can be rewritten as a study of *Sammelbände* and it is here that that the physical nature of a book series is hinted at. *Sammelbände*, books in which multiple items were bound as one volume, were once common, although they are now unfortunately victims of modern library practices with most having been unbound and catalogued as separate items (hiding the history of how they were once read and owned). One example of this, the *Sammelbände* of Caxton's 1476–8 editions, now disbanded and held at Cambridge University Library, contained three of the most pivotal instructional books: *Stans puer ad mensam, Parvus Cato* and the *Book of Curtesye*.[9] Paul Needham has in fact argued that many of Caxton's books were once collected together, citing the financial savings that came with binding several texts as a practical factor in their creation. Utilitarian motives are, however, not the

---

[7] Kuskin, 'Caxton's Worthies', p. 511.
[8] Reading communities and manuscripts have been studied in depth in Huot, *Romance of the Rose*.
[9] S. Lerer, 'William Caxton', in *The Cambridge History of Medieval English Literature*, ed. D. Wallace (Cambridge, 1999), pp. 720–38 (pp. 726–7). A. Gillespie discusses this in *Print Culture and the Medieval Author: Chaucer, Lydgate, and their Books, 1473–1557* (Oxford, 2006), pp. 45–6.

only reason for individual printed texts to be bound together by owners, and Alexandra Gillespie has highlighted the cultural meaning behind the creation of these volumes.[10] Intertextual relationships can also be studied through the compendia nature of printed works; the printed edition of *Stans puer ad mensam* is a case in point, comprising a series of five individual texts, all too short to be printed separately. Equally, printers like Caxton inserted their own glosses into material with the intention of drawing a reader's attention to a passage, inserting their own voice and authority into the narrative and constructing the way in which they believed a reader should approach the text. Such editorial decisions are worth considering. Finally, it is worth projecting forward into the sixteenth century to see how print was a medium used in teaching speciality fields.[11] In relation to this, an early instructional series reveals how manners and good upbringing were, in a similar way, knowledge which authors and printers were professing to hold: behaviour which was sold to consumers in degrees previously unattainable by scribes, although it is true that manuscript production has been seen to be similarly systematic.[12]

What the books in this instructional series looked like in a physical sense is also important. H. S. Bennett has argued that the publication of smaller quarto volumes suggests Caxton was testing the strength of his market ahead of more ambitious folio editions.[13] Risking the publication of cheaper works is financially justifiable, but it is worth noting that of the six courtesy and

---

[10] P. Needham, *The Printer and the Pardoner: An Unrecorded Indulgence Printed by William Caxton for the Hospital of St Mary Rounceval, Charing Cross* (Washington, 1986), pp. 17–21; A. Gillespie, 'Poets, Printers, and Early English *Sammelbände*', *Huntington Library Quarterly* 67 (2004), 189–214; Gillespie, *Print Culture*, pp. 45–54, 67–79, 112–17; A. Gillespie, '"Folowynge the trace of mayster Caxton": Some Histories of Fifteenth-Century Printed Books', in *Caxton's Trace: Studies in the History of English Printing*, ed. W. Kuskin (Notre Dame, 2006), pp. 167–95.

[11] On this see Eisenstein's *Printing Press as an Agent of Change* and also P. J. Voss, 'Books for Sale: Advertising and Patronage in Late Elizabethan England', *Sixteenth Century Journal* 29 (1998), 733–56 (p. 747) which also discusses this idea.

[12] Nicole Clifton finds that some manuscripts testified 'to a serious and sustained production and appreciation of medieval children's literature'. N. Clifton, 'The "Seven Sages of Rome", Children's Literature, and the Auchinleck Manuscript', in *Childhood in the Middle Ages and the Renaissance: The Results of a Paradigm Shift in the History of Mentality*, ed. A. Classen (Berlin, 2005), pp. 185–201 (p. 187).

[13] Quarto volumes include four of Lydgate's poems, what Bennett describes as the more serious *Parvus Cato*, Christine de Pizan's *Morale Proverbes* and *The Book of Curtesye*. Folio editions include the *Dicts or Sayings of the Philosophers*, *The History of Jason* (1477) and Chaucer's *Boethius de consolatione philosophiae* (1478). See H. S. Bennett, *English Books and Readers 1475–1557: Being a Study in the History of the Book Trade from Caxton to the Incorporation of the Stationers' Company* (Cambridge, 1952), p. 13. See also N. F. Blake, 'Caxton Prepares his Edition of the *Morte Darthur*', *Journal of Librarianship* 8 (1976), 272–85. Carol Meale cautions that other factors beyond status may have contributed to the aesthetic design of books. C. M. Meale, 'Caxton, de

instructional books aimed at children, or parents with children or young dependants, only three were in quarto. Size has a flow-on effect on status and Gillespie has suggested that smaller books were symbolically equated with trivial, 'childish' matters with larger books holding greater value and status.[14] Publication of quarto books may suggest that Caxton was testing childhood reading interests by an identifiable physical type. A symbolic connection may have occurred consciously or subconsciously concerning physical appearance and likely audience.

The range and multiplicity of possible interactions between printed texts and readers constitute only one part of the story of early printing culture; evidence of contact between the product of the press and the audience is related to the earlier decisions printers made to print (only) certain texts.[15] Caxton's publications are evidence of the overlooked importance of these decisions. In other words, it is only by looking at the type of courtesy literature that was privileged by the presses in relation to the overall body of courtesy material which existed that we can begin to see changing patterns in the socialisation process. As Carol Meale has shown in relation to English romances, it is worth tracing print culture through this longer-term manuscript awareness, investigating how a genre was represented across manuscript and print, or in other words asking 'is any correlation to be noted between the currency of a particular romance in manuscript and its transference into print'?[16] Indeed, only a small proportion of English romances were printed by Caxton and Wynken de Worde in the fifteenth and early sixteenth centuries. The significance this has for manuscript and print culture is apparent.[17] In this instance, the range of relationships, consolidations and separations that were possible between manuscript and print presents an opportunity to identify the changing role of courtesy and upbringing in the late fifteenth century.

Worde, and the Publication of Romance in Late Medieval England', *The Library* 6th s. 14 (1992), 283–98 (p. 291).

[14] Gillespie, 'Poets, Printers, and Early English *Sammelbände*', p. 204.

[15] A. E. B. Coldiron, 'Taking Advice from a Frenchwoman: Caxton, Pynson, and Christine de Pizan's Moral Proverbs', in *Caxton's Trace: Studies in the History of English Printing*, ed. W. Kuskin (Notre Dame, 2006), pp. 127–66.

[16] Meale, 'Caxton, de Worde, and the Publication of Romance', p. 287; A. S. G. Edwards and C. M. Meale, 'The Marketing of Printed Books in Late Medieval England', *The Library* 6th s. 15 (1993), 95–124 (p. 95); A. S. G. Edwards, 'Chaucer From Manuscript to Print: The Social Text and the Critical Text', *Mosaic* 28 (1995), 1–12.

[17] Edwards and Meale, 'Marketing of Printed Books', p. 95.

Caxton's audience

Child and family reading networks have received little attention from historians of either childhood or book history. The changing market for printed books in the late fifteenth century is an important part of how changes in childhood were perceived. Provincial gentry families and London merchant and bourgeois audiences, including lawyers and officials, were offered new opportunities to purchase and read printed books.[18] In Caxton's case, the prologues he wrote to accompany his books record significant arrangements, or attempts to suggest arrangements, with patrons and audiences. Prologues function as an intermediary stage between a text and an audience, often directing readers to messages within a narrative by citing public figures and political events. This could dramatically bring a text closer to a specifically English context, favouring English ideologies and contemporary contexts over European ones. Knowing and astute readers would have identified with the contemporary nature of prefaces and engaged with them as part of a dialogue with a directly accessible literary figure; frequently this figure was Caxton himself. Numerous examples exist of Caxton writing himself into his books. In the simplest instances he merely referred to himself (*Polycronicon*, *The Golden Legende* and *The Fayttes of Armes*). More elaborate scenarios were constructed when he described the text's 'history' – inventing an authoritative prehistory (*Caton*), explaining how the book came into his hands (*Book of Good Manners*, the *Curial*, *The Royal Book*), or outlining how and why he decided to undertake the arduous task of translating a foreign language text into English (*The Historie of Jason*, *The Royal Book*). Caxton is thus a legitimate 'author' of the book, no longer its scribe or its editor.

Value also continued to be symbolically attached to audiences. Caxton shrewdly utilised royal and noble patronage as a means of advertising certain publications. The *Dicts or Sayings of the Philosophers*, Christine de Pizan's *Morale Proverbes* and *The Cordial* were translated and published at the behest of Anthony Woodville, Earl Rivers, and Caxton went to some lengths to publicise this in prologues. Of course, this became a problem when Woodville later fell from political favour. *Reynard the Fox*, while acknowledging the interests of non-noble readers, symbolically tried to play upon the imagery of elite environments:

> men maye lerne to come to the subtyl knoweleche of suche thynges as dayly ben vsed & had in the counseyllys of lordes and prelates gostly and worldly and also emonge marchantes and other comone peple[19]

---

[18] On this see Y. C. Wang, 'Caxton's Romances and Their Early Tudor Readers', *Huntington Library Quarterly* 67 (2004), 173–88.

[19] *This is the table of the historye of reynart the foxe* (Westminster, 1481), Aiii^v. Caxton's *Le*

Claims of multiple readerships reveal Caxton's experiments with different networks; some of these were no doubt for commercial reasons, yet they revolutionise the often-anonymous relationships between narratives and the networks they were formed by and for. Such claims do not necessarily reflect accurate readerships or even genuine patronage networks. Increasingly they have been read as symbolic and strategic rather than trustworthy.[20] The top-end market was relatively small and limited, while growing gentry, merchant, bourgeois and urban wealth opened up wider business opportunities for Caxton. While parallel evidence from book prices is intriguing, although limited, there is no doubt that printed books were not restricted to the wealthiest members of society.[21] Data on wages show that incunabula were affordable material items for merchants and some craftsmen.[22]

Understanding emendations found in manuscripts and printed books as suiting gentry, merchant and urban bourgeois markets or fostering negotiations between multiple class groups leads us towards the notion that literary culture was capable of fashioning multiple identities. Such was the case with *Reynard the Fox* in that the associations with the nobility and royalty would have appealed to some status-conscious gentry, merchant and bourgeois readers whose purchase of books signalled their participation in elite activities. As already noted, the needs of some readers can be understood by their actions in reworking texts to suit merchant and moral agendas. Fifteenth-century gentry groups were able to seize the chivalric and political texts of the nobility while shifting the thematic interests to suit their own interests.[23] Such measures, while made in relation to adult texts, are nevertheless applicable to courtesy and instructional books. Caxton should be thought of as contributing to this process by singling out particular themes at the outset, and certainly there is evidence from the prologues to suggest conscious decisions were applied to textual choices and audiences.

At the same time, these links between texts and supposed class appropriateness can be misleading. Caxton adeptly created an inclusive public

---

Morte Darthur similarly expanded traditional noble concepts of chivalry to a wider audience.

[20] Blake, *Caxton and his World*, pp. 95–6; Blake, *William Caxton*, pp. 13, 32.

[21] Book prices remain an area needing further study. For some early research into this see F. Madan, 'The Day-Book of John Dorne, Bookseller in Oxford, A. D. 1520', *Collectanea* 1, part. III (1885), 71–177; F. Madan, 'Supplementary Notes', *Collectanea* 2 (1890), 454–78. For comparisons on the cost of paper and manuscript books, see H. E. Bell, 'The Price of Books in Medieval England', *The Library* 4th s. 17 (1936–7), 312–32. Wholesale book prices are noted in Kuskin, '"Onely Imagined"', pp. 204–5.

[22] Dyer, *Standards of Living*, pp. 196, 215. In 1510, five Caxton/de Worde folios were bought for between four pence and two shillings eight pence. Needham, *Printer and the Pardoner*, pp. 19, 80.

[23] On this see R. L. Radulescu, *The Gentry Context for Malory's* Morte Darthur (Cambridge, 2003), p. 39.

readership, rather than an *exclusive* one.²⁴ As has already been seen, increasingly far-reaching and multi-directional engagements were taking place, with gentry, merchant and bourgeois interests overtly driving the production of certain types of socialising literature, even competing with traditionally noble (courteous) values. Merchants and bourgeois groups were not only readers of these books in their final physical form, but were active agents in promoting, supplying and encouraging the publication of some texts, as we see with Caxton and his books.

Older traditions

The content of *Stans puer ad mensam* has been addressed in the previous chapters and Caxton's 1476 edition offers no substantially different reading. Caxton certainly assimilated the fixed courtesy topos into his book, extending the life of courtesy into the new printed medium. These continuities are not unexpected. Early printers made good use of existing texts for the presses as this both sped up the process of preparing an item for publication and offered printers a safe and established avenue for the sale of their books. Bourgeois, merchant, gentry and elite readers were familiar with courtesy literature's suitability for young people and the popularity of the poem in manuscripts would have added to Caxton's belief in its marketability. It is therefore not necessary to re-examine the content of the poem; however, it is worthwhile examining the 1476 edition in terms of the manner in which printed courtesy material was presented to readers.

As we have already seen, hunting through manuscript and printing practices for similarities may be misleading, but here they do serve some purpose. The combination of separate texts in Caxton's 1476 edition is worth exploring. The book begins with *Stans puer ad mensam*, followed by a short verse of simple precepts with the incipit 'Aryse erly'. A religious note is explored in the *Salue Regina*, after which comes a simple verse with the incipit 'Wytte hath wonder'. Six proverbial phrases bring this short book to a close.²⁵ These decisions speak to the use of manuscript strategies in a new form. On the one hand copy-setting these five items was, at its most basic level, an effective way of using available free space: technological advances made it possible for printers to print and sell multiple texts as a single and discrete edition. Yet, the nature of the compilation would have been attractive to the family audiences who were increasingly reading and owning manuscripts and household miscellanies in the fifteenth century. As noted earlier, this was not uni-directional: Richard Hill's household miscellany is evidence

---

[24] S. Lerer, *Chaucer and His Readers: Imagining the Author in Late-Medieval England* (Princeton, 1993), p. 168.
[25] J. Lydgate, *Stans puer ad mensam* (Westminster, 1476).

of the manner in which printed books were taken and reworked back into a manuscript.

Physical similarities between printed books and manuscripts are suggestive of print not radically transforming the reading landscape. Printing a longer courtesy poem with miscellaneous smaller verses reproduced anthologised manuscripts and would have been a familiar extension of material culture to readers. In a pragmatic sense, Caxton was aided by the relative ease of publishing a short volume of multiple items. Simultaneously, the reader also now owned a book that had thematic unity, and this is suggestive of supposed reader interests. In other words, the practical exploitation of available texts helped create a more substantial, yet easy to produce, book. This was an approach taken in the sixteenth century by Wynken de Worde and Johan Redman, both of whom reprinted this edition (barring some textual mistakes which seem to have crept in and excluding the five-line verse at the end of the *Salue Regina* which was removed, although for no obvious reason).[26] Each, however, made two significant additions. The first concerns the inclusion of woodcuts. In 1510, de Worde published this book with a simple image showing adults and children. Redman's 1540 edition included a similar image. While generic in many ways, these woodcuts nevertheless reinforce the text's message of youth and (in)experience. Art historians have typically deciphered visual images by analysing the relative size of figures to distinguish between adult and child portraits. While this can be confused in medieval and early modern artwork because of the use of smaller figures to denote class as well as age differences, the context of the woodcuts in relation to the poem means both readings may have been appropriate, at the very least heightening the reader's experience of owning the book.[27]

While interesting, and certainly altering the visual aspect of the book, these changes are relatively minor. It is the more extensive changes de Worde and Redman made to the intertextual arrangement of the book which draw our attention to the calculated way courtesy texts were reproduced in the early sixteenth century. Both included a second, parallel courtesy poem which Caxton had printed independently in 1477. This was the *Book of Curtesye*, although it now went by a different title, *Lytell Johan*. This poem will be pursued in more detail later in this chapter; however, for now it can be summed up as recasting courtesy values as part of a critique of false courtesy and overly extravagant elite practices. It is the addition of a contradictory narrative on courtesy which alters how the complete edition may have been read; *Lytell Johan* certainly offsets the more traditional themes of

---

[26] *Stans puer ad me[n]sa[m]* (London, 1510); *Stans puer ad mensa[m]. Otherwyse called the boke of Norture, newly imprinted and very necessary vnto all youthe* (London, 1540).

[27] On young people in artwork see M. Pastoureau, 'Emblems of Youth: Young People in Medieval Imagery', in *A History of Young People in the West*, ed. G. Levi and J. C. Schmitt, trans. C. Naish (Cambridge, MA, 1997), pp. 222–39 (pp. 228–31).

Stans puer ad mensam. The similarities between the two poems may, however, account for this publishing decision. As before, the printing of these texts as one substantial edition is an extension of how related material was gathered and presented to readers in manuscripts. Here, the suggestion that late fifteenth century literary culture was fashioned around the publication of books bound by common themes has actual weight.

By 1510 and 1540 parents or any adults buying *Stans puer ad mensam* were effectively purchasing a multi-volume book on courtesy and instructional advice for children. It is tempting to see the presence of visual aids in each edition as emphasising a family-unit readership. As with earlier manuscript anthologies, editions such as these shaped reading habits and responses and were in turn shaped by presumed reader interests. The physical compilation of texts in print removed one aspect of active participation on the part of the reader who could no longer commission which texts would be included, reinforcing the control and influence of printers in creating unified texts which could not be separated. Readers could, of course, choose to bind this with other material or write it out into their own household miscellanies as Hill did and reclaim a measure of independent participation in the way texts were controlled, but it is worth remembering that they could not undo the work of the printers.[28] Technological advances in printing shaped the way the reading community approached literary material, with established narratives reworked for a new buying and reading public. This could still be carried out according to traditional and conventional lines, as we see here.

If *Stans puer ad mensam* was a traditional courtesy text, then Caxton's *Parvus Cato* also sits squarely within a tradition of didactic literature for young people, one in which conventional ethical principles described upbringing. When this book discussed children's behaviour it did so by looking to ethical and moral socialising norms, the first stanza stating that there is a lack of 'vertuous gouernaunce' in people's lives. It is this message which is sold to readers, embedded in a discussion of *thewes*, customs or manners of behaving, in which everyone's conduct is linked to virtue: 'How thy sowle inward shal acqueynted be / With thewes good and vertues in al wyse'.[29] The imagery supports a concern with conduct according to virtuous actions.

It was extremely important that children behaved well and they were

---

[28] For different views see Edwards and Meale, 'Marketing of Printed Books', p. 96 and Gillespie, '"Folowynge the trace of mayster Caxton"', pp. 167–95.

[29] *Hic incipit parvus Catho* (Westminster, 1483) (henceforth *Parvus Cato*), Aii^r. Two earlier editions, in 1476 and 1477 respectively, were not paginated. All quotations and page numbers refer to the third edition. All passages can, however, be found in the earlier editions. An article which discusses the Distichs over the centuries is I. A. Brunner, 'On Some of the Vernacular Translations of Cato's *Distichs*', in *Helen Adolf Festschrift*, ed. S. Z. Buehne, J. L. Hodge and L. B. Pinto (New York, 1968), pp. 99–123. Some comparisons to the manuscript versions of this text are noted in Appendix B of this book.

warned to rise early and 'loue no slogardye', to revere parents and 'drede' their masters, to moderate their eating and drinking and be demure in their speech.[30] It is still somewhat ambiguous how virtue and courtesy were understood to relate to each other. For example, the word courtesy still has a place in a moral text: 'Be thou curteys and demeure of thy langage' or 'To vilayns swalowe of couetyse'.[31] However, what can we make of other lessons which seem to recognise the book's central message of moral conduct? We can, for instance, take the passage 'the first of vertues alle / Ys to be stylle and kepe thy tonge in mewe'.[32] One way to read this would suggest that virtue exists in relation to inner qualities but also as a synonym for public conduct and manners, standards of behaviour which courtesy poems also considered. Despite this, virtue is decidedly more compatible with the book's moral ideas about upbringing:

> Wherwyth he may his sowle fostre and fede
> With vertue and it from vyces vnbynde
> Come nere my chyld therfore and haue in mynde
> Suche doctryne in thyn herte to bere awey and lere[33]

Fundamentally, the relationship that exists here between virtues, vice and religion should be seen as part of a wide-ranging value system in which nurture is identified in terms of complex good behaviour.

It is worth asking how virtue increasingly surpasses courtesy and courteous behaviour. The accepted norms of behaviour underpinning conduct are not necessarily changing in themselves; although it can be noted that in another of Caxton's books, the *Book of Curtesye*, there is evidence of a contemporary understanding of changing manners. In most ways, however, children and young people in the late fifteenth century were still growing up in ways that were recognisable from previous centuries. It is not always the case that the overt display and style of manners change; rather the displacement that courtesy undergoes is part of an alteration in the conceptual way of seeing and of understanding good behaviour, or in other words an expansion of the significance that good manners had in real terms to people.[34] There are parallels between this and other conservative forms of printing. William West has argued that 'far from spearheading the latest in thought, early printing was often quite conservative in content – it produced an explosion of old news'.[35] The relationship between older wisdom and printing culture was more complex and paradoxical than this implies. The reissue of old material

---

[30] *Parvus Cato*, Aiii^v.
[31] *Parvus Cato*, Ciii^r and Ciiii^v respectively.
[32] *Parvus Cato*, Aiii^v.
[33] *Parvus Cato*, Bviii^r.
[34] On this see Elias, *Civilizing Process*, p. 62.
[35] W. N. West, 'Old News, Caxton, de Worde, and the Invention of the Edition', in

in print, far from offering nothing new, actually spearheaded new directions in behaviour by being extremely conservative.

The discussion of social position and identity in *Parvus Cato* is significant for this reason. It engages with a broader understanding of social estates than is commonly found in courtesy poems. As noted earlier, the class-conscious word 'churl' had previously prepared children and young people to be aware of their conduct in terms of social estates and position. A similar division of behaviour and class is evident in didactic literature, but this suggests that identity was not solely predicated upon social position, for this literature even goes so far as to criticise the nature of elitist preoccupations:

> Grace is yeuen to man in many sondry wyse
> Some haue wysedam & some haue eloquence
> The poure folkes also some tyme be ful wyse
> A seruaunt sumtyme may be eke of grete sapyence
> Though al he be had in litel reuerence
> Rewarde his wyt yf it be worth the whyle
> For vertu is hyd vnder many an habit vyle[36]

The class-conscious labelling of people is certainly reinforced, and initially it is this, along with the traditional division of social estates, which is most striking. Nevertheless this passage invites the reader to be aware of the universal capacity for integrity. The impression this gives is one of conflicting ideas about class and identity. Identifying virtue does not alter the separation of people into their predesigned, and natural, estates. Rather, readers are encouraged to recognise that even 'poure folks' are wise and that virtue – note it is not saying good manners – might be hidden within the most socially unlikely candidates. There is evidence of this in a related warning over the danger of valuing self-importance and pedigree over conscience:

> And in effect yf thyn astate be hye
> Though fauel with his crafte wyl blynde thyn eye
> In al thy lyf thou neuer gyf credeuce
> More to thy self than to thy conscience[37]

The tension between a hypothetical social inclusiveness and the maintenance of pragmatic hierarchies is not resolved within the text, just as it could not be resolved in society. Two stanzas later, anxiety over marriage practices is suggestive of idealistic sentiments: 'Wedde not a wyf for hyr enheritaunce'.[38] Caxton's own, later translation of this text emphasised the same problem:

Caxton's Trace: Studies in the History of English Printing, ed. W. Kuskin (Notre Dame, 2006), pp. 241–74 (p. 253).
[36] *Parvus Cato*, Ci^v.
[37] *Parvus Cato*, Av^v.
[38] *Parvus Cato*, Cii^r.

'Thou oughtest not to take a wyf ne to coueyte hir forhyr dowayrfor hir rychesse ne for hir noblesse but thou oughtest to chese and take hyr for hyr vertues &good condycyons and for cause of hir good worshypful & honeste lygnage or kynrede'.[39] Given that marriage was one of the primary channels for social mobility in this period, this idealistic sentiment can be read with certain suspicion.

Reinforcing hierarchical divisions equally reinforces the negative imagery associated with some classes. However, there is also a conflicting idea that virtue, wisdom and wit are potentially present in all people. Granted, this does not mean that knowledge of how to behave at a table or how to serve meat or drink has been transferred. Yet it is possible that identity and status increasingly came to mean more than the knowledge of formal manners conferred by inherited social position or by learning these things through literature or experience. Virtue and grace were available to everyone and late fifteenth century children and young people were educated in how to take note of these qualities in printed books, having to learn that these inherent traits were more and more significant as markers of behaviour. Of course, this was not an original concept. Some earlier courtesy poems, such as *Stans puer ad mensam* in manuscript Ashmole 61, explicitly commented that the lowly born could acquire courtesy. Equally, universal virtue was acknowledged in other types of medieval texts and was not necessarily a concept or an indication of change unique to these instructional works and their audiences. The imagery in *Parvus Cato*, however, encroached upon the narratives of identity, gestures and hierarchy which had been so firmly established within courtesy material and provided an additional perspective on these issues to very much the same audience. That Caxton's books were read within bourgeois and mercantile reading communities lends further weight to this.

Contemporary political events

The mid- to late fifteenth century was a time of acknowledged social and political disruption in England, associated both with the loss of French territories from the 1440s and internally on English soil with the Wars of the Roses. While escalating military and political tension was undoubtedly felt most strongly within inner royal and aristocratic circles, other social groups, including the gentry, merchants and bourgeois we have been analysing in this book, responded to the same anxieties and disorder. London merchants had connections to the Continent and local gentry and lesser nobles had powerful roles as justices of the peace. Even yeomen, craftsmen and prosperous tradesmen were involved with juror presentments in local commu-

---

[39] *Here begynneth the prologue or prohemye of the book callid Caton* (Westminster, after 23 Dec. 1483), Giiii^v.

nities.[40] It is apparent that during the late fifteenth century concerns with government, national identity and acceptable (and legitimate) political order found expression in material that was read by these interested gentry, urban bourgeois and merchant groups. An awareness of social and political turmoil eventually turns into an interest in how to defuse and strategically cope with such problems.[41] Social and political agendas were, in fact, raised and driven by the gentry, local governments and peasants. The rise of critical commentary after the 1450s has been viewed as part of popular suspicion of government and law.[42]

There are connections between these political anxieties and the role of virtue and morality in wider society. Once seen as a puritan movement, moral regulation is in fact noticeable in court records from the mid-fourteenth century onwards.[43] Gender conservatism also became stronger in the late fifteenth century, linked to a tightening moral outlook, which Goldberg sees existing in conjunction with declining economic prospects.[44] Marjorie McIntosh's work on juror presentments reveals active approaches in instilling moral reform and in controlling perceived disorder at an individual community level.[45] The relationship between the regulation of moral order and national events has been interpreted differently, although it does seem that by the late fifteenth century localised community efforts had a more compelling relationship with English national crises in politics.[46] Pragmatic, personal and local interest in moral behaviour was matched by the theoretical and intellectual interest in

---

[40] On this see M. McIntosh, 'Response', *Journal of British Studies* 37 (1998), 291–305 (p. 295).

[41] D. McCulloch and E. D. Jones, 'Lancastrian Politics, the French War, and the Rise of the Popular Element', *Speculum* 58 (1983), 95–138 (pp. 134–5). Fear of political disorder and kingship in gentry circles is discussed in R. Radulescu, 'Yorkist Propaganda and *The Chronicle from Rollo to Edward IV*', *Studies in Philology* 100 (2003), 401–24

[42] Harriss, *Shaping the Nation*, p. 649.

[43] On this see M. McIntosh, *Controlling Misbehaviour in England, 1370–1600* (Cambridge, 1998).

[44] Goldberg, *Women in England*, p. 13. Phillips sees gender conservatism in literary examples which are also linked to conservative merchant audiences: Phillips, *Medieval Maidens*, p. 90

[45] Some of these moral offenses are listed in McIntosh, *Controlling Misbehaviour*, pp. 9–10.

[46] McIntosh in fact argues that before the mid- to late fifteenth century, moral regulation occurred in peaks and troughs often unrelated to wider national events: McIntosh, *Controlling Misbehaviour*, pp. 129–34. Peter Lake has written that McIntosh manages to 'uncouple the phenomenon from many of the national, global events and ideological currents to which it has been hitherto attached', instead concentrating on regional and local factors at work in communities: P. Lake, 'Periodization, Politics and "The Social"', *Journal of British Studies* 37 (1998), 279–90 (p. 283). McIntosh finds that from the 1470s onwards, the language of official national debates concerning order and law resembled the language and phrasing of these lesser local courts,

ethical conduct taken from the literary record. We know that networks of social and political agency did not always begin with the elites and move downward to the masses.[47] Caxton's books were a literary mirror held up to this, as were other contemporary texts like the *De Consulatu Stiliconis* and William Worcester's *The Boke of Noblesse*,[48] the latter correlating national virtue with England's international status, revealing that virtue was necessary not only for the security of the nation but also for its long-term international interests.

These responses demonstrate the mental strategies put in place by individuals to comprehend social change and, often, English nationhood. We can also use literature as a gauge of wider social discourses. Early print culture can itself only be grasped if we understand its engagement with the times. Kuskin reads this as the connections between 'vernacular literary authority, capitalism, and the identity of the English nation'.[49] In this case there was also a strong debate with moral reform.[50] How did these threats become translated not only into adult works, but also into literature for children and young people or, as is often the case, into literature concerned with children and young people? In the eighteenth century French revolutionary literature targeted children in an attempt to create a politically active and morally orthodox society.[51] These children were the future model citizens of the Republic, acknowledged as valuable participants in the imagined community. Even so, it is easier to perceive adult literature as enjoying a more established relationship with political agency. Courtesy and instructional literature may seem peripheral to this, yet it was also a medium accessed by and relevant to a growing body of classes.[52] For gentry, merchant and bourgeois readers we

---

an example of language and ideologies filtering upwards: McIntosh, *Controlling Misbehaviour*, pp. 132–3.

[47] The cultural and political agency of non-elites has been promoted by C. Ginzburg, *The Cheese and the Worm: The Cosmos of a Sixteenth Century Miller*, trans. J. and A. Tedeschi (Baltimore, 1980). See also G. Harriss, 'Political Society and the Growth of Government in Late Medieval England', *Past and Present* 138 (1993), 28–57.

[48] On the former see J. Watts, '*De Consulatu Stiliconis*: Texts and Politics in the Reign of Henry VI', *Journal of Medieval History* 16 (1990), 251–66 (pp. 258–9). Stilico's right to rule was based on his virtuous character and dynastic connections, in a context of political and social crisis. To read Worcester's text see *The Boke of Noblesse, Addressed to King Edward the Fourth on His Invasion of France in 1475, with an Introduction by John Gough Nichols* (London, 1860). On this see also Harriss, *Shaping the Nation*, pp. 128, 159.

[49] Kuskin, '"Onely Imagined"', p. 201.

[50] The relationship between printing and political agendas, and even propaganda, is clearer for the sixteenth century. Edwards and Meale, 'Marketing of Printed Books', pp. 98–9.

[51] Higonnet, 'Civility Books', p. 124.

[52] Carolyn Collette describes something similar occurring in French courtly vernacular literature after Charles V's death in the 'deteriorating political situation' of the time, with a shift away from the 'self' towards social relationships or a moral state: C. P.

should remember that courtesy and instructional literature aimed at children and families had a long and distinguished history and relevance. While it is increasingly recognised that adult texts reflected a supposed national decay, the circulation of similar ideas in the children's genre has not been understood. The following integrates this literature into existing studies on political debates, looking at the manner in which the paradigms of 'childhood' were affected by social changes during the late fifteenth century and at what can be seen of this in the literature.

Different emphases

The higher value ideologies of morality and virtue were not restricted to printed books. As noted previously, earlier poems to some degree supported moral and virtuous lessons in upbringing; this was particularly reflected in the three poems for girls in the *Good Wife* tradition. Equally, didactic and moralising literature circulated in manuscripts which were then used as the basis for early print. In the printed *Book of Curtesye*, the central motif in 'Little John's' education is the association between his behaviour and the parallel constructions of virtue and vice. For Little John, the emphasis on good manners and observable courteous behaviour forms part of a wide-ranging moral discussion. A stylistic and narrative characteristic worth noting in this book is the use of the words 'virtue', 'vice' and 'sin'; this is a vocabulary more directly related to virtuous philosophies and importantly it comprises word choices that are used systematically throughout the poem.

Like a number of Caxton's earliest publications, this book lacks a prologue which could provide clues about audience, patronage and intent. However, both the title and content make direct references to the courtesy genre. Although exposure to European printed books was already occurring, and Caxton himself imported and sold books from the Continent at his shop in Westminster,[53] it is worth remembering that for many printed books were a new and different medium. It is useful, therefore, to consider for a moment how this book would have appeared to English readers largely unacquainted with English printed literature. First, Caxton plays upon familiar concepts of genre with the title. By retaining familiar language Caxton pre-empted demand in his market. Even before reading the poem proper, the potential (buying) audience would have understood the reference to 'courtesy' and its

---

Collette, 'Chaucer and the French Tradition Revisited: Philippe de Mézières and the Good Wife', in *Medieval Women: Texts and Contexts in Late Medieval Britain, Essays for Felicity Riddy*, ed. J. Wogan-Browne, R. Voaden, A. Diamond, A. Hutchison, C. Meale and L. Johnson (Turnhout, 2000), pp. 151–68 (pp. 154–5).

[53] E. Armstrong, 'English Purchases of Printed Books from the Continent 1465–1526', *English Historical Review* 94 (1979), 268–90.

heritage in literature aimed at children. Scribes themselves used 'the book of curtesye' as a generic descriptive title and the repetition of 'courtesy' within many texts would have been familiar and reassuring to potential purchasers. Caxton's business sense is clear and it is evident that he understood his market. Anna Bryson sees the retention of distinct courtesy values and terminology by English printers in the sixteenth century as a failure to adapt to the newer notion of civility.[54] In a sense this is correct, as older courtesy terms remained visible in books. However, this literature did not necessarily use the word 'courtesy' to mean the same things and there were important and pragmatic reasons for reusing 'courtesy'. The service performed by the title may be even more deliberate when a closer reading of the text shows that the word 'courtesy' is not used until the sixth stanza. The lexis readers first encountered is thus one of virtue and vice:

> Vyce or vertue to folowe and enpresse
> In mynde and therfore to styre & remeue
> You from vice and to vertu addresse
> That one to folowe and that other teschewe[55]

Stanza 53 provides hints at the manner in which the courtesy tradition remained a positive selling point to readers. This takes the form of a reminder about Lydgate, cited as the author's 'master'. No doubt Lydgate's connection to *Stans puer ad mensam* increased the chances of a reader creating a link between both poems. Using an author's name to denote genre, status or even authorship is not straightforward; here, however, linking Lydgate's name with the anonymous author of the *Book of Curtesye* can reasonably be seen as a deliberate literary association to imply status and legitimacy.[56]

Before this, the reader or listener had in fact already navigated two traditional courtesy frameworks. As noted above, the title created a deliberate expectation of a traditional courtesy narrative. The second courtesy paradigm comes from the first line of the poem, in which a youthful character, 'lytyl Iohn', is introduced, followed by an age-specific term, 'tendre enfancye'.[57] 'Infancy' usually referred to babies or children below the age of seven years, with overtones relating to children of noble or gentle birth. The case for youthfulness is further emphasised:

---

[54] A. Bryson, *From Courtesy to Civility: Changing Codes of Conduct in Early Modern England* (Oxford, 1998), pp. 47–8.
[55] All quotations are from *Book of Curtesye*, 1ʳ.
[56] On this see Gillespie, *Print Culture*.
[57] *Book of Curtesye*, 1ʳ. The reasons why 'tender age' was used in literature and court records were addressed earlier in this book.

Virtue and Vice

> I have deuysed you this lytyl newe
> Instrucc[i]on acordyng vnto your age
> Playne in sentencebut playner in la[n]gage[58]

On the face of it, these statements recognise that children need suitable texts relevant to them and to their upbringing. More importantly for Caxton, this was a useful marketing strategy which enabled him to extend his market to all ages, not restrict it to adult readers and interests. Further evidence regarding intended audience comes when Little John is told that upon rising he is to cross himself, recite his Pater Noster, Ave Maria and the Holy Creed, with such religious instructions forming the basic spiritual lessons in childhood. The instruction to help the priest when he says mass also confirms a male audience and situates the text within an established religious framework. Young boys were thus introduced to standard religious attributes which were recognised as suitable and appropriate by the wider Christian community. The manner in which this was carried out operates at the same basic and conventional level as socialising norms.

The details provided in these opening stanzas informed the reader of two crucial courtesy frameworks. First, they registered an interest in courtesy in the title and second, they acknowledged the relevance of the courtesy genre to young male children – classic promises made by courtesy texts. Yet, from this point onwards it is apparent that different themes are incorporated into the poem. A daily approach to virtue and morality is emphasised, moving the courtesy ethos towards something new. Virtuous behaviour is described immediately when, for example, the first three stanzas mention 'virtue' four times and three times they also incorporate the word 'vice'. Vice is the opposite of virtue; more specifically, it is a corruption of morals leading to degrading behaviour and dishonesty, or less extremely the word was used to denote a fault in the way of doing something. In manuscript Sloane 1986, *the boke of curtasye* used vice to represent a less extreme sense of incorrect behaviour at the table.[59] Given the correlation between morality and virtue in Caxton's book, the choice of 'vice' should be seen to play deliberately on the association with morality, and we know Caxton used vice in the *Game and Playe of the Chesse* to mean immorality and wickedness.

Of course, for young people patterns of behaviour still rested upon an association between inherited class and conduct, and in one sense conduct which was both necessarily courteous and moral: 'Lerneth to be vertuous and wel thewed / Who wil not lerne nedely he must be lewed'.[60] Failure to

---

[58] *Book of Curtesye*, 1ʳ. 'Sentence' is an obsolete form for the quoted sayings or maxims of eminent persons or more generally, a way of thinking or opinion: *OED*.
[59] It is worthwhile pointing out that these were not the same poems: the title is a common one.
[60] *Book of Curtesye*, 1ʳ.

be 'thewede' (instructed) in both morals and manners would result in being considered 'lewed'. Lewd, a pejorative term meaning untaught, also alluded to the lower orders and vulgarity, similar to the class overtones associated with churl|addressed earlier.[61] Churl associated a lack of good manners with a person's social background. In this instance lewd suggests social estate could be linked with virtue. It is clear that class-consciousness had not disappeared from this instructional literature and it was brought to the forefront of lessons in order to codify and differentiate between behaviours, as it had always done. The regard to moral perspectives is, however, more overtly indicated in this passage, as it was in *Parvus Cato*.

While class ideology informs both the text and subtext of the *Book of Curtesye*, thus establishing parallels to the principles of behaviour addressed in courtesy literature, the emphasis on elite service is limited to the second half of the poem, taking up less than half of the total text, primarily between stanzas 17 and 44. Therefore of the total 76 stanzas, only 28 relate to, or are positioned within, a cluster relating to table manners. Some indications of this theme are found in this passage:

> Awayte my chylde whan ye sta[n]de atte table
> Of maister or souerayn whether it be
> Applye you for to be seruysable
> That no defaute in you founden be[62]

Little John was aware that his service, his behaviour and his application to labour were judged by his social superiors. There is, however, a subversive idea here that this service was not only for the benefit of the master or sovereign. By paying attention to the 'best of gentleman' and by attending them in particular fashion, Little John would find himself in a position to advance: 'who doth bestand hym ensiewe ye / And in especyalvse ye attendaunce / Wherin ye shal your self best auaunce'.[63] It is possible that Caxton himself inserted this idea as these lines are absent in the only comparable manuscript version of the poem, manuscript Oriel 79. In the manuscript's text, the passages on service are more conventional and obscure the self-serving element present in Caxton's book, simply stating 'And specially vseth attendaunce / Whiche is to souereyne thyng of gret plesaunce'.[64] The emphasis

---

[61] 'Lewd': unlearned, unlettered, untaught (1225–1601); rude, artless (1425–1560); belonging to the lower orders; common, low, vulgar, 'base' (1380–1640); ignorant (implying a reproach) and foolish, unskilful, bungling; ill-bred, ill-mannered (1380–1710); and also, of persons, their actions, etc.: bad, vile, evil, wicked, base; unprincipled, ill-conditioned; good-for-nothing, worthless, 'naughty' (1386–1709): *OED*.

[62] *Book of Curtesye*, 3ᵛ.

[63] *Book of Curtesye*, 3ᵛ.

[64] Oxford, Balliol College, MS Oriel 79, stanza 17. Hill's household miscellany, MS

on personal gain, and by implication social mobility, is more evident in the printed edition and is a theme which had meaning, and literal allusions, to merchant and bourgeois readers. This has also been seen in Caxton's *Le Morte Darthur*, which equated virtue with success in an attempt to appeal to commercial interests and the culture of self-advancement and acquisition within merchant/bourgeois classes.[65]

There are obvious allusions to the same social environments in courtesy poems and Caxton's book touches on this. References to the needs of elite groups do occur throughout the *Book of Curtesye*. It should be noted that in terms of vocabulary, there is a distinct difference between Little John and his superiors. For example, the line 'It is a grete plesure to the hyghe estate / To see his seruauntis aboute hym present' subtly implies that the servant is from a different social group to the master. This could indicate a shift in removing the child character, and therefore the audience, from being a part of this high estate themselves. Such wording differentiates between the highly born lord and those who are being addressed; readers or listeners were being told what the elite thought and wanted.[66] Caxton was aware of the potentially conflicting impulses of elite and bourgeois readers, and, as Jennifer Summit argues, 'In his attempt to define a market, Caxton performed a complicated negotiation; while drawing on the book's associations with courtly leisure, he also had to prove its utility to a class of merchants and citizens.'[67] There is similar evidence that the *Book of Curtesye* was tasked with these pragmatic concerns.

The importance of moulding character to meet social demands and expected behaviours was a well-trodden theme in this literature. Such is the case in the *Book of Curtesye* where once again manners and courtesy fostered select behavioural ideals; as already mentioned, this is most noticeable in the cluster of passages between stanzas 17 and 44. Here, for example, Little John learns his behaviour in the great household is dependent upon observing certain conduct norms which may have been familiar to him, or familiar to his father or male relatives from their own youth. For example, he learns that he should not spit upon the table and that he should not let greed provoke him into taking too much food. There were also more abstract concepts regarding his behaviour towards others, including acting companionably and greeting others pleasantly. These notions were conventional and greatly

---

Balliol 354, includes Caxton's line on self-advancement. In Oriel 79, the name Little John is not used; instead the neutral 'childe' appears.
[65] On this see Stroud, 'Chivalric Terminology', p. 330.
[66] *Book of Curtesye*, 3ᵛ.
[67] Although I would omit her final clause, 'who were new to book culture': J. Summit, 'William Caxton, Margaret Beaufort and the Romance of Female Patronage', in *Women, the Book and the Worldly: Selected Proceedings of the St Hilda's Conference, 1993*, ed. L. Smith and J. H. M. Taylor, 2 vols. (Cambridge, 1995), II, 151–65 (p. 155).

treasured and indicate some of the continuing pressures in forming the ideal child or young servant. The development of a moral vocabulary sits alongside these established courtesy values and at this stage there is little evidence of any friction between the concepts. It is notable, however, that the prevalent identification with morality in Caxton's *Book of Curtesye* ensures the text is increasingly silent on the issue of courtesy per se; Little John is never told to *be* courteous. It is possible that it was understood that courtesy was expected, yet the evidence suggests there was a great deal of attention paid to following virtue and loving honesty. In these cases Little John was told to 'Lerneth to be vertuous' and 'To folowe vertu & fro folye declynyng / And waite wel that ye loue honeste'.[68] These passages are not dominated by courtesy terms which are restricted in some degree to manners or descriptions of conventional behaviour. Little John's conduct pointed towards 'virtue' with all its connotations of moral accomplishments. The repeated use of 'virtue', and to a lesser extent 'nurture', instead of 'courtesy' or the ambivalent use of the two terms is evidence of a trend towards the idea of virtue underpinning behaviour. For example, 'Of suche a wight as in *vnmanerly* nyce / And is ful likely disposid vnto *vyce*' and 'This *curtoys* clerk writeth in this wise / Rebukyng the *vice* of vyle detracc[i]on'[69] stress the ambiguities in courtesy and virtue and provide evidence of the manner in which both courtesy and virtue were preoccupied with maintaining favourable public opinions.

As discussed earlier, courtesy and virtue could register on a similar scale. However, it is the extent of references to virtue which renders this book unusual in a socialising sense. This difference is particularly notable in the second half of the text in stanzas that talk about reading habits, eloquence and knowledge of English literature – Hoccleve, Lydgate and Chaucer are singled out. Little John is shown as being a literate young man and one who is possessed of a knowledge of the great English poets. Hoccleve, Lydgate and Chaucer were noted for their blend of virtue and entertainment, suggesting a deliberate assemblage of material thought to suit children's reading habits and needs.[70] Equally, references to these authors invoked an already established literary genre which had long emphasised virtue and ethics in behaviour.

Changing directions

How and why did courtesy texts, normally a bastion of conventional behaviour and a medium resistant to change, develop interests in other conduct? A concern with false behaviour and *over*-courtesy is evidence of where this changing ideology comes from. The nature of over-courtesy indicates a new

---

[68] *Book of Curtesye*, 1ʳ and 12ʳ respectively.
[69] *Book of Curtesye*, 3ᵛ, 4ᵛ. Emphasis is mine.
[70] On these authors see Lerer, *Chaucer and his Readers*, p. 85.

direction in both the literature and in socialising young people. *Parvus Cato's* assessment of behaviour, located within a different ethical and didactic genre, was addressed earlier but it is worthwhile comparing evidence from this to the *Book of Curtesye*. In both, the potential shortcomings and deficiency inherent in 'courtesy' are lamented in a criticism of what ironically had once been praised as adroit flattery: 'Preue thou neuer a man by ouer paynted speche / For vnder fayr wordes is ofte annexid gyle'.[71] There is similar condemnation for those who exploited such courtesy: 'The whistelyng fouler makyth mery songe / And so the byrdes begyleth he amonge'.[72] The reprinting of *Parvus Cato*, three times in an eight-year period, is suggestive of considerable support for this book which attracted gentry, bourgeois and provincial readers.

In the first part of the sixteenth century, courtesy was increasingly associated with negative connotations, particularly over-punctiliousness and standing upon ceremony.[73] By the mid-eighteenth century it was, of course, associated with anxieties about how outward behaviour could legitimately equate to inner character. The 1748 letter written by the earl of Chesterfield to his son promoted a conscious and self-serving exploitation of exterior behaviour, emphasising self-interest and falsity in sponsoring external sociability which was divorced from real morality.[74] The emphasis on etiquette (a term in fact brought into English circulation in 1750 by Chesterfield) stripped conduct of its moral identity and sponsored the idea of behaviour according to class-consciousness which was ruled by a strict adherence to correct social signs. The debates that raged in the eighteenth century suggest a cyclical return to earlier courteous behaviour, whereby observable conduct and courteous manners held value in themselves and assumed a privileged place in elite society and in socialisation.

The capacity to recognise distinctions in courteous behaviour was earlier grappled with in the fifteenth century when overly courteous and suspiciously false conduct was seen as relating to less than appropriate styles of behaving. The *Book of Curtesye* relates to this by showing that Little John learns how his identity is dependent upon a separation of truly virtuous conduct from 'Ruskyn' gallants and foppish attire.[75] The concern with iden-

---

[71] *Parvus Cato*, Avii^v.

[72] *Parvus Cato*, Avii^v.

[73] See the *OED* for 'courtesy'.

[74] P. Carter, 'Polite "Persons": Character, Biography and the Gentleman', *Transactions of the Royal Historical Society* 12 (2002), 333–54 (pp. 334–6, 348–54). More generally, see Arditi's *A Genealogy of Manners*, especially pp. 208–28.

[75] The meaning of Ruskyn is unclear. It could refer to wearing a type of clothing trimmed with fur, 'squirrel and ruskin fur'. Consider also the following line from de Worde's *Treatyse of a galaunt*: 'And Thou ruskyn galaunt, that pouerte dooth menace / For all thy warrocked hoode, and thy proude araye': *Here begynneth a treatyse of a galau[n]t* (London, 1510), no sig. William Harrison writes about young

tifying extremes of courteous behaviour and distinguishing them as 'true' and 'false' alters the dominant perceptions of what children and malleable young people were expected to learn and aspire to. It is easier to distinguish truly honourable conduct from its counterpart if it is linked to 'virtue' and 'virtuous behaviour'. A person's life therefore needed to be lived in virtue and not just with courtesy or, as one line states, 'To ben a man ay vertuous of leuyng'.[76] This divides courtesy into two different dialogues, one positive and the other negative. This is identified in a lengthy passage concerning the nature of manners and conduct. It is worth quoting in full to note how social customs are described as malleable and flexible over time. Malleability is thus a precursor to more specific, socialising changes:

> Thene lityl John I counceyl you that ye
> Take hede to the norture that men use
> Newe founde or auncyent whether it be
> So shal no man your curtoisye refuse
> The guyse & custom my child shal you excuse
> Menys werkis haue often enterchange
> That nowe is norture so[m]tyme had be strange
>
> Thingis whilom used ben now leyd a syde
> And newe feetis dayly ben contreuid
> Mennys actes can in no plyte abyde
> They be changeable and ofte meuid
> Thingis somtyme alowed is now repreuid
> And after this shal thinges up aryse
> That men set now but at lytyl pryse[77]

This comparison of old and new modes of behaving highlights the arrival of new rituals of nurture and courtesy replacing older acts. In this regard, Little John learns that he should be aware of changing manners and behaviours in his own lifetime, and the passage sets the scene for a discussion about behaviour in the next six stanzas. Untrue courtesy is a danger Little John unknowingly faces by aping these 'Ruskyn' gallants with what in a later age would be called foppish behaviour:

> This mene I my childe th[at] ye shal haunte
> The guyse of them that do most manerly
> But beware of vnthryft Ruskyn galante
> Counterfeter of vnconnyng curtoisye[78]

---

wives wearing 'lusty gallant' clothing (light red): W. Harrison, *The Description of England, The Classic Contemporary Account of Tudor Social Life*, ed. G. Edelen (Ithaca, 1968), p. 148.

[76] *Parvus Cato*, Bii^v.
[77] *Book of Curtesye*, 11^r.
[78] *Book of Curtesye*, 11^v.

Virtue and Vice

Here, there is a new understanding of courteous behaviour being branded as a corrupt facade concealing misconduct, furthermore leading the wax-like child into aping similar undesirable mannerisms. The gallant's dress is picked out as showing his over-exaggerated style, 'Braced so strayt that he may not plye'.[79] This is inextricably bound to a fear over change in England and the supposed new effeminacy in men:

> Not apysshe on to mocken ne to mowe
> To nyce araye that is not commendable
> Fetis newe fonuden by foolis vnp[r]uffitable
> That make th[e] world so plainly tra[n]ssormate
> That men semen almoste enfemynate[80]

The figure of the 'gallant' had appeared in medieval literature since the fourteenth century, representing the youthful male embodiment of excess, improper behaviour, vanity and falsely high status. Theresa Coletti has argued that this figure was linked to serious sin through the double-edged sword of moral dissolution and material excess. The combination of internal immorality and tangible appearance made the gallant so dangerous.[81] In the Digby plays this leads to the downfall of Mary Magdalene. In the *Book of Curtesye* it highlights the danger of excess and false conduct for male youths. Anxieties over dress were a recurrent concern in the fourteenth century, escalating after the 1340s when radical shifts in fashion took place in England and Western Europe.[82] The *Book of Curtesye* picks up on these (established) anxieties in true hyperbole, playing on the fear of extravagant clothing being a new and threatening experience. It singles out anxieties over social immorality and class, using the 'gallant' as a catch-cry for concerns. It is worth remembering that this model of behaviour appears here within a supposedly fixed and traditional courtesy text, a genre of literature that did not seek to promote unfavourable associations with elite behaviour.

At the time this shift was occurring in the literature, audiences were also increasingly investing in the purchase and reading of printed books. Those reached by the *Book of Curtesye* would have heeded this theme according to the social and economic circumstances of their positions. Dress was germane to the symbolic differences, or more precisely the lack of visible differences, between young men from elite backgrounds and those from merchant or bourgeois classes. This overlaps with Richard Helgerson's observation that the term 'nobility' was 'primarily a term of difference'.[83] Dress disrupted

---

[79] *Book of Curtesye*, 12r.
[80] *Book of Curtesye*, 12r.
[81] T. Coletti, '"Curtesy Doth it Yow Lere": The Sociology of Transgression in the Digby *Mary Magdalene*', *English Literary History* 71 (2004), 1–28 (p. 8).
[82] Scattergood, 'Fashion and Morality', pp. 255–72.
[83] R. Helgerson, *Forms of Nationhood: The Elizabethan Writing of England* (Chicago,

these differences, as the legal enforcement of dress codes in sumptuary legislation attests. The gallant was dangerous precisely because he threatened this order. This is illuminated in a London context where young gentry men and sons of merchants were criticised for the extravagant clothing they wore.[84] Social relationships between London merchants and gentry groups developed as a result of financial and commercial dealings, while further blurring of the two groups took place through inter-marriages and friendships. Merchants and those of gentle birth did share similar interests and means, demonstrated through their shared inclination for secular education as well as certain domestic lifestyles and social trappings such as family coats-of-arms, the reality of which drew merchant classes further away from the yeomanry.[85] The fifteenth century also saw increasingly elaborate armigerous displays by those below the knightly ranks.

For those concerned with such permeable barriers, another option in constructing firm social relationships was to develop and raise moral behaviour to a higher level. In literary exemplars moral behaviour was an obvious way to represent character without delving into more corruptible forms of outward appearance. This was a manner of living which was available to everyone and was not dependent on being associated with an elite lineage or on exploiting extravagant fashions. It is suggestive, on one level at least, that the literate and morally conscious merchant and bourgeois classes were prompted to distinguish their children in a positive fashion from elite society and its associated behaviour. In a political sense, Christine Carpenter has argued that 'the gentry may well have come to believe in the mid- to late 1450s that they were better off without the nobility'.[86] This may well have extended to a cultural sense of separation which included the socialising of children.

This literature articulated, defined and gave authority to this process. Morality became a way to claim status that was significantly different from and ethically sounder than other means, where status had to be asserted through adherence to superficial social signs or through wearing particular dress. Late fifteenth century printed books increasingly pointed to this positive separation of gentry, merchant and bourgeois customs from elite customs, counting the motifs of dress, lifestyle and codes of courtesy as part of this. London, with its uniquely high proportion of urban gentry owing to the presence of the royal administration and the Inns of Court, was a focal point in this.[87] The emphasis on bourgeois virtue taking shape in printed texts, more so than in manuscripts, can also partly be seen as a result of the easier access

---

1992), p. 205.
[84] Coletti, '"Curtesy Doth it Yow Lere"', p. 9.
[85] On these social divisions see Thrupp, *Merchant Class*, pp. 29–30, 247–69.
[86] Carpenter, *Locality and Polity*, p. 479
[87] Horrox, 'Urban Gentry', p. 23.

these groups had to new printing cultures. The continuation of bourgeois access to literature was now present in conjunction with overt references to bourgeois and merchant groups.

The relationship between virtue and courtesy within these printed books, and even the ambiguity between the two concepts evidenced in the use of a partial moral vocabulary, suggests that advice on virtuous behaviours was emerging alongside established courteous ideologies. The question of whether the son of a London merchant or the son of a provincial gentry family, perhaps the real life equivalent of 'Little John', was aware that behaviour was taking on added significance is harder to determine. What was being instituted was a literary model of children as creatures of moral and immoral behaviour, with public acts of good manners judged in terms of moral nature. The result is that courtesy and instructional literature now promoted a child's public actions as well as their inner character and conduct.

Female virtues

The claim to be able to manipulate and induce women to behave in certain ways through the production and circulation of a literary model of behaviour is at once true and false: true in the sense that, after all, male authors were tempted to write about the socialisation and conduct of wives and daughters in order to have influence over these very groups; yet false in the sense that the creation of gendered patterns of behaviour for young girls and women was contested by women, just as elite behaviour was contested by gentry and merchant readers.[88] Leaving aside the related question of women as producers and writers of books, as users of texts women appropriated patterns of conduct in selective ways.

As patrons, women invested in romance, religious, conduct and even household estate books, and this has been seen as both a devotional and a

---

[88] On women's involvement in reading networks see J. Wogan-Browne, *Saints' Lives and Women's Literary Culture: Virginity and its Authorizations* (Oxford, 2001); R. L. Krueger, 'Love, Honor, and the Exchange of Women in Yvain, Some Remarks on the Female Reader', in *Arthurian Women*, ed. T. S. Fenster (London, 1996), pp. 3–18; J. Weiss, 'The Power and Weakness of Women in Anglo-Norman Romance', in *Women and Literature in Britain, 1150–1500*, ed. C. M. Meale (Cambridge, 1993), pp. 7–23. On *Livre du Chevalier de la Tour* see R. L. Krueger, '"Nouvelles Choses": Social Instability and the Problem of Fashion in the *Livre du Chevalier de la Tour Landry*, The *Ménagier de Paris* and Christine de Pizan's *Livre des Trois Vertus*', in *Medieval Conduct*, ed. K. Ashley and R. L. A. Clark (Minneapolis, 2001), pp. 49–85. Also, D. Bornstein, *Mirrors of Courtesy* (Hamden, 1975); D. Bornstein, *The Lady in the Tower: Medieval Courtesy Literature for Women* (Hamden, 1983); A. M. de Gendt, *L'Art d'eduquer les nobles damoiselles:* Le Livre du Chevalier de la Tour Landry (Paris, 2003).

spiritual act. It is also indicative of the more inclusive engagement women had with the production of literary texts and the arts.[89] Elizabeth Woodville's pseudo-patronage of the *Book of the Knight of the Tower* brings women's investment in literary models of exemplary behaviour to the cluster of courtesy and instructional works printed by Caxton. Translated by Caxton from the *Livre du Chevalier de la Tour* written by Geoffroy de la Tour Landry in 1371–2, the *Book of the Knight of the Tower* added to Caxton's series of conduct books by introducing female socialisation into debates on virtue and morality.

Caxton's prologue has received little attention, which is unfortunate, as it noticeably anchors the original French text to Caxton's English readership. It is worthwhile examining how the prologue considers the meaning and value of virtue. As indicated above, virtue as a discrete concept appears to have had an increasingly important influence on this literature. Caxton's dedication simultaneously represents two readerships. The first is adroitly outlined through a class-based comment that 'a noble lady which hath brought forth many noble & fayr doughters which ben vertuously nourisshed & lerned'[90] has desired the translation of this book into English, stressing its relevance to the nobility, in this case Elizabeth Woodville. There is a logical strategy in using 'noble' and 'lady' to both gain access to and reinforce elite networks. A socially broader model was, however, situated alongside this. Caxton disrupts the very pattern he has established by alluding to a wider gentle audience in simultaneous references to his, still female, readership: 'as moche as this book is necessary to euery gentilwoman of what estate she be'.[91] 'Gentle' still only referred to women of certain social estates and certainly peasant and working women would not be called 'gentle' by Caxton. He is, however, emphasising a female readership which is not necessarily noble or aristocratic, reiterated in the phrase he uses: 'good ensa[m]ples for al maner peple'.[92]

A similarly varied audience has been suggested for the circulation of the original French text; less so, however, the deliberate encouragement of these

---

[89] On this see, for example, *The Cultural Patronage of Medieval Women*, ed. J. H. McCash (Georgia, 1996) which brings together many useful essays exploring women's patronage of literature and other artistic forms. C. M. Meale discusses female book ownership in, '"... alle the bokes that I haue of latyn, englisch, and frensch": Laywomen and Their Books in Late Medieval England', in *Women and Literature in Britain, 1150–1500*, ed. C. M. Meale (Cambridge, 1993), pp. 128–58. Other useful work on the relationship between books and women includes D. Bornstein, 'William Caxton's Chivalric Romances and the Burgundian Renaissance in England', *English Studies* 57 (1976), 1–10; R. Krug, *Reading Families: Women's Literate Practice in Late Medieval England* (New York, 2002), p. 93. Caxton's romances and religious books include *Troilus and Criseyde* (1483), *Paris and Vienne* (1485), *Blanchardin and Eglantine* (1488), *Deathbed Prayers* (1484), the *Psalter* (1483) and *Fifteen Oes* (1491).
[90] la Tour Landry, *Knight of the Tower*, prologue
[91] la Tour Landry, *Knight of the Tower*, prologue
[92] la Tour Landry, *Knight of the Tower*, prologue.

readers evidenced in the text itself.[93] Roberta Krueger makes the point that paper manuscripts of the *Livre du Chevalier de la Tour*, as well as Christine de Pizan's *Livre des Trois Vertus*, can probably be explained by their circulation within bourgeois communities, while the production of more elaborate vellum editions testifies to their parallel circulation amongst elite groups.[94] Caxton's business acumen is not to be underestimated in his own printing decisions, and the gains to be had in reaching a large audience in England were potentially massive. The clever, understated juxtaposition of classes in the prologue reinforces this potentially wide audience while staying faithful to the elite.

As well as defining his audience in his prologue, Caxton also suggests a practical reading strategy, noting that he had completed the English translation that 'it may the better be vnderstonde of al suche as shal rede or here it'.[95] This retains its aural tag, suggestive of the public readings taking place within female reading networks.[96] Textual communities were important in female culture, and women and young girls participated in reading circles arranged within household environments. The households of Lady Margaret Beaufort and Cecily, duchess of York, provided communal aural networks for elite women and female servants. These audiences were defined by gender and, like the prologue, included different status groups crossing hierarchical positions.[97]

The prologue is also evidence of the manner in which 'virtue' develops over the late fifteenth century in English courtesy and instructional texts. It is worthwhile noting that the term virtue is used extensively, appearing no fewer than eight times in a one-and-a-half-page introduction. The following is evidence of the manner in which virtue provides the English reader with a framework to manage their expectations of the text. The prologue includes such phrases as: 'Alle vertuouse doctryne & techynge'; '& vertuouse maners to be gouerned by'; 'al yong gentyl wymen specially may lerne to bihaue them self vertuously'; 'noble & fayr dougters which ben vertuously nouris-

---

[93] Mark Amos, however, discusses contrary indications of merchant advancement in the text: 'Violent Hierarchies: Disciplining Women and Merchant Capitalists in *The Book of the Knyght of the Towre*', in *Caxton's Trace: Studies in the History of English Printing*, ed. W. Kuskin (Notre Dame, 2006), pp. 69–100.

[94] Krueger, '"Nouvelles Choses"', p. 52.

[95] la Tour Landry, *Knight of the Tower*, prologue.

[96] On aural networks see K. Cherewatuk, 'Aural and Written Reception in Sir John Paston, Malory, and Caxton', *Essays in Medieval Studies* 21 (2004), 123–31; J. Coleman, *Public Reading and the Reading Public in Late Medieval England and France* (Cambridge, 1996); R. Rutter, 'William Caxton and Literary Patronage', *Studies in Philology* 84 (1987), 440–70 (p. 461).

[97] On this see Phillips, *Medieval Maidens*, p. 71. See also Meale, '"...alle the bokes that I haue"', p. 133; F. Riddy, '"Women talking about the things of God": A Late Medieval Sub-Culture', in *Women and Literature in Britain, 1150–1500*, ed. C. M. Meale (Cambridge, 1993), pp. 104–27.

shed'; 'more knouleche in vertue'; 'In whiche werk I fynd many vertuous good enseygnementis & lernynges'; 'euery gentilman or woman hauyng such children desyryng them to be vertuously brougt forth to gete & haue this book'; and 'hou they ougt to gouerne them vertuously'.[98] The vocabulary Caxton chooses shows a familiarity with 'virtue' – the single term he applies to what he saw as the book's principle message and purpose. This evidence reveals how embedded a virtuous terminology was becoming for English audiences and authors, and not least for printers. Virtue is itself not a novel concept in literature, but here the novelty is certainly developing out of the context of the courtesy tradition.

Female conduct
The relationship between female conduct and identity in the text is ambiguous. Moral lessons create an image of the ideal aristocratic female. She is temperate in her appetites (both carnal and dietary), peaceable in character, true in her heart, silent and pious. Literature created a sanctioned, and sanitised, picture of female identity, one that was then distributed to parents, authority figures and girls and young women themselves. Although the individual stories in the *Book of the Knight of the Tower* give women ample space to conduct themselves either appropriately or inappropriately, modest and demure conduct, both before and during marriage, is associated with a particular combination of spirituality and pious devotion. Given this, virtue is a useful mechanism for socialising lessons. In four cases the term virtue is used in a precise way directly to parade pious and devout values: 'god and his Angels louen better humylyte than ony other virtue',[99] 'therfore no better vertue maye be in a woman than the vertue of humylyte',[100] 'knowe ye that hit is a noble vertu not to be enuyous'[101] and 'The one pryson was loue the other was drede and the thyrd shame These thre vertues mastryed her'.[102] This does not correspond to other examples from the courtesy and instructional series by Caxton, where virtue describes general conduct and behaviour, as well as occasionally moral actions. Again, it is female readers who are exposed to more layers of meaning in descriptions of virtue and are socialised according to these higher values; critically, this is often part of their training for marriage.

Bornstein's description of female idealisation is worth noting: 'Women are presented entirely as symbols of abstract qualities or psychological states in allegories.'[103] In the *Book of the Knight of the Tower* ideal images of female

[98] la Tour Landry, *Knight of the Tower*, prologue.
[99] la Tour Landry, *Knight of the Tower*, Kii^r.
[100] la Tour Landry, *Knight of the Tower*, Kii^v.
[101] la Tour Landry, *Knight of the Tower*, Mvii^v.
[102] la Tour Landry, *Knight of the Tower*, Ii^r.
[103] Bornstein, *Lady in the Tower*, p. 10.

charity achieve authority and power through representations of the saints: 'And at thexample of her dyd saynt Elyzabeth, saynte Lucye, saynt Cecylle and many other holy ladyes whiche were so charitable that they gaf to the poure & Indygent the most parte of theyr reuenues'.[104] Obedience to husbands also informs behaviour: 'Euery good woman must humbly suffre of her lord that whiche she maye not amende, For she that more suffreth of her lord withoute makynge therof no resemblaunt receyueth therof more worship x tymes'.[105] Equally, we know female readers of French romances were critically reading and resisting the gendered roles presented to them and it is likely that the female readers or aural participants of this book were both consumers and rejecters of gendered models, particularly given the extension of reading networks into mercantile and bourgeois communities.[106]

As discussed earlier in relation to courtesy poems, the internal household space was privileged as a result of the notion that it was a safe and controlled location for both boys and girls: safe because it was controlled. The relationship this has to poems for bourgeois girls has been seen as resulting from external *constraint*, a process different from the notion of *self-restraint*.[107] There is certainly a learned appreciation and understanding of conduct which is privileged in the *Book of the Knight of the Tower*, discouraging inappropriate behaviours through learned historical parallels and moral exemplars.[108] However, de la Tour Landry also limits the environments his aristocratic daughters are permitted to explore within the fictional confines of the narrative, prioritising the household while at the same time categorising and curtailing any excursions into external spaces and social activities which are seen as 'unsafe'. Unsurprisingly, stories about dances and banquets expose a range of threats to a woman's character.[109] This aspect of confinement can be understood in relation to the social and economic activities of higher status girls who did not need to participate in commercial economic activities. The economic and social realities of life are less pressing and therefore do not need to be part of its socialising lessons. Problematically, of course, this also had to be translated to Caxton's merchant and bourgeois readership.

How this subject of female identity was constructed is worth considering. Obviously moral behaviour was promoted through an adherence to chastity

---

104 la Tour Landry, *Knight of the Tower*, Kiii^v.
105 la Tour Landry, *Knight of the Tower*, Hvi^r.
106 Krueger, *Women Readers*, pp. 247–52. Manuscript and printed conduct books were largely owned by the merchant classes in the fifteenth and sixteenth centuries. Ashley, 'The *Miroir des Bonnes Femmes*', p. 88.
107 Phillips, *Medieval Maidens*, pp. 94–6.
108 Many of the Knight's lessons begin with a retelling of a biblical story leading to a contemporary analogy.
109 For example, 'Of them that gladly go to festes and Ioustes' and 'How none ought to abyde allone in a place': la Tour Landry, *Knight of the Tower*, Cii^r–Ciii^r and Eviii^v–Fi^r.

and piety, as well as through the observance of proper hierarchy. The subject of duty to male superiors, including the father and the future husband, is certainly expected in conduct books of this type from this period, crossing class boundaries. The *Good Wife* poems equally extolled obedience through the depiction of the daughter's behaviour before and during marriage. However, the views this posed were revised by parallel depictions which prioritised the physical perfection and beauty of women. The *Good Wife* poems write about the daughter's dress, and the aristocratic daughters of de la Tour Landry are potentially seduced by sumptuous descriptions of clothing.[110] As a result of this, female readers or listeners of the *Book of the Knight of the Tower* negotiated two contrasting but not mutually exclusive identities and ideas about socialisation (one moreover, which would have resonated with both aristocratic and lower-status girls). Both Krueger and Bornstein read these descriptions of women's clothing in conduct and romance books as simultaneously using beauty and dress to suggest identity.[111] In her reading of the original French *Livre* text Susan Udry sees a similar model operating, concluding that by clustering the principles of virtue and modesty with descriptions of beauty, dress, comportment and style the text creates a contradictory and at times violent framework for women to navigate.[112] Indeed, girls reading de la Tour Landry's book (either in the original French or Caxton's translation) were doubly exposed to the importance of dress as passages on clothing in de la Tour Landry's sources were considerably shorter.[113] Leaving the aristocratic element of this to one side, Mark Amos points to de la Tour Landry's negativity about fashion (and its social and ethical problems) with the rising merchant classes, appropriate to Caxton's own readership.[114]

In these ways, the book instructs via both positive and negative reinforcement of behaviour; de la Tour Landry's conservative and elitist concern with French social trappings certainly needs to be read here. However, it remains the case that women of all classes would have absorbed the lessons concerned with beauty and appearance leading to spiritual and moral danger. The subject of exterior modifications, cosmetics and clothing potentially corrupting natural beauty is an example of feminised identity which women were expected to adhere to through their choices and actions. However, it has been widely suggested that by repeatedly using images of feminine beauty to create these moral precepts, these lessons were subverted. Girls

---

[110] For more on this see Krueger, *Women Readers*, p. 178; Krueger, '"Nouvelles Choses"', pp. 49–85.
[111] Bornstein, *Lady in the Tower*, p. 10; Krueger, '"Nouvelles Choses"', pp. 80–5.
[112] S. Udry, 'Robert de Blois and Geoffroy de la Tour Landry on Feminine Beauty: Two Late Medieval French Conduct Books for Women', *Essays in Medieval Studies* 19 (2002), 90–102.
[113] J. L. Grigsby, 'A New Source of the Livre du Chevalier de La Tour Landry', *Romania* 84 (1963), 171–208 (p. 203).
[114] Amos, 'Violent Hierarchies', pp. 84–8.

and women are presented with descriptions of sumptuous dress which, while condemned, are essentially given equal space in the text:

> For I shalle make her kirtels and hoodes alle the furre outward & so she shalle be better pourfylled than ye ne the other. And after this he said Madame thynke ye that I ne wylle wel that she be arayed after the good ladyes of the Countre yes veryly but I wylle not that she chaunge the guyse of good wymmen[115]

Ironically, this seems to have been a concern raised at the time, when in 1534 Anthony Fitz-Herbert pointed out the problem.[116] Of course, there was also disapproval of boys wearing elaborate clothing. Text on dress and physical appearance in the *Book of Curtesye* says of boys that 'To nyce araye … is not commendable'.[117] However, it is evident that the physicality of dress in the *Book of the Knight of the Tower* is more visually imagined through the spectacular descriptions of clothing. There is less emphasis on this in the *Book of Curtesye* where the specifics of fabrics, styles and named attire are ignored. It is worth noting that details of dress are equally absent from the *Good Wife* poems for bourgeois girls. Kim Philips reads the comparatively insistent attention to clothing in the *Book of the Knight of the Tower* as a statement of religious anxieties which was part of a different message aimed at aristocratic girls.[118] To this we can add those messages on clothing for boys in the *Book of Curtesye* which more closely resemble the advice to bourgeois girls. It is tempting to suggest that youth and class, rather than gender, were the dominant factors in these anxieties. This struggle also reveals one more moral message: clothing was all too likely to be dangerous and held too much power and influence over young people, be they aristocratic, mercantile or bourgeois.

As we found in the *Good Wife* poems, in the fourteenth and fifteenth centuries there was a stronger interest in writing about the moral behaviour of women of different social positions and status. This usually called attention to female virtues and closely monitored the behavioural standards of girls, defining conduct according to moral attributes. It should be seen as part of the endorsement of female conduct as a composite of both surface behaviour and inner moral control. The language of this literature equally enjoyed a stronger relationship with virtuous and moral capacities, a particular set of themes which early male courtesy texts did not explore as rigorously. Authors, scribes and printers such as Caxton endowed their narratives with moral terminology and imagery beyond even the messages in the texts, speaking to

---

[115] la Tour Landry, *Knight of the Tower*, Bviii^v.
[116] On this see Adams, 'Medieval Mothers and their Children', p. 274.
[117] *Book of Curtesye*, 12^r.
[118] On this important point see Phillips, *Medieval Maidens*, pp. 92–4.

female virtues as the true objective of upbringing. This was a message that was consistent across earlier and later texts.

Complex 'good behaviours': 'fayr lernynge and notable ensamples' for families[119]

The books examined up to this point have addressed children or young people directly or adults with young people in their care. A wide variety of households can be understood as present or encompassed within these texts, although these households far from constitute what we could call a family audience or these texts a family literature. It is important to accept that the concept of the family is ambiguous, and our definitions more so. David Herlihy reads the medieval family as 'a co-residential unit, with a kin group at its core'.[120] Yet surely a family also requires some kind of ideological understanding and emotional reaction to take place amongst its members? Moreover, the inclusion of apprentices and servants alone means the members of a family unit will not necessarily be related by blood. There must, however, still be some kind of identification of emotional and functional ties existing within this group. In what ways were elite households not prescribed by these emotional ties? It is not difficult to exclude elite young servants of the kind addressed in the earlier courtesy literature from inclusion in the elite family: they were tied by functional roles to the household, yes, but there is very little sense of there being strong emotional ties, although these may have formed over time between servants themselves and between servants and those they served. It may be that only in smaller households did servants, and apprentices, take on the emotional resonance of blood-related family members. In Caxton's literature we can see a new category of family advice books emerging as part of the genre relevant to children. The following analysis addresses two books that develop this understanding of children's literature in relation to an emotionally linked, smaller family audience.

Earlier the point was made that bourgeois audiences found it difficult to imagine a common cultural or intellectual unity. Such a lack of coherence was a consequence of extreme heterogeneity. Caroline Barron has shown that London's merchant class was 'eclectic', coming to settle in England's most urbanised city from across the country.[121] Caxton, as the pre-eminent printer in England, was one of the first figures to capture and characterise this movable, uncertain and ambiguous group in a literary sense. Caxton's prologue to *Caton* fulfils both of the functions which this chapter has addressed. It hints at

---

[119] *Caton*, I^r.
[120] Herlihy, 'Making of the Medieval Family', p. 117; Herlihy, 'Family and Religious Ideologies', pp. 3–17.
[121] Barron, 'Expansion of Education', pp. 241–2.

Virtue and Vice

the cohesion of the merchant class and at another level offers up a revealing familial template:

> Vnto the noble auncyent and reno[m]med Cyte the Cyte of london in Englond I william Caxton Cytezeyn & coniurye of the same & of the fraternyte & felauship of the mercerye owe of ryght my seruyse & good wyll and of very dute am bounden naturelly to assiste ayde & counceille as ferforth as I can to my power as to my moder of whom I haue receyued my noureture & lyuynge And shal praye for the good prosperite & polecye of the same duryng my lyf[122]

The multi-layered message calls out to a London community as well as to a common familial heritage. The confident tone recalls London's municipal kinship: the guilds brought men in particular trades together for work, recreation and religious observance. London's guilds were strongly socio-familial, modelled on existing religious fraternities, making them important centres for male interaction.[123] Along with this civic identity, the notion of the family is itself evident in the conscious allusion to the mother's nurturing, educational role. If anything, Caxton's pairing of London with his reference to his mother is awkwardly placed, but it makes more sense when he returns to the issue of nurture and education later in the prologue:

> And as in my Jugement it is the beste book for to be taught to yonge children in scole & also to peple of euery age it is ful conuenient yf it be wel vnderstanden. And by cause I see that the children that ben borne within the sayd cyte encreace and prouffyte not lyke theyr faders and olders but for the moost parte after that they ben comen to theyr parfight yeres of discrecion and rypenes of age how wel that theyre faders haue lefte to them grete quantite of goodes yet scarcely amonge ten two thryue[124]

Caxton provides the means of seeing the audience as a united group and also offers the same audience a chance to share in a clear ideological vision of the city and the family-household.

Caxton's prologue to *Caton* is much celebrated for its opening dedication addressed to the city of London.[125] It allows us to gain some insight into contemporary London society and merchant networks. Moreover, *Caton* was published at a time of political turmoil in which Caxton may have played a part; equally problematic for him, he was at least named and implicated in the failed gentry rebellion. He expediently sued for pardon in 1483/4 (although

---

[122] *Caton*, Ai^r.
[123] On this see *Guilds, Society and Economy in London 1450–1800*, ed. I. A. Gadd and P. Wallis (London, 2002), particularly the chapter by P. Gauci: 'Informality and Influence: The Overseas Merchant and the Livery Companies, 1660–1720', pp. 127–39.
[124] *Caton*, Ai^{r–v}.
[125] See for instance 'Amos, 'Violent Hierarchies', p. 71.

this was a common move among other recognised servants of Edward IV).[126] Fortunately or unfortunately for Caxton, his own epilogues and prologues fashioned a well-known relationship with the Woodvilles which was indicative of the elite political and royal circles to which he called attention.[127] The recent move to assign merchant patronage to his books is largely irrelevant in this context; Caxton publicised seemingly personal connections with many of the leading and ill-fated magnates of the day.[128] In light of this, the dedication to 'the city of London' has been read as a sign of disillusionment with aristocratic patronage, possibly even as a pragmatic mark of self-survival to create distance from contentious noble sponsorship during a charged political time.[129] In many respects there is no reason why Caxton would not have felt it useful to combine multiple marketing strategies for his different publications. He was, after all, a businessman and a strategic manipulator of his audience.

The prologue to *Caton* reinforces a message of concern with behaviour, particularly the behaviour of London children: 'that the children that ben borne within the sayd cyte encreace and prouffyte not lyke theyr faders and olders'.[130] This concern with the state of the youth of the day precedes the 'body and soul' conceptual framework, explicitly spelt out as 'they shal moche the better conne rewle them self ther by For among all other bookes this is a synguler book and may well be callyd the Regyment or gouernaunce of the body and sowle'.[131] The moral and ethical discussion that follows is overtly linked to the London scene and is a tactical device that gives the traditional text, taken from an older French version of the *Distiches of Cato*, a contemporary urban and specifically London relevance. *Caton* is thus promoted in the light of contemporary fears. Reasons for these fears are varied but may originate with concerns that children were inheriting excessive wealth from their fathers, a combination of conservative anxieties mixed with attacks on merchant culture.[132] Mending these ills required men (and children) to rule

---

[126] L. Gill, 'William Caxton and the Rebellion of 1483', *English Historical Review* 112 (1997), 105–18.

[127] Anthony Woodville, as well as his sister, Elizabeth Woodville, to whom we know *The Book of the Knight of the Tower* was dedicated. On Caxton and the Woodvilles see Blake, *William Caxton*, pp. 30–2. Also, S. C. Weinberg, 'Caxton, Anthony Woodville, and the Prologue to the Morte Darthur', *Studies in Philology* 102 (2005), 45–65 (p. 49).

[128] George, duke of Clarence (to whom the first edition of *The Game and Playe of the Chesse* was dedicated) was executed on 18 February 1478 and Anthony Woodville was executed on 25 June 1483.

[129] Blake, *Caxton: England's First Publisher*, pp. 49–50. Alternatively, Rutter argues that royal and noble patronage was never very important to Caxton and that it was always incidental rather than calculated: 'Caxton and Literary Patronage', pp. 440–70.

[130] *Caton*, Ii^{r-v}.

[131] *Caton*, Ii^v.

[132] On this see Painter, *William Caxton*, p. 138.

and govern themselves in a temporal and spiritual sense, hence leading to the dual references to the body and the soul. At the same time, this off-putting condemnation is tempered by a flattering gloss on London youth: 'but fayrer ne wyser ne bet bespoken children in theyre yongthe ben now-her than ther ben in london'.[133] Like the astute salesman he was, Caxton demonstrated that his book was essential reading at a period of supposed social crisis, while at the same time being careful that his criticism did not overly offend the people he was relying on to purchase his book.

A significant portion of the text is more accurately described as relating to older individuals, particularly adult men with their own households; this warns against categorising texts as either solely for young people or for adults in this period. Prohibitions on gambling and drinking wine and the need to monitor household servants reflect adult concerns, although older youths no doubt existed on the fringes of this audience. In these cases the reading theory of 'double address' and 'dual address' suggests how this material was accessed by, and accessible to, different age and status groups. In examining texts that seem to have addressed both children and adults, and more specifically in terms of this type of literature that addressed dependent children and parents, distinguishing between double and dual address is useful. Developed in the study of modern children's literature, double address directs the text to adults over the top of children, while dual address occurs more rarely when the messages for adults and children coincide.[134] Multiple reading networks are a useful way of considering a text such as *Caton* that includes passages consistent with at least two audiences differentiated by age, although united by their gender.

The 'body and soul' philosophy which is so overtly stressed in *Caton* was not novel, nor is there any automatic relationship with a growing interest in moral socialisation. The texts examined earlier in this book warn us that in certain limited ways religious observance had equally been expressed in courtesy poems and this includes the literature found in manuscripts prior to the arrival of the presses in England. It was texts such as *the boke of curtasye* (especially in the second book), Peter Idley's *Instructions to his Son* and *The Lytylle Childrene's Book* which acknowledged that socialisation required dual social and religious training. Idley's poem, particularly in manuscripts which contain both *Liber Primus* and *Liber Secundus*, is the most complete example of a social and religious text and likewise duplicated something of a 'body and soul' principle. Of all courtesy poems, Idley's text is also the closest to being

---

[133] *Caton*, Ii^v. George Painter believes Caxton felt he may have gone too far in his attacks and needed to sweeten his criticism of the city. Painter, *William Caxton*, p. 138.

[134] B. Wall, *The Narrator's Voice: The Dilemma of Children's Fiction* (New York, 1991), p. 35. Clifton discusses these reading theories in relation to medieval texts in '"Seven Sages of Rome"', p. 196.

written for non-elite audiences from the outset, focusing on the interests of professional officials. Care needs to be taken in extending these similarities as Idley was not writing for a merchant audience. Nevertheless we can see that Idley was writing in a period close to, if not contemporaneous with, Caxton's edition of *Caton*, and was very much a part of mid- to late fifteenth century debates over social mobility, manly duties and English character.

The integration of virtuous principles into this social-religious narrative comes early in the prologue to *Caton* and relates to a highly imaginative Christian heritage:

> There was a noble clerke named pogius of Florence And was secretary to pope Eugenye & also to pope Nycholas whiche had in the cyte of Florence a noble & well stuffed lybrarye whiche alle noble straungyers comynge to Florence desyred to see And therin they fonde many noble and rare bookes And whanne they axyd of hym whiche was the best boke of them alle and that he reputed for best He sayd that he helde Cathon glosed for the best book of his lyberarye[135]

This opening is as hyperbolic as the opening stanzas of *The Lytylle Childrene's Book*, which stated that courtesy was a gift from Heaven and linked to Christ's birth. It is more significant, however, that the relationship between virtue, conduct and religious adherence is here extended and treated as a fully developed tool in socialisation. The double emphasis on morality and religious values as a function of daily living swings the socialising lessons towards morality, with 'virtue' attached to the themes of sin and transgression. The result is a double representation of religious-social conduct: 'Wherfore thou must be first with out synne and vertuous than for to wyl make the other to be vertuous and without synnes'.[136] Substantially the same message is found in the relationship between behaviour and religious meaning: 'By cause that they that lyue vertuously Vse reson Justice & equyte & haue praysyng of god and of alle the world'.[137] 'Sin' and 'vice' are explicit cautionary terms which are consistent with these statements.

This provides the foundation for the subsequent discussions about behaviour and conduct, directly affecting how the 'courtesy' topos is reformulated as a socialising principle. Conservative courtesy poems valued hierarchical obligations in practical terms. Several examples focused on seating arrangements and expressions of honour and respect to superior lords. The theme of the duty of children to God and parents was also highly popular and influential and can likewise be found in *Caton*. Discussions of hierarchy and politeness are equally cited but are not associated with a detailed aristocratic structure and are probably consistent with a merchant and bourgeois

---

[135] *Caton*, Ii^v.
[136] *Caton*, Cv^v. A later passage states 'and falleth in to many vyces and synnes': Cvi^r.
[137] *Caton*, Aii^r.

Virtue and Vice

perspective. In *Caton*, children are advised to show respect to anyone who is 'auncient' or honourable or, more broadly still, to any who held a dignity or office.[138]

Similarly generic are the lessons on table manners which lack a specific application to elite households. In *Caton*, children are warned to be temperate in eating and drinking and to pay attention to their speech lest they be taken for gossips. Lessons also include how to behave in a tavern, where loud voices and everyone speaking at once are censured. Young people in medieval and early modern England were not barred from drinking alcohol. Instead it was the relationship to locations such as alehouses and taverns and not the actual consumption of alcohol which preoccupied authorities. Moderation rather than abstinence was desired for youths and there was less of an interest in distinguishing between the behaviour of adults and young people in this regard in this period.[139] Goldberg has shown, however, that there were particular concerns in the late fifteenth and early sixteenth centuries with one group of young people, namely servants, frequenting alehouses; this threatened the good order of the household and the community.[140] As a general trend, concerns with alehouses in the late fifteenth century are more frequently found in extant presentments, probably associated with a rise in unemployment and vagrancy.

It was common for courtesy poems to be concerned with the principle of moderation. This was conveyed through detailed strictures on gluttonous eating and drinking, although always more specifically on the manner of eating. Early medieval guides for the religious houses were critical of gluttony as a sin and extolled moderation.[141] The difference in *Caton* is more readily found in the desire for the reader or listener to understand why moderation and suppressing greed are key principles in socialising people. Drunkenness is not itself linked to a display of bad manners, rudeness or poor comportment. Instead it corresponds to theoretical, medical, pious and practical accounts explaining why excessive wine drinking is not a profitable activity for men. The 'evils' of 'over much drinking of wine' include carnal appetites, shakes of the body, liver problems and a damaging effect on memory and 'wit'. The 'body and soul' philosophy, as already mentioned, is also held in higher regard as over-indulgence 'maketh feble alle the vertues bothe of the bo-dy and of the sowle'.[142] This is not connected to rudeness,

---

[138] *Caton*, Aiiii^v–Aiiii^v.
[139] On this see J. Warner, 'Historical Perspectives on the Shifting Boundaries around Youth and Alcohol: The Example of Pre-Industrial England, 1350–1750', *Addiction* 93 (1998), 641–57.
[140] Goldberg, *Medieval England*, p. 257.
[141] Nicholls, *Matter of Courtesy*, pp. 22–44.
[142] *Caton*, Bviii^r.

manners or sociability. Rather, there is a preoccupation with virtue, as well as a more fundamental concern with physical injury.

A later lesson calls for moderation in speech, similarly linked to vice and sin, 'for ouer many wor-des may not be wythout vyces and synnes'.[143] While *Caton* touches upon some of the core principles of courtesy poems – honour, respect, duty and a sense of hierarchy – it does not consider respectable manners, hygiene or protocol to be the core of socialising values. The parallels between socialising lessons make the specific differences all the more apparent.

Addressing children?

Double address is established through passages speaking about fatherly conduct and the father's role in raising male children. Taking responsibility for actions, as discussed in an earlier chapter, is generally shown in courtesy literature in terms of the child's actions towards their parents, elders or superiors. This is part of the broader issue concerning the individual responsibility of each young person in governing and monitoring public conduct.

Caton instead woos fathers and considers parental roles rather than children's roles as the dominant factor in parent–child relationships. Classical analogies validated the role of fathers in teaching their children. Allegories were also made of religious 'fathers' who held spiritual authority over young people. These household responsibilities were founded upon the notion of parental and adult self-control. Adult gamblers were warned to avoid dice and playing, especially if they were married and had children as this would lead them to put their 'wyues and daughters to grete dyshonoure and shame'.[144] The emphasis on youthful autonomy is subsumed into the idea of parental authority and in particular the role of the father as head of his household. The lengthening of the time of childhood in the sixteenth century is a significant issue and will be pursued later. For now, however, it is worth noting that the time between dependence (as felt by children) and independence (a common marker of adulthood) increased, providing parents and authority figures with a longer timeframe to instruct and govern youths.[145]

According to *Caton*, the father's responsibility to children and servants is central to any normal household. A comparable idea can be found in the late sixteenth-century poem *How to Rule one's Self and one's House* in manuscript Harley 787. The poem comprises two parts. Half of the text falls under the heading *Domus* and half under the heading *Temperance*; each section depicts a father's responsibility towards his children and his household, echoing the make-up of a small household and reinforcing the idea of the normal

---

[143] *Caton*, Cvii^v.
[144] *Caton*, Biii^r.
[145] Rappaport, *Worlds Within Worlds*, pp. 322–9. See also, Griffiths, *Youth and Authority*, pp. 294–5.

family hierarchy in which the father, mother and their children participate in a daily domestic routine. In this short poem, fathers rather than children are addressed. The sense of the family as a unit is described more clearly than in older courtesy narratives. The conscious appeal to 'the family' rather than an individual touches on the role of the 'moral household' that is invoked in the sixteenth century.[146] In this literature children are part of the audience within the family, but the sense that they are directly addressed is lost:

> Bring up thy children in uertuous callinge
> Teach them to knowe & feare God
> Keep them in due obedyence
> Nourish them not in delicacye[147]

According to this, the behaviour of children lies in the hands of parents who have responsibility for upbringing. It is entirely different from the voice heard in earlier courtesy poems addressing children as the main protagonists of lessons and, importantly, where they were given a high degree of responsibility over their own actions.

Caxton's *Caton* shows a late fifteenth century picture of the idealised father. A further element is added through a conservative discourse on household servants. In court records we find household servants and apprentices discussed in terms of the male head of the house and his religious, social and legal duties and responsibilities.[148] In *Caton* this is evidenced through a similar conceptual understanding of domestic labour and household structures, associated with religious duty: 'Thou oughtest to haue the care and the gouernement of thy famylle or seruauntes for thou arte callede fader of thy seruaunte bycause that amonge alle thy seruauntes thou arte lyke a fader and gouernour & of thys thou shalt rendre and yelde a counte before god'.[149] Caxton inserts a specific London reference into this, turning what is a standard didactic dialectic into a highly relevant book for his urban and London readership: 'and euery man that hath any gouernemente or rewle upon his house-

---

[146] S. D. Amussen, *An Ordered Society: Gender and Class in Early Modern England* (Oxford, 1988).

[147] London, BL, MS Harley 787, fol. 9ʳ, *Domus*.

[148] See S. Rees Jones, 'The Household and English Urban Government in the Later Middle Ages', in *The Household in Late Medieval Cities: Italy and Europe Compared*, ed. M. Carlier and T. Soens (Louvain, 2001), pp. 71–87; C. Beattie, 'Governing Bodies: Law Courts, Male Householders and Single Women in Late Medieval England', in *The Medieval Household in Christian Europe, c.850–c.1550: Managing Power, Wealth and the Body*, ed. C. Beattie, A. Maslakovic and S. Rees Jones (Turnhout, 2003), pp. 199–220. Also, Goldberg, *Medieval England*, pp. 21–4; P. J. P. Goldberg, 'What Was a Servant?', in *Concepts and Patterns of Service in the Later Middle Ages*, ed. A. Curry and E. Matthew (Woodbridge, 2000), pp. 1–20.

[149] *Caton*, Aviiᵛ.

hold in lounden'.[150] It is possible to overstate London's hold on the printing market as 'London' may have had a symbolic and celebrated status within provincial reading networks. London, however, had the only major urban population in England and although it had rivals in York, Norwich and Coventry, it constituted a larger market than anywhere else in England. The tone, subject and, again, the prologue produce a feeling that merchants and bourgeois audiences were being provided with a book to suit their interests. Such concerns are part of this book's household utility. By contrast, courtesy poems set within the elite environment elided such household dynamics, rarely even speaking of areas outside the interior space. Of course the *Good Wife* poems, with their mercantile basis, confidently addressed the subjects of taverns and urban centres. In these poems the smaller household context and the more personal dynamic between servants and other household members were equally addressed.

In a similar way the *Book of Good Manners* can be read for its relevance to English urban environments. This English context is introduced, as before, in the prologue. As was the case with *Caton*, the prologue to the *Book of Good Manners* is doubly significant as the text of the book itself does not come from within an English literary tradition; it is translated out of an older French manuscript widely attributed to Jacques Legrand. It is worth commenting on the nature of the original text. Although it is not directly stated by Caxton, the anonymous French source he uses is Legrand's early fifteenth century *Livre de bonnes moeurs*. Difficulties in relating French culture to English culture exist, and French court guides cannot be directly transplanted onto the English court.[151] For Caxton, what was of concern to Legrand and his audiences may not have resonated in England. There was, however, an allure in England in using French as well as Burgundian court standards as a benchmark of behaviour.

A reference in the prologue to the *Book of Good Manners* to a Londoner, William Pratt, mercer and 'friend' of Caxton, establishes two important local connections: the first to London's guild system and the second to Caxton's personal London connections. William Pratt was a member of the Mercers' Company at the time when Caxton was also a member.[152] The prologue is also significant in taking into account the separation of the book from traditional noble patronage networks. Caxton's prologue advertises the familiar refrain of 'maners make man', linked to the rude conditions of 'comyn people whiche

---

[150] *Caton*, Aviiᵛ.
[151] A. E. B Coldiron suggests that literary translations 'disrupted' national boundaries: 'Translation's Challenge to Critical Categories: Verses from French in the Early English Renaissance', *Yale Journal of Criticism* 16 (2003), 315–44.
[152] A. F. Sutton, *The Mercery of London: Trade, Goods and People, 1130–1578* (Aldershot, 2005), p. 169

without enformacion & lernyng ben rude and not manerd lyke vnto beestis',[153] ostensibly moving the book towards a non-noble position and dropping the sometimes standard themes of noble patronage at the outset. Edwards and Meale read the move towards general sponsorship, rather than named noble figures, as part of Caxton's change from 'patronage' to 'endorsement'.[154] Emphasising this, Caxton uses his friendship with the Londoner Pratt to explain how he acquired the text, playing upon his merchant networks and commercial business arrangements, even going to the trouble of explaining that the French text had been given to him by 'An honest man & a specyal fren[d]e of myn a Mercer of london named wyllia[m] praat'.[155]

The focus on 'common people' and the association with a mercantile reading and transmission network can be overstated as the text itself contrasts this initial grouping of people with frequent references to princes and their behaviour. This is characterised in the discussion of the three estates of the Church, the nobility and the common people. Yet the prologue certainly suppresses the elite association. The reader is introduced to the book via more inclusive conditions, learning that manners have a broad application to all people. This is specifically stated in terms of virtuous behaviour. Such is the case in the line 'it is requesite and necessary that euery man vse good & vertuous maners. And to thende that euery man shold haue knowledche of good maners'.[156] Caxton achieves the effect, mentioned earlier in this chapter, concerning the role of books in disseminating knowledge to others, or as Eisenstein and Voss would have it, the transmission of 'expertize' to the community.[157] It is worth noting that de Worde reprinted Caxton's prologue verbatim when he published this book in 1497 and 1526, re-emphasising these issues to his own audiences some ten and thirty-nine years later.

Thematically, the *Book of Good Manners* is deeply religious in tone and ideology. In character one should be humble and patient. In actions one should go on pilgrimage, be abstinent, chaste or remain a virgin. While the first three actions were classed explicitly under virtue and its practice, the epithet honourable was applied to the estate of being a virgin. Good (courteous) manners are only vaguely reported: 'And therefore noo man ought to be a prelate. but yf he be wyse. Vertuous and of right good maners and lyf'.[158] The behaviour of princes is measured according to broader 'good manners' in the sense that 'Thus thene ought a prynce to fore alle thyng gete to hym good

---

[153] Legrand, *Book of Good Manners*, Aii[r].
[154] Edwards and Meale, 'Marketing of Printed Books', p. 97.
[155] Legrand, *Book of Good Manners*, Aii[r].
[156] Legrand, *Book of Good Manners*, Aii[r].
[157] Eisenstein, *Printing Press as an Agent of Change*, pp. 554–5. Voss, 'Books for Sale', pp. 746–7.
[158] Legrand, *Book of Good Manners*, Dvi[r].

ma-ners for to gyue good example to alle them that ben in hys gouernance.'[159] For merchant and bourgeois readers there was the opportunity to extend these values to their own social and business networks, reconfiguring the ethical behaviour of rulers to bourgeois and mercantile communities. In this way, manners are acknowledged as a helpful aid to government. Bourgeois and merchant readers could reproduce this message by taking princely behaviour as a model for business behaviour. This goes beyond proper manners at a table or observable actions, and it is this which moves socialising values in this period beyond the prescription of arranged formalities. However, this should not be overstated; manners are used in a particularly vague way in this book and it is difficult to ascribe any particular activity to the 'good manners' listed. We are unable to know completely what Legrand or Caxton may have intended to allude to or what readers would have understood by this term. However, more usefully we can approximate a reading of 'manners' by comparing it with other narratives which paralleled 'good manners' in different ways. The discussion about service, for example, contrasts with the narrative in courtesy poems. Servants, and particularly young servants, were supervised for their conduct at the table, in serving food and in interacting with others. Honour, obedience and duty may have been the subtext of courtesy lessons but what was of primary importance was the observable element of conduct. The *Book of Good Manners*, like *Caton* before it, focused on internal qualities that supported outward behaviour. In one case a discussion of the qualities that servants were expected to comply with to meet worldly and spiritual values contains a clear distinction from previous socialising values. Six are listed: honour (for their master), faithfulness, truth, obedience, diligence and patience.[160] Scriptural examples of servants obeying their masters reinforce the message and promote this in ways that ascribe different values to good behaviour.

We should also consider the overall context of the different discourses on manners and elite service. It becomes clearer in later lessons that neither protocol nor observable actions are monitored and privileged. Princes are warned not to be avaricious, nor covetous, to maintain and keep justice and to be humble: 'Thene ought the prynces to be ashamed. The whiche demannde no thyng but wyn ande mete. And holden longe dyners. And yet more longe soupers'.[161] Soberness and chastity are also part of the idealisation of principles governing behaviour, at odds with aristocratic feasting and lifestyles in this period and qualities we know were relevant to both French and English court cultures. Unlike courtesy literature, which described elite standards of living in terms of extravagant gestures of public hospitality, feasting and courtly behaviour, the *Book of Good Manners* instead looked to

[159] Legrand, *Book of Good Manners*, Eii^r.
[160] Legrand, *Book of Good Manners*, Gii^v–Giii^v.
[161] Legrand, *Book of Good Manners*, Evii^r.

Virtue and Vice

the genre of princely guides to describe virtuous qualities. Simultaneously there is an emphasis on the contractual obligations a monarch bears to his people. Given Richard III's defeat at Bosworth two years prior to this and Henry VII's accession to the throne, publishing this work was an interesting decision on Caxton's part. In the prologue to the *Order of Chivalry* Caxton had previously praised English kings for their conduct, virtue and chivalry, beginning with Richard I and continuing with Edward I and III and Henry V. Richard III was conspicuously absent. Orientating printed books towards political and social subtexts provided alert readers with opportunities to engage with wider national debates.

A discourse on kingly rule and responsibilities is not, of course, unique to this period. Literary guides had long been used in discussions about kingship, morality and governance. This literature, which includes the *Secretum Secretorum* (mid-twelfth century), Gower's *Vox Clamantis* (1378–81), *Confessio Amantis* (1390) and Hoccleve's *Regement of Princes* (1411), expressed dissatisfaction with corruption and political manoeuvrings.[162] In terms of early printing, there was now the added potential for a wide dispersal of texts and ideologies to a range of (anonymous) social groups. Caxton's agency in publishing politically sensitive works occurred at a time when printing culture is increasingly seen as engaging with national identity.[163] Caxton's translation of *The Curial* (1483 and 1484) from Alan Chartier's earlier text emerged in politically sensitive times.[164] Chartier's moral critiques of court life would have found some relevance among English audiences in the mid-1480s when they were experiencing their own disruption to the English royal succession with the death of Edward IV, the disappearance and possible murder of the two princes and Richard III's contentious rise to the throne. Of course, the fact that Caxton felt able to publish in this vein suggests anxieties and alarm were not at such a fever pitch that this text would have ignited unrest. Given this, the subtexts of undeserving kingly rule and shameful noble conduct would

---

[162] The 'mirrors for princes' genre is important in relation to the upbringing of the nobility and as a guide to medieval political writing. See, W. Fałkowski, 'Carolingian *speculum principis* – The Birth of a Genre', *Acta Poloniae Historica* 98 (2008), 5–27. A mid-sixteenth century guide, *Mirror for Magistrates*, written in the early 1550s, is discussed by P. V. Budra, A Mirror for Magistrates *and the* de casibus Tradition (Toronto, 2000); J. Winston, '*A Mirror for Magistrates* and Public Political Discourse in Elizabethan England', *Studies in Philology* 101 (2004), 381–400; S. C. Lucas, A Mirror for Magistrates *and the Politics of the English Reformation* (Amherst, 2009).

[163] Kuskin looks not so much towards Caxton but towards late fifteenth and early sixteenth century printing in general as 'representative of a much larger relationship between the material production of goods and the symbolic production of national identity': '"Onely Imagined"', pp. 199–200.

[164] Coldiron suggests literary translations 'disrupted' national boundaries in, 'Translation's Challenge', pp. 315–44.

have held meaning for Caxton and been interpreted by his audience as covert allusions to current rule, if the audience chose to read them this way.

As first outlined by Legrand in *Livre de bonnes moeurs*, order and harmony are surveyed according to the Church, the elite and the common people. The fourth book in particular focuses on multiple social estates not limited to the clergy and the gentry, refocusing merchant and bourgeois readers to their own set of values and experiences. Here the text serves to remind readers of the divisions of the world and passages range from poverty, age, children, servants and pilgrims to merchants and fathers. The correspondence to the inclusive social framework first identified in the prologue is particularly visible. This also shows a clear identification with the thematic topic of the family and it is no surprise that Chilton Powell once said that 'Among the very earliest books printed in England, we find the first on the family. This is Caxton's *Boke of Good Manners*.'[165]

This bears closer examination. Apart from describing the qualities children and youths should have, the book appended the highly traditional and popular concept of youthful softness to its notion of youthful character. Here it overlaps with the semi-medical and religious tradition: 'And therefore saynt Anselme in his boke of symylitudes compareth Infancye or chyldehode to ware whiche is softe'.[166] In other words, infancy is compared to soft, mouldable wax. Conduct, then, whether it is seen as being meek, obedient, dutiful or any number of other conventional actions, was enabled through the unformed nature of the child. Courtesy poems understood this message; learning needed to begin early.

A final point is that children and young people are integrated directly into the book through discussions about parent and child relationships, specifically the mutual obligations that exist between the two. Any adult who has the governance of children should not hesitate to chastise and reprove them; misbehaviour, in terms of disobedience towards parents, was, and still is, a deeply felt anxiety for adults, and it is this which informs many of the preoccupations and anxieties of socialising lessons. Countering this are scriptural examples of obedient children: David obeyed his father and Christ himself was a dutiful son. However central this message is, youthful responsibility is not completely suppressed and there is an awareness that adult governance could only accomplish so much, with children ultimately responsible for their actions and their salvation: 'For syth they haue wytte and vnderstondyng they ben [...] be repreuyd & they shal be pugnysshid of god yf they doo ouy uyll.'[167] Equally disturbing to our modern sensibilities is the customary

---

[165] Powell, *English Domestic Relations*, p. 102.
[166] Legrand, *Book of Good Manners*, Fvi^r.
[167] Legrand, *Book of Good Manners*, Fvi^v.

warning about the stark reality of infant death, and young people are warned not to think their age will protect them from death and judgement.[168]

This partial revision of child responsibility is developed progressively in the literature through the increasing articulation of parental duties. Fathers and mothers are directed to think of their children because it is by their 'good doctrine' that the children learn.[169] Three years earlier Caxton's translation of Cato (*Caton*) had explored this theme, discussing the role of parents and especially the father as the dominant factor in parent–child relationships. The implied role of parents in their children's lives is increasingly direct. That is, these books present a scenario where it is parents who are in habitual contact with their children. Unlike courtesy poems which addressed children living away from the natal household – even though, as we saw in earlier chapters, for some gentry and middling classes this would not have been the case – the evidence from the *Book of Good Manners* and *Caton* is that it is parents who are in a dominant position to monitor the behaviour and moral identity of their children on a regular, if not daily, basis. Goldberg has shown that adolescent children were more likely to be found in the natal home in prosperous households.[170] The changes in reading networks and particularly the increasing readership within prosperous urban households which this chapter has suggested explains why we hear more of the responsibility of parents within these books and equally why it is books such as these that were acquired by the printing presses. The explicit references to a household environment in both *Caton* and the *Book of Good Manners* are suggestive of the importance of these 'family' books which could be read or heard by dual audiences made up of adults and children living within the same space. Elias saw this focus on family life as fashioning the interest in interior responses, no longer exterior responses, and this can be seen in this English literature.[171]

In these two decades of printing in England the choice of texts has been shown to be both conservative and different, simultaneously suggesting a new direction in socialisation while harking back to older forms of literature. Good manners are certainly not displaced within individual texts or across the printed corpus. It is more the case that socialisation in moral matters is increasingly articulated in the literature to which children were exposed. In the previous chapters these adaptations from the courtesy format took the form of competition from gentry and bourgeois consumers anxious to appropriate elements of the elite household and elite courtesy into their own spheres, modifying beliefs and concepts on an ad hoc, instinctive basis. The period shows this developing towards a more considered and conscious,

---

[168] Legrand, *Book of Good Manners*, Fvi^v.
[169] Legrand, *Book of Good Manners*, Giiii^r.
[170] Goldberg, *Medieval England*, p. 20.
[171] Elias, *Civilizing Process*, pp. 116–17.

positive separation of bourgeois from elite ideologies during times of political and social stress.

Caxton's books seem also to anticipate the family reading audiences that became commonplace in the sixteenth century. The voice of the family in the small natal household is clearly identified in this period, as it is in later sixteenth century literature. In the following chapter the roles of the family, the father and the household are analysed in relation to other literary examples focusing on children and upbringing. Sixteenth-century books also reflect, even more overtly, the gentry, merchant and bourgeois readerships addressed here, with this perhaps even extending to artisan classes and more prosperous yeomen as books began to circulate more widely and in greater numbers. The responsiveness of this literature to developments in family relationships and the social and religious role of the small natal household also developed in the next few decades and are the subject of the next chapter.

CHAPTER FOUR

Sixteenth-Century Books

'Lerne: or be lewde folowe the proued mannes advyse'[1]

By the late fifteenth century there was a growing ideal within literature that boys and girls should be subject to moral, virtuous and courteous guidance. Caxton's publications told of young people being 'fed with virtue' and 'removed from vice'.[2] These books defined their responsibilities towards socialising both sexes as the instilling of courteous and virtuous manners. Before this the common theme in courtesy literature for boys had represented socialisation in multi-directional class lines, although it always began with an explicit focus on elite behaviour. Quite distinct differences between poems for boys and those for girls show that there had been a well-developed sense of moral female behaviour prior to this. By the close of the fifteenth century the archetype accentuating moral characteristics was emerging more strongly in material for boys. In the previous chapter Caxton's publications, with their parallel accounts of virtue and sin, were shown as substantially contributing to this development in response to social and political turmoil in England. What, then, of the literature in the century after Caxton, which circulated at a time when disruption to the social and political order was attributable to religious turbulence? Bryson has argued that manners are evidence of changing social strategies.[3] This chapter addresses the nature of sixteenth-century strategies in the light of childhood upbringing, domestic household policy and religious values.

Considerably less attention has been paid to print culture in the century after Caxton's death, and yet the sixteenth century saw a massive uptake in printing.[4] It is the increasing publication of books over this period that allows us to examine how socialisation was articulated across different contexts and paradigms: by secular or clerical authors, by English or Continental writers

---

[1] H. Rhodes, *The boke of nurture for men, seruantes and chyldren, with Stans puer ad mensam, newly corrected, very vtyle and necessary vnto all youth* (London, 1545), Biiii^v.
[2] *Parvus Cato* and *Book of Curtesye*.
[3] Bryson, *Courtesy to Civility*, p. 276.
[4] On this see, *The Cambridge History of the Book in Britain*, vol. III, ed. Hellinga and Trapp and *The Cambridge History of the Book in Britain, vol. IV, 1557–1695*, ed. J. Barnard and D. F. McKenzie with the assistance of M. Bell (Cambridge, 2002).

and for the socialisation of girls or boys. We should also be more attentive to the pressures brought to bear by changing religious policies upon people's engagement with literate culture and particularly books that addressed English family affairs. Unlike previous chapters, this one begins by addressing texts which emphasise virtue in socialisation. The profound anxiety with the moral and chaste identity of girls in the status-conscious book *The Instruction of a Christen Woman* by Juan Luis Vives (1523, first English publication 1529) shows how texts originally from Continental Europe enjoyed success in England. Vives's book has attracted most of the attention historians have paid to the issue of female education; however, it was only one of a number of didactic treatises imported into England from the Continent and any reading of Vives needs to be placed alongside texts with which it shares similar characteristics.[5] Two English translations of Giovanni Michele Bruto's *La institutione di una fanciulla nata nobilmente*, translated in 1579 by Thomas Salter and in 1598 by William Phiston, are part of the context which sees a young English girl's upbringing expressing a culturally conservative Italian perspective.

Sixteenth-century writers addressed moral patterns in relation to boys as well as girls. Moral and virtuous counsel was cultivated through relationships that existed, or were seen as ideally existing, between children and family members, usually with an emphasis on patriarchal relationships. This built on the emerging family-household genre of the late fifteenth century, taking the message of socialisation out of the realm of the elite household and putting it firmly into the gentry and merchant household. The parental voice had occasionally been used in earlier courtesy material, with Idley's lessons to his son in the *Instructions* as well as the poem *How the Wise Man Taught his Son* existing within the limits of this parental genre. Both poems also belonged to a separate tradition of courtesy literature that developed independently from the elite styling of most courtesy texts. By the sixteenth century it was this non-elite family which was dominating the literature written about children's social norms and customs.

Three key points are raised in this chapter in terms of this parent-child relationship. First, we must consider the commercial reasons books were published; secondly, the reading locations these books both described and anticipated; and, thirdly, the manner in which socialising patterns were represented. The development of a genre on household affairs was dependent upon households where parents, step-parents and siblings lived in closer proximity to one other. This was not necessarily a nuclear kin-family, as high death rates meant extended family networks were important in caring for children; families including both siblings and step-siblings were common.[6]

---

[5] On Vives see *The Instruction of a Christen Woman*, ed. V. Walcott Beauchamp, E. H. Hageman and M. Mikesell (Chicago, 2002); *The Education of a Christian Woman: A Sixteenth-Century Manual*, ed. and trans. C. Fantazzi (Chicago, 2000).

[6] J. Kermode, 'Sentiment and Survival: Family and Friends in Late Medieval English

Importantly, however – and something which will be picked up later in this chapter – literature rarely referred to the reality of these blended families, preferring instead relationships between fathers, mothers and children (although the servants were also included). The exception to this was the parallel drawn between adults standing *in loco parentis* to young people. The role of these works in socialising real children also depended on families being willing to purchase books that spoke to them and to their preoccupations and interests. Decreasing book prices in the sixteenth century created a relatively wide culture of individual and communal reading amongst the gentry and wealthy merchant classes. English print runs extended to substantial figures of between 1250 and 1500 copies,[7] and while book scholars have debated whether reprints were less expensive than first-run printings, there were fewer economic barriers in place preventing households from purchasing books. The picture we have of book circulation across this entire period is largely masked, while difficulties in extrapolating print runs from existing figures complicate matters further. More work needs to be done on book prices and circulation in general in this period.[8]

Two developments saw the voice and responsibility the householder had in family affairs increasingly favoured over children's experiences. Firstly, there was an increase in the scale of production of books addressing parents, and secondly, the family was increasingly characterised in court proceedings as representing social order.[9] Lessons were still discussed through a fairly conventional social hierarchy similar to that seen in medieval texts. However, parents (on the whole it is fathers who are described in terms of governing dependent children) needed to be in direct contact with young people before it could be assumed that they would be the primary arbitrators of the household's conduct. As Caxton had done, sixteenth-century printers catered to a market that masked variations of this model.

In the previous chapter I noted the reading theory of 'dual address' and 'double address' as one which identifies multiple reading networks, important

---

Towns', *Journal of Family History* 24 (1999), 5–18.

[7] Noted for Vives's book: Vives, *Instruction*, ed. Beauchamp, Hageman and Mikesell, p. xcii.

[8] On sixteenth-century print runs and editions see J. A. Dane, *The Myth of Print Culture: Essays on Evidence, Textuality, and Bibliographical Method* (Buffalo, 2003) and A. Weiss, 'Casting Compositors, Foul Cases, and Skeletons: Printing in Middleton's Age', in *Thomas Middleton and Early Modern Textual Culture: A Companion to the Collected Works*, ed. G. Taylor and J. Lavagnino (Oxford, 2007), pp. 195–225. On how books were sold outside London see G. Pollard, 'The Company of Stationers Before 1557', *The Library* 4th s. 18 (1937), 1–38.

[9] G. J. Schochet, *Patriarchalism in Political Thought: The Authoritarian Family and Political Speculation and Attitudes Especially in Seventeenth Century England* (New York, 1975). Amussen re-addressed many of the ideas on the family and its political role in *An Ordered Society*.

when considering family reading groups. This chapter explicitly presupposes these audiences and it should be read in the light of the earlier discussion of potential reading practices. It is therefore a premise in the following discussion that 'family' narratives and 'parental advice literature' had audiences amongst both children and adults, as well as amongst employers and servants. This also contributed to the aural engagement people had with literate culture.

Household instruction for girls

A continuing process of translation and reproduction of Continental European ideas by English translators and printers throughout the sixteenth century means that, as we saw in the previous chapter, it tended to be conservative attitudes to women which remained popular in commercially produced books. Popularity is, of course, difficult to judge from the distance of centuries. The question of seeing 'either acquiescence or resistance to texts' is a challenge historians face when any prescriptive material is analysed.[10] The insight we gain into contemporary responses to texts and particularly into this question of acceptance and recognition by looking at the activities of printers should not be underestimated. As suggested in the previous chapter, printers were entrepreneurial figures who selected books based on a range of commercial (and admittedly sometimes personal and religious) strategies. There should never be the assumption of an automatic equation between commercial value and the uptake of ideas by readers or the application of ideas from texts to private family situations. Attentiveness to printing history can, however, suggest that particular notions of social behaviour and upbringing dominated the social discourse. Once this picture is constructed there is a greater possibility of gaining more insight into occasions where parents chose to act on or resist didactic practices, although one is still hampered by questions of evidence.

When in 1529 Richard Hyrde translated Juan Luis Vives's *De Institutione Foeminae Christianae*,[11] he brought the medieval pedagogical convention of

---

[10] Here, J. F. Ruys, 'Introduction' in *What Nature Does Not Teach*, p. 19, is particularly insightful. Ursula Potter's essay contrasts Vives's book with other parental attitudes to children: 'Elizabethan Drama and The Instruction of a Christian Woman by Juan Luis Vives', in *What Nature Does Not Teach: Didactic Literature in the Medieval and Early-Modern Periods*, ed. J. F. Ruys (Turnhout, 2008), pp. 261–85.

[11] R. Hyrde, *A very frutefull and pleasant boke called the instructio[n] of a Christen woma[n], made fyrst in Laten, and dedicated vnto the quenes good grace, by the right famous clerke mayster Lewes Vives, and turned out of Laten into Englysshe by Rycharde Hyrd. whiche boke who so redeth diligently shal haue knowlege of many thynges, wherin he shal take great pleasure, and specially women shall take great co[m]modyte and frute towarde the[n]creace of vertue [and] good maners* (London, 1529).

moralistic and improving literature into what has been described as the 'developing genre of the domestic conduct book'.[12] While this genre would eventually become sharply associated with non-elite family reading circles in Protestant England, the influence of puritan ideology on English society and moral behaviour has been overstated.[13]

The *Instruction* develops conventional medieval ideas about girlhood and womanhood. Be chaste. Be demure. Be devout. Be meek. All of these were qualities which medieval moralising authors addressed and much has been made of the medieval tradition which lies behind Vives's book.[14] Such attributes were nevertheless extremely brittle and limited by both external and internal corruptibility. Vives explains that it is the external environment which is the first potential hazard for infant girls. Instructions for parents begin with the obligation for mothers to breastfeed their children in preference to putting them out to wet nurses, a practice embraced by the elite and affluent bourgeois in England and which extended to the landed gentry and some rich merchant families.[15] It was a commonplace belief that milk was a potential contaminant, acting as a bodily carrier for disposition, character and temperament. Contemporary medical and social texts upheld the view that wet nurses imparted more of their character to a child than any hereditary imperatives – as was baldly stated by Vives: 'They that have ben nurced with sowes mylke have rolled in the mier.'[16] The innately virtuous quality of mothers' milk had been extolled in Trevisa's fourteenth-century translation of *De Proprietatibus Rerum*: 'and so the childe is bettir and more kindeliche ifedde with his owne modir melk thanne with othir melke'.[17] Breastfeeding was likewise advocated by Edward Grant as a maternal duty, but one moreover that was deeply emotional, 'bicause wyth a certain intier loue, & mere affection they tender them which they haue born & bred: and loue euen the nailes of their fingers'.[18] Maternal attachments are presented

---

[12] Vives, *Instruction*, ed. Beauchamp, Hageman and Mikesell, p. xl. Powell discusses the book's importance in England in *English Domestic Relations*, pp. 102–19, 154.
[13] On this see M. Spufford, 'Puritanism and Social Control?', in *Order and Disorder in Early Modern England*, ed. A. Fletcher and J. Stevenson (Cambridge, 1985), pp. 41–57; McIntosh, *Controlling Misbehaviour*, pp. 1–19.
[14] See for instance, Potter, 'Elizabethan Drama', pp. 261–85.
[15] V. Fildes, *Wet Nursing: A History from Antiquity to the Present* (Oxford, 1988). For further European evidence on wet nursing see H. M. Jewell, *Women in Late Medieval and Reformation Europe, 1200–1550* (Basingstoke, 2007), pp. 71–3. Vives acknowledges that most children will, in fact, be sent to wet nurses.
[16] Vives, *Instruction*, Book 1, C1^v.
[17] *Properties of Things*, ed. Seymour, I, 303.
[18] E. Grant, *A president for parentes, teaching the vertuous training vp of children and holesome information of yongmen. Written in greke by the prudent and wise phylosopher Choeroneus [sic] Plutarchus, translated and partly augmented by Ed. Grant: very profitable to be read of all those that desire to be parents of virtuous children. Anno. 1571. Seene and allowed according to the Quenes iniunctions* (London, 1571), Biiii^r.

in emotive language, elevating this as a formative emotional characteristic of womanhood.[19]

The formation of gendered behaviour has often been viewed as taking place at a later stage in the youthful life cycle, typically starting in earnest when a child was around seven years. Shulamith Shahar has suggested that contemporary writers referred to both sexes equally in the first stage (*infantia*) of life, with separate tracts and instructions developing only once the *pueritia* stage (seven to twelve for girls and seven to fourteen for boys) had been reached.[20] The often repeated distinction between the ages of twelve (for girls) and fourteen (for boys) relates to canonical ages of consent for marriage, based partly on medieval biological understandings of childhood. Kim Phillips suggests that gendering began in earnest at puberty, with girls 'learning' how to become women at this time.[21] There is no doubt that this later dividing of girls from boys affected the socialising process. However, Vives writes of virtuous character formation as a gendered concept to be vigorously enforced from the moment of birth.[22] The crafting of a virtuous environment from the very beginning of development was necessary for the long and slow process of forming a girl's moral character:

> But the mayde, whom we wolde have specially good, requireth al intendaunce both of father and mother, lest any spotte of vice or unclenlynes shulde stycke on her: Let her take no suche thynges neither by her bodily senses and wyttes, nor by her norishyng and bryngyng up. She shal fyrst here her nurce, fyrst se her: and what so ever she lerneth in rude and ignorant age, that wyl she ever labour to counterfete and folowe counnyngly[23]

---

[19] Linda Pollock analysed emotional attachments connecting parents to children in the sixteenth century: *Forgotten Children*, pp. 33–67, 96–142. This was one of a wave of analyses of childhood which questioned the perceived lack of emotional attachment between parents and children. Lloyd deMause and his later adherents had argued that children were largely neglected and overlooked by adults and by society at large. Pollock's study revised these perceptions. It is surprising that historians have overlooked Vives's writings: 'Or what a crueltie is hit, nat to love them that thou hast borne?', *Instruction*, Book 2, M2r.
[20] Shahar, *Childhood in the Middle Ages*, pp. 23–6, 29–30.
[21] Phillips, *Medieval Maidens*, pp. 61–2. Phillips is not suggesting that there were no gendered notions in early childhood, just that 'Adolescence was the time at which the differences between the sexes began to be delineated with greater sharpness … Although gender differentiation had some place in childhood roles and identities, the distinction of sexes was far less important than later in life': *Medieval Maidens*, p. 9.
[22] On how gender was understood during conception and fetus development see *Properties of Things*, ed. Seymour, I, 298. See also D. T. Kline, 'Female Childhoods', in *The Cambridge Companion to Medieval Women's Writing*, ed. C. Dinshaw and D. Wallace (Cambridge, 2003), pp. 13–20.
[23] Vives, *Instruction*, Book 1, C2r.

Though this effectively directed parents to consider a gendered model of upbringing from infancy onwards, the notion of seven years of age being an important marker in the life cycle remained an idea that most medieval writers and pedagogues upheld. Vives himself introduces concrete ages by referring to seven years as the traditional point when learning should begin, although he cautions that no hard-and-fast rule should determine this and suggests both fathers and mothers pay attention to the particular aptitudes of their child. It is important not to overstate this personal parental attention. Such comments could just as easily be a convenient narrative device that suited Vives's discussion of parental roles, and even then one only appropriate to families with the financial resources to offer such personal attention to the education of their children.

In the past much was made of Vives's attitudes towards educating young girls.[24] Yet education across the medieval and early modern periods was profoundly inexact for girls, partly seen as beneficial to the growth of their moral character but also considered detrimental. For moralising writers, education could reinforce internal qualities recognisably attributable to women, including chastity and moral character, yet it was equally chronicled as being a negative mechanism for socialising young women. On the one hand it was possible for a well-educated girl to stand firm against evil influences.[25] However, any schooling taking place outside the home and the study of eloquence, rhetoric and some of the more dubious classical authors were viewed as sure threats to a girl's chaste character. Lurking beneath many of these notions was a view that education was unnecessary for girls who were to become wives and mothers, although this attitude may not have been as pervasive as these moralising writers implied. While restricting learning for 'practical' reasons would have had a profound effect on the educational standards achieved by many young women, other accounts reveal that up to the late fifteenth century the study of French (for aristocratic girls) and English (for both aristocratic and gentry girls) was seen as both enjoyable and necessary to complete an education.[26] Learning the English alphabet could be achieved within a short space of time; for girls from artisanal and merchant groups this could have taken place at elementary schools, while for the higher status families of which Vives writes it was more likely to have been carried out in the household.

Equally problematic is the way we view literacy, and particularly women's literacy, in the medieval and early modern periods. Malcolm Parkes expanded

---

[24] For instance see F. Watson, *Vives and the Renascence Education of Women* (London, 1912); J. Simon, *Education and Society in Tudor England* (Cambridge, 1966), p. 161. For a feminist perspective see G. Kaufman, 'Juan Luis Vives on the Education of Women', *Signs* 3 (1978), 891–6.
[25] Vives, *Instruction*, Book 1, E1^r.
[26] Meale, '"... alle the bokes that I haue"', pp. 139–41.

how we think of literacy by looking at models of (reading) engagement across a spectrum. The literate ability of the professional reader was not the same as that of the cultivated or pragmatic reader.[27] James Daybell also writes of literacy as being either 'functional' or having a 'spiritual impetus'. While didactic treatises and formal educational records may overlook girls' education, the extensive evidence of female letter-writing demonstrates a functional literacy.[28] The mid sixteenth century educational abilities of Margaret Willoughby, the daughter of a Nottingham gentry family, may have been functional, with her training in casting accounts part of her preparation to manage household records. Her brother Francis Willoughby's education was different: it included both Greek and Latin texts and was spent in formal grammar schools and later at Cambridge. Yet this did not produce 'a new world of male authority which pushed women into the ranks of the disadvantaged',[29] as Alice Friedman argues. This view assumes that a humanist education which revived classical learning was of a higher value than the practical learning more likely to be attained by girls. I am not suggesting that it was academically better only to learn English and not Latin (or even Greek), or that girls would not have flourished had they been given the opportunities to study. However, a comprehensive grounding in an elementary curriculum presented a range of opportunities for some young women. The value in knowing how to read English in the sixteenth century was greater than ever before, given the multitude of books on a range of topics which had been printed by this time. Reading literacy in English would have opened up many worlds for female readers.

The preceding paragraph describes education in the somewhat narrow sense of reading literacy, less so writing literacy. For Vives, education is more correctly understood as one piece in an ongoing process of socialisation. As with the issue of literacy addressed above, Vives clearly does not accommodate aristocratic and middling women occupied with running households, estates and businesses.[30] For him, household duties instead included dressing wool and cooking, good housekeeping and holy study.[31] Education as a tool which promoted moral character was also part of wider educational practice which saw the curriculum aligned with moral and religious duties. The final chapter of this book addresses the connections between schools and manners and virtue in more detail; however, it is worth noting that Vives's writing

---

[27] Parkes, 'Literacy of the Laity', pp. 555–77.
[28] J. Daybell, 'Interpreting Letters and Reading Script: Evidence for Female Education and Literacy in Tudor England', *History of Education* 34 (2005), 695–715.
[29] A. T. Friedman, 'The Influence of Humanism on the Education of Girls and Boys in Tudor England', *History of Education Quarterly* 25 (1985), 57–70 (pp. 65, 67).
[30] L. Pollock, '"Teach her to live under obedience": The Making of Women in the Upper Ranks of Early Modern England', *Continuity and Change* 4 (1989), 231–58.
[31] Vives, *Instruction*, Book 1, C3^r.

shows how this educational–moral duality was identified for young girls, with chastity, purity and involvement in the domestic spheres dominating and defining the majority of educational options open to young women. The exceptions to this, such as Margaret Roper's Latin and Greek education, should not be overstated.[32]

It follows that all of this takes place in the home and a Spaniard's sense of the value of sequestering females is present in what Vives writes.[33] The public nature of misbehaving, already mentioned in earlier chapters, as well as the damage done to a reputation if a girl was seen taking part in an unsuitable activity were as important as the attributes themselves. Vives speaks of how a girl's kin and community would react to a damaged reputation; and guilt and shame play an important part in this:

> What mournyng, what teares, what wepynge of the father and mother and bringers up? Dost thou quite them with this pleasure for so moche care and labour? Is this the rewarde of thy bryngyng up? What cursyng wyl ther be of her aquayntance? What talke of neighbours, frendes, and companyons, cursynge that ungratyous yonge woman? What mockyng and bablynge of those maydens, that envyed her before?[34]

The desire to lock daughters safely away in the household is raised in many didactic books from the Continent.[35] It was seen in the *Book of the Knight of the Tower*, less so in the English *Good Wife* poems where economic realities establish a female presence within the town and as participants in urban trade activities, although these texts also aspired to curtail free movement. Of course, representations of autonomy, authority and external monitoring would have been comprehended, followed and dismissed according to the social and economic pressures facing particular groups of readers. Lower income families were logistically unable to keep daughters sequestered in the natal house, or mistresses their servants in their houses. Equally, these terms were not unique to medieval Catholic literature and Protestant authors across the early modern period borrowed heavily from this model.[36]

Gauging the frequency with which moralising ideas were taken up by families is frustratingly difficult, as already mentioned (the Pastons provide

---

[32] Another often commented on exception is Bunbury, Cheshire, which famously mentions young girls in the 1594 school statutes, provided they attended before they reached the age of nine and only learnt English. Cheshire and Chester Archives, P40/16/1.
[33] Vives, *Instruction*, Book 1, K4^r.
[34] Vives, *Instruction*, Book 1, G2^v. Tadmor, 'Friends and Neighbours', pp. 150–67; McIntosh, *Controlling Misbehaviour*, p. 24.
[35] On this see A. P. Coudert, 'Educating Girls in Early Modern Europe and America', in *Childhood in the Middle Ages: The Results of a Paradigm Shift in the History of Mentality*, ed. A. Classen (Berlin, 2005), pp. 389–413 (pp. 400–1).
[36] Coudert, 'Educating Girls', pp. 407–13.

some sense of varying success in managing the marriages of daughters).[37] The popularity of Vives's book in Tudor England can, however, be used to answer other questions.[38] The reprinting over subsequent years (1529, 1531, 1541, 1547, 1557, 1567, 1585, 1592) presupposes the ability of readers to approach books from their Catholic past and from staunchly Catholic countries in order to appropriate themes which transcended overt religious and national forms. It also suggests that social norms and customs for children were based on even deeper social, medical and commonplace notions which the outward form of religion was unable to alter in the short term. Others have written on the measured progress of Protestantism under Elizabeth; Patrick Collinson and Kenneth Hylson-Smith have both pointed out that neither the Church nor the Crown sought to alter society radically or even to institute fully labelled religious ideologies at this time.[39]

By the last quarter of the sixteenth century the scope and interests of readers aware of a moral literature for girls were extended through two translations of Bruto's 1555 *La institutione*; the earlier of the two English translations by Thomas Salter appeared in 1579, *A mirrhor mete for all mothers, matrones, and maidens, intituled the Mirrhor of Modestie*,[40] and it was followed nearly two decades later by *The necessarie, fit, and conuenient education of a yong gentlewoman* attributed to William Phiston.[41]

The duties of medieval and early modern translators were complex. In part they were to remain faithful to the original text even when it lacked cultural relevance to the new location.[42] Salter, in fact, anglicises Bruto's Italianate focus, adding several significant amendments which directly address English readers while also making relatively trivial changes such as omitting the names of painters 'Albert Dure', 'Raphael Vrbin' and 'Michel Angell' (used to parallel advice on choosing a good instructor). Other amendments are suggestive of a deeper responsiveness to English cultural and religious values. Salter glosses Protestant beliefs and at one point introduces a virtuous text for the Maiden to read, John Foxe's *Acts and Monuments*. Although in its

---

[37] *Paston Letters*, ed. Fenn, II, 28–30.
[38] The book is generally perceived as being very popular in England; however, Potter suggests its reception was less favourable, in 'Elizabethan Drama', pp. 261–85.
[39] P. Collinson, *Godly People: Essays on English Protestantism and Puritanism* (London, 1983), pp. 335–6; K. Hylson-Smith, *The Churches in England from Elizabeth I to Elizabeth II, Vol. 1: 1558–1688* (London, 1996), pp. 31–47.
[40] T. Salter, *A mirrhor mete for all mothers, matrons, and maidens, intituled the Mirrhor of Modestie, no lesse profitable and pleasant, then necessarie to bee read and practiced* (London, 1579).
[41] W. P[histon], *The necessarie, fit, and conuenient education of a yong gentlewoman. written both in French and Italian, and translated into English by W. P. And now printed with the three languages togither in one volume, for the better instruction of such as are desirous to studie these tongues* (London, 1598).
[42] Coldiron, 'Taking Advice from a Frenchwoman', p. 140. An interesting study on translation is U. Eco, *Experiences in Translation*, trans. A. McEwen (Toronto, 2001).

own right this was an important moralising and religious book, it echoes a comment Salter makes concerning the ongoing nature of the Catholic threat facing English Protestants: 'I trust that at this presente, in whiche tyme especiallie emong us here in Englande, where the Gospell is so freely and sincerely preached, I neede not to declare from the beginnyng to the ende, where in the one is different from the other, I meane true religion, from falce superstition'.[43] Salter was making his translation at a time when Elizabeth I had been excommunicated from the Catholic Church and when the Spanish were seen as a real threat to England's national security.

Although there were sound religious reasons for Salter to refer to Foxe, it is more valuable to consider the tactical advantage that he builds by citing Foxe's well-known religious book as suitable reading material for English girls. The inclusion of *Acts and Monuments* creates a literary network that poses a symbolic and even a physical union between the two books. *Acts and Monuments*, moreover, is determinedly 'English' in its focus and religious intent. We must be careful not to overstate this. Janis Butler Holm has argued that Salter's Protestantism is only a 'veneer' and that he remained content to retain original Catholic imagery, leaving descriptions of saints' lives in the book.[44] Later in this chapter minor textual changes made by another moralising writer, Hugh Rhodes, show that writers and printers often deleted only the most overt Catholic references in books for family and child audiences. In fact, there was more continuity between Catholic and Protestant literature than is often recognised. Phiston's literal translation of Bruto's text in 1598, in a context of his own Calvinist leanings, suggests the same.

On the whole, two types of household have tended to be identified in conduct literature. One of these strands (including courtesy poems and the *Good Wife* poems) fashions socialising lessons by looking at the fostering environment and the other focuses on the kin-related family (*Book of the Knight of the Tower*, Idley's *Instructions*, the *Book of Good Manners*). While there is no rigid correlation between these environments and the status of girls, there is a tendency for kin homes and familial socialising techniques to represent higher status groups in Continental literature, even though English aristocratic girls were often educated elsewhere.[45] This is the case for the noble Marietta who resides at her family estate. Here, though, she is alone and is supervised by a female chaperone of good repute.[46] In Salter's English context the maiden is similarly guided by an older woman, but there is a new

---

[43] Salter, *Mirrhor of Modestie*, Ciiii^r.
[44] *A Critical Edition of Thomas Salter's The Mirrhor of Modestie*, ed. J. B. Holm (New York, 1987), p. 6.
[45] S. D. Michalove, 'The Education of Aristocratic Women in Fifteenth-Century England', in *Estrangement, Enterprise and Education in Fifteenth-Century England*, ed. S. D. Michalove and A. Compton Reeves (Stroud, 1998), pp. 116–39 (p. 123).
[46] Phiston, *The necessurie, fit, and conuenient education*, C4^r.

and different relationship between the maiden and matron: 'for Matrones to knowe how to traine up suche young Maidens as are committed to their charge and tuission'.[47] It is unclear where this will happen, although there is certainly a strong inference that young girls will receive this training away from their own household. The practice of sending children away from natal families ostensibly stemmed from a concern about over-affectionate parents: 'Prudence, is ouercome and blynded by affection, therefore I thinke it more meete and conuement, for Parents to set their Children forthe to be taught, but under whom? under euery one that beares the name of a teacher'.[48] We can compare this to the affectedly critical views of the Venetian traveller in the late fifteenth century who censured the English practice of sending children into foster care.[49]

The tone of books in terms of status imagery did vary, and in the Bruto/Phiston text clear references to the nobility are retained with the direct naming of Lord Cattaneo and his daughter, as well as sumptuous descriptions of their country garden and estate. The text is peppered with phrases invoking noble connections – 'gentlewoman', 'daughter of noble birth' and 'notable families'. However, audiences of Salter's *Mirrhor* are presented with an expansion of noble interests suiting a middling status audience. In the *Mirrhor*, 'gentlewoman' becomes the simpler and less elite 'Maiden' and Salter avoids naming Lord Cattaneo and Marietta altogether. Salter's engagement with the text through his position as translator suggests that he felt a new English context was necessary to convey English anxieties.[50]

In Salter's translation the behaviour and character of the instructress are specifically portrayed through recognisably female characteristics and charged with distinctly gendered language: 'she ought what so euer she be, to be Graue, Prudent, Modest, and of good counsell, to thende that suche Maidens ... maie learne her honeste and womanlie demeanoure'.[51] Unsurprisingly, this maps a strategy for socialisation tailored to ideal female attributes, emphasised in the discussion of well-trodden female vices which might taint the Maiden: 'if she beyng by Nature of beautifull forme, in deakyyng her self by a Christall *Mirrhor*'.[52] Gendered social networks could be problematic and there was a common fear that young girls formed corrupt habits through

---

[47] Salter, *Mirrhor of Modestie*, Avi^v. Phiston occasionally uses these terms but with a different emphasis.
[48] Salter, *Mirrhor of Modestie*, Aviii^r.
[49] See *Women in England*, ed. Goldberg, pp. 87–8.
[50] The mirror device in literature has been discussed in H. Grabes, *The Mutable Glass: Mirror-Imagery in Titles and Texts of the Middle Ages and English Renaissance*, trans. G. Collier (Cambridge, 1982). Despite this, Vives's book was more commercially successful in England, even though it criticised practices which were popular there, such as dancing. On English practices see Potter, 'Elizabethan Drama', p. 262.
[51] Salter, *Mirrhor of Modestie*, Avii^v.
[52] Salter, *Mirrhor of Modestie*, Avii^v.

association with other women.[53] Gossiping, by no means a petty vice, was also warned against. A misericord at Ely Cathedral (1341–2) depicts Tutivillus, the medieval patron demon of scribes, with two gossiping women. Marjorie McIntosh has compiled records of local authorities prosecuting women (and men) for gossiping and scolding.[54] On the whole, however, these gender-specific definitions are in accord with conventional ideas about female education, disorder and social-domestic activities. Needlework and household duties are encouraged, as are piety and religious obedience. As before, the favoured female virtue of chastity, as well as the related values of modesty, humility and silence, is highly visible and the reader or listener is asked to accept this through constant repetition. Opposing this are 'feminine' sins of pride, opulent dress, vanity, reading inappropriate books and ballads and keeping the company of gossips. There is a sense of worldliness in some of these feminine vices, largely concerning the possession of material items and the coveting of possessions. In terms of a courteous ideology only one passage declares the need for courteous behaviour, as part of a discussion on how a young girl is to interact graciously with people, whether they are from her own estate or lower. However, even this develops into an opportunity for the girl to display virtue: 'to thende that suche seyng her greate courtesie to be commendable, maie by example of her vertue, haue Pride in hate as a moste pernitious euell'.[55]

In both books, and particularly the revised *Mirrhor*, environment is central to understanding how the upbringing of these adolescent women was ideally represented. Both noble and non-noble socialising practices were concerned with women's social interactions even within the 'safe' household. Lessons in both books contain warnings concerning the danger that came from, as Salter says, consorting with 'kitchine Servauntes, or suche idle housewives, as commonly and of custome, doe thruste theim selves into the familiaritie of those of good callyng'.[56] A similar case is made in Phiston's translation, focusing on women who 'haunt the houses of gentlewoman of accou[n]t'.[57] In high status households girls needed to be aware of over-familiarity with personal servants.[58] The *Good Wife* poems have likewise been read as lessons for young girls living away from home, although these poems are more directly associated with the conduct of servants (and possibly daughters)

---

53 Salter, *Mirrhor of Modestie*, Cv^v. On female gendered groups inciting disorder, but also providing mutual support, see B. Capp, 'Separate Domains? Women and Authority in Early Modern England', in *The Experience of Authority in Early Modern England*, ed. P. Griffiths, A. Fox and S. Hindle (New York, 1996), pp. 117–45.
54 McIntosh, *Controlling Misbehaviour*, pp. 58–65.
55 Salter, *Mirrhor of Modestie*, Dii^r.
56 Salter, *Mirrhor of Modestie*, Biiii^r.
57 Phiston, *The necessarie, fit, and conuenient education*, D8^r.
58 Phiston, *The necessarie, fit, and conuenient education*, K4^r.

rather than the fostering or guardianship of young girls from middling status backgrounds.[59]

It would seem from didactic treatises that men were largely absent from these socialising strategies and for most young maidens interaction with other women in a domestic, although not necessarily kin-related, household formed the core of socialising customs. Emulating the mistress or matron is affirmed, while mixing with servants, gossips and idle housewives demonstrated serious errors in judgement. The absence of male figures may be a residual echo from the absent paternal Lord Cattaneo in the original text, yet it is still worth noting that female interaction is encouraged almost exclusively and that the socialisation of girls is represented inside a single-gendered environment. For Salter, and to an extent Phiston, upbringing was better organised by women, although we need to remember that this was a picture filtered through the pen of male writers and translators and that influential men existed in women's lives.[60] Yet writers continued to insist to parents that socialisation was best accomplished when it took place inside female networks, not only for practical reasons, but for their capacity to foster moral character in a young woman.

Continuity and change in sixteenth-century courtesy

The shift in socialising sensibilities was not one all writers shared. It is important to realise that courtesy remained desirable in the socialisation of gentry and merchant children and that young people's cultural values in the sixteenth century were influenced by social norms and customs which stretched back to the literary examples from the early and late medieval periods. It is clear that images of courtesy and service were brought into play in several influential books in this century and we gain a sense of how courtesy and formulaic gestures were introduced to a new generation of children. This provides valuable information on the manner in which customary courtesy themes were interpreted at a time of religious change, when conventional behaviour would have been a safe and reassuring way of guaranteeing new generations were fittingly brought up. The market for books conceivably embraced prominent local families. There is enough evidence that the dispersal of monastic lands occurred with some rapidity after 1536 and that people from the gentry, merchant classes and also royal servants sought to buy property, establishing themselves as secular landlords in the countryside in place of monastic landlords. Overwhelmingly these new owners paid market rates

---

[59] Girls in the Paston family were sent to live in other households, including Elizabeth in 1458, Margery in 1469 and Anne c. 1470. *Paston Letters*, ed. Fenn.
[60] Phillips, *Medieval Maidens*, pp. 76–7.

to the Court of Augmentations for the lands they purchased, meaning they were men of considerable means.[61] They may have been a likely readership for books on gentry manners.

Although in the fifteenth and sixteenth centuries economic and political fluctuations destabilised elite social groups, noble households retained their status as privileged environments, continuing to employ gentle servants and to fashion ideal models of behaviour. Discussing the nobility's position in politics and society, Gerald Harriss has written that while the late medieval aristocracy had to share political leadership, they nevertheless retained their place as economic leaders and presumably as custodians of social niceties, although Harriss is not referring to this aspect of social power.[62] There is no doubt that some aristocratic modes of behaving remained desirable to others, even when elite households no longer operated on the scale they had once enjoyed. While this literature retained some aspects of elite imagery, socialising lessons were increasingly removed from the original context of the elite household and high status service. As we saw with Caxton, English printers tended to retain the word 'courtesy', a point Anna Bryson has made about book culture in the sixteenth century. The inclusion of this single word does not necessarily indicate that 'courtesy' in the sixteenth century was the same 'courtesy' used in the fourteenth and fifteenth centuries. The word needs to be understood as a flexible idea. Equally, these shifts do not necessarily equate to a movement towards 'civility' with its overtones of sociability and citizenship.[63]

One of the characteristic features of courtesy books as opposed to moral household literature is the centrality of domestic service, and more precisely where this service takes place. It is apparent that for two sixteenth-century writers, Francis Seager and Hugh Rhodes, references to young people's training as servants are intended for houses of middling status (for Seager this includes children serving at their parents' table), while elite household characteristics are reduced. Rhodes tries to retain both elements in a confusing arrangement of both domestic and higher status households, a problem which appears to arise from the source material he used (all editions refer to *Stans puer ad mensam* in the title) and which lends his book something of an incoherent quality.[64] Caxton also retained courtesy titles to lend validity to some of his early books.

---

[61] J. Youings, *The Dissolution of the Monasteries* (London, 1971), pp. 129–31.
[62] Harriss, *Shaping the Nation*, p. 94.
[63] Bryson's argument is that English printers were hesitant to embrace the term 'civility' until the seventeenth century, preferring instead the older terms 'courtesy' and 'nurture': *Courtesy to Civility*, pp. 47–8. On civility see Elias, *Civilizing Process*, pp. 47–52. Bryson discusses civility in *Courtesy to Civility*, pp. 70–1.
[64] For example, *boke of nurture*. The book was popular enough to be printed six times in the sixteenth century. The analysis here attempts to account for its popularity. See Appendix C of this book for details on the editions. All references are to the

A shift to a joint parental-courtesy tone is most evident in Seager's book, which grafts a domestic, kin-household perspective onto common courtesy themes. Some aspects of Seager's *The schoole of virtue* notably focus on courtesy values while others correspond more directly to moral issues in discussions about the vices of anger and envy. The chapters which deal with courtesy, however, play on particularly prominent and traditional courtesy tropes: two chapters discuss table manners, while in another there are further references to service and to young people running errands.[65] Obvious mechanisms continued to be used to describe good upbringing and socialisation. At least seventeen practical rules for the child to follow are listed by Rhodes. These include some general injunctions such as flee sin, dread God and avoid pride. However, there is also an emphasis on practical activities. Children are told to rise by six o'clock, wash themselves and brush their clothes. They need to walk with decorum when they go into the town or street. They also need to remember to sit where appointed at the table and to hold their cap in their hands when their master talks to them.

Like earlier courtesy poems Rhodes's book claims that observing conduct was the best way to socialise young boys: gazing at people in the street was frowned upon and the idea of sitting where appointed at the table (as your sovereign watches over you) was still held in regard. Yet, unlike late medieval didactic texts, there is no doubt that parental roles were now more prominent in the literature. Parents are prioritised as readers of the text over children, cited even within the framework of the conventional *Stans puer ad mensam* poem which had once spoken directly to young people. Rhodes begins a passage with references to parents and adults: 'All that hath yonge people good maners let them to lerne ... A good father maketh good chyldre[n]'.[66] This is not the only occasion parents are privileged as an authority in socialising their children. Mothers and fathers are identified both in direct address and in several lines referring to children greeting their parents in the morning. A parental household with dependent children can certainly be recognised within this, but the book would also have been relevant in households where young children were fostered or sent to live, work and learn, as well as those where orphans and poor kin were living with relatives, friends and patrons.[67]

1545 edition unless otherwise noted. In the 1560 and subsequent editions passages on serving a superior are included under 'The maner of seruing a knight, squire, or gentleman' and 'Howe to ordre your maisters chamber, at night to bedwarde'. These are absent from the 1545 edition. Parents are referred to in other passages in all editions.

[65] F. Seager, *The schoole of virtue, and booke of good nourture for chyldren, and youth to learne theyer dutie by. Newely persued, corrected, and augmented by the fyrst auctour. F. S with a briefe declaration of the dutie of eche degree* (London, 1557). These chapters are described in Appendix C of this book. It was published steadily until 1687.

[66] Rhodes, *boke of nurture*, Aiiii^r.

[67] Tarbin discusses arrangements for the care of orphaned or destitute children in

The introductory passage in Rhodes's book has few references to servants of any kind and what are presumably the biological children of the household are initially identified. We do read of household servants in the context of the children of the house – servants and children are paired in terms of how they are to dress appropriately.[68] The presence of household servants is acknowledged as a moral concern: 'And take good hede of any newe seruau[n]tes that ye take in to your house & howe ye put them in any auctorite amonge your chyldren: and what ye gyue them take hede howe they spende it'.[69] What else were parents to do when overseeing their households of children and servants? For the most part parents were told of the importance of fostering a religious creed in the home, and of dressing children and servants modestly so that the sins of pride and obstinacy were not engendered. Parents were also encouraged to monitor where their children went and whom they met.[70] Young people were to help serve food to their parents. Part of these tasks included making sure trenchers and napkins were available and seeing to the delivery and removal of food. Mealtimes also contributed to the daily religious performance of the household and children played important roles in this by reading or reciting prayers.

In the fifteenth and sixteenth centuries, the notion that governors, masters and mistresses were *in loco parentis* to young people who as orphans, destitute children or servants had other living arrangements was a dominant one.[71] Stephanie Tarbin has drawn attention to occasions where people saw this as a proper way to explain their relationships with younger people, citing seven-year-old Joan who was informally adopted by an older widow who promised to raise the child as if she were her own biological daughter.[72] Prolonging the responsibility of parents and masters contributed to the lengthening of childhood in the sixteenth century, with longer periods of socialisation delaying the transition of young people into full adulthood.[73] At the very end of the period analysed in this book, a Church of England clergyman and writer, Robert Shelford, saw responsibility for upbringing firmly placed upon a variety of adult shoulders:

S. Tarbin, 'Caring for the Poor and Fatherless Children in London, *c.* 1350–1550', *Journal of the History of Childhood and Youth* 3 (2010), 391–410.

[68] In Rhodes, *boke of nurture*, Aiii^v. In later editions the portion of the book dealing the most closely with courtesy and good manners is given an additional heading, 'Here foloweth the booke of nurture of good maners for man and childe', from which the title is taken. In later editions 'the book of nurture' appears midway through the book and is bracketed by sections on service not found in the first extant edition.

[69] Rhodes, *boke of nurture*, Aiii^v.

[70] Rhodes, *boke of nurture*, Aiii^r–Aiiii^v.

[71] On this there is *Dives and Pauper*, printed in 1493 by Pynson and J. Dod and R. Cleaver, *A godlie forme of householde gouernement* (London, 1610).

[72] Tarbin, 'Caring for the Poor', p. 400.

[73] Rappaport, *Worlds Within Worlds*, pp. 322–9.

But now because this duty of parents is comunicated to many, as to Rectors of Schooles, to masters of families, to dames, to patrons and guardians, and such like: let all they here understand whosoeuer they be, that haue the gouernment of children or any youth committed to their charge, that they are here bound by the voice of the Almightie, and that they must doe the duetie of parents unto them, as if they were their naturall children[74]

Shelford tactically links these roles to the role of biological parents: 'as if they were their naturall children'. These didactic texts may have reminded people of their duties, perhaps as a result of sensitivity that guardians were not caring for the young people who lived with them.[75] There is a suggestion that Shelford views the array of people now governing malleable youths negatively – 'But now because this duty of parents is communicated to many' – almost as if this were a modern phenomenon to be criticised. He also broadens the concept of adults *in loco parentis* to include any who interact with children.

The contribution different adult figures made to socialising dependent children, as well as the numerous living arrangements represented, were recognised in this literature and contribute to our understanding of medieval and early modern notions of youthful dependency. Parental language was clearly powerful in early modern England.[76] It was also an image adults could use when they desired the veracity and authority of family and parental relationships to govern young people.

While these lessons hint at multiple socialising situations, it was primarily the idealised parent–child dynamic which was entrenched in literature. We can see this when Rhodes sets up the premise of non-working children living in or coming home to a domestic household. At a recreational level there are even indications of some of the activities available to children from relatively prosperous homes, and sports and games are encouraged while children are warned not to read 'fayned fables, or vayne fantasies'.[77] There is also an expectation concerning formal educational opportunities: 'yf ye put them to scole awaye frome you, se ye put them to a dyscrete mayster'.[78] This could account for the presence of 'governors' within the book's lessons if the

---

[74] R. Shelford, *Lectvres or readings vpon the 6. verse of the 22. chapter of the Prouerbs, concerning the vertuous education of youth: a treatise very necessary for all parents in this corrupt and declining age of the world* (London, 1596), p. 8. The book was reprinted twice.

[75] Servants and apprentices were often at risk from their masters. The Court of Chancery heard cases in which young apprentices alleged neglect and failure to honour contracts on the part of their masters. For example, see TNA C1/998/41, TNA C2/Eliz/C11/10 and TNA C2/Eliz/C20/15. Of course, masters just as often sued their apprentices for theft, misbehaviour and absenteeism.

[76] Amussen, *An Ordered Society*, pp. 38–47, 54–66.

[77] Rhodes, *boke of nurture*, Aiii^v.

[78] Rhodes, *boke of nurture*, Aiii^r. The mention of formal education, the type of activities the servants are expected to perform and the comment 'To help a preest to say

term is read in a strictly educational sense. Addressing recreational activities – sports, games and reading fables – and referring to formal schooling are consistent with Rhodes speaking to an audience above subsistence level, probably responding to the interests of families from the middling and lower ranks of society. Both Seager's and Rhodes's books were in steady publication throughout the sixteenth century, representing significant continuity in the available literature relevant to manners and conduct. This is valuable evidence that books reflecting practical manners and behaviour, mixed with a little morality, remained viable publishing ventures in England.

Writers themselves sometimes seem confused about how to cope with different households in terms of socialising lessons. Pragmatic working considerations are one of the ways they accommodated the reality of different class-based households, balancing high status domestic service in courtesy poems with middling and artisanal class households. Rhodes is willing to acknowledge the potential range and diversity of households where young people might ultimately find work: 'if your soueraigne be a knight or squier set downe your dishes couered and your cup also'.[79] This is far removed from the large elaborate households identified and idealised in elite clusters of literature, even when, as we know, the latter was being read by families from the merchant and gentry classes. This can also be contrasted to Russell's *Boke of Nurture* which played upon elite associations even when professional work was outlined. The once all-too-familiar high status household is supplanted – the lessons are on how to serve groups who are part of the gentry classes, including knights, esquires and gentleman, although these classes still did not explicitly include yeoman and artisan groups.[80] Rhodes also advises young servants on what to do if any more than one or two courses are served at dinner, suggestive of households where the three-course meal was not served as the norm, but where such pretensions to gentility might be of interest and used occasionally.[81]

This is not to say that important continuities did not remain between these lessons and older ones. Directions regarding the behaviour of children and youths at mealtimes reveal anxieties about the practical moment of consuming food – anxieties exacerbated, once again, by the observable and public nature of this communal activity. It remained important to break bread off with a knife and not to tear it, not to gnaw at meat bones and to

---

masse / it is greatly to be co[m]mended' are all pertinent to boys and not to girls: Aiiii^v.

[79] From the 1560 edition of Hugh Rhodes, *The boke of nurture for men seruauntes, and children, with Stans puer ad mensam, newelye corrected, virye vtyle and necessarye unto all youth*, Aiii^v.

[80] In the 1560 and subsequent editions. Rhodes, *boke of nurture* (1560), Aii^v.

[81] Rhodes, *boke of nurture* (1560), Aii^v. On the order of messes in households by the fifteenth century see Woolgar, *Great Household*, p. 159.

wipe fingers clean on a napkin. Given the communal nature of dining and the arrangement of food on large platters from which people took individual portions, these lessons (particularly concerning greediness) made practical sense and betrayed awareness about how one person's conduct impacted upon others. These precepts were based upon the symbolism of gestures and like earlier courtesy literature situated observable manners at the forefront of youthful socialisation.

The nature of courtesy was not, however, restricted to its social value. Shelford wrote of social lessons in terms of deeper, religious values. For example, piety could now be incorporated into polite behaviours, equated with standing to greet elders, taking your hat off and behaving well towards others. These were simple but symbolically and socially important gestures and they were made substantially more influential than they might otherwise have been. Shelford makes a clear point about the means by which these manners were different from superficial courteous behaviour and court conduct: 'Wherein I minde not to trouble you with courte fashions, and new fangles, and toyes of curious heades; but onely to teach such nourture and seemely behauiour, as Gods word commendeth'.[82] There is also a wonderful reference to French manners: 'but if it bee toyish, new-fangled, or french-like, it hath no warrant out of Gods worde'.[83] It is overly simplistic to suggest that the aristocracy and court-based French culture were seen as lacking moral character while middling class conduct represented morality. However, it does seem that the distance between court behaviour, and by implication the conduct of the aristocracy and peerage, and pious and more genuine good conduct was articulated in contemporary commentary.[84] The position the aristocracy found themselves in with regard to their moral character is raised again later in this chapter.

Good manners could also be promoted as important acts in themselves, even when they were linked to Christian values. Shelford's commentary on love binding all behaviour serves to remind us that the exchange between outward conduct and inner intent was still ambiguous at the end of the sixteenth century:

> Without this all our curtesies & manners are but shadowes of curtesies and pictures of manners, and there is no more life in them then is in a dead carkasse: but if thy curtesie commeth from a loving and willing minde, it moueth all men, and stirreth up others to renderthe like dutie againe[85]

---

[82] Shelford, *Lectvres*, p. 43.
[83] Shelford, *Lectvres*, pp. 57–8.
[84] Antony Taylor summarises anti- and pro-aristocratic sentiment in *Lords of Misrule: Hostility to Aristocracy in Late Nineteenth- and early Twentieth-Century Britain* (Basingstoke, 2004), pp. 1–16.
[85] Shelford, *Lectvres*, p. 58.

Were these the 'shadowes of curtesies' privileged in earlier courtesy verses and even within Rhodes's and Seager's books? Shelford himself understood that there was a variety of semi-religious meanings in behaviour; his commentary on surface conduct, which was identified with 'court' behaviour and with French culture, contrasts with more 'natural' courteous manners.

Shelford in fact reused strategies from the courtesy narrative to identify the importance of social behaviour but with a new sense of influence which blends religion with behaviour more keenly. The connection between social actions and religious values in a contemporary context is seen when he refers to the English practice of removing headgear. While this was not a social custom mentioned in the Bible, it is such an important social ritual in England that God surely would approve:

> The sixt duetie, is to uncouer the head. And though wee finde no example for this in holy Scripture, as being not used in those former times: yet seeing the thing is ciuill and comely, & one of the speciall curtesies of our daies, we will confirme it also with the authoritie of Gods word Phil 4. *What soeuer things are honest, what soeuer things are of good report, those things due.* And againe, 1 Cor. 14. *Let all things be done decently and according to order.* But this kind of ciuilitie is both decent and according to order, as also honest and of good report & therefore warranted and commended by Gods word, and so worthie to bee followed[86]

It is worth pointing out that the reiteration of social hierarchy remains a common feature in socialisation and is one of the core principles adapted to the new medium of moral instruction, retaining its place in the elite as well as the smaller family household. While Shelford does not neglect courteous manners, or perhaps what he would have called 'honourable' manners, there is a strong subordination of these values to religious concerns. This indicates that rules for conduct and behaviour were partially separated out of some instructional texts, just as they were incorporated into others, often in thought-provoking new ways, by religious writers.

What can we make of youthful socialisation when it so deliberately attempted to include two different household environments – on the one hand the kin-focused domestic home complete with parents, but on the other a return to an older courtesy tradition of young people in service? The self-consciously referential tone of many of these books, heightened by Rhodes's explicit declaration that *Stans puer ad mensam* is 'newly corrected', is suggestive of a self-conscious appropriation of traditional courtesy narratives and a desire to indicate a continuity with older texts. To an extent we need to be aware that the guidelines on service are out of place in a text that begins with the everyday behaviour of children and youths in kin or small homes. It is the duplication of common socialising lessons which circumvents potential fric-

---

[86] Shelford, *Lectvres*, p. 57. It also showed respect for the social hierarchy.

tion. Cultural affinities and experiences for young people were thus shared across kin and non-kin households. The 'family' information contains the same type of subject matter about manners and proper behaviour as appears in passages for young servants. The two household settings are thus not at odds in terms of the socialising lessons directed at young people. We can also read this as suggesting that age rather than status exerted considerable influence. Young servants and children were expected to demonstrate similar (although not identical) qualities because of their age and life inexperience, with socialising lessons playing upon their imagined propensity to misbehave. The relationship between courtesy and virtue extended many of these books' relevance and perhaps at the same time the relevance of courtesy to sixteenth-century readers. Rhodes and Seager present their discourses on youthful upbringing with an adept hand, preserving the authority and status that courtesy had but regulating them through an understanding of parental authority and the family home.

In several respects writers such as Seager, Rhodes and Shelford were in the process of shoring up older ideas about courtesy and showing them to be important in the sixteenth century. They created stability in what was an often unstable world. The injection of good manners into the debate on upbringing and religious observance (and vice versa) exposes a continuing preoccupation with formal behaviour and the desire to retain a coherent set of mannerly actions that defined 'good' conduct. The ongoing popularity of these beliefs, running parallel and sometimes in conjunction with moral and religious literature, is noticeable in the revival of what is essentially a 'courtesy' genre in the sixteenth century. The unquestionably prolific publication of Rhodes's and Seager's books suggests that parents and authority figures were attracted to the values of mannerly behaviour and believed in having consistent definitions for conduct that described well-behaved children and young people, sometimes in the home, sometimes in public or sometimes as servants. The often dramatic religious changes in the sixteenth century would also have influenced the desire for conservative and orthodox values.

At first glance there are intriguing parallels between the sixteenth century and the eighteenth century, which saw shifts in the concepts of politeness, sensibility and finally etiquette; however, there are key differences in the sixteenth century's rhetoric on manners and morality. Society's views on manners and virtue in the eighteenth century incorporated not only Christian ethics but also an awareness of a 'natural' desire to socialise with other human beings – in other words, we are describing Addison's 'Sociable Animal'.[87] What is apparent in the sixteenth century is not Addison's take on moral character. Rather it is Shelford's paradigm, equating personal character

---

[87] J. Addison, *Spectator* 9 (10 March 1711) quoted in E. A. Bloom and L. D. Bloom, *Joseph Addison's Sociable Animal: In the Market Place, on the Hustings, in the Pulpit* (Providence, 1971), pp. 4–5.

with religious principles, that serves to explain the manner in which sociability was viewed at this time. The shifts and balances occurring between these moral and mannerly standards are a reminder that codes of behaviour, and the dominant ideologies on which they were based, were continuously fluctuating and flexible.[88] This literature never fixed or settled upon a single concept of behaviour or code of conduct for children but echoed variant ideologies and principles which modified, supplanted, superseded and even reinforced different messages at different moments.

The religious household

The family and the kin household became the central platforms in socialising lessons from the late fifteenth and very early sixteenth centuries, long before puritan writers would take their pens to the combined issues of family life, marital relationships and social order.[89] Family life in this literature was constructed partly through the relatively simple repetition of the word 'household' as well as through sensitive descriptions of household activities, with a clear sense that this was now a fully realised physical environment, anchoring socialising lessons to a specific and singular location. In other words, readers were invited to the idea that proper socialisation could take place through family activities and interactions. Family audiences would have been sensitive to their own households in the discussions about specific prayers they could recite upon rising and before and during meals. It is evident that this literature presented readers with activities that could be easily replicated in their own homes. This evidence also raises the important question of religious values in social norms and customs for young people.

Although the increase in English vernacular reading (and writing) literacy in the fifteenth and sixteenth centuries was uneven and varied according to occupation and social status, reading literacy contributed to the extension of religious teaching into the lay household.[90] It is not the case that religious lessons were separated from social lessons in literature. Throughout the

---

[88] Children's literature in eighteenth-century revolutionary France likewise suggested a cyclical interest in courtesy, at a time of broader political and social developments. See for instance, Higonnet, 'Civility Books', p. 131.

[89] For example, H. Smith, *A preparative to marriage* (London, 1591); Dod and Cleaver, *A godlie forme of householde gouernement*; W. Gouge, *Of domesticall duties* (London, 1622). K. M. Davis, 'The Sacred Condition of Equality – How Original were Puritan Doctrines of Marriage?', *Social History* 5 (1977), 563–80. Humanist writers had provided early precedents for this. M. Todd, 'Humanists, Puritans and the Spiritualized Household', *Church History* 49 (1980), 18–34.

[90] E. Duffy, *The Stripping of the Altars: Traditional Religion in England, 1400–1580* (New Haven, 1992), pp. 68–87; D. Cressy, *Literacy and the Social Order: Reading and Writing in Tudor and Stuart England* (Cambridge, 1980), p. 3.

sixteenth century there was acceleration in the development of this religious and social literature, progressing alongside printed sermons which gained popularity in the late sixteenth and seventeenth centuries in England. Both of these genres were printed at a time of religious disruption on the Continent and in England, when familiar and established Catholic devotional practices and beliefs were slowly supplanted by Protestant ideologies.[91] At the level of childhood social norms and customs these books would have been of service to householders and parents confused by changing religious standards.

Modifications between Catholic and Protestant texts were one way writers and printers accommodated developing Church beliefs, but the changes could be somewhat mechanical, as is seen in Seager's book whose later editions included minor alterations from the original (printed in 1557 during Mary I's reign): the 1582 and 1593 editions included new prayers and graces for Elizabeth I and her government. Although the 1557 edition does begin with a prayer to use in the morning and describes how to behave in Church, in both cases the advice is general and Seager avoids mentioning the Catholic mass. Later editions were responsive to a distinct political and religious climate, with added passages by Seager and Robert Crowley (Church of England clergyman and also a poet and printer) working in references to Elizabeth. Given Seager's and Crowley's Protestant beliefs, the overt support of Elizabeth's reign is not surprising. A similar and very simple Catholic to Protestant doctoring appears in Rhodes's book, where directions concerning the priest and helping at mass were removed from later editions to reflect changes in official policy regarding the celebration of the Catholic mass.[92] While writers like Seager and Crowley held deep religious, and specifically Protestant, beliefs, many people, including printers, may have felt it expedient to conform to required expectations, adopting an adaptable strategy to cope with changing demands.[93]

Protestantism might have been the 'religion of the Word' but Catholicism was also interested in lay devotional practices. A culture of writing about and for the household preceded Protestant books of instruction, most memorably with the volume for which Richard Whitford is best known, *A werke for*

---

[91] On the extensive sermon tradition see G. R. Owst, *Preaching in Mediaeval England: An introduction to Sermon Manuscripts of the Period c.1350–1450* (Cambridge, 1926); G. R. Owst, *Literature and Pulpit in Medieval England: A Neglected Chapter in the History of English Letters and of the English people*, 2nd edn (Oxford, 1961); S. Volk-Birke, *Chaucer and Medieval Preaching: Rhetoric for Listeners in Sermons and Poetry* (Tübingen, 1991); H. Leith Spencer, *English Preaching in the Late Middle Ages* (Oxford, 1993).

[92] For how word changes in Cranmer's 1548 catechism are important see P. Tudor, 'Religious Instruction for Children and Adolescents in the Early English Reformation', *Journal of Ecclesiastical History* 35 (1984), 391–413 (p. 408).

[93] E. H. Shagan, *Popular Politics and the English Reformation* (Cambridge, 2003), p. 306.

housholders, described as 'the devotional best-seller of the 1530s'.[94] This book is indicative of a Catholic writer's pursuit of the lay household as an audience for literature about internalised religious experiences and social duties. While Whitford may have had no personal experience of the type of household life he writes about so evocatively, he was exceptionally well qualified to speak as a spiritual guardian for both the religious and lay members of the Catholic community, being a lay brother of the Bridgettine Order at Syon Abbey, Middlesex, a community well known for its intellectual scholarship and extensive library, as well as for the literary careers of its members.[95]

The 1531 edition of Whitford's book includes Catholic commentaries, passages on the beatitudes, the saints, the collects and occasional prayers for the day. Religious lessons reinforce the emphasis on the lay household as a religious environment and point to a robust understanding of lay spiritual values for individuals in Catholic households. In these terms, Whitford directs the text to the attention of 'housholders' or to any who are responsible for the governance of others. It is clear that 'householder' can be seen as an alternative to 'father', addressed earlier in terms of adults who stood *in loco parentis* to young people. This is partly based on the assumption that the 'father' will monitor his own character before turning to others:

> Howe be it we thynke it nat sufficie[n]t nor ynough for you to lyue well your selfe but that all other christians also lyue the better for you and by your example and specially those that you haue in charge & gouernaunce that is to say: your chylder and seruauntes[96]

The reality of social and economic pressures, deaths and blended families meant this ideal was not one which was relevant to every household. Instructional writers paid no heed to elements outside this perfect household group.

---

[94] R. Whitford, *The conte[n]tes of this boke. A werke of preparacion, or of ordinaunce vnto co[m]munion, or howselyng. The werke for houcholders with the golden pistle and alphabete or a crosrowe called an A.B.C. all duely corrected and newly prynted* (London, 1531). Parts of this book were printed in *A werke for houshoulders*, various editions between 1530 and 1537. See Appendix C of this book for details. The inclusion of multiple texts makes the 1531 edition particularly noteworthy and it is this edition which will be discussed in this chapter. On the book's popularity see J. T. Rhodes, 'Whitford, Richard (d. 1543?)', *DNB*. See also A. Walsham, '"Domme Preachers"? Post-Reformation English Catholicism and the Culture of Print', *Past and Present* 168 (2000), 72–123.

[95] On Syon see 'Religious Houses: House of Bridgettines', in *A History of the County of Middlesex*, ed. J. S. Cockburn, H. P. F. King and K. G. T. McDonnell, 13 vols. (London, 1969), I, 182–91; J. Hogg, 'Richard Whytford, A Forgotten Spiritual Guide', *Studies in Spirituality* 15 (2005), 129–42; J. T. Rhodes, 'Syon Abbey and its Religious Publications in the Sixteenth Century', *Journal of Ecclesiastical History* 44 (1993), 11–25. Several useful chapters are in *Syon Abbey and its Books: Reading, Writing and Religion c. 1400–1700*, ed. E. A. Jones and A. Walsham (Woodbridge, 2010).

[96] Whitford, *The werke for housholders*, B^r.

Households headed by widows, single people or those who rented rooms within a property are largely rendered invisible in didactic material.

The obligation of parents to supplement religious instruction had been defined in a thirteenth-century religious statute.[97] Whitford wrote of parents teaching children how to say their prayers, cross themselves in the morning and know the Creed and Saints through rote learning: 'Than must you teche them to knowe by ordre the preceptes or comaundementes of god the names of the vii. princypall synnes and of theyr v. wyttes'.[98] If we look forward several decades to 1547 we can see the reappearance of this in Edward VI's injunction which confirmed that parents were to teach their children and servants the Pater Noster, the Creed and the Ten Commandments in English, reinforcing the efforts made by parish priests in providing instruction in these same prayers.[99]

In an age when people engaged with literacy in assorted ways books in vernacular English would have appealed to a broad audience. Whitford's preface to the Epistle of St Bernard (the 'Golden Epistle') was purportedly written in English 'to the encrease of the deuotio[n] of them that can rede Englishe and understande not latyn tonge'.[100] A sense of who Whitford is writing for is established through his explicit endorsement of a non-Latinate, lay readership. Alphabet books, or ABCs, were also intended to provide dual religious and social lessons and the relationship between ABCs and children is obvious, although not exclusive.[101] These lessons were always brief and simple and related to basic religious principles. Whitford's example of 'many prety and devoute lesons set forth by saynt Bonauenture after the order of the Alphabete',[102] for example, provides guidance on (D)iligence, (M)ercy, (P)leasure and (S)obriety. Whitford's statement at the end of the ABC – 'Let euery feythfull persone wryte this Alphabete A.B.C or crosrowe: in the boke of his hert as in the boke of lyfe. And euery daye by day: loke there upon

---

[97] 'Because parents are perilously negligent about this matter, they are advised that they should instruct their children and their household in these things, just as God will have inspired them.' Richard Poore, Salisbury Statutes I, *Councils and Synods II*, I, 61, in Spencer, *English Preaching*, pp. 210–11, 445.

[98] Whitford, *The werke for housholders*, Bvi^v – Bvii^r.

[99] *Tudor Royal Proclamations*, ed. P. I. Hughes and J. F. Larkin, 3 vols. (New Haven, 1964), I, 394.

[100] Whitford, *The werke for housholders*, Bii^v.

[101] On their religious and devotional roles see Orme, *Medieval Children*, pp. 246–54. In 1552, Richard Huloet's dictionary, *Abcedarium anglico latinum*, included 'ABC' as an identifiable term: 'A.B.C. a boke for chylderne, so called Abcedaerium'. Thomas Fuller gave a contemporary assessment of ABCs when he wrote 'many who had one foot in their grave, had their hand on their primer'. See R. Huloet, *Abcedarium anglico latinum, pro tyrunculis Richardo Huloeto exscriptore* (London, 1552), Ai^r and T. Fuller, *The Worthies of England: Edited with an Introduction and Notes by John Freeman* (London, 1952), p. 55.

[102] Whitford, *The werke for housholders*, Ivii^r.

and use the maners and effecte conteyned in the same'[103] – was taken literally by one owner. The copy now held at Cambridge University Library has the alphabet written by hand after this, followed by 'est amen'.[104] The usefulness of ABCs to various ages, as well as to those at different stages of learning, would, of course, sit well with a family audience, with children of various ages living within the household.

Not all clerics saw an automatic connection between instructing children and pastoral care, despite preparation for the communion being a core duty of the Church. The thirteenth- century pastoral syllabus of Archbishop Pecham was confirmed in the mid-fifteenth and early sixteenth centuries and identified a cycle of quarterly instruction in the Pater Noster and Ave, the Creed, the Ten Commandments, the seven sins and five wits and possibly the seven works of mercy.[105] The requirement for children to learn the basic elements of faith, as taught by priests, was equally adopted. Robert Shelford, however, thought that churchman should be excluded from supervising children as their duties lay with instructing parents. At odds with older religious statutes, this also contradicts contemporary ecclesiastical records which document the extensive role clerics played in youthful instruction. This took the form of teaching the catechism as well as the alphabet and other simple lessons. Certificates for pensioners of Chaddesley Corbet in Worcestershire (1548) reveal that there was a 'preste that did use to teache children'.[106] In the chantry certificates of Blisworth, Northamptonshire, for the same year the priest was also 'to be a schole m[r] to teache a free schole there';[107] the documents reveal that thirty scholars received their education from him. When the chantries were dissolved under Edward VI many of the educational interests of the ordained clergy were taken over by schoolmasters. However, there was considerable overlap between these two groups: the canon of 1604 states that the local curate was to be given priority in taking the position of local schoolmaster.[108]

The idea of communal literacy has changed how we think about the nature of literacy and the use of texts in an aural way. Brian Stock uses the term 'textual communities' to refer to these groups.[109] At a local parish level one

---

[103] Whitford, *The werke for housholders*, Kvii^v.
[104] Cambridge University Library, Syn. 8. 53. 35, Kviii^r. It is not possible to tell if this was the work of a young child, an adolescent or an adult. It was common for books to be used as paper for 'practice' lettering, often beginning with writing the alphabet.
[105] These are described in Spencer, *English Preaching*, pp. 196–227.
[106] TNA, E 301/61/17.
[107] TNA, E 301/35/31.
[108] *Synodalia: A Collection of Articles of Religion, Canons, and Proceedings of Convocations in the Province of Canterbury, From the year 1547 to the year 1717: With Notes Historical and Explanatory by Edward Cardwell*, ed. E. Cardwell, 2 vols. (Oxford, 1842), I, 291.
[109] B. Stock, *The Implications of Literacy: Written Language and Models of Interpretation in*

literate person could affect the whole community by guaranteeing access to books and texts. Whitford exposes how communal literacy was integral to a religious and moral programme of work, simultaneously combining his religious message with reading networks that existed in households and neighbourhoods. Those who could read could gather people to hear lessons found in good English books; particularly important were those lessons which took the form of learning the Pater Noster, the Ave Maria and the Creed, which were the essential building blocks of lay religion. Specific passages reveal that young people clearly formed a part of this audience. Young people were immersed in local communities and in the fashioning of moral responsibility. Unlike some courtesy narratives, often aimed at adolescent boys, which imply a reasonable degree of mental sophistication, these religious and moral lessons were seen as necessary for every age and gender: 'Unto some craftes or occupacions a certayne age is required in chylder but vertue and vyce may be lerned in euery age.'[110] We have seen that the formation of a virtuous identity, first in infancy, was of paramount importance to medieval and early modern writers and resonated throughout life stages. Vives himself suggests character could be formed from infancy, long before the stages of speech and cognitive thought. The community was also involved in this process. Young people were a legitimate part of religious networks, neither marginalised nor separated from adult community contacts and responsibilities.[111] These texts emphasise how moral socialisation was understood in terms to do with the interests not only of the family but also of the nation and the religious community. On the whole, courtesy texts did not use language which implied a similar national interest in young people or in upbringing.

Manners at the close of the sixteenth century

The unease Shelford had with 'court' manners reveals a correlation between upper-class manners, which were influenced by Continental fashions (a topic easily targeted by moralists), and an absence of authentic virtuous morality. William Vaughan, a writer who was part of the Welsh landed gentry with connections to parliament and to the royal family through his brother (later made earl of Carbery), identified the elite classes with a need for stronger virtuous conduct. Moral reformers perceived the nobility to be lagging behind in the prioritisation of virtue and ethics. Reformers such as Vaughan viewed truly virtuous behaviour and chivalry – in the uncorrupted sense of fighting for just causes, mercy and so forth – as failing to be instilled in young gentlemen and aristocratic youth. Many of the texts which have

---

the Eleventh and Twelfth Centuries (Princeton, 1983).
[110] Whitford, *The werke for housholders*, Bii^r.
[111] S. Brigden, 'Youth and the English Reformation', *Past and Present* 95 (1982), 37–67.

Sixteenth-Century Books

been discussed in this chapter indicate that moral issues were increasingly promoted and accessible to other classes. When John Locke discussed interior and exterior behaviour in *Some Thoughts Concerning Education* (1693), he was writing for the gentry, although his focus on moral identity made the work suitable for all individuals.[112]

The close of the sixteenth century saw the end of the great household and by extension the end of hospitality on a large scale, with the nobility finding different avenues for spending capital.[113] Vaughan offers insights into this from the perspective of a contemporary observer, albeit one with an agenda of decrying the current state of social decay. Vaughan confirms that noble and rich men now spent their money on other pursuits, citing their preoccupation with buying costly clothes, living in London or abroad, as well as the disintegration of local neighbourhood ties.[114] The ease of travel to London and the movement of many gentry away from their native areas towards larger cities, attracted by commerce and merchant opportunities, could explain this breakdown of community ties at a local level which led to the termination of hospitable bonds.[115] One issue specifically raised by Vaughan is the cost of building new stately homes, tying up money in expensive projects which diverted economic resources away from charity and hospitality.[116] During Elizabeth I's reign, the construction of elaborate houses for the elite classes mostly stopped, with newly rich merchants and the gentry instead taking up the reins of construction. This was often achieved through the purchase of lands and goods formerly belonging to religious houses. These new houses showed all of the trappings of wealth and prosperity in overt displays designed to match elite houses of old. Vaughan may have been uncomfortable and uneasy with increasing merchant and bourgeois wealth.[117]

Vaughan is preoccupied with the conduct of young gentlemen, a social group he very carefully distinguishes as different from the 'Commanaltie'.

---

[112] Carter, 'Polite "Persons"', pp. 336–7.
[113] Woolgar, *Great Household*, p. 204.
[114] W. Vaughan, *The golden-groue, moralized in three bookes: a worke very necessary for all such, as would know how to gouerne themselues, their houses, or their countrey. Made by W. Vaughan, Master of Artes, and student in the ciuill law* (London, 1600). Second Book, Chapter 26.
[115] Although some wills of affluent London merchants record charitable bequests to native parishes, suggesting these ties were not broken. For example, Thomas Jenyns, Thomas Thomlynson and Cuthbert Buckle all left money to their native parishes. John Watson left money to Clyf Chapel in the parish of North Cave, Yorkshire 'where he went sometime to school'. *Calendar of Wills Proved and Enrolled in the Court of Husting, London: Part 2: 1358–1688*, ed. R. R. Sharpe, 2 vols. (London, 1890), pp. 634–51.
[116] Vaughan, *The golden-groue*, Second Book, Chapter 26.
[117] M. Girouard, *Robert Smythson and the Elizabethan Country House*, rev. edn (New Haven, 1983), pp. 4–5; J. Summerson, *Architecture in Britain, 1530–1830* (Harmondsworth, 1953).

His method of stratifying social classes tells us something about the manner in which early modern society was organised, with peers, knights, esquires, lawyers and, now, those with university degrees called 'gentlemen'. The 'Commanaltie' included citizens, artificers, merchants and yeomen. Tellingly, the term 'gentleman' is one he uses synonymously with 'youth'. The gentlemanly classes were required to demonstrate virtue as a core aspect of their character. This ideal of gentlemanly behaviour was identified with certain characteristics, including affability and courteous speech, the willingness to fight for just causes (as indicated above) and generosity. This echoes older courtesy narratives where elite conduct was demonstrated through some of these behaviours; chivalry and generosity were associated specifically with hospitality. Vaughan writes of corruption, poor schoolmasters, lack of parental interest in children (parents are instead preoccupied with mindless acquisition and material gain) and, conversely, the over-affection and indulgence of fathers and mothers as leading to decay in these qualities. Salter suggested similar problems in the *Mirrhor of Modestie*. Vaughan also links a lack of interest in virtuous behaviour to extravagantly elite lifestyles.[118] He goes on to point out that gentlemen who fail to demonstrate virtue 'deserueth but the title of a clowne, or of a countrie boore'.[119] This is reminiscent of traditional courtesy themes, although Vaughan cites a new figure who now represented churlishness, the 'countrie boore'. The interest in being seen as part of the gentlemanly estate in the sixteenth century and the increasing proportion of people who identified themselves as 'gentlemen' account for Vaughan's concern with the status of some country figures – Vaughan may have been thinking of rural squires when he wrote this. The rapidity of the dispersal of monastic lands, with over fifty per cent of religious estates sold by the end of Henry VIII's reign, had helped the pace at which secular landlords in the countryside were drawn from London's affluent classes, or otherwise helped launch provincial families who selectively purchased monastic lands and in so doing raised their local profile.[120]

The ancient practice of hospitality remained important in elite lifestyles as it had in courtesy poems and in chivalric literature. Vaughan encouraged the practice of hospitality, 'the chiefest point of humanity',[121] but decried its corruption by some rich men who focused only on the superficial elements of elaborate feasting and the preparation of exclusive foods. Ironically this was the point much of the earlier literature had highlighted. While hospitality was valuable as a public gesture towards others, it was also related to

---

[118] Vaughan, *The golden-groue*, Third Book, Chapter 33.
[119] Vaughan, *The golden-groue*, Third Book, Chapter 15.
[120] Youings, *The Dissolution of the Monasteries*, pp. 117–18; G. Williams, 'The Dissolution of the Monasteries', in *The Agrarian History of England and Wales: Volume 4, 1500–1640*, ed. J. Thirsk, (Cambridge, 1967), pp. 383–87.
[121] Vaughan, *The golden-groue*, Second Book, Chapter 24.

honour and public shame, revealing someone's generosity or lack thereof in extensive cycles of give and take.[122] Vaughan overtly reflected on that 'which an housholder ca[n] shew, not only vnto his frie[n]ds, but also vnto straungers & way-faring men'.[123] However, he writes of hospitality in a way that is significantly different from courtesy narratives or even romances and chivalric tales, harking back to the medieval seven works of mercy: 'Good hospitality therefore consisteth not in gluttonous diuersities, but rather in one kind of meat, in clothing the naked, and in giuing almes vnto the poore'.[124] This emphasis is very different from earlier courtesy poems, where even if charitable giving was acknowledged as the core function of hospitality, it was the public lavishness and pomp of the event, as well as the proper order of behaviour, which generated the most concern.

Vaughan explicitly concerns himself with the interests of an elite audience and privileges the finer thoughts and feelings of his own class. He returns us to the contexts first identified in courtesy literature. However, there is a distinctly different emphasis on manners and upbringing in this text. To an extent, many of these differences are accounted for in terms of particular audiences: sons living at home as opposed to gentle servants and family environments as opposed to large non-kin households. Vaughan's book, however, also indicates a different theoretical framework for elite upbringing which acknowledged the importance of virtue in elite social norms and character. Perhaps most striking was Vaughan's belief that the lack of virtue in early modern elite society was of concern. This may simply be a narrative conceit and a way of focusing on the poor state of the day's youth (a perennial topic for conservative writers); however, it is suggestive of a more direct attack on the specifics of elite upbringing and a real acknowledgement of the deficiency in and lack of attention paid to virtue within elite social groups.

In this chapter we have seen the development of a new perspective on socialisation and upbringing, anticipating readerships within the smaller kin household and projecting the parental voice into this. Can we imagine parents eagerly reading these texts to learn how to bring up their children and can we see these strategies as anything more than idealistic representations of learned authors? We can never be sure just how these texts were read, or even by whom, beyond the reconstruction of audiences based on thematic interests, book prices and print-runs. There is strong evidence, however, of books deliberately addressing multiple, class-based reading networks. We can also note that the ideological concerns expressed by these authors had commercial merit. Additionally we can see that some of the elements

---

122 Kerr, 'Open Door', pp. 322–35.
123 Vaughan, *The golden-groue*, Second Book, Chapter 24.
124 Vaughan, *The golden-groue*, Second Book, Chapter 24. Vaughan's definition of hospitality encompassed the good works prescribed by Matthew 25. 34–6.

visited in this literature, namely the awareness of the kin-family household and the responsibilities of male householders, are borne out in legal and religious sources, matching preoccupations expressed by contemporaries elsewhere. More importantly, these literary models were indicators of prevailing trends and fashions for people, especially parents, indicating as they did an ideal world not bound by bureaucracy or mediated by pragmatic realities. These ideal worlds, populated by ideal children and their parents in model family households, revealed highly desirable qualities to their readers. These concerns were, however, constrained by the strong commercial interests of printers and authors and were often set within identifiably realistic contexts, lending them a valuable credibility.

The books examined in this chapter demonstrate both remarkable change and continuity in the manner in which children's upbringing was understood and conceptualised by contemporary authors and translators, often being written within periods of religious ferment. As before, the socialisation of girls took moral parameters into consideration and emphasised moral behaviour as vital in development. At the same time, these concerns were increasingly part of the literature aimed at boys. Young boys and men were instructed in the manner in which they should develop a moral identity, with this question increasingly raised and emphasised for parents. These moral concerns reflected developments taking place in English society, particularly in household networks, religious education and family groups. The small domestic household was increasingly spoken of in literary sources as an environment germane to the good and proper upbringing of children, with the preoccupations of parents privileged within narratives. This led to the previously dominant voice of children in earlier courtesy poems being drowned out by the voice of parents.

This literature maps an increasing interest in moral concerns as essential for both boys and girls, and one which was not always viewed as relevant to elite interests or affairs. But what of manners and courtesy in upbringing in this century? If moral and ethical narratives were represented in the printed record, courtesy too found its place within youthful socialisation. The value of this literature lies in identifying trends and patterns promoted over time that indicate and reflect new emphases in what was seen as important in socialisation, based on religious uncertainties and changing social contexts. In the following chapter these trends will be considered in relation to childhood socialisation in one other arena: the educational institution.

CHAPTER FIVE

The School

'For education properly, is nothing else but a bringing vp of youth in virtue'[1]

In 1502–3, Sir John Percyvale's will revealed the manner in which the endowment of the grammar school in Macclesfield, Cheshire, was to have a long-term socialising effect on scholars 'whose lernyng and bryngyng forth in Conyng and vertue right fewe Techers and scolemaisters been in that Contre whereby many Children for lak of such techyng & draught in conyng fall to Idlenes And so consequently live disolately all their daies'.[2] His sentiments reflect a commonplace desire among pedagogues, moralising adults and parents that the educational curriculum instil social, moral as well as educational skills in young people.

These sentiments are found in educational institutions elsewhere in pre-Reformation England. The almoner of the almonry and grammar school of St Albans, Hertfordshire, perceived his duties as including the promotion of appropriate table manners: 'He usually also, for the sake of good manners, not because he is obliged to do so, maintains table-cloths and napkins for the boys' and servants' table there.'[3] The similarity of these rules to the lessons found in courtesy poems reflects the importance of fashioning an environment, and particularly an elite environment, where good manners, refined behaviour and the exclusive trappings of wealth created material differences in the behaviour of young people.

Whereas households contained childhood upbringing and socialisation within the restricted and limited environment of a single space, the socialising remit of schools, as well as how school spaces fashioned interactions between youthful peers and their superiors, was equally vital for many young people. Patterns in socialisation in household literature existed according to status and to the functional roles of children, whether they were young gentry servants of the elite household, the children or apprentices of the urban merchant household or the offspring of a small household where children

---

[1] Vaughan, *The golden-groue*, the third book, Chapter 32.
[2] Cheshire Archives, SP3/14/1. For the school's history see D. Wilmot, *A Short History of the Grammar School, Macclesfield, 1503–1910* (Macclesfield, 1910).
[3] *c.* 1330. Leach, *Edu Chtr*, p. 299.

and parents lived for part of the year as co-habitants. The household location had a symbiotic relationship with the literature and with socialisation; the household structure formed, and informed, the required codes of conduct and sustained the interests of particular audiences. Schools, because of their nature as training grounds for young people, approached issues of normative conduct from the perspectives of the Church, the State and the Crown, as well as of parents and pedagogues interested in youthful learning processes.

In this chapter education is not restricted to the formal academic remit that was carried out by tutors and schoolmasters across counties. Grammar schools obviously had an academic responsibility for teaching Latin grammar for clerical and university careers, as well as practical skills in English literacy and in some cases writing and casting accounts.[4] However, the school was also a transmitter of social values and this occurred alongside academic lessons. Stephen Jaeger's analysis of early medieval European cathedral schools situated educational activity within an ethical context and in his statement we can see precedents for the English experience:

> Learning for its own sake had no legitimate role in this period. Studies had to be subordinated to a higher goal. For secular studies this goal was virtue and 'composed manners' ... all the disciplines and arts could serve that purpose and ideally were pursued 'for the sake of learning virtue'.[5]

Humanistic influences in England were visible by the late fifteenth and sixteenth centuries. The revival of classical Latin works was matched by an interest in personal character as part of a multi-layered model of teaching. While this forms part of the background to the interest in youthful behaviour and identity in sixteenth-century schools, schools taught moral lessons prior to humanism, and for other reasons than those of a revised classicism.[6] In England the context of sixteenth-century religious change also places school objectives within a wider State-Church goal of creating religious orthodoxy. Integrating the contemporary perception of social behaviour into this allows us to see how education fitted children for adulthood and, during Elizabeth I's reign, for responsible roles within the emerging Protestant state.

---

[4] Jo Ann Moran arrives at literacy levels through book ownership while David Cressy focuses on evidence from signatures and marks, an approach which assesses writing literacy. J. A. H. Moran *The Growth of English Schooling, 1340–1548: Learning, Literacy, and Laicization in Pre-Reformation York Diocese* (Princeton, 1985), pp. 150–79; D. Cressy, 'Educational Opportunity in Tudor and Stuart England', *History of Education Quarterly* 16 (1976), 301–20; Cressy, *Literary and the Social Order*, pp. 42–61.

[5] C. S. Jaeger, *The Envy of Angels: Cathedral Schools and Social Ideas in Medieval Europe, 950–1200* (Philadelphia, 1994), p. 118.

[6] For studies on humanism see C. Shrank, *Writing the Nation in Reformation England, 1530–1580* (Oxford, 2004); D. Wakelin, *Humanism, Reading, and English Literature, 1430–1530* (New York, 2007).

Forms of education

The extent of access to education is a vexed issue for historians, important here in the sense that it shows the extent of the interest in virtue and courtesy beyond elite classes. There was no single form of schooling in England. Different categories, ranging from private tutoring for the nobility to ecclesiastical schooling within religious houses as well as the increasing involvement of the laity in school foundations, created an ad hoc arrangement for educating children, primarily male.[7] Elementary schooling was so fluid and variable across this period that identifying an elementary curriculum is problematic, and it remained so largely until the seventeenth century. Fortunately grammar schools habitually created records of foundation, established a curriculum and sometimes documented more personal information about schoolmasters, ushers (under-masters) and scholars. Optimistically, it seems that a grammar school education was open to multiple class groups, certainly from the fifteenth century. In the late 1380s school endowments – such as Lady Catherine Berkeley's school at Wotton-under-Edge in Gloucestershire (1384) – supported two poor students, while generally it was common for grammar schools across England to adopt a mixed model of fee payments.

Access to schooling was presumably easy for wealthy bourgeois and merchants as well as for the lower gentry in the late fifteenth and sixteenth centuries, yet for the middle ranks, including tradesmen, yeomen, professionals, prosperous yeoman and artisans, it was also achievable.[8] The number of schools which were founded also touches on the question of access to education (although these two issues are not precisely the same). It does appear that while school foundations were irregular, with periods where new foundations peaked followed by times of decline, we can cautiously say that the number of educational institutions increased over the late fifteenth and sixteenth centuries. This makes the ideologies of courtesy and virtue powerful models for many more families with young children. Orme talks of a 'national' endowment of schools by the 1480s, with founders following existing endowment models in the creation of educational institutions.[9] This 'national' endowment can be seen in school statutes which tend to follow common formats: evidence of national patterns affecting education at a local level.

How did the school affect the traditional socialising role of the household, given the strong emphasis which was placed on the household in social-

---

[7] The debate on the laicisation of schools is a long one. For literature on it see, Orme, *Education and Society*, pp. 23–31.

[8] Historians who have seen education in terms of expansion include Moran, *Growth of English Schooling*; M. V. C. Alexander, *The Growth of English Education 1348–1648: A Social and Cultural History* (University Park, 1990).

[9] Orme, *Education and Society*, pp. 14 15

ising young people? We are increasingly cognisant of the processes by which a physical environment shapes behaviour and does not simply mirror it.[10] Extending this to schools reveals how the space of the school, and particularly the grammar school, shaped behaviour and specifically socialisation. With favour increasingly being given to household spaces that encouraged privacy, and with specialist rooms for cooking, food storage, sleeping and dedicated servants' areas increasingly preferred, the socialisation of young people devolved onto schools which remained public and civic spaces.[11] The point made here is not about elite children attending public schools but the manner in which multiple social groups below the elite classes participated in environments similar in some senses to the large household. Most schools were built or adapted around a large single room, with separate domestic chambers for the master and usher attached to the main space. Semi-fixed features divided and altered the internal area, although before the seventeenth century internal partitioning was minimal.[12] While larger schools such as St Paul's divided scholars into forms through the manipulation of semi-fixed features and moveable objects, the communal nature of schools largely did not change. These schools echoed the make-up of large houses where socialisation was focused on monitoring public conduct and visible behaviour.

Schools experienced similar pressures and social tensions to those felt in large households; both contained sizeable (youthful) populations which were organised along hierarchical lines. Like large households, schools required social rules to be strictly observed to make the community function smoothly. In both arenas adults monitored youthful behaviour according to pre-set, acknowledged principles. In elite households positions of authority were filled by the lord and by senior officials holding key household positions. In smaller households the male householder assumed control over his children, apprentices and servants. In the school multiple people, including the schoolmaster, usher, school governors, as well as older pupils, fulfilled these func-

---

[10] Jane Grenville looks at the social activities of York households in terms of social space in 'Houses and Households', p. 320. Also on architecture see B. Hillier and J. Hanson, *The Social Logic of Space* (Cambridge, 1984); S. Kent, 'Activity Areas and Architecture: An Interdisciplinary View of the Relationship Between Use of Space and Domestic Built Environments', in *Domestic Architecture and the Use of Space: An Interdisciplinary Cross-Cultural Study*, ed. S. Kent (Cambridge, 1990), pp. 1–8; A. Rappaport, 'Systems of Activities and Systems of Settings', in *Domestic Architecture and the Use of Space: An Interdisciplinary Cross-Cultural Study*, ed. S. Kent (Cambridge, 1990), pp. 9–20.

[11] M. E. James, *Family, Lineage, and Civil Society: A Study of Society, Politics, and Mentality in the Durham Region, 1500–1640* (Oxford, 1974), pp. 13–15, 102–3.

[12] Rappaport, 'Systems of Activities', p. 13. For school architecture see M. Seaborne, *The English School: Its Architecture and Organization 1370–1870* (London, 1971), pp. 1–61.

The School

tions. Grammar schools could be substantial institutions. Up to 100 scholars were admitted to the grammar school in Guildford, Surrey; in fact more could be admitted if there were additional children residing in the town who were guaranteed access to education, much the way modern catchment areas operate. Similar numbers of scholars are listed in the governor's accounts for Rivington Grammar.[13] Smaller households did not share the same pressures of these environments and therefore did not focus on socialisation through predetermined rules according to the demands of observable courtesy and the needs of others. This may explain why guidelines for courtesy and good manners were jointly maintained in school statutes during the sixteenth century, at a time when they were disappearing from some household books. Educational records are evidence of a broader ideological preoccupation with the environments in which children were found.

School records charted prosaic concerns including school hours, fees and wages. How are we to gauge the 'spirit' of the school when it comes to the more unstructured and fluid concept of 'good behaviour'? The importance of a scholar's social conduct in educational records can be difficult to track accurately, with sources obscuring these elements and prioritising complex financial settlements and the like, probably in a proactive bid to stave off future legal quarrels and entanglements. Schools often became embroiled in complex and convoluted legal battles running over years, if not decades, concerning initial endowments, incomes from land and other financial matters. It is necessary to tease out information concerning social conduct from these descriptions of school organisation.

Occasionally it is clear that details relating to conduct were consciously documented and recognised as occurring in the school. In some cases legal records provide information on what was expected of young people, allowing us to move closer to the experiences of the child. In the Court of Chancery (1538–44) John Aleyne, the son of a husbandman, brought a case against his mother and stepfather for failing to put him to school during his minority. The defendants' answer is striking in the indication it gives of John's agency in his educational choices, with the mother and stepfather arguing that they 'offeryd to ffynde hym at Scole at lernyng & often tymes sent hym to brystoll & to westvery wher good scoler ar keppyd … w[hi]ch sayd co[m]playnit refused to be a Scole[r] & wondryd abroade & woulde not take lernyng'.[14] In an age where the paramount authority of parents or the householder was so idealistically described in literature and conduct books, misbehaviour of this sort suggests childhood actions could easily destabilise parental control. The ineffectuality of John's mother and stepfather and their lack of success in correcting his behaviour suggest they were powerless in the face of his

---

[13] Surrey History Centre, 1775/2/2 and Lancashire Record Office, DDX 94/94 respectively.
[14] TNA, C1/723/7–8.

youthful disobedience. Whether these accusations and counter-accusations were true or not, it is clear that John felt entitled to take up this matter within the court on the basis that his educational needs as a child had not been met by his immediate kin family.

This personal account of schooling (or lack thereof) is the exception rather than the rule. Informal schools predictably offer even fewer resources for educational standards, although it is possible to outline elementary educational networks through licensing records, as well as through printed books which were written to provide basic elementary education and training.[15] As noted earlier, it can be difficult to uncover systematic elementary school records prior to the beginning of the seventeenth century when charitable endowments for elementary schools became more regular.[16] Parish records and licensing records offer ways to reconstruct elementary teaching, both licensed and unlicensed. The lack of evidence on elementary schools before the seventeenth century particularly limits what we can tell about the education of girls who were customarily excluded from grammar institutions. Girls from the middling classes more likely continued to receive their education in the home from mothers and unlicensed elementary teachers, to whom there are some surviving references. Girls from the upper gentry and nobility received some schooling in the nunneries and were introduced to functional learning, in addition to the French and Latin acquired in the home, as was noted in the previous chapter. While education for girls was achievable, it remained firmly attached to the household or the nunneries.

'bryngyng forth in Conyng and vertue':[17] sociability, courtesy, virtue and religion in the grammar schools

Earlier we saw that the St Albans almonry and grammar school placed a great deal of emphasis on behaviour at the table. This directive did not teach manners, although manners would have been developed by association, but focused on forming an environment similar to the great household and imposing on the grammar scholars some of the discipline of the monastery.[18] We are not looking at a direct correlation between this record and courtesy poems, but rather a circular movement of corresponding values and beliefs based on high status contexts. An ordinance for poor scholars from *c.* 1339 enlarges on this association by discussing educational provisions in terms of behaviour: 'Likewise, whosoever is convicted or notorious for being incon-

---

[15] The ephemeral nature of elementary education is discussed in W. B. Stephens, 'Literacy in England, Scotland, and Wales, 1500–1900', *History of Education Quarterly* 30 (1990), 545–71.
[16] The exception to this was London's Christ's Hospital (founded 1552). This institution is not studied in this chapter because of its unique nature.
[17] Sir John Percyvale's will. Cheshire Archives, SP3/14/1.
[18] Nicholls, *Matter of Courtesy*, pp. 22–44.

tinent, a night walker, noisy, disorderly, shall be wholly expelled.'[19] Immoral and uncontrollable behaviour, particularly when it was immoral sexual conduct, would certainly have impacted on the community. This religious setting locates these rules in a different context to later secular grammar schools. Yet, these accounts were carefully written down in the statutes and indicate that the almonry and its grammar school were concerned that the site of education should recognise manners and courtesy.

The association between education and long-term socialisation also formed part of the interests of the refounded cathedral school at Canterbury (refounded 1541). Documents associated with this cathedral school identify the multiple skills that were to be developed in students, ranging from a moderate learning of Latin to general good behaviour.[20] Contemporary audiences and parents may have valued the promise of good behaviour just as highly as academic lessons. Certainly, behaviour was further emphasised in rules describing conduct at the table and the need for all of the minor canons and other ministers, grammar scholars, grammar schoolmasters and choristers (ten choristers were maintained at Canterbury, 'For their instruction and education, as well in good behaviour as in skill in singing')[21] to dine together. Again, communal sociability is identified, with wayward behaviour monitored and controlled as it was likewise discussed in courtesy poems: 'The Precentor shall be overseer of manners in hall ... and shall rebuke any grown-up person who behaves badly, but the boys shall be rebuked only by their masters, that all may be done in hall in silence and good order.'[22] By the mid- to late sixteenth century smaller and less prestigious grammar schools were incorporating rules for table manners and general behaviour into their own statutes, indicating a continuing and perhaps escalating emphasis on behaviour as part of the school's responsibility. It also extended these qualities to children from lesser gentry, merchant and artisan classes.

Detailed grammar school statutes from this later period are invaluable when searching for the social objectives of schools. Increasing documentation certainly reflects the institutional nature of education in this later period and the better survival of records.[23] At Guildford (established 1509)[24] we can see how academic skills were monitored and tested during a yearly examination

---

[19] Leach, *Edu Chtr*, p. 297. 'Incontinent': Wanting in self-restraint: chiefly with reference to sexual appetite: *OED*.
[20] Leach, *Edu Chtr*, p. 455.
[21] Leach, *Edu Chtr*, p. 455.
[22] Leach, *Edu Chtr*, p. 461. Again there is a high status religious context to this.
[23] On foundations of schools in the late fifteenth and sixteenth centuries see N. Orme, *Medieval Schools: From Roman Britain to Renaissance England* (New Haven, 2006), pp. 236, 254.
[24] Statutes date to a period later than this. See Appendix D. The school's architectural plan can be found in Seaborne, *The English School*, pp. 17–19.

where two examiners questioned scholars over a three-hour period.[25] This annual examination process was part of the school's educational responsibilities; however, academic skills were also associated with moral values at a core level. The skill of memorisation, the core of a grammar education, held moral value. Mary J. Carruthers has written that memory was 'co-extensive with wisdom and knowledge, but it was more – a condition of prudence, possessing a well-trained memory was morally virtuous in itself. The medieval regard for memory always has this moral force to it.'[26]

This educational, moral accountability existed alongside other responsibilities. At Guildford social values were legitimised and fully documented within the statutes and proclaimed alongside the rules for the curriculum; the schoolmaster was given equal authority in both areas. The rules are based on both traditional courtesy and moral and religious lessons. Of the thirty-one statutes, seven deal directly with the curriculum and the learning requirements expected of scholars. These include references to exercises in grammar and rhetoric and the study of Latin and Greek. A significant number of statutes, thirteen in total, govern the employment conditions of the schoolmaster and usher, a preoccupation itself linked to social conduct as we shall later see. An additional six statutes incorporate directions for the moral and religious observance of scholars, statistically on a par with the rules for the curriculum. Among these six 'socialising' statutes we find guidelines to kneel for prayers at the start and end of the school day, judgements concerning bad behaviour (including disobedience to the schoolmaster or usher and violence or threatening speeches to the same) and rules over swearing and blasphemy. We can read this as part of an agreed contract between the school and scholar concerning observable conduct. Statute twenty-five comments on swearing, blasphemy and violent behaviour: 'yf any Scholler shalbe a common picker, stealer, usuall swearer or blasphemer of the name of God and cannot be reformed by often admonitions and moderate corrections … thereof shall immediately take him from the schoole'.[27] Statute twenty-nine further clarifies this and correlates good conduct with a slightly different set of values: 'honesty and cleanes of lyfe, gentle and decent speeches, humilitie curtesye and good manners'. These elements were to be 'established by all good meanes'.[28]

---

[25] Surrey 1775/2/2.
[26] M. J. Carruthers, *The Book of Memory: A Study of Memory in Medieval Culture* (Cambridge, 1990), p. 71. Memorisation is discussed in U. A. Potter, 'Performing Arts in the Tudor Classroom', in *Tudor Drama Before Shakespeare, 1485–1590: New Directions for Research, Criticism and Pedagogy*, ed. L. E. Kermode, J. Scott-Warren and M. Van Elk (New York, 2004), pp. 143–65 (pp. 145–7).
[27] Surrey 1775/2/2.
[28] Surrey 1775/2/2.

The School

It was obvious to the (biased) observer of schools in the 1558 Gloucester Boy-Bishop sermon that grammar schools included a strong socialising remit. More importantly still, the supposed failure of schools in carrying this out resulted in the development of children who lacked social graces and virtuous character:

> but yet I dare not warant yow to folow the childer of the grammer scoles, for, how so ever it happ, nurturyd thei are as evill or rather worse then the other. Yf yow will have a profe herof, mark ther maners in the temple, and at the table; mark ther talkes and behavior by the wayes at such tymes and houres as thei leave scole and go home to ther meales, specially on holydays and campos dayes, when thei are sett a litill at libertie … yow find the most of them most ongracious grafftes, ripe and redy in all lewd libertie[29]

Boy-Bishop sermons were occasions for satire and for the inversion of normal roles and character. Since satire caricatures what it depicts, this was most likely an exaggerated picture of youthful disobedience, and probably – given the audience – a deliberately comic one. Even so, the themes singled out resonate with commonplace perceptions about the value of conduct for young scholars. The sermon can be compared to the statutes for the prestigious Westminster School (1560), which reveal the legitimate concerns the institution had with the social behaviour and the general activities of the boys. The statutes represent the far-reaching hold schoolmasters looked for in academic and social dynamics, as well as in external, non-school locations. Here the themes of conduct and behaviour that had been chosen by the author of the Boy-Bishop sermon are represented:

> Their duty shall be not only to teach Latin, Greek and Hebrew, Grammar … but also to build up and correct the boys' conduct, to see that they behave themselves properly in church, school, hall, and chamber, as well as in all walks and games[30]

The diligence with which these environments and activities were registered shows that concerns with male misconduct were publicly addressed by schools but also reveals a deeper desire for influence. In addition Westminster scholars were monitored for hygiene and dress via detailed lists of responsibilities:

> that their faces and hands are washed, their heads combed, their hair and nails cut, their clothes both linen and woollen, gowns, stockings and shoes

---

[29] *The Camden Miscellany, Volume the Seventh, Containing Two Sermons Preached by the Boy-Bishop* (London, 1875), p. 24. E. K. Chambers discussed these unusual ceremonies in which young people had a legitimate place in religious affairs in *The Mediaeval Stage*, 2 vols. (London, 1903), I, 337–43.

[30] Leach, *Edu Chlr*, p. 499.

kept clean, neat, and like a gentleman's, and so that lice or other dirt may not infect or offend themselves or their companions[31]

This associates behaviour with the conduct of gentlemen and encourages boys to aspire to gentlemanly status. For the boys at Westminster this was a class that was theirs by birthright. It is not surprising that conduct is defined in terms of gentlemanly status, nor that the statute appropriated some of the forms of courtesy literature in order to describe gentry identity.

Characterising education in this way, in the sense of involving morality and virtue, was an objective for England's elite and governing classes. At least that is the impression we receive from Roger Ascham's *The Scholemaster*, in which moral conduct and actions are of considerable importance in preparing young people for ruling positions within the commonwealth. As royal tutor to Princess Elizabeth between 1448 and 1550 he, just like Sir Thomas Elyot, who decades earlier had dedicated his own educational treatise, *The Boke named the Gouernor*, to Henry VIII, reveals the strategic thinking that was taking place amongst educationalists regarding the educational and moral provisions for England's elite, strategies which were already deeply embedded in the grammar schools attended by the middling and gentry classes. Similar ideals can be seen in relation to less prestigious county grammar schools which monitored physical appearance along comparable but not identical lines. The school at Rivington distinguished between costly clothing and clothing that was merely unsoiled, 'though their apparell need not to be costli yet it is shame to were it slovenli', presumably referring to the middling classes who made up its approximately 100 scholars.[32] Statute five of the 1592 statutes of Sherborne School, Dorset, regulates overall good conduct under the general provision 'that good manners & behaviour maie by hadd & increased w[i]th good learnyng as it is seamly', specifying that the scholars 'wear their apparel cleane & decently w[i]thout wilful spoiling'.[33] Further guidelines which describe modest neatness and cleanliness are better seen as appropriate to all classes, lacking the overt gentlemanly association noted at Westminster. It is to these schools that we now turn.

The school's desire for control was raised earlier. It was the schoolmaster's authority which was most often directly invoked, although school governors played powerful roles which will be discussed later in this chapter. The elementary style of schooling at Dame Alice Owen's school in Middlesex (1613) monitored physical appearance according to pre-determined standards, with the statutes going so far as to specify the type of haircut required of male scholars: 'That the Schoolmaster haue a care that the faces & hands

---

[31] Leach, *Edu Chtr*, p. 499.
[32] Lancashire Record Office, DDX 94/100, fol. 8ᵛ. This is the number of scholars listed in the Governor's Accounts for the school *c*. 1574. Lancashire DDX 94/94.
[33] Dorset History Centre, S235/A1/2(2).

of his Schollers be washed, their heads polled & their garments kept cleane. And that hee appoint every day two of his Schollers in order, to sweepe the schoole that the place maybe swept & clean at all times.'[34] 'Polled' refers to having hair cut short, or shaven, probably in an attempt to stop the spread of lice. The school's statutes spoke about authority over scholars in ways similar to grammar school documents, although Owen's school was certainly unlike Westminster which attached status to physical appearance. There is a downward movement of values from grammar schools to other schools, with elite language and ideals modified to suit economic contexts. Of course, while some London apprentices were from gentry backgrounds, this school clearly distinguished between its more affluent scholars and its poorer ones: 'That all children that shall be taught freely in the Schoole shall be children of poore people.'[35] The school's thirty poor scholars were educated in grammar, fair writing and ciphering, specifically in relation to future employment, 'to traine up young beginners whereby they may be fitt to be Apprentices, or to take some other honest course for the obtaining of their living'.[36] These freely taught scholars were educated at the school in addition to fee-paying scholars. There are comparable references to fundamental elementary learning in the orders of Dame Elizabeth Periam's School (1609), where scholars learnt to read, write and perform basic numeration. This was also specifically associated with fitting poor scholars for apprenticeships 'Whereby to get their Living'.[37] Practical lessons in book-keeping and writing were suitable for a number of professions in trade.

The reference to physical and manual labour in the second half of the above passage concerning Dame Owen's school ('two of his Schollers in order, to sweepe the schoole') reveals the pressures that could be placed on poorer scholars to contribute to the school environment: such tasks are rarely imposed on fee-paying scholars. At Almondbury, it was the poorer, non-fee-paying boys who were required to gather moss for the school roof and to clean desks.[38] Practicalities in admitting poorer scholars are acknowledged in Dame Owen's school documents, where it is noted in a statute that poor children might be absent for sickness or for employment, recognising that children from less affluent households held additional responsibilities for their family's financial well-being, a sentiment absent from grammar school statutes. The cost of schooling involved not only school fees but also the loss of

---

[34] London Metropolitan Archives, CLC/L/BF/G/071/MS05480A.
[35] LMA CLC/L/BF/G/071/MS05480A.
[36] LMA CLC/L/BF/G/071/MS05480A.
[37] Oxfordshire History Centre, S128/1PB2/A1/2.
[38] U. A. Potter, 'Pedagogy and Parenting in English Drama, 1560–1610: Flogging Schoolmasters and Cockering Mothers' (unpublished doctoral dissertation, University of Sydney, 2001), p. 21.

any income that might be generated by the child's activities, which impacted upon the regularity of school attendance and consequently on literacy.[39]

The references in these statutes suited the lower class status of the scholars more readily than the higher status of their grammar counterparts. However, it is important that these differences are not overstated. All statutes shared the same basic desire to enforce certain behaviours within the school grounds and they were careful to ensure that authority over the immediate school environment was possessed by adults. There was, however, no formal decision to have the school's power end at the school door, as it were, or any conscious or accepting awareness of limited (educational) authority. This question – how schools were to extend their influence beyond customary school hours when scholars were physically bound by school precincts – stands out in statutes and contemporary accounts. An obvious place to begin the process of extending educational power was the street, a place which was of deep concern to educators. The street was a place between two centres of adult authority: one being the home and the other the school. Moreover it was a potentially disruptive place, an observation which had been made in the Boy-Bishop sermon. It is to the street that we now turn.

The street held a fascination for commentators on youthful behaviour. It found a place within early courtesy texts, as we saw earlier. Conventions about how to behave in the street were relevant to both boys and girls, although the extant courtesy literature aimed at female audiences made particular use of the potential disruption and damaging location of the street. By the sixteenth century instructional authors used the activity of walking through the street on the way to school as part of their guidelines on household affairs. Transferring concerns with the street – as a place a young person walked through when they left the household or on their way to market – to a different set of concerns over loitering before school indicates uncertainty over who held authority over youths at this ambiguous moment which was neither wholly part of the domestic home nor inside the school proper. Francis Seager's *The schoole of vertue* reveals the ways in which the street functioned as a site of public courtesy, joined to the visibility of the school:

Howe to behaue thy selfe in going by the streate and in the schoole. ii.

> In goynge by the way
> and passynge the strete
> Thy cappe put of
> Salute those ye mete
> In geuynge the way
> to suche as passe by
> It is a poynte
> of siuilitie

---

[39] Stephens, 'Literacy in England', p. 562.

> And thy way fortune
> so for to fall
> Let it not greue thee
> thy felowes to call
> When to the schole
> thou shalte resort
> This rule nore well
> I do the exhort[40]

This advice is reminiscent of courtesy poems, particularly *Stans puer ad mensam*, which used the public space of the street to present instructions about the appropriate behaviour of young gentle servants when they went outside the structured environment of the household. Edmund Coote in *The English Schoole-maister* likewise reiterates conventional courtesy themes when he writes 'Vnto all men be curteous, and mannerly in towne and field.'[41] He also identifies the street as a key space in the school day, although it is worth noting that he does not comment on the street's physical characteristics; the street is a temporal space that exists between leaving home and arriving at the school, charged with the vices of absenteeism and loitering:

> If to the schoole you do not goe,
> when time doth call you to the same:
> Of if you loyter in the streetes,
> when we do meet, then look for blame[42]

For young boys, the interval between leaving the household and arriving at the school must have represented a short period of freedom, outside the monitoring gaze of both parents and schoolmasters. The boy in the poem *The Birched School-Boy* also plays truant and is beaten by his schoolmaster for his insolence.[43] The public space of the street was an important arena for scholars (as well as the young girls, young gentle servants and youths mentioned in courtesy poems) as a space and time that existed beyond habitual adult control. The recurrence of rules relating to the street in both literature and in school statutes is a clear indication of its significance. The author of the Gloucester Boy-Bishop sermon also observed this, using satire to criticise grammar scholars, and by implication grammar school authorities, for the conduct of scholars outside the school.

School authorities in fact tried hard to monitor children outside of the school. In 1309 the statutes for St Albans restricted the times when male scholars could go into public areas: 'Also the Master forbids any scholar

---

[40] Seager, *The schoole of virtue*, Av^{r-v}.
[41] E. Coote, *The English Schoole-maister, teaching all his scholars the order of distinct reading and true writing of our English tongue* (London, 1596), I4^v.
[42] Coote, *The English Schoole-maister*, I4^v.
[43] MS Balliol 354, fol. 250^r.

henceforth to wander or run about the streets and squares without lawful and reasonable cause.'[44] At Sherborne the awareness of the street's potential danger is shown when the school authorities wrote, 'And also passing by the Streats to be courteous to all men, to use reverence to their elders & betters, not to swear nor use ribaldry nor filthie communication nor to frequent Taverns and Victualling Houses nor to plaie at dize cardes nor other unlawful Games.'[45] Some school statutes identified quite alarming vices associated with activities outside the physical boundaries of the school. A list of unacceptable behaviours drawn up at Rivington is ominously detailed: 'alehouse haunters truands gammers daliers with women harlot haunters, gadders on the night, troblers of their fellowes, pikers brallers, swearers liers taletellers, not given to praier nor resorting to the church'.[46] This was a refrain picked up in a later comment on courteous behaviour towards elders: 'unreverent users of their elders and betters in not shewing some curtesie as oft a thei passe bi theim, or when thei speak unto them'.[47] These attitudes were partially pragmatic: grammar schools were usually to be found in urban environments and rules governing the street were especially relevant to both school and civic authorities. Painted in these terms it appears that schools and school authorities were concerned with the question of public order and disobedience but it is not difficult to see that exerting control over other environments was equally a matter of self-interest for schools.

Statutes for Rivington School systematically extended school authority beyond the school precincts.[48] The following looks at the manner in which this was carried out through attention to a scholar's clothing, their household activities and boarding. One highly detailed passage not only concerns the behaviour of scholars in the street but extends even further, into the household: 'And if there be ani number of scholers to gether in one house at bourd, eueri one in course shall rede often whan the household is most to gether a chapter of some piece of the Scriptures.'[49] Household behaviour has been allied to religious instruction. Scholars boarding in houses were singled out probably because they were living outside the normal socialisation structure

---

[44] Leach, *Edu Chtr*, p. 243.
[45] Dorset S235/A1/2(2).
[46] Lancashire DDX 94/100, fol. 5ᵛ. Where parts of the original Rivington documents are illegible or torn, I have turned to the transcript in M. M. Kay, *The History of Rivington and Blackrod Grammar School* (Manchester, 1931). In *A president for parentes* Grant identified similar vices and activities. These were perhaps relevant to older scholars: 'So studentes (least they fall into the detestable vice of drunkennesse, and contamynate them selues wyth filthie pleasures) had their delightes, musike and other bodily exercises, wherewith theyr mynde (being tired with study) myght be moste pleasantly recreated': *A president for parentes*, Fiiiᵛ.
[47] Lancashire DDX 94/100, fol. 9ᵛ.
[48] Lancashire DDX 94/100, undated but about 1570.
[49] Lancashire DDX 94/100, fol. 8ᵛ.

of the kin home and were more susceptible to perilous influences. This advice was tailored for scholars who boarded by themselves in a house: 'and though there be but one scholer in a house, yet he shall on the holi daies and the long winter nyghtes, and other idle times whan most compani is to gether rede some what of the Scripture or other godli booke, to the rest of the household where he is lodged'.[50] The literate status of the scholar is deliberately highlighted and the school reinforces the scholar's high status within a household by encouraging him to take on the role of reading scripture to assembled household members. In parental advice books children performed much the same function for the family.

The question of spiritual and pragmatic tasks for young people was settled differently in the opening statement of Alexander Nowell's *Catechism*, sometimes called the *Larger Catechism*, which John Day printed in 1570. The emphasis in this is on spiritual learning and not practical guidance, although Nowell expresses the idea of the schoolmaster as a father figure: 'For asmuch as the maister ought to be to his scholars a second parent and father, not of theyr bodyes but of their mydnes, I see it belo[n]geth to the order of my dutie, my dere child, not so much to instruct thee ciuilly in learnyng and good maners, as to furnish thy mynde, and that in thy tender yeres, with good opinions and true Religion.'[51] The importance of catechisms lies not only in the religious content they taught (vital for seeing the beliefs the Protestant Church espoused) but also in the techniques of learning and instruction aimed at young and older people. Ian Green is right to point out that the catechising 'question and answer' technique has much in common with medieval and early modern teaching methods. Latin grammar scholars opposed one another and elementary educators took up similar methods.[52]

In contrast, however, to Nowell's claim that he was only concerned with the mind of the scholar, grammar school statues often referred to washing hands, making beds and saying morning prayers. Pragmatic lessons of this type had also been cited in courtesy poems dating back centuries, and these too were directed at young children and adolescent boys. The school had no direct authority over this environment or these activities but it assumed jurisdiction in dictating behaviour in all arenas of a scholar's life. This control was emphasised when Rivington School ordered that the master and the usher were to question scholars to see whether these actions were being performed.[53] The question of boarding, already mentioned, needs to be

---

[50] Lancashire DDX 94/100, fol. 8ᵛ.
[51] A. Nowell, *A catechisme, or first instruction and learning of Christian religion. Translated out of Latine into Englishe* (London, 1570), Biʳ. After 1571 schoolmasters were ordered to use Nowell's catechism. On catechisms see I. Green, *The Christian's ABC: Catechisms and Catechizing in England c. 1530–1740* (Oxford, 1996).
[52] For example Coote used this in *The English Schoole-maister*.
[53] Lancashire DDX 94/100, fol. 8ᵛ.

raised again. These rules may be said to have had an immediate relevance to scholars who were boarders. An earlier statute had paid specific attention to boarders in private houses, and schools might reasonably have expected to intercede in these environments. There is other evidence, however, that a more insistent sense of authority was developed in relation to the parental home. It is worth noting that an indiscriminate attitude towards the school's authority can be found in William Fiston's *The schoole of good manners* (1595) in which these principles were paraphrased in a way the Rivington authorities would have applauded. 'When thou goest to the Schoole, remember that the Schoole is the very nurserie of all vertues: the workehouse of framing thy minde and body to a right fashion: the pathway to knowledge and the very direct entrance into a happy & well ordered life,' writes Fiston.[54]

These attitudes were given direct expression in statutes. School authorities called upon adult figures, inviting parents, tutors and hosts to regulate conduct in conjunction with the school's own power and sense of responsibility. It was the schoolmaster's duty to 'entreat their Parents tutors & hostes to be amended to demeane them honestly & soberly at their meals & otherwise in their parents tutors & hostes houses,' wrote the authors of the Sherborne statutes.[55] The monitoring gaze of parents supported the authority of the schoolmaster but it did not detract from it. Authorities made a conscious decision that the school had a duty to monitor all behaviour. By enlarging the scope of their remit educators took on more and more important roles, extending into the household and into the parental sphere, and adjusting the relationships that existed between children and parents to include a schoolmaster's authority. Shelford's comment on community responsibility in *Lectures*, discussed in the previous chapter, is pertinent in this educational context. Of course, a core difference between the literary sources and school records relates to who arbitrates behaviour. Statutes habitually ignored, under-emphasised or, more cleverly, subverted the role of parents and other adults to augment the schools' own authority. Co-option of this type can be seen in the Rivington statutes that included parents and householders, or landlords, in a contract with the school. In effect it made scholars subject to the oversight of the school governors outside the school as well as within the household:

> Their [governors'] duite also is to serch spie and learne how eueri scholler behaue himself in the house where he lies towardes the women or seruants; and also in their coming to or going from the schole, and when they be abroad ... and also the governours shall sharply with words correct his

---

[54] W. Fiston, *The schoole of good manners. Or, a new schoole of virtue. Teaching children & youth how they ought to behaue themselues in all companies, times, and places. Translated out of French. By W. F.* (London, 1595), C4ᵛ.

[55] Dorset S235/A1/2(2). Sherborne School.

The School

ill-behaviour, and cause the Schoolmaster or Usher to warn the parents of suche a disordered p[er]son and owners of the house where he lies in their names if the fault be great.[56]

Sherborne School attempted something similar. It included parents and hosts in a contract with the school to monitor the scholar's conduct: 'that the M[aster] & Usher themselves must enquire & diligently search in the Houses of the Parentes & Houses of all Schollers w[i]th in the Towne of their misdemeanors, and to give due punishment & correction accordingly'.[57]

Another of the educational writers who was successful in this period also discussed education in relation to household and parental roles. William Kempe was a long-time master at the grammar school in Plymouth, governing there for two decades (1581–1601). It was during his tenure that he wrote an educational treatise, *The Education of children in learning*, addressing the sons of merchants and yeomen as well as the gentry.[58] It is his position as both schoolmaster and author which is significant. These dual roles made it necessary for him to preserve his professional authority while appealing to his readership and he was particularly inclusive of the role of parents and their agency in upbringing. Kempe declared that children were socialised into proper, virtuous behaviour 'partly by the helpe of the Parents, and partly by the diligence of the teacher'.[59] However, he deliberately emphasised the unique and distinctive role of schoolmasters who were able to offer the child something parents could not: 'Therefore when the child is about fiue yeares old, the Father for the causes before alleadged, shall commit him to some Phoenix ... that can teach him all things.'[60] The father's role, and we can note the exclusion of the mother in this, was further subordinated to the schoolmaster through the new responsibility the father bore to his school-age child: 'His second care is to keepe his Child *being now a Scholler*, in good order at home, and there to exercise him in such things as he learneth, or hath learned in the Schoole.'[61] The child is now specifically identified by his status as a scholar, no longer just by his chronological age or by his position

---

[56] Lancashire DDX 94/100, fols. 6r-v. School governors often had an intimate role in a school's organisation, including the management of financial matters, the hiring and firing of schoolmasters and more detailed 'hands-on' management of the school and scholars. The Rivington governors are discussed in more detail later in this chapter.
[57] Dorset S235/A1/2(2).
[58] W. Kempe, *The Education of children in learning, declared by the dignitie, vtilitie, and method thereof. Meete to be knowne, and practised aswell of parents as schoolemaisters* (London, 1588).
[59] Kempe, *Education of children*, E3v.
[60] Kempe, *Education of children*, E4v.
[61] Kempe, *Education of children*, F1r. My emphasis. Ursula Potter discusses the manner in which schools privileged the role of the schoolmaster over that of parents, especially over the mother. However, she demonstrates that literary evidence

in the household. Kempe identifies a child's admission into a grammar school as something setting him apart from 'childhood' and family life in general. Edmund Coote's recurring emphasis on the 'scholar' in *The English Schoolemaister* also emphasised the status of education by singling out school-age children and scholars in contrast to more generic terms such as child or son.[62]

One passage in Kempe's book condenses many of these principles while also paralleling themes found in contemporary household books written about the good upbringing of children. Although long, it is worth quoting in full:

> The Father therefore must keepe his fatherly authoritie ouer his Child, and ioyntly with the Maister prescribe vnto him a good order for manners and behauiour, for repairing home, for attendance, for diet, for apparell, for exercise in learning, that his behauiour be godly and honest, in seruing God, in keeping his Church, in humilitie towards his superiors, in humanitie towards all men, that he repaire home aswell from Schoole as from play in time conuenient: he giue attendance to do seruice either at the Table, or any other way: that he be sober and temperate in his diet, well mannered in taking the same: that he be cleanly and frugall in his apparell: that he employ the vacant time in reading, in writing, in all good exercises for the gaine of learning.[63]

The comprehensive nature of these rules shows how far the framework for social activities and mannerly conduct expected from the child, or more accurately from the scholar, had developed over two centuries. It now included aspects as diverse (but also as connected) as apparel, diet, modesty towards elders, service at meal times, punctual attendance at church, moderation in eating and educational learning. Of course, these were 'guidelines of perfection' rather than the reality of boys' behaviour. However, we can conclude from comparison with the earlier courtesy poems which had discussed only some and not all of these issues that the understanding of socialisation within the household was turning to new principles. The later sixteenth-century literature aimed at household audiences also took up some of the additional descriptions about behaviour as well as serving at the family table, often arbitrarily incorporating occasional courtesy lessons. Kempe integrated education into this, adding a further dimension to good upbringing. It is striking that schools participated in teaching across this range of social tasks, with these matters relevant to the school environment just as they were relevant to the household.

(principally school plays) reveals a different side of parental control: 'Pedagogy and Parenting', pp. 36–90.
[62] Coote, *The English Schoole-maister*.
[63] Kempe, *Education of children*, F1r.

'When all in a towne generally, shall murmure against vs':[64] the schoolmaster as moral example

A scholar's social conduct and moral fibre were only as strong and well developed as the social conduct and moral fibre of those around him. Socialisation in part depended on the conduct of other scholars and also on the conduct of the adults with whom young people were in daily contact. The schoolmaster as an embodiment of *cultus virtutum* arose early on in medieval European schools.[65] The influence of a schoolmaster on his scholars in English grammar schools was keenly felt to serve the wider social value of the school, while the urge to monitor adult behaviour was part of the broader ongoing anxiety with issues of community order.

The conduct of the schoolmaster as a living witness to virtue finds a place in English school records, although we would find it hard to come across any notion of the 'cult' of the schoolmaster or the impact of their individual presence and charisma on scholars. The author of the Boy-Bishop sermon deliberately spoke of schoolmasters in terms that are certainly suggestive of this even if they do not allude to it directly:

> I must have a word or ii with the scolemaisters, which, at some of your handes, take your childer in cure to teach and nurture them, as well in vertue as in prophane learning. Therfor I say now to yow scolemasters, that have the youth under your handes to make or marr them not by your neglygence, but make them to God ward with your diligence ... so the scolemaster do or owght to fascion the soule of the child by good educacion in learnyng of good nurture and vertue[66]

Practical measures were taken by school authorities to ensure schoolmasters conducted themselves appropriately. School documents, particularly statutes, were written to include parallel guidelines about the schoolmaster's

---

[64] J. Brinsley, *A Consolation for Ovr Grammar Schooles: Or, A faithfull and most comfortable incouragement, for laying of a sure foundation of all good Learning in our Schooles, and for prosperous building thereupon. More specially for all those of the inferiour sort, and all ruder countries and places; namely, for Ireland, Wales, Virginia, with the Sommer Ilands, and for their more speedie attaining of our English tongue by the same labour, that all may speake one and the same language. And withal, for the helping of all such as are desirous speedilie to recouer that which they had formerlie got in the Grammar Schooles; and to proceed aright therein, for the perpetuall benefits of these our Nations, and of the Churches of Christ* (London, 1622), G2^r.

[65] On this see Jaeger, *Envy of Angels*, p. 76.

[66] *Camden Miscellany*, pp. 27–8. This connection between the schoolmaster and virtue exists across periods. Jewell cites a 1306 testimonial for a schoolmaster at Beverley which emphasises his learning and behaviour: '"The Bringing Up of Children in Good Learning and Manners": A Survey of Secular Educational Provision in the North of England, *c*. 1350–1550', *Northern History* 18 (1982), 1–25 (p. 11).

behaviour, and the similarities between the rules directed at students and those directed at their teachers create striking connections between moral behaviour and the non-school activities of young people and adults. While scholars would have certainly felt the watchful eye of their teachers and the community upon them, their schoolmasters and ushers were in fact subject to similarly strict and specific monitoring. The public display of statutes in schools enforced these philosophies, and it is worth remembering that schools could require statutes to be read aloud to scholars and parents throughout the year.[67] The poor conduct of grammar school masters did not escape contemporary comment from pedagogues either. Richard Sherry, in his translation of Erasmus's *De pueris statim ac liberaliter instituendis*, paints a picture of a four-year-old child being sent to a grammar school where the master is unlearned, rude in his manners and ridden with the 'fallyng sycknes, or frenche pockes' or worse, mentally unstable 'often lunatike'.[68] There the child is terrorised by the petty tyrannies of the schoolmaster who sees himself as a king in his own domain. Erasmus's comments on the physical punishment meted out to scholars probably reflect the realities of often harsh school discipline. However, his censure of the 'howlynge and sobbinge and cruell threatnynges' that went on in schools brings to attention the fact that this was neither universally accepted nor commended by parents or other observers. Rather than ignoring scholars, especially young scholars, who are treated in this way or tacitly accepting that it was a customary practice of schools, Erasmus calls attention to these acts as harming children and turning them away from the joy of learning. This is a more sympathetic perception of childhood which makes us balance the discipline that probably was enforced in many schools across England with evidence that some writers opposed the more extreme disciplinary practices. Even the frequently harsh and strict puritan writer Edward Hake included elements of these sentiments in his own translation of Erasmus, although it needs to be acknowledged that he did still err on the side of emphasising discipline and correction.[69]

School statutes openly discussed the issue of the schoolmaster's behaviour, providing communities with the written authority to 'murmure against' these figures, as John Brinsley would later write.[70] We can compare this insistence on the schoolmasters' moral conduct to the poor reputation they had in Shakespeare's works. At Rivington the authorities insisted that the school-

---

[67] D. M. Sturley, *The Royal Grammar School Guildford* (Guildford, 1980), p. 74.

[68] Sherry, *Schemes and tropes, [Part Two]*, Lvii^v. On this and other negative aspects of school life see Alexander, *Growth of English Education*, p. 199.

[69] E. Hake, *A touchestone for this time present, expresly declaring such ruines, enormities, and abuses as trouble the Churche of God and our Christian common wealth at this daye. VVhereunto is annexed a perfect rule to be obserued of all parents and scholemaisters, in the traynyng vp of their schollers and children in learning. Newly set foorth by E. H.* (London, 1574), F6^v.

[70] Brinsley, *A Consolation for Our Grammar Schooles*, G2^r.

master and usher were not to go to alehouses, were not to be negligent in their teaching, were not to swear, gamble or be seen with whores, or, as they say later, '[they] shall corrupt the youth'.[71] The accent laid on their activities both inside the school (consider the command concerning negligence in teaching) and outside the school (which is often given more attention, including references to alehouses and gambling) is precisely documented. Every Rivington schoolmaster and usher took a formal oath at his appointment to abide by the statutes, formally promising that 'I shall also teach my Scholars, and bring them up in learning and good nurture.'[72] The orders for Dame Owen's school are likewise unambiguous in the connection they make between the schoolmaster's behaviour and far-reaching moral consequences for the scholars: 'least his euill example breed any discredit to the Schoole & infeccon also to the Schollers to whom he ought to be a patterne of vertue honesty and piety'.[73] The character of schoolmasters was in fact a major anxiety for contemporary observers. The people of Blisworth in Northamptonshire considered they had the right to legal recourse over their anxieties with the local school and the difficulties faced there by their children, eventually bringing an action against the schoolmaster, Francis Wiggington. In depositions, Thomas Andrewe was asked if Wiggington was 'a com[m]en Alehouse haunter'.[74] This is reminiscent of the wording used in school statutes and probably a cue which had distinctive meaning and significance. The moral positions taken up in statutes spoke directly of these concerns.

Not only were schoolmasters watched by parents and the community but the school governors' role in monitoring the master's behaviour could be equally extensive, if not intrusive. Unusually for school statutes at this time, Rivington School's orders extensively document the role of the governors in the school's management, organisation and administration, suggesting that relationships formed not only between schoolmasters and parents but between school governors and the community as well. The position of governors in educational provision has been largely overlooked in favour of the more visible schoolmaster who was in daily and therefore more obvious contact with scholars. Rivington School governors were directly identified through their task of monitoring the schoolmaster's behaviour, and they were able to call on the community to ensure this did not fall below acceptable standards:

> If the Schoolmaster or Usher be negligent in teaching, keep not their due hours ... be gamesters, swearers, hore-hunters quarrellers, resort not to common praiers and the Church at appointed times ... the Governours

---

[71] Lancashire DDX 94/100, fol. 5ʳ. The same rules applied to scholars.
[72] Lancashire DDX 94/100, fol. 13ᵛ. The oath for the school governors also survives.
[73] LMA CLC/L/BF/G/071/MS05480A.
[74] TNA, E 134/36 Eliz/Hil10.

shall severely warne him of it ... If in this time there appear not good hope of amendment, the governours shall take unto them six of the discreetest neighbours dwelling within the six towns of their corporation ... and shall with sharp words both rebuke him or them for their misbehaviour.[75]

If the schoolmaster or the usher failed to correct these social or academic breaches, the entire parish would be told and another person found to replace him or them. Academic criteria, holding a BA or MA, were less often cited or required in a schoolmaster.[76]

Similar rules applied not only to schoolmasters in formal institutions. Thomas Elyot, writing in this period, discussed the behaviour of tutors who resided within high status households. Elyot was aware that good education was related to the master's moral character, which was to be sober and virtuous and demonstrate affability and the important quality (for any teacher) of patience.[77] As with school statutes, Elyot's views were based on a concern for the environmental influences children were exposed to and their propensity to absorb lessons and behaviours from those around them.[78]

What was occurring in schools was also of religious significance. Records from ecclesiastical courts disclose that schoolmasters were regularly investigated for suspect religious practices. This occurred in addition to the systematic process of licensing which was already in place to supervise orthodox religious views. This was related, in part, to fears of the corruption of the young and the desire to secure allegiances to the Protestant Church. The watchful eyes of the community, already mentioned in the context of moral disorder, would have presented a real concern for many schoolmasters caught in religious change, unsure as most were of which way to turn.[79] State Papers of 1591 show that Mr Yates, schoolmaster at the Blackburn School, was implicated in charges of recusancy along with his wife, daughter and maid. We know about this as during John Bancroft's testimony about his brother's suspected Catholic leanings, Bancroft responded to the question about 'What papists you know' with a damming accusation against Yates: 'There is no house worse in Lancashire that I knowe than Mr Yates Schollemaster at Blackburn whose wife daughter and mayd are recusants, his mayde is known to have done much hurt among the Schollers.'[80] It is not clear from this testi-

---

[75] Lancashire DDX 94/100, fol. 5ʳ.
[76] Moran, *Growth of English Schooling*, pp. 71–2. There is some evidence that the larger and more prestigious schools demanded MA qualifications after the sixteenth century. Orme, *Medieval Schools*, pp. 170–72.
[77] T. Elyot, *The boke named the Gouernour, deuised by Thomas Elyot knight* (London, 1531), Diiiiʳ.
[78] Elyot, *boke named the Gouernour*, Diiiiʳ.
[79] P. Collinson, *The Religion of Protestants: The Church in English Society 1559–1625* (Oxford, 1982), pp. 189–241.
[80] TNA, State Papers 1591, SP 12/240 (105). Yates was also accused of harbouring a Catholic priest.

mony exactly what influence the maid had over the scholars. George Alfred Stocks noted that five scholars from Blackburn later fled overseas after their involvement in the Counter-Reformation, indicating that schools could be significant breeding grounds for turmoil and religious dissent as the authorities feared.[81]

Intervention in schools was particularly noticeable after the Reformation.[82] The terminology used in these policies also reveals the manner in which moral values were integrated into educational matters. The re-drafted Chantries Act, passed 21 and 22 December 1547, ensured chantry endowments were converted to 'good and godlie uses, as in erecting of Grammar Scoles to the educacion of Youthe in vertewe and godlinesse'.[83] The act's emphasis on religious values and virtues is not surprising given the attempt to stabilise religious change after Henry VIII's death and during Edward VI's minority. Schools were intended to support this religious reform. Similar statements of intent (if not actual practice) concerning academic and social responsibilities can be seen in the letters patent of numerous schools. The grammar school of Cheveley in Cambridgeshire (1568) confirmed in official language that it was to be engaged with good morals as well as academic education: 'for the education of boys and youths, as well in good morals as grammar'.[84] Additional religious and political controls were in place by 1559, when Elizabeth I issued a royal injunction commanding all schoolmasters and teachers to teach from the official grammar set out by Henry VIII and Edward VI and ordering that all teachers were to be licensed by the ordinary under the criteria of good academic prowess, sober disposition and their understanding of Protestant doctrine.[85] This was clearly an attempt to remove masters who remained faithful to Catholic doctrine. In 1563, the Oath of Supremacy was also extended to schoolmasters (from the 1559 Act of Supremacy) to ensure that there was introduction at the official level of allegiance to the emerging Protestant Church and specifically to Queen Elizabeth I as the Supreme Governor of the Church of England. Schoolmasters also had to subscribe to the Thirty-nine Articles at this time.

Licensing was one of the methods of control which held a schoolmaster's social and religious conduct to a higher standard than it did their academic proficiency. Since the thirteenth century licences granted by the bishop had been required for teachers. The value of this was apparent to Mary I and

---

[81] G. A. Stocks, ed., *The Records of Blackburn Grammar School*, 3 vols. (Manchester, 1909), I, xviii.
[82] H. M. Jewell, *Education in Early Modern England* (New York, 1998), p. 22.
[83] Cited in Leach, *Edu Chtr*, p. 473.
[84] *Report of the Commissioners for Inquiring Concerning Charities: Cambridgeshire, 1815–1839* (London, 1837), pp. 94–5: Transcript of Letters Patent of Queen Elizabeth I, 6 July 1568.
[85] Leach, *Edu Chtr*, p. 495.

Elizabeth I for essentially the same social and religious reasons.[86] It guaranteed that bishops and their deputies had the mechanisms in place to maintain contact with schools, and by extension with young and malleable scholars. There was also a financial incentive for schoolmasters and schools to monitor any educational provisions taking place locally. Loss of income for authorised schools would have created a healthy dislike for unlicensed teachers.[87] The rigorousness of licensing varied over the mid-sixteenth century, although it does seem that by the 1570s harsher penalties were recorded against unlicensed teachers following the failed Counter-Reformation.[88] The monitoring of recusant schoolmasters is noticeable in records dating to the 1580s, with penalties for recusant teachers reaching £10 for every month they remained actively teaching students, either in schools or in private houses. Archbishop Grindal's letter on this subject notes with some alarm the influence of recusant teachers on young scholars:

> And for as much as a great deal of the corruption in religion, grown throughout the realm, proceedeth of lewd schoolmasters, that teach and instruct children, as well publicly as privately in men's houses, infecting eachwhere the youth.[89]

Schools themselves understood this, with statutes noting the behaviour of schoolmasters and ushers in relation to their influence over younger people.

Records of licences also documented more prosaic deviations. These were not necessarily always related to religious beliefs, although such records did often refer to religious conformity in some way. In the *Libri Cleri of Synods* for the Ely Diocese several reports were made concerning problems with local educational provisions. In an entry c.1584, Thomas Newcomyn, vicar of Lynton, was reported for teaching reading and religious lessons that were contrary to the Book of Common Prayer.[90] In other cases unauthorised teaching could be retrospectively authorised on the basis of religious soundness:

> that Thomas East privately in his hous and Thomas Sandborne in Edward Pikhams house teach children both latyn and English and that (as far as he

---

[86] Licences as a Protestant measure against Catholic teachers is discussed in Alexander, *Growth of English Education*, pp. 191–4.

[87] Jewell '"The Bringing up of Children"', pp. 10–11. For the monopoly of schools see Barron, 'Expansion of Education', p. 232.

[88] J. P. Anglin, *The Third University: A Survey of Schools and Schoolmasters in the Elizabethan Diocese of London* (Norwood, 1985), p. 63.

[89] 1580: Leach, *Edu Chtr*, pp. 524–5. Moments of turmoil produce stricter controls. The Gunpowder Plot in 1605 also produced a renewed interest in licensing and an increase in penalties: Leach, *Edu Chtr*, p. xlvi.

[90] Cambridge University Library, EDR D2/16, fol. 4^r.

The School

knoweth) they teach noo bookes but such as bee lawfull, and the parties bee likewiese of good religion.[91]

There was no single sentence for unlicensed teaching. In fact penalties were handed out according to a number of factors including the rigorousness of the bishop and his deputies, the poverty of the schoolmaster and the age of students taught; anyone teaching very young children seems to have been let off more lightly. A comment on religious orthodoxy is present more often than not, usually recorded along the lines of the following example: 'licens he hath none, in that his master will aunswer for him, he is of good behaviour and sound of relygyon'.[92] It also seems to have been common for unlicensed teachers to have acted with the cooperation and support of the local community. Equally, it is highly probable that private and unlicensed education took place in communities within the vicinity of authorised grammar schools. John Joanes received testimonial letters after teaching boys in Kirdford between 1582 and 1585, while Peter Joanes received similar testimonials from the parishioners of Shipley which allowed him to teach anywhere in the archdeaconry of Storrington.[93] Penalties for unlicensed teaching could, however, be harsh. In 1575 William Bullaker was excommunicated for teaching after being forbidden to do so, probably because of suspected Catholic leanings.[94]

The licensing system did provide guidelines that allowed certain informal teaching to take place without intervention. Teachers, including women, were allowed to give basic elementary lessons to groups of fewer than six children provided no boys over the age of ten were present and that the teaching did not resemble a formal school.[95] The question of women as teachers has certainly preoccupied historians. Could women earn their livelihood as teachers? How often did it occur? The image of St Anne teaching the Virgin to read circulated widely in devotional books and sculptures and certainly contributed to the ideology of education as a nurturing act which was part of domestic household duties.[96] The practice of women, particularly mothers, teaching young children in the household appears to have been consistent across classes, and it even led to some women taking this up professionally or as a way to augment income from other sources. Nicholas Orme has noted several references to female educators in the early fifteenth century.[97]

---

[91] West Sussex Record Office, EpI/23/5, fol. 1ᵛ.
[92] West Sussex EpI/23/5, fol. 3ʳ. Likely to date *c.* 1570s.
[93] West Sussex Record Office, STC III/C fol. 110ᵛ and STC III/B fol. 64ᵛ respectively. Chichester had an authorised and long-established grammar school supervised by the local cathedral.
[94] West Sussex Record Office, EpIII/4/3, fol. 38ᵛ.
[95] Anglin, *The Third University*, p. 86–90.
[96] P. Sheingorn, '"The Wise Mother": the Image of St Anne Teaching the Virgin Mary', *Gesta* 32 (1993), 69–80.
[97] Orme, *Education and Society*, p. 50.

Visitation and subscription books also include references to unlicensed female teachers, suggestive of their role in informal educational networks. In 1616 Anna Hassall was recorded as teaching boys, although she was eventually excommunicated after being found to be a recusant. In the proceedings of the archdeaconry of Colchester (1593–6) Robert Glascock of Beaumont and his wife are reproached for teaching without licence.[98] In the register of presentments for Chichester, William Sharpe blamed his wife for teaching in an attempt to absolve himself.[99] The professionalisation of women in formal school institutions, as opposed to informal arenas, was more prominent by the mid-seventeenth century, particularly in boarding or finishing schools.[100]

The elasticity of licences reflects an appreciation of the work women carried out as teachers of young children. However, the lowly status of such teachers is equally indicated by the lack of interest in documenting and licensing their activities. This informal teaching did not require the same moral standards in its practitioners, just a basic 'soundness' and religious observance. The State and community interest in schools as sites of courteous and virtuous socialisation was more conspicuous when the education of adolescent boys of the middling and upper classes was raised. For lower status boys and girls, and particularly girls, socialisation remained centred on what was learnt in the household augmented by some schooling, which often also took place in similar small local households. Social status remained a telling factor in the systematic and institutionalised interest in virtue and good manners.

Published educational books provide additional insight into the nature of the work carried out by female teachers in semi-formal educational settings. It is important not to overstate the gendered nature of elementary teaching as both men and women were employed to teach young children basic reading and religious lessons. Female teachers, however, could not make the leap beyond the elementary level until much later. In the literature, elementary teachers received their fair share of criticism, although it is worth noting that criticism tended not to be gender specific. This is the case with the 'rude and ignorant' teachers described by Francis Clement in *The Petie School*, in which he criticises both men and women who teach young children privately in houses before they attend formal schools.[101] It is likely that early education along these lines often took place outside the control and direction of the Church and Crown, although basic learning could often be carried out

---

[98] Essex Record Office, D/ACA 21, fol. 147^v.
[99] West Sussex Record Office, EpI/17/6 fol. 138^r. 1588. There were legitimate joint ventures between husbands and wives: see Anglin, *The Third University*, p. 87.
[100] R. O'Day, *Education and Society 1500–1800: The Social Foundations of Education in Early Modern Britain* (London, 1982), pp. 183–95.
[101] F. Clement, *The Petie Schole With and English Orthographie, wherein by rules lately prescribed is taught a method to enable both a childe to reade perfectly within one moneth, & also the vnperfect to write English aright* (London, 1587), Aii^v.

under the direction of parish priests or minor parish officials. Even within grammar schools the basic education of petty scholars was not a priority, with Rivington School ordering 'pettys' to be taught either by the usher or by other scholars, who themselves probably had very little understanding of what they were teaching.

A final point on religious conformity is that equally extensive strategies to deliver religious lessons were made internally in grammar schools. These often responded to official regulations issued by the crown and ecclesiastical courts. But, as we have seen, they were equally likely to be a consequence of the school's intensive interest in social activities and behaviour. The statutes for Sherborne made church service integral to the weekly school routine. Scholars were also required to attend school as normal until the end of the day when they were to go to church accompanied by the master and usher.[102] Schoolmasters could themselves be presented to church officials for failing to abide by these regulations. In 1580 Mr Etheryng, the schoolmaster from Clapham, was recorded in the presentment book for failing to go to the sermons with his scholars.[103] These religious responsibilities had been confirmed in 1571 in the Canons for the Church of England in which schoolmasters were directed to teach from the Bible and from the catechism, as well as accompany scholars to church services.[104] Religion had always been part of the school system and was viewed as a tool for religious preservation. The newly emerging Protestant Church did nothing to separate the ties between education and religion. The integration of church attendance into educational practices during Elizabeth I's reign was strategic in securing allegiance to the Church against its attackers and critics. Hylson-Smith talks of the emotional battle during the Elizabethan Settlement, when people's emotional attachment to Protestantism had yet to be decided.[105] Securing the younger generation to Protestantism would have seemed a vital way of stabilising religion along with political and community networks at a time when allegiances were still open.

---

[102] Dorset S235/A1/2(2).
[103] West Sussex EpI/17/5, fol. 73ᵛ.
[104] Alexander has argued that after 1571 statutes became increasingly detailed when it came to religious matters: *Growth of English Education*, pp. 190–1. However, the Oath of Supremacy had also been extended to schoolmasters some years earlier in 1563.
[105] Hylson-Smith, *The Churches in England*, I, 31–47. See also Collinson, *Godly People*, pp. 335–6.

Printing education

Most of this chapter has been occupied with unveiling the social directives inside schools. However, elsewhere this book has demonstrated that the contemporary literature, mostly didactic, demonstrates an active interest in organising and explaining the manner in which childhood was understood through the printed medium. Can the evidence from school documents, then, be linked to a discrete set of published educational books? What can printed educational sources reveal about socialisation as a matter that interested pedagogues and parents which is either absent from or minimised in the archival record?

In fact, where institutional records are unavailable or silent on issues such as language acquisition and elementary teaching, turning to printed sources which were published in England from the 1480s onwards is invaluable. Educational books were published on a wide range of topics and although they differed from books for the household with their focus on the theory and practice of learning, they clearly underpinned the commonplace idea of young people being subject to external, adult influence. In fact, the influence of adults which was so firmly incorporated into household manuals from the late fifteenth century was a cornerstone of pedagogical books which emphasised the child as obedient to all adults and particularly to teachers. It followed, then, that educational books incorporated both aspects of socialising lessons, first in terms of the theoretical duties children owed to adults and society, and second, by adopting practical educational training seen as sufficient to the class and gender of the child.

These links begin with alphabet books. This was a genre distinctively associated with children (although at any time unlearned adults could find value in their simplicity). These books were composed along religious-educational lines, mirroring the multiple socialising and academic tasks which existed within households and schools. Parchment ABCs on alphabet tablets and primers were two of the ways the English vernacular was taught after the thirteenth century and they combined religious lessons with practical literacy skills in the form of the alphabet and prayers. The simplicity of the religious content made them suitable for very young children. By the fourteenth century the ABC characteristically began with a cross followed by the alphabet and finished with 'est Amen'. Some primers did go into more complex religious lessons in the form of the Creed and the Pater Noster.[106] This was connected to the religious syllabus taught to all lay people. Children who used these tablets and books, either in the home or sometimes at school, were thus exposed at a young age to basic, although shallow, learning.

---

[106] Orme discusses changing patterns in ABCs in *Medieval Children*, pp. 246–51.

The School

ABCs and primers became increasingly complex over the sixteenth century. The 1561 *A.B.C for chyldren* included rhymes to illustrate the correct pronunciation of words which were simple enough for even the youngest child to follow: 'I brake my hed: I go to bed: I hurt my leg: this ma[n] doth beg'.[107] Advice on 'good living' completed the lessons and included both overt religious comments, 'Trust in the mercy of god',[108] as well as social and courtesy related advice, 'Be sobre of meat & drink', 'Reuerence thyne elders' and 'Washe cleane'.[109] Courtesy manuals connected religious precepts with courteous advice in equally uncomplicated ways. Here these issues were raised for the young child as part of their educational training, tellingly suggestive of the lack of distinction drawn between education and social customs.

The transition from using ABCs to Latin grammars precluded social groups below gentry level. However, the blurring of educational training with social messages is clear in Latin grammars, a genre which is remarkable for its longevity as an educational source. Manuscript grammar books were used within schools by the master and perhaps owned by scholars themselves, printing making this increasingly possible.[110] Published Latin grammars developed from two principal printing networks: Oxford with the early printers Rood and Hunt and London with Pynson and, slightly later, de Worde. It was, of course, necessary to teach Latin using vernacular English. The 1496 grammar *Peruula*, printed by de Worde, began with the question 'What shalt thou doo whan thou haste an englissh to be mad in latin. I shal reherce myn englissh first ones. twyes or thryes.'[111] Grammars are linked to the history of language acquisition but they exploited social activities and childhood interests as methods of teaching young boys how to form Latin sentences. It is this approach which reveals the complex socialising customs endorsed by educators and which contemporary educational sources have demonstrated within specific schools. The claim that grammar books made to detail social activities and youthful interests reinforces previous evidence that grammar schools blurred educational lines with social ones.

The late fifteenth century grammar *Vulgaria quedam abs Terencio in Anglica[m] linguam traducta* united practical and familiar English sentences with Latin equivalents, at times emphasising distinctly secular tones: 'women luff or desyre to be mich made off'.[112] School life could also be extended as a family metaphor, 'Scolers shuld loue to gyder lyke as thei were bredyr',[113] describing

---

[107] *An A.B.C for children* (London, 1561?), Aiii^v. Alphabet tablets were also covered in thin sheets of horn by the late sixteenth century.
[108] *An A.B.C for chyldren*, Biiii^v.
[109] *An A.B.C for chyldren*, Biiii^v.
[110] Moran, *Growth of English Schooling*, pp. 34–6.
[111] Wrongly attributed to John Stanbridge. *Peruula* (London, 1496), Ai^v.
[112] Terence, *Vulgaria quedam abs Terencio in Anglica[m] linguam traducta* (Oxford, 1483), Aiiii^v.
[113] Terence, *Vulgaria*, Biii^r.

the relationship between fellow scholars as comparable to that of kin. There were other references to family environments as well as kin relationships proper, in which maternal emotions and character are negatively emphasised through over-affection and favouritism: 'The modyr makyth moste of hyr yongist son[e]' and 'All modyrs help their sonnys offendynge ageyns their faders.'[114] This touches on one component of domestic society which treated mothers as potential disrupters of conventional household order. This idea was juxtaposed by turning to patriarchal norms which maintained that fathers were the titular heads of households: 'I yelde me to the fader' and 'A fadere shulde use his chylde to do wele by his own will or of his own accorde rather than by drede.'[115] On the one hand the repetition of phrases such as these in school environments introduced English-speaking children to Latin. More significantly, on the other it instilled and reinforced social and gendered codes of behaviour in young and impressionable minds, through their memorisation of these phrases.

The vitriolic 'grammarians' war' conducted through increasingly venomous publications over the 1520s between William Horman and Robert Whittington has been described by others in considerable detail.[116] It is a curious event in itself, demonstrating the prominence of educationalists in the period and the importance of status and rank within academic circles. Of interest, however, are the different marketing techniques used by Horman and Whittington. Horman's 1519 *Vulgaria* sold for approximately 5 shillings while Whittington's books were sold as individual titles (on different parts of the grammar) for much cheaper prices. Whittington's grammars were in frequent publication through to the early 1530s.[117] Horman's 1519 book is of special interest, however. It contains thirty-seven chapters on topics which range from religious material to education, manners and social life. The text spells out that behaviour was judged in terms of how it demonstrated courtesy: 'It was a sayenge full of louly courtesy' and 'This was vncourtesly done.'[118] The maxim 'Vnclenlye langage is the messanger of vnclenlye mynde'[119] combines elements of outward behaviour with inner virtue. Horman's book includes themes as diverse as religion, behaviour, manners, clothing and family relationships, all within the framework of Latin exercises. It is particularly noteworthy in demonstrating a continuing use of courtesy terms. This becomes still more interesting when the status of learning Latin grammar is compared

---

[114] Terence, *Vulgaria*, Aiiii^v and Eii^v.
[115] Terence, *Vulgaria*, Bii^v and Eiii^v.
[116] On this see B. White, *The Vulgaria of John Stanbridge and the Vulgaria of R. Whittinton, Edited with an Introduction and Notes by B. White*, EETS OS 187 (London, 1932).
[117] N. Orme, 'Horman, William, (1447–1535)', *DNB*; N. Orme, 'Whittington, Robert (c.1480–1553?)', *DNB*.
[118] W. Horman, *Vulgariauiri uiri doctissimi Guil. Hormani Cæsariburgensis* (London, 1519), Liii^v and Miii^v respectively.
[119] Horman, *Vulgaria*, Lviii^r.

to the emphasis on courtesy and the elite context it gained from the household location. It seems likely that courtesy remained associated with elite contexts and higher academic lessons for some time, even while morality developed across other contexts.

William Lily effectively ended the earlier influence of grammarians such as John Holte, John Stanbridge and John Anwykyll. By the mid-sixteenth century, Lily had become the most famous of all the early humanist grammarians with the increasing monopoly enjoyed by the text 'Lily's Grammar' or *The Royal Grammar*. Lily's reputation, built partly as master of St Paul's School, was confirmed in 1543 roughly two decades after his death when the text was authorised by royal proclamation.[120] However, the long-term effect this had on grammar education is much harder to establish. The records from grammar schools reveal that school libraries comprised miscellaneous titles, not just the official grammar.[121] Older and still perfectly tenable grammars in fact continued to be used in schools by scholars, and grammar masters dipped into any available grammar; the diversity of grammars had been an acknowledged problem since the 1520s. The preface of the 1567 edition of Lily's *Brevissima institutio* confirms this: 'The varietie of teaching is dyuers yet, and always will be that euery Scholemaister lyketh that he knoweth, and feeth not the use of that he knoweth not.'[122] As late as 1612 the question of multiple grammars in schools was identified as a problem, with Brinsley referring to it in his 1612 *Ludus Literarius*.[123] Grammar scholars continued to be taught from a variety of sources, as the ongoing debate over acceptable grammar textbooks in the seventeenth century makes clear.

---

[120] R. D. Smith, 'Lily, William (1468?–1522/3)', *DNB*. Lily's book was a composite work of earlier grammatical texts, many of which are no longer extant in their first editions. There were additional injunctions issued by Edward VI in 1547 and Elizabeth I in 1559 regarding Lily's grammar, as well as ecclesiastical canons in 1571 and 1604. For Henry VIII's royal injunction see *Tudor Royal Proclamations*, ed. Hughes and Larkin, I, 317.

[121] For instance, a memorandum for the Blackburn Grammar School, dating to September 1605, listed sixteen books donated to the school including *Cooperi Dictionarium, Baretti Dictionarium, Lexicon graecolatinum Johis Scapula* and *Johis Ravisii Textoris Epitheta*: Lancashire Record Office, DDBk 3/10.

[122] W. Lily, *Brevissima institutio, seu, Ratio grammatices cognoscendae, ad omnium puerorum utilitatem praescripta, quam solam regia maiestas in omnibus scholis profitendam praecipit* (London, 1567), Aii^v. Brinsley repeated this quotation in *A Consolation for Ovr Grammar Schooles*, D3^r.

[123] J. Brinsley, *Ludus literarius: or, the grammar schoole; shewing how to proceede from the first entrance into learning, to the highest perfection required in the grammar schooles, with ease, certainty and delight both to masters and schollars; onely according to our common grammar, and ordinary classical authours: begun to be sought out at the desire of some worthy fauourers of learning, by searching the experiments of sundry most profitable schoolemasters and other learned, and confirmed by tryall: intended for the helping of the younger sort of teachers, and of all schollars* (London, 1612).

It was over the course of the sixteenth century that pedagogical texts changed in purpose from Latin grammars to books written in English on a wider variety of topics. This same period saw the growth in books on family affairs for middling status households and certainly these households would have been a valuable market for some of these educational texts, although this picture is complicated by the fact that elementary education was frequently singled out by writers. These households in many respects were too well off to be interested in elementary schooling. It seems, instead, that there was a wider domestic market for books than was catered for by household themes and that education was seen as a growing market for groups below the middling strata. Over the sixteenth century printers came to place increasing value on educational texts. The printer who dominated the educational market was de Worde; he created something of a new market for educational books in the early sixteenth century. de Worde also established relationships with provincial markets which may have had an impact on the dispersal of educational material throughout England and not just the immediate London area.[124] As the sixteenth century wore on educational books were increasingly represented within other printers' corpus of works, notably that of Pynson who had had early success with Latin grammars.

In some cases these books were intended for children, for example ABCs, and sometimes for older scholars, as instanced by Peter Bales's *The Writing Schoolemaster* (1590). However, many of the more interesting examples were written as aids for adult teachers, mainly focusing on elementary teaching, for instance Coote's *The English Schoole-maister*, John Hart's *A Methode or comfortable beginning for all unlearned* (1570)[125] and Clement's *The Petie Schole*. Some of these books focused on reading, some on writing and others, more rarely, on arithmetic. In practice, arithmetic was not emphasised in the medieval and Tudor period to the same extent as reading, Latin grammar or other subjects in the *studia humanitatis*, often being relegated to the final few pages of educational books. Strikingly, Francis Clement incorrectly adds up the sums in *The Petie Schole* and Coote's *The English Schoole-maister* allocates less than a page to the study of numbers. This is remarkable given that his market included craftsmen and merchants who desired to teach young people and apprentices. John Withals's *A Short dictionarie*, published first in 1553 and then again in 1556 (another nineteen editions were published before 1634), included ruthlessly brief sections on numeration which were expanded only in the 1586 edition. William Kempe's translation of Ramus's *The Art of Arithmeticke in Whole numbers and Fractions* (1592) is exceptional in being a thorough and extensive textbook on arithmetic.

---

[124] Edwards and Meale, 'The Marketing of Printed Books', pp. 117–18.
[125] J. Hart, *A methode or comfortable beginning for all vnlearned, whereby they may be taught to read English, in a very short time, vvith pleasure: so profitable as straunge, put in light, by I. H. Chester Herald* (London, 1570).

The School

As noted above, educational textbooks written for adults form a distinct category within this broader anthology. Some echoed theoretical arguments concerning the value and worth of education (for example, Kempe) while many more approached education from the practical viewpoints outlined above, intending to show parents and would-be teachers how to educate children. These texts suggest that, just as books on family affairs appealed to reading communities in the sixteenth century, there was an equally zealous interest in laying out educational matters. It is remarkable that many teachers chose to put their ideas to paper. In the case of Richard Mulcaster, another schoolmaster and writer of educational treatises, tensions are revealed between theoretical educational strategies and the realities of the day.[126] While much has been made of Mulcaster as a proponent of girls' education beyond the elementary level, he did not propose that they should be educated in formal institutions alongside boys. The disciplinary action brought against him when he was master of the Merchant Taylors' School over his admission of extra scholars for the payment of fees to boost his salary reveals his own difficulties as a professional educator. These books, by teachers such as Mulcaster and also William Kempe, framed educational theories through references to commonplace notions about childhood, noting the importance of virtue and good behaviour for scholars. It is important not to overstate the saturation of the market by these books – they were overshadowed by other genres such as law texts, religious works and literature. However, the links between literary sources and school records paint a picture of education as a concern of various class groups. If Latin grammars and grammar schools catered to the middling strata then other educational books expanded this market considerably.

The final word on the relationship between education and conduct in printed sources belongs to the humanist scholar Erasmus, when he spoke of childhood, from infancy, as a time of both academic learning and the learning of manners. Childhood was a serious enough subject that this most renowned humanist scholar of the early sixteenth century penned three books relevant to young people and education.[127] Erasmus's care for and interest in chil-

---

[126] R. Mulcaster, *Positions vvherin those primitive circumstances be examined, which are necessarie for the training vp of children either for skill in their booke, or health in their bodie. VVritten by Richard Mulcaster, master of the schoole erected in London anno. 1561. in the parish of Sainct Laurence Povvntneie, by the vvorshipfull companie of the merchaunt tailers of the said citie* (London, 1581); R. Mulcaster, *The first part of the elementarie vvhich entreateth chefelie of the right writing of our English tung, set furth by Richard Mulcaster* (London, 1582). On Mulcaster see R. L. DeMolen, *Richard Mulcaster (c.1531–1611) and Educational Reform in the Renaissance* (Nieuwkoop, 1991), pp. 61–4.

[127] These were: *De Ratione Studii* (1511), *De Civilitate Morum puerilium* (1526) and *De pueris statim ac liberaliter instituendis* (1529). In England *De Civilitate Morum*

dren's upbringing are apparent when his writing expresses concern for children who are neglected by parents and abused by teachers, a topic touched on earlier in this chapter. More importantly, Erasmus describes a tri-fold scheme based on three related mechanisms (nature, training and practice) which were part of the process of education and socialisation. This is suggestive of the careful way some theorists tried to explain the socialising process.[128] Erasmus's views are at the heart of the relationship between the household, education, behaviour and religious obedience, counselling fathers to put their sons into the care of both nurses and male teachers so that from the time of infancy children (in this case sons) would be imbued with good learning and wholesome values. The value of this was profound: 'but ryghte bryngynge up helpeth muche more to wysedome, then pronunciacion to eloquence. For diligente and holy bringing up, is the founteyne of al vertue'.[129] 'Bringing up' in the sense described by Erasmus very clearly included religious values as a precursor to the creation of virtuous behaviour. This united the themes, so often articulated in literature and paralleled in school statutes, which promoted these mutual values during a scholar's time at the school. While relevant to education, Erasmus's ideas on parental duties also overlap with the focus on a parent's role in children's conduct cited earlier, while his understanding of young children as soft and clay-like ('fashion thys claie while it is moist') places him in an ongoing tradition of writing about youthfulness and malleability of character.[130]

In this chapter we have seen that English schools systematically claimed to offer boys the opportunity to learn academic skills while also seeking to provide an equally valuable and productive education in courtesy, morality, virtue and religious character. That school guidelines even went so far as to comment on clothing, cleanliness and hygiene suggests a strong and developed interest in the completely formed, well-mannered and socialised child. Fifteenth- and sixteenth-century educational sources, as well as educational books, picked up and developed the issues raised so insistently in literature and brought socialisation back full circle to a discussion of conduct and youthful identity that was dependent on both outward appearance and inner

---

    puerilium was translated by R. Whittington, *De ciuilitate morun [sic] puerilium per Des. Erasmum Roterodamum, libellus nunc primum & conditus & æditus. Roberto VVhitintoni interprete. A lytell booke of good maners for chyldren, nowe lately compyled and put forth by Erasmus Roterodam in latyne tonge, with interpretacion of the same in to the vulgare englysshe tonge, by Robert whytyngton laureate poete. Cum priuilegio* (London, 1532). *De pueris statim ac liberaliter instituendis* was translated by Richard Sherry: *A treatise of schemes [and] tropes.* See Appendix D of this book for details.

[128] Ruys explores the role of experience in educating young people. 'Practice', as used by Erasmus is not the same as 'experience', but there are some interesting parallels. Ruys, 'Didactic 'I's', pp. 129–62.

[129] Sherry, *Schemes and tropes,* [Part Two], Cv^r.

[130] In Sherry, *Schemes and tropes,* [Part Two], Dv^r.

behaviour. The astute political decisions of Elizabeth I in maintaining licensing also ensured that the development of Protestantism was absorbed into these environments. Schools did not lag behind when it came to observing religious change and, as we have seen, they had a particular role in religious ideology. Licensing, the 1563 Oath of Supremacy and the Church of England's 1571 Canons all ensured the schools had an outward conformity to Elizabeth's doctrines. Children absorbed this from their teachers, and from Elizabeth's reign onward they grew up knowing no other belief system, unless contested in the home or by strong-willed Catholic teachers like Blackburn School's Mr Yates.

While the effectiveness of this 'complete' education may sometimes have fallen short, as suggested in the Boy-Bishop sermons, schools themselves nevertheless set lofty goals to achieve these desired ends. They saw the school environment as vital in creating the well-socialised, educated and mannered child necessary for the school, the commonwealth and, indeed, necessary for the household itself.

CONCLUSION

Parents and adults, the State and the Church were obsessively preoccupied with the behaviour and conduct of children in medieval and early modern England. They saw childhood not as a spontaneous and natural time of life, but rather one to be structured, developed and moulded. At the core of their beliefs was the staple that the process of socialisation was necessary to produce a well-behaved child and then eventually a well-adjusted adult who had thoroughly absorbed the current conventions of society and could meet its demands.

This book's chronology, moving from the late medieval to the early modern period, shows this fundamental belief was never shaken. Rather, it was the manner in which socialisation was achieved and perceptions of what was important that were subject to revision and amendment. A shift in expectations is suggested by the evidence rather than radical new approaches to the socialisation of children. Key issues in upbringing, such as obedience, meekness and duty, remained consistent. More compellingly, the evidence examined in this book suggests a cyclical tendency in social norms; courtesy appears to lose ground to morality in the late fifteenth century but is then reinvented in sixteenth-century books. These books reminded people that observable conduct and the *appearance* of good behaviour still held social value and importance. Schools also continued to emphasise basic courtesy and hygiene while at the same time calling attention to higher moral and religious values. Socialisation, as with all social and cultural systems, rode the wave of shifting political and religious dynamics, putting pressure on the manner in which childhood was experienced across the late medieval and early modern periods.

The emphasis on outward behaviour in courtesy literature achieved what it set out to do. Courtesy poems introduced children, especially boys, to the world of the court and noble household *whether they belonged there or not*. Social and political networks which were based on land ownership and inheritance rights were buttressed by inter-marriages and by the fostering of children in greater houses. Every class participated in these networks in their own ways. Consider again the heated comments of a late fifteenth century Venetian visitor to England on the practice of fostering and sending children away from the natal home: 'For everyone, however rich he may be, sends away his children into the houses of others, whilst he in return, receives those of strangers into his own ... they answered that they did it in order that their children might learn better manners.'[1] Courtesy poems held out a promise

---

[1] In Goldberg, *Women in England*, pp. 87–8.

Conclusion

to their conservative middling status audience of the future prosperity, advancement and success that would be theirs, pledging that a knowledge of courtesy, of knowing how to behave in the right way (as a young elite man would) to the right people (both superior and inferior) would benefit the young person, and his family, in meaningful ways. Only in their failure to follow these guidelines did the reader or listener risk all of this; they would be considered no better than 'churls', 'Felde men' and 'glotons'. Courtesy was an avenue and a means to avoid failure and impoverishment and to be placed at the forefront of social advancement and worldly success in the household and in life.

Readers influenced by these courtesy poems clearly extended beyond the noble classes, although the ephemeral circulation of courtesy *ideas* within and around elite households should not to be discounted, ideas these poems sought to lay out in logical and systematised order. Some authors were legitimate participants in elite networks. John Russell was one such figure, as was Robert Grosseteste, the original author of *Stans puer ad mensam*, in the thirteenth century. These authors were participants in elite worlds and wrote about youthful upbringing as knowing observers of its specific requirements. The development from a Latin (religious) perspective to a secular English vernacular perspective in the fifteenth century is emblematic of the changes taking place in society and reading literacy and the increasing importance of vernacular literature to reading communities and to authors as a chosen mode of expression.

A change comes when courtesy poems framed other social and political anxieties of concern not to the nobility but to those just outside this social group. Throughout, this book has demonstrated that the context in which texts circulate manifests itself in the form modifications and revisions take. The courtesy poems incorporating bourgeois issues and citing work and mercantile occupations were responding to concerns about ethical business practices and not elite anxieties about hospitality, table manners and serving food. These narrative choices reflect the economic conditions of families owning manuscripts or buying printed books, seen in Hill's manuscript and with the groups who purchased Caxton's books in the 1470s and 1480s. Merchant groups had distinctive interests in the ideology of upbringing. It was this that brought about responses to concerns beyond those of the elite, responses embracing themes and topics that pushed socialisation in new directions. The social lessons which were taught to young people at this time were different from earlier lessons but, paradoxically, also fundamentally the same. The evidence this book has examined unveils a shift in expectations over the late medieval period rather than a radical new approach to the socialisation of children. Again, expectations of childhood were rewritten, with new tactics at play, but not ones suggestive of a radical new approach to socialisation.

The division between manuscript and print culture has also been shown as less of a concern to contemporary readers and publishers than to later historians of book culture. Such changes as there were in the type of family and household literature prioritised in print were the consequence not of technological changes and the agency of the presses but of the abiding responsiveness of literature to historical events and attitudes. *Print* did not change what was read by people; it had no inherent impact on literary types and culture beyond the production of books in greater numbers, which could itself be meaningful. The relationship(s) between manuscript and print culture and the ideals of courteous and moral socialisation put forward by authors were more complex and sophisticated than the manuscript–print division allows for. It requires us to examine changes and transformations at the individual level and not according to a predetermined picture of the agency of the presses.

This book has gone some way towards answering questions about the progression of English literature over the centuries by giving childhood and family books a stronger voice. Broader conclusions and statements can be drawn from this study in terms of the shifting and variable relationship(s) between manuscript and print culture, the nature of production and technology on literature and how vernacular writings explored English family identity and social contexts better than Latin literature was able to do. Early printed books clearly allowed an expansion in audiences who were interested in socialising children, by setting lessons within a wider range of household contexts. Young people were now less likely to be described as gentle servants than as dependent members of the smaller household; *Caton* discussed fatherly duties and the *Book of Good Manners* inaugurated a household/ family genre that would later flourish in England. The social values upheld in courtesy literature concerning the display of good behaviour themselves underwent a change. Parents rather than lords were the overseers of youthful conduct and identity. Highlighting moral conduct, as Caxton's books and to a lesser extent some manuscripts did, gave socialisation new vitality and scope. Concerns with outward manners turned to concerns with inner character. However, even while over-courtesy was explored, value continued to be placed on elite service. Likewise, 'Ruskyn gallants' could be criticised even as courteous behaviour remained privileged. For boys, socialisation became increasingly confused and complex, with a new interest in higher objectives. The right mindsets as well as the right practices were now required for these social objectives to work in a merchant and bourgeois environment. Yet while these manners changed in specific form, adult alarm with unruly children (dictating the wish to have concrete rules in place as counter-measures) remained the same.

Paradoxically, the literature for girls did not show comparable development accentuating moral and ethical conduct in the fifteenth century. There is clear evidence of an ongoing and persistent preoccupation with (im)moral female behaviour from fourteenth- century literature and even further back

Conclusion

than this. In extant texts for girls, virtuous socialisation was unimaginatively, although consistently, written about as a concern with chastity, a concern absent from courtesy poems for boys. Patristic writers promoted virginity, less so marriage, and this fed into society's preoccupation with the terms of moral behaviour for women. *How the Good Wife Taught her Daughter*, associated with clerical writers, signalled this early concern with female moral conduct at the bourgeois level. It was repeated consistently in manuscripts in the fifteenth and sixteenth centuries with similar themes embraced in its two sister poems, *The Good Wyfe Wold a Pylgremage* and *The Thewis off Gud Women*. Strikingly these writers were disturbed by realistic dangers. Teaching girls how to behave in credible scenarios, in essence how to navigate dangerous situations, was a key function of this literature. The bourgeois attention to moral female conduct touched upon class-specific concerns with marketplaces, the conduct of live-in servants and reputable working careers, and this was matched by the attitudes if not the exact rules of the elite writings of de la Tour Landry (translated by Caxton in 1484). The tone de la Tour Landry took was echoed by Vives, in the expression of a desire to protect vulnerable girls. Regardless of status and reading groups, the emphasis on moral conduct was upheld.

In fact, girls, regardless of status, were socialised according to virtue and morality in ways alien and perhaps unnecessary for boys to follow, at least until the strict moral atmosphere of the late fifteenth and sixteenth centuries saw youthful male behaviour more judiciously linked to moral anxieties. At some point, probably at the close of the fifteenth century but more likely over the sixteenth century, socialisation for boys and socialisation for girls grew closer together, when bourgeois and merchant groups professed a strong interest in moral conduct and morality for their sons. Their daughters, and the daughters of the nobility, were already accustomed to this.

In view throughout this book has been the periodisation of history: the margins between the late medieval and the early modern. The evidence gathered shows clear changes in how socialisation was imagined over the long term although it would be unwise to say there were clear-cut divides between 'medieval' and 'early modern' notions of behaviour and socialisation. Rather, manners and behaviour responded to contemporary political disruptions and religious confusion. In the late fifteenth and sixteenth centuries the forms of upbringing reflected a society in which patterns of manners were repeated but understood through changed objectives, at least at the theoretical and idealised level represented in the literature and in school documents. A desire to hold fast to conventional notions of good courtesy and polite conduct explains why conservative commentators such as Caxton, Rhodes and Seager could achieve commercial success with books echoing the need for conservative courteous behaviour against a background of change. At the same time, moral conservatives achieved even greater commercial success with books aimed at fears over moral incontinence and divergent religious expressions. Authors and publishers, such as Shelford, Vaughan and ironically Caxton again, reflected on contemporary social issues with a knowing and keen awareness of just how deeply connected youthful socialisation was to society's concern with future stability and order. The political disquiet of the Wars of the Roses and uncertainty about how the Reformation would affect traditional patterns of life, both religious and secular, made compelling contexts for the development of new mental and social strategies that dealt with change.

The literature from the sixteenth century tells us that the dynamics of family life were central to society's view of itself, articulated in tandem with a moral/virtuous thread uniting behaviour, manners and conduct. Books by Whitford, Vives, Phiston and Salter were relevant only to boys and girls living in a smaller household. The shift away from large elite houses to texts about smaller houses represents a profound change in English society as the momentum swung away from the nobility to the dynamism of the middling classes. The importance of the household as a private and interior space, but also one with communal and commonwealth values, set in place particular perspectives through which young people were socialised. At the same time, parents replaced children as the central figures addressed by books, and lessons were filtered through elaborate discourses exclusively addressing the father and less often the mother, or perhaps even an anonymous third (but necessarily adult) person.

This was also a time which witnessed socialisation's increasing subordination to religious obligations, something both Catholic and Protestant writers saw a chance to explore in print. The household became a site of religion. As this book has insisted, the study of early sixteenth century literature explains how religious writers were able to play upon parental anxieties to promote religious ideologies long before the Elizabethan and Stuart puritan emphasis on the religious household. Simultaneously there was also a striking generic factor at play in youthful socialisation. No sixteenth-century religious reformer was prepared to suggest radical new approaches to socialising children when the reforming acts of the Crown and Church were positively conservative in some ways. A Protestant child of Protestant parents behaved in the same dutiful, obedient and well-mannered way that the Catholic child of Catholic parents did. Rhodes's and Seager's books, and the publishers who released edition after edition, saw this perhaps more clearly than do we who are so conditioned to look for differences between Catholic and Protestant cultures.

The school environment was one place where courteous values and manners maintained their importance in youthful male behaviour and it was also an arena that secured religious values. During the Elizabethan Settlement the school helped to establish the Protestant nation through careful consolidation and the placement of outwardly conforming teachers into educational institutions. Children, and parents through their children, were shown how Protestantism could develop in parallel with attendance at parish churches.

Conclusion

Schools were certainly perceived as locations preparing young male children for adulthood. Just as significant is the idea of the school as an arena where boys learnt how to interact with their peers and with adults and where they were socialised to 'fit' them for life as young adult men of Elizabeth's Protestant nation. By the sixteenth century a 'good education' was one that saw a scholar leave school imbued with religious doctrine and the knowledge of how to behave in society, complementing and augmenting the lessons that were part of the household. Girls lacked this secondary socialising location, although they learned similar if not identical social lessons based on the three cornerstones of manners, virtue and religion inside the household. The forms of socialisation, if not their location, grew closer together for boys and girls in the sixteenth century.

Chaucer's squire and von Eschenbach's Parzival now fade gracefully into the background in the face of the sixteenth-century child, particularly the boy, who was adept not only at showing courtesy but in serving in any number of household types, in conducting himself with virtue and in participating in years of educational study at the school. Courtesy poems which began the basic lessons of socialisation for the elite male classes now existed along with other lessons, as virtue, religion, morality and academic skills became increasingly relevant for an array of social groups and for both genders. As Erasmus noted, nature was effectual but 'educacion more effectual'.[2] Households and schools were the locations where this socialisation took place, as authors and authorities were intimately aware. By the sixteenth century, 'education' either in the household or in the school, or in both, was sophisticated and complex enough to cope with anything society could demand of the child, be they male or female. As to why socialisation was important and of such persistent and enduring concern to parents, pedagogues, the Church and the State, Erasmus himself had the answer:

> For we reme[m]ber nothynge so well when we be olde,
> as those thynges th[at] we learne in yonge yeres.[3]

---

[2] Sherry, *Schemes and tropes*, [Part Two], Bvii^v.
[3] Sherry, *Schemes and tropes*, [Part Two], Bi^r.

APPENDICES

A survey of the source material used in this book appears in the following appendices. Appendix A surveys courtesy material circulating in manuscripts and is presented in (general) order according to the structure of Chapters 1 and 2. Another useful appendix of English courtesy texts has been compiled by Jonathan Nicholls.[1] Nicholls's definition of 'courtesy material' omits several of the courtesy poems that have been identified in this study. However, it provides a useful secondary aid to this book and may be a helpful source for manuscripts not studied here.

Appendices B and C document printed books of the late fifteenth and sixteenth centuries respectively. Of Caxton's books, the first, *Stans puer ad mensam*, was printed in the same year Caxton opened his business in Westminster, while the last used in this study, the *Book of Good Manners*, was published only five years before Caxton's death in 1492. The books are listed chronologically for ease of reference. These appendices provide relevant bibliographical information not included within the chapters, including dates for later editions and information on translations. For additional bibliographical information the English Short Title Catalogue Online, the Incunabula Short Title Catalogue and Early English Books Online are useful databases, as are the Bibliographical Society's reissue of E. Gordon Duff's *Fifteenth-Century English Books* in 2009 and Lotte Hellinga's *Catalogue of Books Printed in the XVth Century now in the British Library, Part XI, England*.

For ease of reference the educational material used in this book has been compiled and summarised separately in Appendix D, which is divided into two sections. Appendix D, *Educational Sources*, differs from the format of the previous appendices in order to reflect the particular quirks and idiosyncrasies of documentary evidence. Where possible this material is listed by date. Only the principal educational material examined in Chapter 5 is included. School statutes are themselves rich sources of information, although it can sometimes be the case that original records have not survived to the present day. Eighteenth- and nineteenth-century transcripts offer one way of reconstructing these records. For more detailed information on schools and licensed teachers in pre- and post-Reformation England, see the useful tables

---

[1] Nicholls, *Matter of Courtesy*, pp. 191–6.

compiled by Elizabeth Key, Helen M. Jewell and Nicholas Orme.[2] Founding dates reflect available evidence which may obscure earlier institutions at the site.

The latter part of Appendix D returns to the familiar ground of printed sources. Relevant bibliographical information concerning school textbooks and other educational texts circulating in the late fifteenth and sixteenth centuries is listed here.

---

[2] Key, 'A Register of Schools and Schoolmasters', pp. 136–89; Jewell, '"The Bringing Up of Children"', pp. 22–5 and Orme, *Medieval Schools*, pp. 346–72.

Appendix A
English Vernacular Courtesy Poems

Uniform title: *Stans puer ad mensam* (SPAM), Lydgate.[3]

Manuscript reference	Author/scribal evidence A = Author S = Scribe T = Translator	Date of original composition	Notes on dating of individual manuscripts	Notes on manuscript, text and textual differences
	John Lydgate (A, T).	Early fifteenth century.		Rime royal stanzas. Approximately 99 lines. The poem is concerned with elite households, particularly manners while at the table. It also includes a passage on childlike characteristics, making it a useful poem for identifying childlike behaviours. The first 4 stanzas follow closely from Grosseteste's original; however, other features are mostly altered by Lydgate. His reworking is consistent with the concerns of an elite secular household: a secular trope common to the other courtesy poems. It is worth noting this trend in one of the most widely copied courtesy poems.
London, British Library, MS Stowe 982, fols. 10r–11r.			Late fifteenth century.	Titled *the boke of curtesye* and not SPAM. The manuscript also contains *Rules for preserving Health* (Lydgate's *Dietary*) and *The Boke of Keruynge*.

[3] There are over twenty extant manuscripts containing Lydgate's *Stans puer ad mensam*. Not all manuscripts are identified in this appendix; only those which offer the opportunity to study intertext or which have significant interpolated stanzas have been included. Manuscripts which are not included in this study are: Oxford, Bodl., MS Bodley 48; Oxford, Bodl., MS Bodley 686; Oxford, Bodl., MS Ashmole 59; Oxford, Bodl., MS Laud Misc. 683; Oxford, Bodl., MS Rawlinson C.48; Oxford, Bodl., MS Rawlinson C.86; Oxford, Bodl., MS Rawlinson D.328; Oxford, Bodl., MS Deposit Astor A.2; Cambridge University Library, MS Ff.4.9; Cambridge University Library, MS Hh.4.12; Cambridge, Jesus College, MS 56; Cambridge, Pembroke College, MS 120; Washington D.C., National Library of Medicine, MS 4; Leydon University, MS Vossius 9.

Manuscript	Scribe/Dialect	Date	Notes
London, Lambeth Palace Library, MS Lambeth 853, pp. 150–7.	Written in middle English. Dialect probably central Midlands, possibly Cambridge.	c. 1430 or c. 1450. Possibly the earliest version discussed in this book.	References from this manuscript are typically given as page numbers rather than folio numbers. The poem concludes with 'Thus eendith the book of curteisie. Th[a]t is clepid stans puer ad mensam', p. 155. Possibly for a middle-class audience.[4] Contents also include didactic material – *ABC of Aristotle*, *How the Good Wife Taught her Daughter*, *How the Wise Man Taught his Son* – as well as a collection of religious items.
London, British Library, MS Harley 2251, fols. 148r–149r.	Possibly John Shirley (d.1456) (S), who was closely associated with Lydgate's works, or by the 'Hammond' scribe, based on a Shirleian example.	c. 1460. This manuscript may be contemporaneous with Add. MS 5467. See below.	Lacks the first stanza. Contents also include a collection of Lydgate's poems, among them the *Dietary* and 4 Latin Distichs on the 'general Degeneracy of Mankind, and Dissolution of Manners' and 'Prudential maxims ... for the same young noble youths'. The title is not used in this manuscript.
Cambridge, Jesus College, MS Q.G.8, fols. 77r–78v.		Fifteenth century.	Contents also include poems by Lydgate.
London, British Library, MS Additional 5467, fols. 67r–68v.	John Shirley (S, T). See above.	Mid- to late fifteenth century. Most likely after 1461.	A paper quarto volume. Contents also include passages on courses to set for a royal table, suggesting an interest in courtly protocol and elite activities. The title is not used in this manuscript. Various owners have been identified, including Thomas Wilson, a merchant (before 1697). Also includes *Livre de Bones Meurs* in English and *Secretum Secretorum*.

4 J. Kluewer, 'The Lambeth Lyrics: A New Edition of Lambeth Palace MS 853' (unpublished doctoral dissertation, State University of New York at Stony Brook, 1975), p. xxvii.

Manuscript	Date	Description
Oxford, Bodleian Library, MS Ashmole 61, fols. 17ʳ–19ᵛ.	c. 1480s. The dating of watermarks fixes the paper to approximately the 1480s.	Rate (S). North-east Midlands, possibly associated with Leicestershire. Thought to be a 'one book library' for a family, similar to Edinburgh, National Library of Scotland, MS Advocates 19.3.1. Rate frequently modified the texts he was copying to suit a family audience.	Quatrains abab. 250 lines. Large and narrow English miscellany (418 × 140mm). *SPAM* is significantly altered with the addition of a 47-line prologue. Also contains references to Dr Palere as well as Grosseteste. The title is not used. A visible cue of larger and more ornate capital letters separates the opening stanzas from the rest of the text, possibly to instruct the reader on how to approach the poem. These initials have been done in the same ink as the text and separate and emphasise the opening stanzas. This may have provided a cue to anyone reading the text aloud to pause at this moment. Contents also include romances, saints' lives, prayers and comic tales.
London, British Library, MS Cotton Caligula A ii, fols.14ʳ–15ᵛ.	Second half fifteenth century.	Completed by a single scribe, probably south-east England or south-east Midlands area.	Contents also include *Ypotis*, a moral tale of a wise child, and the romances *Emaré* and *Isumbras*. *Stans puer ad mensam* is combined with Lydgate's *Dietary*. The title *SPAM* is not used.
London, British Library, MS Harley 4011, fols. 1–1ᵛ.	c. 1460.		Contents also include a collection of Lydgate's poems as well as John Russell's *Boke of Nurture*. It has an abbreviated version of *SPAM*. It concludes abruptly, leaving off several stanzas commonly found in other manuscripts. Given its close resemblance to the text found in other manuscripts there is no valid reason to suppose the scribe deliberately overlooked the final stanzas. It is likely he was interrupted or was working from an incomplete copy.
London, British Library, MS Lansdowne 699, fols. 83ᵛ–85ʳ.	Fifteenth century.		Contains no significant textual differences. Also contains verses by Lydgate, including the *Dietary*, which appears directly after *SPAM*

London, British Library, MS Additional 37075, fols. 20r–v.	Written by a grammar school boy, possibly associated with the school of St Anthony, Threadneedle Street, London.	Fifteenth century.	Latin text of *SPAM*.
Oxford, Balliol College, MS 354, fols. 157v–159r.	Household miscellany of Richard Hill (S). Demonstrates merchant connections, particularly with London.	1503–36.	Contains *SPAM* followed by 5 lines of verse beginning 'A Rise erly / serve god devoutly', as well as the *Holy salue regina*, another set of simple maxims beginning 'Wytt hath wonder & kynde ne can' and, finally, the text of Caxton's *Book of Curtesye* (1477). Caxton's 1476 printed edition of *SPAM* also contained these multiple texts (although the *Book of Curtesye* was not part of the 1476 printed edition as it was when de Worde reprinted it in 1510). Hill transposes the order of stanzas in *SPAM*, inserting stanzas 10 through to 12 between stanzas 6 and 7. There is no textual reason for this and it most likely indicates a scribal error.

Hill was made free of the Merchant Adventurers in 1508 and was sworn at the Grocers' Hall, London, in 1511.[5] Hill's wife was the niece of John Wyngar, one-time Mayor of London, with whom Hill had served his apprenticeship. His father-in-law was Harry Wyngar, a haberdasher in London. The names Dame Agnes Wyngar and John Wyngar appear in the manuscript as godparents to a number of Hill's children.[6] A further gloss on fol. 176r notes that Hill was 'servant with Wynger, alderman'. |

---

[5] MS Balliol 354, fol. 107r. By 1511 he also had the freedom of Bruges and Antwerp.
[6] MS Balliol 354, fol. 17r.

Uniform title: *The Babees Book*

Manuscript reference	Author/scribal evidence A = Author S = Scribe T = Translator	Date of original composition	Notes on dating of individual manuscripts	Notes on manuscript, text and textual differences
The Babees Book.	Unknown.	Mid-fifteenth century.		Rime royal stanzas. 217 lines. Possibly written in Latin prior to being translated into English vernacular. A reference to 'Facet' in the poem points to the *Facetus* tradition as a source. Concerns the elite household. Occasionally uses 'virtue' as a synonym for 'courtesy'. Contains an interesting line telling children to take note of difficult words and ask other, presumably adult and learned, people what they mean.
London, British Library, MS Harley 5086, fols. 86ʳ–90ʳ.			c. 1475.	Extant only in this manuscript.

Uniform title: *Urbanitatis*

Manuscript reference	Author/scribal evidence A = Author S = Scribe T = Translator	Date of original composition	Notes on dating of individual manuscripts	Notes on manuscript, text and textual differences
Urbanitatis.	Unknown.	End of the fourteenth century.		Rhyming couplets. Approximately 98 lines. Concerned with the elite household and particularly manners to use while at the table. Thematically similar to *SPAM*.

Manuscript	Description	Date	Notes
London, British Library, MS Cotton Caligula A ii, fols. 88ʳ–90ʳ.	Completed by a single scribe, probably south-east England or south-east Midlands area.	Second half fifteenth century.	Contents also include *Ypotis*, a moral tale of a wise child, and the romances *Emaré* and *Isumbras*. *Stans puer ad mensam* is combined with Lydgate's *Dietary*.
London, British Library, MS Royal 17 A. I, fols. 29ʳ–32ᵛ.	Recardum Heege (S).	Fifteenth century.	Catalogued as part of the preceding Regius Freemasonry poem. There is no break in the manuscript to signal the beginning of *Urbanitatis*. Lacking the opening three lines.
Edinburgh, National Library of Scotland, MS Advocates 19.3.1, fols. 28ʳ–29ᵛ.	John Hawghton (S). North-east Midlands. Believed to have been for family use, possibly forming the complete household library of the late fifteenth-century Sherbrooke family, Nottinghamshire.[7]	Late fifteenth century. The paper in quire 13 can be dated from watermark evidence to 1478.[8]	Omits first 2 lines. Incorrectly called *SPAM*. Contents also include *The Lytylle Childrene's Book*, medieval romances, religious material, nonsense verses, medical receipts and verses by Lydgate.
London, British Library, MS Egerton 2257, fol. 136ʳ.		Nineteenth-century transcript of MS Cotton Caligula Aii.	Discounted in this study.

---

[7] T. Turville-Petre, 'Some Medieval English Manuscripts in the North-East Midlands', in *Manuscripts and Readers in Fifteenth-Century England: the Literary Implications of Manuscript Study*, ed. D. Pearsall (Cambridge, 1983), pp. 125–41 (p. 139). Also, Shaner, 'Instruction and Delight', pp. 5–15.
[8] Hardman, 'A Medieval "Library in Parvo"', p. 264.

Uniform title: *The Lytylle Childrene's Book*. It has occasionally been titled *the book of curtesye*.

Manuscript reference	Author/scribal evidence A = Author S = Scribe T = Translator	Date of original composition	Notes on dating of individual manuscripts	Notes on manuscript, text and textual differences
The Lytylle Childrene's Book.	Unknown.	Mid-fifteenth century.		Rhyming couplets. Approximately 112 lines. Begins by describing the correlation between courtesy and religion. Occasionally uses 'virtue' as a synonym for 'courtesy'. Predominantly concerned with table manners and the elite household. The religious preface is also used in a separate courtesy poem, *The Young Children's Book*, extant only in MS Ashmole 61.
London, British Library, MS Egerton 1995, fols. 58ᵛ–60ᵛ.			After mid-fifteenth century.	Rubricates the opening letters which emphasises the opening 2 stanzas. The poem concludes with the lines 'Here endythe the boke of Curtesy that ys fulle necessary vnto yonge chyldryn that muste nedys lerne the maner of curtesy', fol. 60ʳ. Contents also include items on London, medical and historical pieces. See also entry on Oxford, Balliol College, MS 354.
London, British Library, MS Additional 8151, fols. 201ᵛ–203ᵛ.			Mid- to late fifteenth century. Quires containing *The Lytylle Childrene's Book* date to the late fifteenth century.	Written in a different hand from the rest of the manuscript. The poem is not titled. Contents also include *Speculum Vitae* in English verse.

Cambridge University Library, MS Ee.4.35, fols. 22ᵛ–23ᵛ.	Comprises 2 parts. Owned by Ricardo Calle.	Fourteenth century and early sixteenth century (after 1503).	The poem concludes with 'Explicit the Boke of cortesey'. Contents also include fables and tales: *The Cheylde and hes Step-Dame* and a tale of Robin Hood. Also includes *the vii vertuys agyn the vii dedly synys*. The older part of the manuscript contains *The Prick of Conscience*.
Edinburgh, National Library of Scotland, MS Advocates 19.3.1, fols. 84ᵛ–86ᵛ.	Recardum Heege (S). John Hawghton (S).	See above.	Contents also include *Urbanitatis*, medieval romances, religious material, nonsense verses, medical receipts and verses by Lydgate.
London, British Library, MS Harley 541, fols. 210ʳ–213ʳ.	A booklet in the manuscript belonged to Sir Thomas Frowyk (c. 1460–1506).	About the time of Henry VI or Edward IV. Also contains items from the late sixteenth and early seventeenth centuries.	Lydgate's *Dietary* (or *Rules for Preserving Health*) has been inserted into the text of *The Lytylle Childrene's Book*. This may have been an accidental inclusion by the scribe or a deliberate addition to add another layer to the poem proper.
Oxford, Balliol College, MS 354, fols. 142ᵛ–143ʳ.	Hill (S).	c. 1503–36.	Ends 'here endith ye boke of Curtasie'. English, with French translations after each line. Another poem in Hill's manuscript, the *Siege of Rouen*, is found in Egerton 1995, which also contains *The Lytylle Childrene's Book*. The catalogue of Balliol manuscripts notes that fol. 62ᵛ of Egerton 1995 was signed 'Quod Hylle'.[9]

---

9   R. A. B. Mynors, *Catalogue of the Manuscripts of Balliol College Oxford* (Oxford, 1963), p. 353.

Uniform title: *How the Wise Man Taught his Son*

Manuscript reference	Author/scribal evidence A = Author S = Scribe T = Translator	Date of original composition	Notes on dating of individual manuscripts	Notes on manuscript, text and textual differences
How the Wise Man Taught his Son.	Unknown.	Furnivall speculates on similarities with a poem found in the Exeter Book.		Varying length between 100 and 188 lines. Uses the device of a father addressing his son. Eschews elite manners and advice concerning eating at the table in favour of more general instructions on behaviour, proper living and good conduct. Many of the manuscripts begin 'Listen Lordylings'.
London, Lambeth Palace Library, MS Lambeth 853, pp. 186–193.			c. 1430 or c. 1450.	Contents also include lyrical and religious material as well as several didactic poems. See also earlier entry.
Oxford, Bodleian Library, MS Ashmole 61, fols. 6^{r–v}.	Rate (S).		c. 1480s.	The poem is catalogued as 'A Father's moral and religious instructions to his son'. Contents also include *How the Good Wife Taught her Daughter*, *SPAM* and *The Young Children's Book*. See also earlier entry.
Oxford, Balliol College, MS 354, fols. 152^r–153^r.	Hill (S).		c. 1503–36.	Contents also include *SPAM*, Caxton's *Book of Curtesye* and *The Lytylle Childrene's Book*. See also earlier entry.
London, British Library, MS Harley 5396, fols. 297–300^v (Ritson mistakenly identified this as MS Harley 1596 and Furnivall as MS Harley 4596).			1456.	This version does not begin with 'Lordylings'. Meale ascribes the manuscript to a middle-class, probably merchant/trade environment.[10]

Manuscript reference				Notes on manuscript, text and textual differences
Cambridge University Library, MS Ff.2.38 fols. 53r–54r.	A miscellany. Probably associated with Leicestershire.		End fifteenth century, beginning sixteenth century.	Shares 6 texts with MS Ashmole 61. Also related to London, British Library, MSS Harley 1706, 2339 and 5396 and Cambridge, Magdalene College, MS Pepys 1584. Identifies the interests of a bourgeois readership.

Uniform title: *the boke of curtasye*

Manuscript reference	Author/scribal evidence A = Author S = Scribe T = Translator	Date of original composition	Notes on dating of individual manuscripts	Notes on manuscript, text and textual differences
the boke of curtasye.	Unknown.	Mid-fifteenth century.		Rhyming couplets. 848 lines. The poem is divided into three sections concerning manners at table (Book One), school and religious instruction (Book Two) and the duties and offices within a large household including almoners, butlers and stewards; all of these were senior household positions (Book Three). Book One is solely concerned with commonplace table manners. Books One and Three share similarities with Russell's *Boke of Nurture*.
London, British Library, MS Sloane 1986, fols. 12r–27v.			Dated by Furnivall 1430–40. Dated by Rickert c. 1460.	Extant only in this manuscript. Contents of manuscript are a mixture of Latin and English verse and prose. Included are medical receipts, a chronicle of English kings and a later English translation of what may be a letter by Adam Marsh to Bishop Grosseteste on the management of his household.[11]

[10] C. M. Meale, 'Romance and its Anti-Type? The *Turnament of Totenham*, The Carnivalesque, and Popular Culture', in *Middle English Poetry: Texts and Traditions. Essays in Honour of Derek Pearsall*, ed. A. J. Minnis (York, 2001), pp. 103–28 (pp. 113–15).

[11] The relations between Adam Marsh and Robert Grosseteste are discussed in *The Letters of Adam Marsh*, ed. C. H. Lawrence, 2 vols., Oxford Medieval Texts (Oxford, 2006–10), I, pp. xviii–xxx.

Uniform title: John Russell's *Boke of Nurture*

Manuscript reference	Author/scribal evidence A = Author S = Scribe T = Translator	Date of original composition	Notes on dating of individual manuscripts	Notes on manuscript, text and textual differences
Boke of Nurture.	John Russell (A). Usher and servant to Humphrey, duke of Gloucester (d. 1447).	Early to mid-fifteenth century.		A detailed poem of the various occupations and offices within a large elite household. Of varying length from 832 lines in Sloane 1315 to 1250 lines in Harley 4011. Russell's poem is unusual in that it creates central characters. In Harley 4011 references are given to older source material: 'This tretyse that I haue entitled if it the entende to p[ro]ve / I assayed me self in youth w[i]th] outen any grewe / While I was young I nough & lusty in dede / I enioyed these maters foreseid & to lerne I toke good hede': fol. 188ᵛ. Furnivall and Rickert have speculated he was referring to the *boke of curtesye*.[12] Russell fashions a narrative which identifies courtesy literature as a tool for the dissemination of behaviour. The symbolism of his statement is perhaps as important as the veracity of the comment itself.
London, British Library, MS Sloane 1315, fols. 1ʳ–15ᵛ.			Before *c.* 1460s.	Contains no envoi and concludes with 'Explicit', leaving room for several further stanzas on the leaf before the start of the next poem on the following page.

---

12 Furnivall & Rickert, p. 195.

Manuscript reference	Author/scribal evidence (A = Author, S = Scribe, T = Translator)	Date of original composition	Notes on dating of individual manuscripts	Notes on manuscript, text and textual differences
London, British Library, MS Harley 4011, fols. 171ʳ–189ʳ.			c. 1460.	Passages on general courtesy are separated from the rest of the poem through visual indicators. An inter-title 'Symple condicions' is written in a larger hand. The 'S' is rubricated in red ink, fol. 174ᵛ. This manuscript also contains menus for various dinners, recipes for Hippocras and detailed passages on various types of meats and other food, including baked meats, fried meats and potages, a range which accords with the framework of elite household management. Contains a unique 16-line envoi citing Russell's name.
London, British Library, MS Sloane 2027, fols. 37ʳ–52ʳ.			Before c. 1460s.	Contains no envoi, but begins 'An usscherre y am as ye may se / To a prynce of hygh degre', fol. 37ʳ. Contents also include *Secretum Secretorum*.
London, British Library, MS Royal 17. D. xv, fols. 333–348ᵛ.	Various hands.		Third quarter fifteenth century.	The opening stanza is missing and it begins 'Off such thinge as here be taught by diligence', fol. 333ʳ. Given that the 'O' is elaborately rubricated and is flush with the top of the leaf, it is unlikely that the first lines were ever included in this manuscript. It is possible that some leaves at the end of manuscript have been lost. Contents also include Chaucer's *Canterbury Tales*.

Uniform title: *The Young Children's Book* (variant title, *Dame Courtesy*)

Manuscript reference	Author/scribal evidence (A = Author, S = Scribe, T = Translator)	Date of original composition	Notes on dating of individual manuscripts	Notes on manuscript, text and textual differences
The Young Children's Book.	Unknown.	Unknown.		Rhyming couplets. 152 lines. Indexed in the catalogue of Ashmolean manuscripts as 'Dame Curtasye's moral instructions'.

Oxford, Bodleian Library, MS Ashmole 61, fols. 20ʳ–21ᵛ.	Rate (S).	c. 1480s.	Extant only in this manuscript. Contains striking allusions to a mercantile readership. This poem is broader in its themes than many courtesy poems and considers table manners as well as some moral and ethical issues. There are specific references to 'young children'. The prologue is adapted from *The Lytylle Childrene's Book*. See also earlier entry.

Uniform title: *How the Good Wife Taught her Daughter*

Manuscript reference	Author/scribal evidence A = Author S = Scribe T = Translator	Date of original composition	Notes on dating of individual manuscripts	Notes on manuscript, text and textual differences
How the Good Wife Taught her Daughter.	Supposition that the author was a male cleric.	Unknown.		
Cambridge, Emmanuel College, MS I.4.31, fols. 48ᵛ–52ʳ. Text E.			c. 1350.	This describes an urban bourgeois or mercantile household. It is concerned with the social conduct and moral behaviour of girls, particularly relating to reputation. Between 169 and 215 lines. The earliest of the manuscripts, but probably not the original.[13] It contains only one stanza on how the girl is to bring up her own children, while later manuscripts have further stanzas concerning this.

---

[13] Mustanoja, pp. 117–22.

California, Henry E. Huntington Library, MS HM 128, fols. 217ᵛ–220ʳ. Text H.		First half fifteenth century.	Along with Text E, this probably resembles the original text.
London, Lambeth Palace Library, MS Lambeth 853, pp. 102–12. Text L.		c. 1430.	Similar to Text T. Contents also include lyrical and religious material as well as several didactic poems. See also earlier entry.
Cambridge, Trinity College, MS R.3.19, fols.211ᵛ–213ʳ. Text T.		1463–90.	The text is similar to Text L.
Printed edition from a manuscript in Norfolk. Text N.		Printed 1597.	Printed as *The Northern Mothers Blessing*, along with *The Way to Thrift*. The transcript in Mustanoja's book has been used. Original page numbers are not listed by Mustanoja, hence their absence from footnotes.
Oxford, Bodleian Library, MS Ashmole 61, fols. 7ʳ–8ᵛ. Text A.	Rate (S).	c. 1480s.	This manuscript contains the most textual variations, completely omitting the proverbs between stanzas. Contents also include numerous courtesy texts. See also earlier entry.

Uniform title: *The Good Wyfe Wold a Pylgremage*

Manuscript reference	Author/scribal evidence A = Author S = Scribe T = Translator	Date of original composition	Notes on dating of individual manuscripts	Notes on manuscript, text and textual differences
The Good Wyfe Wold a Pylgremage.				Uses a parental advice format of a mother addressing her young daughter on the management of a household in her absence. The advice is relevant to urban/mercantile households. 84 lines.
National Library of Wales, MS Brogyntyn ii.1, fols. 135ᵛ–138ᵛ. Formerly MS Porkington 10.	Up to 16 scribes have been identified as working on this manuscript. Described as a household miscellany. Dialect is mostly West Midlands.		Late fifteenth century. Watermarks suggest late 1460s.	Extant only in this manuscript.

Uniform title: *The Thewis off Gud Women*

Manuscript reference	Author/scribal evidence A = Author S = Scribe T = Translator	Date of original composition	Notes on dating of individual manuscripts	Notes on manuscript, text and textual differences
The Thewis off Gud Women.		Probably no earlier than c. 1450.		A Middle Scots poem. Written in the third person and lacking the parental advice format of the previous two poems. Advice within this text is more generic and not specific to a bourgeois or mercantile audience. It again addresses young girls and provides advice on reputation, behaviour and conduct. Between 306 and 316 lines.

Cambridge University Library, MS Kk.1.5, fols. 49-53r. Text C.		Late fifteenth century.	Contents also include *Ratis Raving*, *The Foly of Fulys* and the *Thewis of Wys Men*, as well as *The Consail and Teiching of the Vys Man Gaif his Sone*.
Cambridge, St John's College, MS G.23, fols. 164r-167v. Text J.		1487.	Titled *Documenta Matris ad Filiam*. It is preceded by Barbour's *Bruce* and followed by Lydgate's *Dietary* and is written in the same hand, suggesting the compilation of similar texts within one manuscript. Contains additional lines relating to dress and clothing not found in Text C.

Uniform title: Peter Idley's *Instructions to his Son*

Manuscript reference	Author/scribal evidence A = Author S = Scribe T = Translator	Date of original composition	Notes on dating of individual manuscripts	Notes on manuscript, text and textual differences
Instructions to his Son.	Peter Idley (A).	1445-50.		This parental advice poem is divided into 2 books, *Liber Primus* and *Liber Secundus*. Each of the 8 extant manuscripts differs in content and length and in all probability they were based on a now lost copy from which these texts derived.[14] Of these 8 manuscripts only Texts D, E, P and Additional 57335 include both *Liber Primus* and *Liber Secundus* in varying degrees of completeness. Of the other 4 manuscripts, 2 contain only the first book (B1 and H)

---

[14] For a more detailed discussion of the relationships between seven of these manuscripts see *Instructions*, d'Evelyn, pp. 60-75. d'Evelyn appears to have been unfamiliar with London, British Library, MS Additional 57335, containing both books, which begins 'Spies (Species) prudencie' (On guarding the tongue).

and 2 only the second book (A and B2). The poem is primarily concerned with social behaviour, upbringing and religious teaching and does not discuss elite socialisation relevant to the great households. Its emphasis falls on gentry behaviour, with isolated information on courteous behaviour and dress. The poem seems to be showing a relationship between non-noble class backgrounds and an interest in morality.

Oxford, Bodleian Library, MS Digby 181, fols. 10ᵛ–30ᵛ. Text B1.	Second half fifteenth century.	*Liber Primus.*
Oxford, Bodleian Library, MS Laud. Misc. 416, fols. 1–65ᵛ. Text B2.	1459.	*Liber Secundus.*
Cambridge University Library, MS Ee.4.37, fols. 1ʳ–109ʳ. Text E.	Second half fifteenth century.	Both *Liber Primus* and *Liber Secundus*. It is the most complete of all the texts.
Cambridge, Magdalene College, MS Pepys 2030, fols. 19ʳ–133ʳ. Cited as Text P (Magdalene) to differentiate it from Text P, *The Good Wyfe Wold a Pylgremage*.	Sixteenth century.	Both *Liber Primus* and *Liber Secundus*.

Manuscript reference	Author/scribal evidence A = Author S = Scribe T = Translator	Date of original composition	Notes on dating of individual manuscripts	Notes on manuscript, text and textual differences
London, British Library, MS Harley 172, fols. 21ʳ–51ᵛ. Text H.			Fifteenth century.	*Liber Primus*. Includes biographical information on Idley which has been added in a later hand by John Stowe.
London, British Library, MS Arundel 20, fols. 43ʳ–70ᵛ. Text A.			Late fifteenth century	*Liber Secundus*.
Dublin, Trinity College, MS 160 (D.2.7), fols. 14–55ᵛ. Text D.			Fifteenth century.	Both *Liber Primus* and *Liber Secundus*.
London, British Library MS Additional 57335, fols. 1ʳ–97ʳ.			Early sixteenth century.	Both *Liber Primus* and *Liber Secundus*. Opening stanzas are absent.

Other

Manuscript reference	Author/scribal evidence A = Author S = Scribe T = Translator	Date of original composition	Notes on dating of individual manuscripts	Notes on manuscript, text and textual differences
London, British Library, MS Harley 787, fol. 9ʳ.		Late sixteenth century		*How to Rule one's Self and one's House*. Split across two sections: *Domus* and *Temperance*.

Appendix B
Incunabula

Uniform title: *Stans puer ad mensam* (SPAM)

Title	Author/printer evidence A = Author S = Scribe T = Translator P = Printer	Date of edition/s examined in this book	Select publishing information	Other notes
Stans puer ad mensam.	Lydgate (A, T). Caxton (P).	1476. STC 17030.[15]	Quarto in type 2.	Caxton's edition comprises *SPAM* as well as devotional material. This was reprinted in the most part by Wynken de Worde and Johan Redman. Both include a woodcut showing male and female adults surrounded by children and the text of the *Book of Curtesye* (*Lytell Johan*) reprinted from STC 3303, the original 1477 edition printed by Caxton.

---

[15] For continuity, all references are to the Short Title Catalogue (2nd edn). However, the dating of incunabula has been confirmed with the Incunabula Short Title Catalogue (ISTC) and, in places, the revised *Printing in England in the Fifteenth Century, E. Gordon Duff's Bibliography with Supplementary Descriptions, Chronologies and a Census of Copies* by Lotte Hellinga (London, 2009). Where discrepancies occur, dates from the ISTC and Duff's revised *Bibliography* have been taken as the more authoritative.

Uniform title: *Parvus Cato*

Title	Author/printer evidence A = Author S = Scribe T = Translator P = Printer	Date of edition/s examined in this book	Select publishing information	Other notes
Hic incipit parvus Catho.	Benedict Burgh (d. 1483) (T). Caxton (P). This text has been wrongly attributed to Marcus Porcius Cato. It probably dates from imperial times and was most likely written by Dionysius Cato in the third or fourth century.	1476, 1477 and 1483. STC 4851, 4850, 4852.	The first and second editions were quarto in type 2. The third was in folio, since the addition of two woodcuts made it better suited to a larger design.[16] Either the first or second of Caxton's books to be printed with woodcuts.	The *Distichs* is found in numerous manuscripts, in both the original Latin and, after the mid-fifteenth century, in English, following Benedict Burgh's translation. A familiar text in grammar schools where it was used in teaching Latin literacy.[17] Caxton's edition considerably expands these audiences. The popularity of the book, which ran to three editions in 1476/7, 1477 and 1483, indicates an interest among late fifteenth century audiences in this type of moral socialisation. Burgh paraphrased the original Latin text to rime royal stanzas. He retained the emphasis on youthful upbringing in the *distich* style. A variation within the Burgh/Caxton edition was the removal of *fili carissime* (beloved son) to the general 'leue child', suggesting a change in projected audience.[18]

---

16 Blake, *Caxton: England's First Publisher*, pp. 63, 75, 92.
17 Orme, *Medieval Children*, p. 279.
18 See Brunner, 'On Some of the Vernacular Translations', pp. 99–123.

Uniform title: the *Book of Curtesye*

Title	Author/printer evidence A = Author S = Scribe T = Translator P= Printer	Date of edition/s examined in this book	Select publishing information	Other notes
Explicit the book of curtesye.	A= unknown, identified as a student of Lydgate: 'my mastire'. Caxton (P).	1477/8. STC 3303. (ISTC, about 1477).	Quarto in type 2. MS Balliol 354 includes a handwritten copy of Caxton's text.	Rime royal stanzas. Probably written after 1449/50 as Lydgate's death is commemorated. Emphasises vice and virtue. Praises Lydgate, Chaucer and Hoccleve (particularly *Regiment of Princes*, c. 1411). Caxton's book contains no pagination. For the sake of convenience I have adopted Furnivall's page references from his 1868 edition of the text.
Oxford, Balliol College, MS Oriel 79, fols. 88–89r and 78r [leaves misplaced].		Second half fifteenth century.	Not a scribal copy of Caxton's printed edition.[19]	The *Book of Curtesye* is found in a 21-leaf paper booklet inserted into the manuscript. Contents also include the wards in London and their taxes, and a list of parish churches within and outside the walls. Probably produced in London. The manuscript has an additional verse commemorating Lydgate that does not appear in Caxton's edition or in the Balliol copy. The phrase 'Little John' is not used. It is unlikely this was copied and emended from Caxton's book; nor, given textual differences, is it likely that Caxton used the Oriel manuscript as his copy-text. A more precise provenance has yet to be established for the Oriel manuscript or for Caxton's copy-text.

[19] Blake, *Caxton and English Literary Culture*, p. 299.

Uniform title: *Caton*

Title	Author/printer evidence A = Author S = Scribe T = Translator P= Printer	Date of edition/s examined in this book	Select publishing information	Other notes
Here begynneth the prologue or prohemye of the book called Caton.	Caxton (T, P).	1484. STC 4853. (ISTC, after 23 Dec. 1483).	Folio. From the French *Distichs of Cato*.	This prose translation of the *Distichs* by Caxton differs from Burgh's verse translation printed as *Parvus Cato*. The prologue addresses the city of London.

Uniform title: the *Book of the Knight of the Tower*

Title	Author/printer evidence A = Author S = Scribe T = Translator P= Printer	Date of edition/s examined in this book	Select publishing information	Other notes
Here begynneth the booke which the knyght of the toure made, and speketh of many fayre ensamples and thensygnementys and techyng of his daughters.	Geoffroy de la Tour Landry around 1371/2 (A). Caxton (T, P).	1484. STC 15296. (ISTC, 31 Jan. 1484).	Folio. Taken from the text of the French *Livre du Chevalier de la Tour*. Numerous French manuscripts exist, as does one English manuscript dating to Henry VI. A German edition was published in 1493 and was extensively reprinted over	Caxton's prologue emphasizes 'virtue'. The dedication is most likely a reference to Elizabeth Woodville.

the following years. The first French printed edition dates from 1514, some 30 years after Caxton printed his English translation.[20]

Uniform title: *Book of Good Manners*

Title	Author/printer evidence A = Author S = Scribe T = Translator P = Printer	Date of edition/s examined in this book	Select publishing information	Other notes
Here begynneth the table of a book entytled the book of good maners.	Jacques Legrand (A). Caxton (T, P).	1487. STC 15394. (ISTC, 11 May 1487).	Folio. From a French text, *Livre de bonnes moeurs*. A mercer, Wyllia[m] praat, is named as supplying the text to Caxton.	The Cambridge University Library copy (Inc. 3. J. 1. 1. [3521]) was formerly bound with *Royal Book* (Inc. 3. J. 1. 1. [3520]), the *Dicts or Sayings of the Philosophers* (Inc. 3. J. 1. 1. [3526]) and the *Doctrinal of Sapience*.

[20] *Book of the Knight of the Tower*, ed. M. Y. Offord, EETS SS 2 (London, 1971), pp. xix–xxiii.

Appendix C
Sixteenth-Century Books

Uniform title: *The Instruction of a Christen Woman* or simply the *Instruction*

Title	Author/printer evidence A = Author T = Translator P = Printer	Date of edition/s examined in this book	Select publishing information	Other notes
A very frutefull and pleasant boke called the instructio[n] of a Christen woma[n], mayde fyrst in Laten, and dedicated onto the quenes good grace ... and specially women shall take great co[m]modyte and frute towarde the[n]crease of vertue [and] good manners.	Juan Luis Vives (A). Richard Hyrde (T). Thomas Berthelet (P).	Vives's 1523 *De Institutione Foeminae Christianae*. Printed England, 1529? STC 24856.	It was printed nine times before 1600 (1529?,1529?, 1531, 1541, 1547, 1557, 1567, 1585, 1592).	Vives's book is situated within the genre of educational treatises aimed at noble children. Vives dedicates the book to his Spanish countrywoman Katherine of Aragon. The English 1529 edition retains this dedication, while Richard Hyrde adds a reference to the education of Sir Thomas More's daughter to emphasise his own pedagogical standing in England. It is worth noting that from 1541 references to Katherine and More were removed from editions to align the text with changing political circumstances. Henry VIII's divorce from Katherine in 1533 and Mary I's unpopular Spanish marriage in 1554 overtook the previous value of royal Spanish patronage. Many medieval and early modern books were dedicated to influential nobles and royals but this should not be interpreted to represent the book's audience or textual message.

Uniform title: *The werke for housholders* (1531 edition)

Title	Author/printer evidence A = Author T = Translator P= Printer	Date of edition/s examined in this book	Select publishing information	Other notes
The conte[n]tes of this boke. A werke of preparacion, or of ordinaunce vnto co[m]munion, or howselyng. The werke for housholders with the golden pistle and alphabete or a crosrove called an A.B.C. all duely corrected and newly prynted.	Richard Whitford (A). Robert Redman (P).	1531. STC 25412.	*The werke for housholders* was printed by de Worde, STC 25422; Robert Redman, STC 25421.8, STC 25422.5, STC 25423.5; Johan Waylande, STC 25425.5; also Peter Treueris, STC 25422.3. Of the publications, Redman's editions comprising the two books are the longest (1531,1537, 1537). STC 25412, STC 25425, STC 25413	Redman's 1531 edition comprises two books: *A werke of preparacion* and *The werke for householders*. Pagination begins again at Ai and there is a new title page with the colophon *The werke for householders*. *A werke of preparacion* is a reprint of Whitford's earlier translation of St Bernard's *Epistola de perfectione vitae*, STC 1912, which had been published by de Worde in 1530 as *Here begynneth a goodly treatyse, and it is called, A notable lesson, otherwyse it is called The golden pystle*. Also included in this 1531 edition was Whitford's earlier St Bonaventura with an ABC which had been published by Richard Fawkes in 1530: *Here foloweth .ii. opuscules or smale werkes of saynt bonaue[n]ture moche necessarye, and profytable vnto all Chrystyanes specyally vnto religyous [per]sones put in to Englyshe by a brother of Syon Rycharde Whytforde*, STC 3273.3. Also STC 1915, the Godfray version of St Bernard with St Bridget's revelations. The 1531 edition concludes with Bernard Silvestris's *Epistola*, STC 1967.5.

Uniform titles: *Mirrhor of Modestie*, or simply *Mirrhor*, and *The necessarie, fit, and conuenient education* respectively

Title	Author/printer evidence A = Author T = Translator P = Printer	Date of edition/s examined in this book	Select publishing information	Other notes
A mirrhor mete for all mothers, matrons, and maidens, intituled the Mirrhor of Modestie, no lesse profitable and pleasant, then necessarie to bee read and practiced.	Giovanni Michele Bruto (A). Thomas Salter (T, A). J. Kingston for Edward White (P).	Printed, Antwerp 1555, *La institutione di vna fanciulla nata nobilmente*. Printed, England 1579. STC 21634.		A translation of the Italian treatise. Concerns female education and upbringing. Salter 'Anglicises' the text and introduces a Protestant theme. Thomas Salter was probably the schoolmaster at Upminster, Essex, in 1583/4–5.[21]
The necessarie, fit, and conuenient education of a yong gentlewoman. written both in French and Italian, and translated into English by W. P. And now printed with the three languages togither in one volume, for the better instruction of such as are desirous to studie these tongues.	Giovanni Michele Bruto (A). William Phiston/ Fiston (T). Adam Islip (P).	Printed, England 1598. STC 3947.	Similarities with the Antwerp edition which has a French translation on the facing page.[22]	Concerns female education and upbringing. A trilingual translation, including Italian and French, with English on the facing page. This edition retains more of Bruto's Italianate focus. Phiston seems to have been unaware of Salter's earlier translation. Phiston also translated the French *L'ABC ou instruction pour les petis enfans* as *The schoole of good manners. Or, a new schoole of vertue. Teaching children & youth how they ought to behaue themselues in all companies, times, and places. Translated out of French. By W. F. Printed by I. Danter for William Ihones*, 1595. STC 10922.5. Considers manners in relation to religious matters, with some educational content.

[21] Cressy, *Literary and the Social Order*, p. 15.

[22] In 1592 John Wolfe recorded his intention in the Company of Stationers Register to publish 'an instruction for yonge gentlewomen'. Wolfe was a specialist publisher of Italian language books and Continental translations and an associate of Adam Islip who published this book in 1598. *A Critical Edition of The Mirrhor of Modestie*, ed. Holm, p. 12.

Phiston's literary works include the translation of French and Italian texts aimed at adult religious audiences, with a particularly strong Protestant tendency noticeable in his books.

Uniform title: *Lectvres or readings*

Title	Author/printer evidence A = Author T = Translator P= Printer	Date of edition/s examined in this book	Select publishing information	Other notes
Lectvres or readings vpon the 6. verse of the 22. chapter of the Prouerbs, concerning the vertuous education of youth: a treatise very necessary for all parents in this corrupt and declining age of the world.	Robert Shelford (A). Widow Orwin for Thomas Man (P).	1596. STC 22401.5.	Printed again in 1602 and 1606.	The text is based on a verse in Proverbs: 'Teach a child in the trade of his way, and when he is old he shall not depart from it.' Links behaviour with religious values. Shelford was educated at Cambridge and served as deacon in the Peterborough diocese 1587–99. He was later rector of Ringsfield parish, Suffolk, until his death in 1638/9. He wrote his only other book, *Five Pious and Learned Discourses* (1635), on the subject of religious belief and doctrine.

Uniform title: *The golden-groue*

Title	Author/printer evidence A = Author T = Translator P = Printer	Date of edition/s examined in this book	Select publishing information	Other notes
The golden-groue, moralized in three bookes: a worke very necessary for all such, as would know how to gouerne themselues, their houses, or their countrey. Made by W. Vaughan, Master of Artes, and student in the ciuill law.	William Vaughan (A). Simon Stafford (P).	1600. STC 24610.	Revised and printed in 1608.	No pagination. Considers the role of the commonwealth and the family. Frequently uses the word 'gentleman' to identify audience and thematic topics. Vaughan's father was a member of Parliament, and his brother was earl of Carbery. Vaughan attended Oxford and later became a doctor of law. He was heavily involved in the promotion and establishment of Newfoundland in the early seventeenth century. By the time *The golden-groue* was published he was already well known as a poet and literary figure.[23] Vaughan was sympathetic to the interests of yeomen and labourers, writing with considerable insight into the difficulties faced by yeomen farmers after the conversion of tillage lands into grazing lands: *The golden-groue*, Second Book, Chapter 26. Vaughan refers to 'Slibber-sauces' which was a specialist term for 'A compound or concoction of a messy, repulsive, or nauseous character, used esp. for medicinal purposes': *OED*. Vaughan was also interested in writing medical books and in 1600 published *Naturall and Artificiall Directions for Health*, which was probably where he became familiar with this somewhat obscure term.

[23] See, C. Davies, 'Vaughan, Sir William (c. 1575–1641)', *DNB*.

Uniform title: *The boke of nurture*

Title	Author/printer evidence A = Author T = Translator P = Printer	Date of edition/s examined in this book	Select publishing information	Other notes
The boke of nurture for men, seruantes and chyldren with Stans puer ad mensam, newly corrected, very vtyle and necessary vnto all youth.	Hugh Rhodes (A). Thomas Petyt (P).	1545. STC 20953.	The editions are quite distinct from each other.	Rhodes writes that he is a member of the King's Chapel. Contains traditional courtesy information relevant to young servants. Also contains advice for children at home. The 1545 edition is shorter than later editions and lacks the passages 'The maner of seruing a knight, squire, or gentleman' and 'Howe to ordre your maisters chamber, at night to bedwarde'. This is the only work known to have been written by Rhodes, making further comparisons to other material impossible.
The boke of nurture for menseruants and chyldren (with Stans puer ad mensam), newly corrected, very vtile and necessary vnto all youth.	Hugh Rhodes (A). Abraham Veale (P).	1560. STC 20954.		
The boke of nurtur for men seruauntes, and children, with Stans puer ad mensam, newelye corrected, verye vtyle and necessarye vnto all youth.	Hugh Rhodes (A). Thomas Colwell in the house of Robert Wyer (P).	1560. STC 20955.		

Title	Author (Printer)	Date/STC	Notes
The Booke of Nurture for man seruauntes, and children: (with Stans puer ad mensam) Herunto is annexed, our Lords Prayer, our Beliefe, and the. x. Commaundements: with godly Graces, to be sayde at the Table, before and after meat. Very vtile and necessary for all youth to learne.	Hugh Rhodes (A). Thomas East (P).	1568. STC 20956.	This edition is the most markedly different in terms of physical appearance and content. It includes specific religious material including graces for before and after dinner and upon rising and retiring.
The boke of nurture for men, seruauntes, and children.	Hugh Rhodes (A). s. n. (P).	1570. STC 20957.	This edition is physically distinctive. It is narrow, only 8.5cm wide, and uses extensive decorative borders and woodcuts.
The boke of nurture, or, Schoole of good maners for men, seruants, and children: with Stans puer ad mensam.	Hugh Rhodes (A). H. Jackson (P).	1577. STC 20958.	Imperfect. Begins page Aii.

Uniform title: *The schoole of virtue*

Title	Author/printer evidence A = Author T = Translator P = Printer	Date of edition/s examined in this book	Select publishing information	Other notes
The schoole of virtue, and booke of good nourture for chyldren, and youth to learne theyer dutie by. Newely persued, corrected, and augmented by the fyrst auctour. F. S with a briefe declaration of the dutie of eche degree.	Francis Seager [Segar] (A). Wyllyam Seares (P).	1557. STC 22135.	Popular throughout the sixteenth and seventeenth centuries. The first three editions only have been discussed in this book.	Looks at the behaviour of young servants as well as children living in the family home. Some educational content. Later editions include additional prayers and graces for Queen Elizabeth I. Suggestive of malleability and flexibility to meet contemporary political conditions and events. The book may have been popular with 'humble readerships'.[24] Seager was involved with reworking Chartier's *The Curial* in 1549. This was a text that was particularly reflective of turbulent social and political changes and responsive to people's concerns and anxieties. Chapters on courtesy are: Chapter One (Howe to order thy selfe when thou rysest, and in apparelynge thy body); Chapter Two (Howe to behaue thy selfe in going by the streate and in the schoole); Chapter Three (Howe to behaue thi selfe in seruynge the table); Chapter Four (Howe to order thy selfe syttynge at the table); Chapter Seven (How to behaue thy selfe in talkynge with any man); and Chapter Eight (How to order thy selfe being sente of message).

[24] J. N. King, 'Seager, Francis (*fl.* 1549–1563)', *DNB*.

F. S. The schoole of vertue and booke of good nurture, teaching children and youth their duties. Newlie perused, corrected, and augmented. Hereonto is added a briefe declaration of the dutie of ech degree: also certaine praiers and graces compiled by R. C.	Francis Seager [Segar] (A). H. Denham (P).	1582. STC 22136.	Chapters on courtesy, with some moral lessons, are: Chapter Five (Howe to order thy selfe in the Churche); Chapter Eleven (Againge the horrible vice of swearynge) and Chapter Twelve (Againste the vice of filthy talkynge). Chapters on moral issues are: Chapter Six (The fruites of gamynge, vertue and learnynge); Chapter Nine (Againste anger, enuie, and malice); Chapter Ten (The fruites of charitie, loue, and pacience) and Chapter Thirteen (Againste the vice of lyinge). See above. Some evidence suggests this edition (and presumably others) was sold at the stalls of ballad singers. Both the 1582 and 1593 editions list Robert Crowley as an additional compiler whose name is used in an acrostic poem with Seager's. Crowley was a Protestant poet and bookseller with whom Seager had a strong working relationship.
The schoole of vertue & booke of good nurture, teaching children & youth their duties. Newlie perused, corrected and augmented. Hereunto is also added a briefe declaration of the dutie of each degree. Also, certaine praiers and graces compiled by R. C.	Francis Seager [Segar] (A). John Charlewood for Richard Iones (P).	1593. STC 22137.	See above.

Appendix D
Educational Sources

Name of school, county	Relevant dates	Catalogue references and location of document	Additional notes
St Albans Almonry, Hertfordshire.	1330	Leach, *Edu Chtr*, pp. 296–9.	Records a distinct interest in behaviour and conduct. Some references to table manners are reminiscent of courtesy poems.
Jesus College, Rotherham, West Riding, Yorkshire.	1483	Leach, *Edu Chtr*, pp. 423–33.	References scholars in terms of virtue.
Grammar School, Macclesfield, Cheshire.	Founded 1502/3	Cheshire Archives, SP3/14/1 (copy of will), SP3/14/2 (copy foundation deed), SP3/14/5 (charter).	Established in the will of Sir John Percyvale (1502/3).
Guildford Grammar School, Surrey.	Established 1509. Refounded Edward VI.	Surrey History Centre, 1775/1/1 (copy letters patent), 1775/2/2 (copy statutes).	Established in the will of Robert Beckingham, London grocer (1509). After the Chantries Act of 1547 the school petitioned for additional endowments. The letters patent of Edward VI allowed for statutes to be drawn up, although it is possible that statutes had been made prior to this. The 1608 statutes analysed in this book were drawn up by George Austen, mayor of Guildford, and were an adaptation of Colet's statutes (1518) for St Paul's. They were approved by the Bishop of Winchester in 1608. By this time the school was charging a fee for attendance.
Canterbury Cathedral and Grammar School, Kent.	Refounded 1541.	Leach, *Edu Chtr*, pp. 452–71.	Emphasises behaviour and conduct.

School	Date	Source	Notes
Sherborne Grammar School, Dorset.	Refounded 1550. Statutes 1592. Account books mid-1550s.	Dorset History Centre, S235/A1/1–2, also S235/A2/5/1, S235/B1/2, S235/C2/4/1, S235/D1/1/1–2	Refounded with chantry lands from Martock and St Katherine in Gillingham. Extensive building works were undertaken in c. 1555.
Westminster School, Middlesex.	Statutes 1560.	Leach, *Edu Chtr*, pp. 496–525.	Reminds scholars that their appearance and conduct should reflect their status as gentlemen.
Rivington Grammar School, Lancashire.	Foundation charter 1566. Governor's accounts 1574. Amalgamated with the Blackrod School, founded 1568.	Lancashire Record Office, DDX 94/94 (Account Book, including list of scholars) and DDX94/100 (statutes).	Charged fees on a scale depending on whether the scholar was from the surrounding area or outside it. Rich and very detailed statutes. References to a school at Blackrod first appeared in the will of its founder John Holme, dated 10 September 1560: 'one Learned & discret Schoolmaster which shall teach a free Gram[mer] School at or within y[e] Towne of Blackrode in y[e] Church there or as near unto it as they shall think meet'. Lancashire, DDX 94/163.
Dame Alice Owen's School, Islington, Middlesex.	Founded 1613.	London Metropolitan Archives, CLC/L/BF/G/071/MS05480A, 'Dame Alice Owen's Charity: Deeds, Papers and Sundry Correspondence' (1608–1923).	The curriculum was based on grammar, ciphering and casting accounts and was specifically identified with training people for apprenticeships. Poor scholars were taught without fee.
Dame Elizabeth Periam's School, Oxfordshire.	1609.	Oxfordshire History Centre, S128/1PB2/A1/2 (statutes).	Elementary training.
Libri Cleri of Synods, Ely Diocese.	Various, sixteenth and seventeenth century.	Cambridge University Library, Ely Diocese Records (EDR).	'Sacra Synodus'. '*Libri Cleri* of synods, county only, celebrated before Richard Bridgewater and Andrew Perne, delegates of the Archbishop, followed by condemnations of absentees.' Records schoolmaster licences.

Register of Presentments, Chichester.	1571–1682.	West Sussex Record Office, EpI/17/5–12, EpI/23/5.	Records schoolmaster licences.
1558 Gloucester Boy-Bishop sermon	1558	*The Camden Miscellany, Volume the Seventh, Containing Two Sermons Preached by the Boy-Bishop* (London, 1875)	It is unlikely that a student wrote any of the boy-bishop sermons. The ceremony, important in Catholic festivities, was associated with St Nicholas's day, 6 December and with the feast of Childermass or Holy Innocents' Day, 28 December. Choristers would elect a 'boy-bishop' who was invested with the dignity of the bishop and who carried out the religious services in the cathedral for that day, with the exception of saying the mass. This was an opportunity for young people to have a legitimate place in religious affairs. The ceremony came under attack by Protestant reformers, was briefly revived under Mary I, but banned again under Elizabeth I.

Printed educational sources

Grammars

Title	Author/printer evidence A = Author S = Scribe T = Translator P= Printer	Date of edition/s examined in this book	Select publishing information	Other notes
Vulgaria quedam abs Terencio in Anglica[m] linguam traducta.	Terence (A). Theodoric Rood and Thomas Hunt (P).	1483. STC 23904.	Bodleian copy is preceded by John Anwykyll's *Compendium totius*, STC 696.	English/Latin. Uses familiar phrases often relating to social interactions and family relationships.

Title	Author/Printer	Date/STC	Notes
Lac puerorum. M. Holti. Anglice mylke for children.	John Holte (A). de Worde (P).	1508 edition. STC 13604.	The 1505 edn STC 13603.7 is a fragment. Contains three woodcuts.
Uulgaria sta(n)brige.	John Stanbridge (A). de Worde. (P).	1509. STC 23195.5.	STC lists 175 editions associated with Stanbridge. English/Latin. Uses familiar phrases, some relating to serving at the table.
Various.	Robert Whittington (A).	1511 through to 1554.	Noted for selling his books individually and cheaply. Critical of William Horman, leading to the 'Grammarian's war' of the 1520s.
Vulgaria uiri doctissimi Guil. Hormani Caesariburgensis.	William Horman (A). Richard Pynson (P).	1519, STC 13811. Reprinted 1530, STC 13812.	Horman's contract survives and shows he paid Pynson 8s per ream to publish 800 copies. Sold for 5s. Criticised by Robert Whittington. Part of the 'Grammarian's war'. English/Latin. Has an extensive thirty-five chapters, some concerning social matters and behaviour.
'Lily's Grammar' or *The Royal Grammar*.	William Lily and others (A). Various printers.	1548–9 onwards.	England's official grammar. The history of this book is involved and sometimes unclear. Lily wrote only part of the grammar. It was consolidated in 1548 and comprised two texts: *A shorte introduction of grammar generally to be used in the kynges maiesties dominions, for the bryngynge up of all those that entende to atteyne the knowledge of the Latine tongue* and *Brevissima institutio, seu, Ratio grammatices cognoscendae, ad omnium puerorum utilitatem praescripta, quam solam regia maiestas in omnibus scholis profitendam praecipit* (1549). For a full description see R. D. Smith's entry in the *DNB*.[25]

---

[25] Smith, 'Lily', *DNB*.

Other published educational books

Title	Author/printer evidence A = Author S = Scribe T = Translator P= Printer	Date of edition/s examined in this book	Select publishing information	Other notes
The school of virtue.	Francis Seager (A).			See earlier entry.
The English Schoolemaister, teaching all his scholars the order of distinct reading and true writing of our English tongue.	Edmund Coote (A). Widow Orwin for Ralph Jackson and Robert Dextar (P).	1596, STC 5711.	Runs to thirty-eight editions between 1596 and 1737.	Brief tenure as schoolmaster at King Edward VI Free School in Bury St Edmunds and later at Hunsdon, Hertfordshire. Manual for elementary teachers as well as grammar masters. John Brinsley identifies Coote's book as a helpful preparatory text for future grammar scholars in his own 1622 educational tract, *A Consolation for Ovr Grammar Schooles*. Brinsley personally acknowledges his own debt to Coote, suggestive of a curious fluidity between elementary and grammar schools.
The schoole of good manners.	William Phiston/Fiston (A).			See earlier entry.
The Education of children in learning, declared by the dignitie, vtilitie, and method thereof. Meete to be knowne, and practised aswell of parents as schoolemaisters.	William Kempe (A). Thomas Orwin, for Iohn Porter and Thomas Gubbin (P).	1588, STC 14926.		Schoolmaster Plymouth Grammar School, 1581–1601. Considers the interaction between parents and schoolteachers.

Passages on Socrates, a parent's duties towards children and a master's duties, are comparable to chapters in Elyot's book. Further details are in R. D. Pepper (ed.), *Four Tudor Books on Education* (Gainesville, 1966), p. xii. |

An A.B.C for children.	Unknown (A). John King (P).	1561, conjecture, STC 19.4	Entered into the Stationers' Registers for J. Walley in 1557–8 and T. Purfoot 1561–2.	Educational and religious. Conservative Catholic grouping of passages. ABCs were popular and came in different forms.
Ludus literarius: or, the grammar schoole; shewing how to proceede from the first entrance into learning, to the highest perfection required in the grammar schooles, with ease, certainty and delight both to masters and scholars …	John Brinsley (A). Humphrey Lownes for Thomas Man (P).	1612, STC 3768.	Cross promotes this and other books in press.	Schoolmaster at Ashby, 1600–17. Later licensed to teach in London. Served as curate in two parishes in Leicestershire.
A Consolation for Ovr Grammar Schooles: Or, A faithfull and most comfortable incouragement, for laying of a sure foundation of all good Learning in our Schooles, and for prosperous building thereupon …	John Brinsley (A). Richard Field for Thomas Man (P).	1622, STC 3767.	No further editions are known to have been printed.	See above.

De ciuilitate morun [sic] puerilium per Des. Erasmum Roterodamum, libellus nunc primum & conditus & æditus. Roberto VVhitintoni interprete. A lytell booke of good maners for chyldren, nowe lately compyled and put forth by Erasmus Roterodam in latyne tonge, with interpretacion of the same in to the vulgare englysshe tonge, by Robert whytyngton laureate poete. Cum priuilegio.	Desiderius Erasmus (A). Robert Whittington (A) (T). Wynken de Worde (P).	1532, STC 10467.	A translation of *De ciuilitate morum puerilium*. Whittington's translation was printed again in 1534, 1540, 1554 and 1555.
A treatise of schemes [and] tropes very profytable for the better vnderstanding of good authors... Wherunto is added a declamacion, that chyldren euen strapt fro[m] their infancie should be wel and gently broughte vp in learnynge. Written fyrst in Latin by the most excellent and famous clarke, Erasmus of Roterodame.	Desiderius Erasmus (A). Richard Sherry (A) (T). John Day (P).	1550, STC 22428.	Includes a translation of Erasmus, *De pueris statim ac liberaliter instituendis*. Erasmus's text is very clearly identified as separate from Sherry's text. Pagination begins again at Biv; there is also an opening title complete with a decorative initial 'I'. Sherry's own text is a summary of grammatical rules and precepts, including proper word order, the construction of sentences and other linguistic rules. This would have been relevant to academic scholars and probably schoolmasters needing to learn or re-learn grammatical rules for use in grammar schools. The lessons are formulaic and there are few pedagogical glosses on the nature of education. Erasmus's text was printed in Antwerp in 1529. It was not one of Erasmus's most famous works in England. An unacknowledged borrowing occurs in Roger Ascham's *The scholemaster*.[26]

---

[26] See M. F. Vaughan, 'An Unnoted Translation of Erasmus in Ascham's "Schoolmaster"', *Modern Philology* 75 (1977), 184–6.

BIBLIOGRAPHY

Manuscript sources

California, Henry E. Huntington Library
MS HM 128

Cambridge, Emmanuel College
MS I.4.31

Cambridge, Jesus College
MS Q.G.8

Cambridge, Magdalene College
MS Pepys 2030

Cambridge, St John's College
MS G.23

Cambridge, Trinity College
MS R.3.19

Cambridge University Library
EDR D2/16
Syn. 8. 53. 35
MS Ee.4.35
MS Ee.4.37
MS Ff.2.38
MS Kk.1.5

Cheshire Archives
P40/16/1
SP3/14/1
SP3/14/2
SP3/14/5

Dorset History Centre
S235/A1/1–2
S235/A2/5/1
S235/B1/2
S235/C2/4/1
S235/D1/1/1–2

Dublin, Trinity College
MS 160 (D.2.7)
Edinburgh, National Library of Scotland
MS Advocates 19.3.1

Essex Record Office
D/ACA 21

Lancashire Record Office
DDBk 3/10
DDX 94/94
DDX 94/100

London, British Library
MS Additional 5467
MS Additional 8151
MS Additional 37075
MS Additional 57335
MS Arundel 20
MS Cotton Caligula A ii
MS Egerton 1995
MS Egerton 2257
MS Harley 172
MS Harley 541
MS Harley 787
MS Harley 2251
MS Harley 4011
MS Harley 5086
MS Harley 5396
MS Lansdowne 699
MS Royal 17 A. I
MS Royal 17 D. xv
MS Sloane 1315
MS Sloane 1986
MS Sloane 2027
MS Stowe 982

London, Lambeth Palace Library
MS Lambeth 853

London Metropolitan Archives
CLC/L/BF/G/071/MS05480A

National Library of Wales
MS Brogyntyn ii.1

Oxford, Balliol College
MS Balliol 354
MS Oriel 79

Bibliography

Oxford, Bodleian Library
MS Ashmole 61
MS Digby 181
MS Laud. Misc. 416

Oxfordshire History Centre
S128/1PB2/A1/2

Surrey History Centre
1775/1/1
1775/2/2

The National Archives, Kew
C1/723/7–8
C1/998/41
C2/Eliz/C11/10
C2/Eliz/C20/15
C 116/151
E 134/36 Eliz/Hil10
E 301/35/31
E 301/61/17
SP 12/240 (105)

Warwickshire County Record Office
DR(B)16/52

West Sussex Record Office
EpI/17/5–12
EpI/23/5
EpIII/4/3
STC III/B
STC III/C

Printed primary sources

An A.B.C for chyldren (London, 1561?).
Explicit the book of curtesye (Westminster, 1477).
Here begynneth a treatyse of a galau[n]t (London, 1510).
Here begynneth the prologue or prohemye of the book callid Caton whiche booke hath ben translated in to Englysshe by Mayster Benet Burgh, late Archedeken of Colchestre and hye chanon of saint stephens at westmestre ... and by cause of late cam to my hand a book of the said Caton in Frensshe, whiche rehercheth many a fary lernynge and notable ensamples, I haue translated it oute of frensshe in to Englysshe, as al along here after shalle appiere, whiche I presente vnto the cyte of London (Westminster, after 23 Dec. 1483).

Bibliography

Here endith a compendiouse treetise dyalogue. of Diues [et] paup[er]. that is to say. the riche [and] the pore fructuously tretyng vpon the x. co[m]man mentes (London, 1493).

Hic incipit paruus Catho (Westminster, 1476/7).

Hic incipit paruus Catho (Westminster, 1477).

Hic incipit paruus Catho (Westminster, 1483).

Peruula (Westminster, 1496).

The Boke of Noblesse, Addressed to King Edward the Fourth on His Invasion of France in 1475, with an Introduction by John Gough Nichols (London, 1860).

The Camden Miscellany, Volume the Seventh, Containing Two Sermons Preached by the Boy-Bishop, ed. J. G. Nichols, with an introduction by E. F. Rimbault (London, 1875).

This is the table of the historye of reynart the foxe (Westminster, 1481).

Ascham, R., *The scholemaster or plaine and perfite way of teachyng children, to vnderstand, write, and speake, the Latin tong, but specially purposed for the priuate bryngyng vp of youth in ientlemen and noble mens houses, and commodious also for all such, as haue forgot the Latin tonge, and would, by themselues, without à scholemaster, in short tyme, and with small paines, recouer à sufficient habilitie, to vnderstand, write, and speake Latin* (London, 1570).

Blamires, A., ed., with K. Pratt and C. W. Marx, *Women Defamed and Women Defended: An Anthology of Medieval Texts* (Oxford, 1992).

Brinsley, J., *A Consolation for Ovr Grammar Schooles: Or, A faithfull and most comfortable incouragement, for laying of a sure foundation of all good Learning in our Schooles, and for prosperous building thereupon. More specially for all those of the inferiour sort, and all ruder countries and places; namely, for Ireland, Wales, Virginia, with the Sommer Ilands, and for their more speedie attaining of our English tongue by the same labour, that all may speake one and the same language. And withal, for the helping of all such as are desirous speedilie to recouer that which they had formerlie got in the Grammar Schooles; and to proceed aright therein, for the perpetuall benefis of these our Nations, and of the Churches of Christ* (London, 1622).

Brinsley, J., *Ludus literarius: or, the grammar schoole; shewing how to proceede from the first entrance into learning, to the highest perfection required in the grammar schooles, with ease, certainty and delight both to masters and schollars; onely according to our common grammar, and ordinary classical authours: begun to be sought out at the desire of some worthy fauourers of learning, by searching the experiments of sundry most profitable schoolemasters and other learned, and confirmed by tryall: intended for the helping of the younger sort of teachers, and of all schollars* ... (London, 1612).

Calendar of Wills Proved and Enrolled in the Court of Husting, London: Part 2: 1358–1688, ed. R. R. Sharpe, 2 vols. (London, 1890).

Cardwell, E., ed. *Synodalia: A Collection of Articles of Religion, Canons, and Proceedings of Convocations in the Province of Canterbury, From the year 1547 to the year 1717; With Notes Historical and Explanatory by Edward Cardwell*, 2 vols. (Oxford, 1842), I.

Caxton, W., *Caxton's Own Prose*, ed. N. F. Blake (London, 1973).

Caxton, W., *The Prologues and Epilogues of William Caxton*, ed. W. J. B. Crotch, EETS OS 176 (Oxford, 1928).

Chaucer, G., *The Works of Geoffrey Chaucer*, ed. F.N. Robinson, 2nd edn (Oxford, 1957).

Bibliography

Clement, F., *The Petie Schole With an English Orthographie, wherein by rules lately prescribed is taught a method to enable both a childe to reade perfectly within one moneth, & also the vnperfect to write English aright* (London, 1587).

Coote, E., *The English Schoole-maister, teaching all his scholars the order of distinct reading and true writing of our English tongue* (London, 1596).

Dod, J., and R. Cleaver, *A godlie forme of householde gouernement* (London, 1610).

Elyot, T., *The boke named the Gouernour, deuised by Thomas Elyot knight* (London, 1531).

Fantazzi C., ed. and trans., *The Education of a Christian Woman: A Sixteenth-Century Manual* (Chicago, 2000).

Fiston, W., *The schoole of good manners. Or, a new schoole of virtue. Teaching children & youth how they ought to behaue themselues in all companies, times, and places. Translated out of French. By W.F.* (London, 1595).

Fuller, T., *The Worthies of England: Edited with an Introduction and Notes by John Freeman* (London, 1952).

Furnivall, F. J., ed., *Early English Meals and Manners: John Russell's Boke of nurture, Wynken de Worde's Boke of keruynge, The boke of curtasye, R. Weste's Booke of demeanor, Seager's Schoole of vertue, The babees book, Aristotle's A B C, Urbanitatis, Stans puer ad mensam, The lytylle childrenes lytil boke, For to serve a lord, Old Symon, The birched school-boy, &c., &c., with some forewords on education in early England, Edited by Frederick J. Furnivall*, EETS OS 32 (London, 1868).

Furnivall, F. J., ed., *Queene Elizabethes achademy (by Sir Humphrey Gilbert). A booke of precedence; the ordering of a funerall, &c, Varying versions of The good wife, The wise man, &c.; Maxims, Lydgate's Order of fools. A poem on heraldry, Occleve on lord's men, &c. / ed. by F.J. Furnivall, with essays on early Italian and German books of courtesy, by W.M. Rosssetti & E. Oswald*, EETS ES 8 (London, 1869).

Furnivall, F. J., and E. Rickert, eds., *The Babees' Book, Medieval Manners for the Young, now first done into modern English from Dr. Furnivall's Texts by Edith Rickert* (New York, 1913).

Goldberg, P. J. P., ed., *Women in England c. 1275–1525: Documentary Sources, Translated and Edited by P. J. P. Goldberg* (Manchester, 1995).

Gouge, W., *Of domesticall duties eight treatises. I. An exposition of that part of Scripture out of which domesticall duties are raised. II. 1. A right coniunction of man and wife. 2. Common-mutuall duties betwixt man and wife. III. Particular duties of wiues. IV. Particular duties o husbands. V. Duties of children. VI. Duties of parents. VII. Duties of seruants. VIII. Duties of masters* (London, 1622).

Grant, E., *A president for parentes, teaching the vertuous training vp of children and holesome information of yongmen. Written in greke by the prudent and wise phylosopher Choeroneus [sic] Plutarchus, translated and partly augmented by Ed. Grant: very profitable to be read of all those that desire to be parents of virtuous children. Anno. 1571. Seene and allowed according to the Quenes iniunctions* (London, 1571).

Hake, E., *A touchestone for this time present, expresly declaring such ruines, enormities, and abuses as trouble the Churche of God and our Christian common wealth at this daye. VVherevnto is annexed a perfect rule to be obserued of all parents and scholemaisters, in the trayning vp of their schollers and children in learning. Newly set foorth by E.H.* (London, 1574).

Harrison, W., *The Description of England, The Classic Contemporary Account of Tudor Social Life*, ed. G. Edelen (Ithaca, 1968).

Bibliography

Hart, J., *A methode or comfortable beginning for all vnlearned, whereby they may be taught to read English, in a very short time, vvith pleasure: so profitable as straunge, put in light, by I. H. Chester Heralt* (London, 1570).

Holte, J., *Lac puerorum. M. Holti. Anglice mylke for children* (London, 1508).

Horman, W., *Vulgaria uiri doctissimi Guil. Hormani Cæsariburgensis* (London, 1519).

Huloet, R., *Abcedarium anglico latinum, pro tyrunculis Richardo Huloeto exscriptore* (London, 1552).

Hyrde, R., *A very frutefull and pleasant boke called the instructio[n] of a Christen woma[n], made fyrst in Laten, and dedicated vnto the quenes good grace, by the right famous clerke mayster Lewes Vives, and turned out of Laten into Englysshe by Rycharde Hyrd. whiche boke who so redeth diligently shal haue knowlege of many thynges, wherin he shal take great pleasure, and specially women shall take great co[m]modyte and frute towarde the[n]creace of vertue [and] good maners* (London, 1529).

Kempe, W., *The Education of children in learning, declared by the dignitie, vtilitie, and method thereof. Meete to be knowne, and practised aswell of parents as schoolemaisters* (London, 1588).

Idley, P., *Peter Idley's Instructions to his Son*, ed. C. d'Evelyn (Boston, 1935).

la Tour Landry, G. de, *Book of the Knight of the Tower translated by William Caxton*, ed. M. Y. Offord, EETS SS 2 (London, 1971).

la Tour Landry, G. de., *Here begynneth the booke which the knyght of the toure made and speketh of many fayre ensamples and thensygnementys and techyng of his daughters* (Westminster, 1484).

Leach, A. F., ed., *Educational Charters and Documents 598–1909* (Cambridge, 1911).

Legrand, J., *Here begynneth the table of a book entytled the book of good maners* (Westminster, 1487).

Lily, W., *Brevissima institutio, seu, Ratio grammatices cognoscendae, ad omnium puerorum utilitatem praescripta, quam solam regia maiestas in omnibus scholis profitendam praecipit* (London, 1567).

Lily, W., *A shorte introduction of grammar generally to be used in the kynges maiesties dominions, for the bryngynge up of all those that entende to atteyne the knowledge of the Latine tongue* (London, 1549).

Lydgate, J., *Stans puer ad mensam* (Westminster, 1476).

Lydgate, J., *Stans puer ad me[n]sa[m]* (London, 1510).

Lydgate, J., *Stans puer ad mensa[m]. Otherwyse called the boke of Norture, newly imprinted and very necessary vnto all youthe* (London, 1540).

Malory, T., *Thus endeth thys noble and joyous book entytled Le morte darthur ... which book was reduced in to Englysshe by Syr Thomas Malory ... and by me deuyded in to xxi bookes ... Caxton me fieri fecit* (Westminster, 1485).

Mulcaster, R., *Positions vvherin those primitive circumstances be examined, which are necessarie for the training vp of children either for skill in their booke, or health in their bodie. VVritten by Richard Mulcaster, master of the schoole erected in London anno. 1561. in the parish of Sainct Laurence Povvntneie, by the vvorshipfull companie of the merchaunt tailers of the said citie* (London, 1581).

Mulcaster, R., *The first part of the elementarie vvhich entreateth chefelie of the right writing of our English tung, set furth by Richard Mulcaster* (London, 1582).

Mustanoja, T. F., ed., *The Good Wife Taught Her Daughter; The Good Wyfe Wold a Pylgremage; The Thewis of Gud Women* (Helsinki, 1948).

Bibliography

Nowell, A., *A catechisme, or first instruction and learning of Christian religion. Translated out of Latine into Englishe* (London, 1570).

Paston Letters: Original Letters Written During the Reign of Henry VI., Edward IV., and Richard III, ed. J. Fenn, 2 vols. (London, 1849).

Pepper, R. D., (ed.) *Four Tudor Books on Education* (Gainesville, 1966)

Phiston, W., *The necessarie, fit, and conuenient education of a yong gentlewoman. written both in French and Italian, and translated into English by W.P. And now printed with the three languages togither in one volume, for the better instruction of such as are desirous to studie these tongues* (London, 1598).

Rhodes, H., *The boke of nurture for men, seruantes and chyldren, with Stans puer ad mensam, newly corrected, very vtyle and necessary vnto all youth* (London, 1545).

Rhodes, H., *The boke of nurture for menseruants and chyldren (with Stans puer ad mensam), newly corrected, very vtile and necessary vnto all youth* (London, 1560).

Rhodes, H., *The Boke of Nurture for men seruauntes, and children, with Stans puer ad mensam, newelye corrected, virye vtyle and necessarye vnto all youth* (London, 1560).

Rhodes, H., *The Booke of Nurture for man seruauntes, and children: (with Stans puer ad mensam) Herunto is annexed, our Lords Prayer, our Beliefe, and the. x. Commaundements: with godly Graces, to be sayde at the Table, before and after meat. Very vtile and necessary for all youth to learne* (London, 1568).

Rhodes, H., *The boke of nurture for men, seruauntes, and children* (London, 1570)

Rhodes, H., *The boke of nurture, or, Schoole of good maners for men, seruants, and children: with Stans puer ad mensam* (London, 1577).

Salter, T., *A Critical Edition of Thomas Salter's The Mirrhor of Modestie*, ed. J. B. Holm (New York, 1987).

Salter, T., *A mirrhor mete for all mothers, matrons, and maidens, intituled the Mirrhor of Modestie, no lesse profitable and pleasant, then necessarie to bee read and practiced* (London, 1579).

Seager, F., *The schoole of virtue, and booke of good nourture for chyldren, and youth to learne theyer dutie by. Newely persued, corrected, and augmented by the fyrst auctour. F.S with a briefe declaration of the dutie of eche degree. Anno. 1557* (London, 1557).

Seager, F., *The schoole of vertue and booke of good nurture, teaching children and youth their duties. Newlie pervsed, corrected, and augmented. Herevnto is added a briefe declaration of the dutie of ech degree: also certaine praiers and graces compiled by R.C.* (London, 1582).

Seager, F., *The schoole of vertue & booke of good nurture, teaching children & youth their duties. Newlie perused, corrected and augmented. Hereunto is also added a briefe declaration of the dutie of each degree. Also, certaine praiers and graces compiled by R.C.* (London, 1593).

Seymour, M., ed., *On the Properties of Things, John Trevisa's translation of Bartholomaeus Anglicus De Proprietatibus Rerum, A Critical Text*, 3 vols. (Oxford, 1975).

Shelford, R., *Lectvres or readings vpon the 6. verse of the 22. chapter of the Prouerbs, concerning the vertuous education of youth: a treatise very necessary for all parents in this corrupt and declining age of the world* (London, 1596).

Sherry, R., *A treatise of schemes [and] tropes very profytable for the better vnderstanding of good authors, gathered out of the best grammarians [and] oratours by Rychard Sherry Londoner. Whervnto is added a declamacion, that chyldren euen strapt fro[m] their infancie should be wel and gently broughte vp in learnynge. Written fyrst in*

Bibliography

Latin by the most excellent and famous clearke, Erasmus of Roterodame (London, 1550).
Shuffelton, G., ed., *Codex Ashmole 61: A Compilation of Popular Middle English Verse*, (Kalamazoo, 2008).
Smith, H., *A preparatiue to mariage. The summe whereof was spoken at a contract, and inlarged after. Whereunto is annexed a treatise of the Lords Supper, and another of vsurie. By Henrie Smith* (London, 1591).
Stanbridge, J., *Uulgaria sta(n)brige* (London, 1509).
Stocks, G. A., ed., *The Records of Blackburn Grammar School*, 3 vols. (Manchester, 1909).
Terence, *Vulgaria quedam abs Terencio in Anglica[m] linguam traducta* (Oxford, 1483).
Tudor Royal Proclamations, eds. P. I. Hughes and J. F. Larkin, 3 vols. (New Haven, 1964), I.
Vaughan, W., *The golden-groue, moralized in three bookes: a worke very necessary for all such, as would know how to gouerne themselues, their houses, or their countrey. Made by W. Vaughan, Master of Artes, and student in the ciuill law* (London, 1600).
Vives, Juan Luis, *Juan Luis Vives, The Instruction of a Christen Woman*, eds. V. W. Beauchamp, E. H. Hageman and M. Mikesell (Chicago, 2002).
White, B., ed., *The Vulgaria of John Stanbridge and the Vulgaria of R. Whittinton, Edited with an Introduction and Notes by B. White*, EETS OS 187 (London, 1932).
Whitford, R., *The conte[n]tes of this boke. A werke of preparacion, or of ordinaunce vnto co[m]munion, or howselyng. The werke for householders with the golden pistle and alphabete or a crosrowe called an A.B.C. all duely corrected and newly printed* (London, 1531).
Whittington, R., *De ciuilitate morun [sic] puerilium per Des. Erasmum Roterodamum, libellus nunc primum & conditus & æditus. Roberto VVhitintoni interprete. A lytell booke of good maners for chyldren, nowe lately compyled and put forth by Erasmus Roterodam in latyne tonge, with interpretacion of the same in to the vulgare englysshe tonge, by Robert whytyngton laureate poete. Cum priuilegio* (London, 1532).

Secondary sources

Adams, T., 'Medieval Mothers and their Children: The Case of Isabeau of Bavaria in Light of Medieval Conduct Books', in *Childhood in the Middle Ages and the Renaissance: The Results of a Paradigm Shift in the History of Mentality*, ed. A. Classen (Berlin, 2005), pp. 265–89.
Alexander, M. V. C., *The Growth of English Education 1348–1648: A Social and Cultural History* (University Park, 1990).
Amos, M. A., '"For Manners Make Man", Bourdieu, de Certeau, and the Common Appropriation of Noble Manners in the Book of Courtesy', in *Medieval Conduct*, ed. K. Ashley and R. L. A. Clark (Minneapolis, 2001), pp. 23–48.
Amos, M. A., 'Violent Hierarchies: Disciplining Women and Merchant Capitalists in *The Book of the Knyght of the Towre*', in *Caxton's Trace: Studies in the History of English Printing*, ed. W. Kuskin (Notre Dame, 2006), pp. 69–100.
Amussen, S. D., *An Ordered Society: Gender and Class in Early Modern England* (Oxford, 1988).

Bibliography

Amussen, S. D., 'Punishment, Discipline, and Power: The Social Meanings of Violence in Early Modern England', *Journal of British Studies* 34 (1995), 1–34.

Anglin, J. P., *The Third University: A Survey of Schools and Schoolmasters in the Elizabethan Diocese of London* (Norwood, 1985).

Arditi, J., *A Genealogy of Manners: Transformations of Social Relations in France and England from the Fourteenth to the Eighteenth Century* (Chicago, 1998).

Ariès, P., *Centuries of Childhood*, trans. R. Baldick (London, 1962).

Ariès, P., *L'enfant et la vie familiale sous l'ancien régime* (Paris, 1960).

Armstrong, E., 'English Purchases of Printed Books from the Continent 1465–1526', *English Historical Review* 94 (1979), 268–90.

Ashley, K., 'The *Miroir des Bonnes Femmes*: Not for Women Only?', in *Medieval Conduct*, ed. K. Ashley and R. L. A. Clark (Minneapolis, 2001), pp. 86–105.

Barber, R., 'Chivalry and the *Morte Darthur*', in *A Companion to Malory*, ed. E. Archibald and A. S. G. Edwards (Cambridge, 1996), pp. 19–35.

Barnard, J., and D. F. McKenzie, eds., with the assistance of M. Bell, *The Cambridge History of the Book in Britain, vol. IV, 1557–1695*, 6 vols. (Cambridge, 2002).

Barron, C., 'The Expansion of Education in Fifteenth-Century London', in *The Cloister and the World: Essays in Medieval History in Honour of Barbara Harvey*, ed. J. Blair and B. Golding (Oxford, 1996), pp. 219–45.

Beattie, C., 'Governing Bodies: Law Courts, Male Householders and Single Women in Late Medieval England', in *The Medieval Household in Christian Europe, c.850–c.1550: Managing Power, Wealth and the Body*, ed. C. Beattie, A. Maslakovic and S. Rees Jones (Turnhout, 2003), pp. 199–220.

Beer, B. L., 'Stow, John (1524/5–1605)', *Oxford Dictionary of National Biography* (Oxford, 2004, online edn, 2006).

Bell, H. E., 'The Price of Books in Medieval England', *The Library* 4th s. 17 (1936–7), 312–32.

Bennett. H. S., *English Books and Readers 1475–1557: Being a Study in the History of the Book Trade from Caxton to the Incorporation of the Stationers' Company* (Cambridge, 1952).

Bennett, J. M., *Ale, Beer, and Brewsters in England: Women's Work in a Changing World, 1300–1600* (Oxford, 1996).

Bennett, J. M., 'Medieval Women, Modern Women: Across the Great Divide', in *Culture and History, 1350–1600: Essays on English Communities, Identities and Writing*, ed. D. Aers (Detroit, 1992), pp. 147–75.

Blades, W., *The Life and Typography of William Caxton, England's First Printer: With Evidence of his Typographical Connection with Colard Mansion, the Printer at Bruges* (London, 1861–3).

Blake, N. F., *Caxton and his World* (London, 1969).

Blake, N. F., *Caxton: England's First Publisher* (London, 1976).

Blake, N. F., 'Caxton Prepares his Edition of the *Morte Darthur*', *Journal of Librarianship* 8 (1976), 272–85.

Blake, N. F., *William Caxton and English Literary Culture* (London, 1991).

Blanchfield, L. S., 'Rate Revisited: The Compilation of the Narrative Works in MS Ashmole 61', in *Romance Reading on the Book: Essays on Medieval Narrative Presented to Maldwyn Mills*, ed. J. Fellows, R. Field, G. Rogers and J. Weiss (Cardiff, 1996), pp. 208–20.

Bloom, E. A., and L. D. Bloom, *Joseph Addison's Sociable Animal: In the Market Place, on the Hustings, in the Pulpit* (Providence, 1971).

Boffey, J., *Manuscripts of English Courtly Love Lyrics in the Later Middle Ages* (Cambridge, 1985).

Boffey, J., and J. J. Thompson, 'Anthologies and Miscellanies: Production and Choice of Texts', in *Book Production and Publishing in Britain 1375–1475*, ed. J. Griffiths and D. Pearsall (Cambridge, 1989), pp. 279–315.

Bornstein, D., 'Courtesy Books', in *Dictionary of the Middle Ages*, ed. J. R. Strayer, 13 vols. (New York, 1982–9), III.

Bornstein, D., *Mirrors of Courtesy* (Hamden, 1975).

Bornstein, D., *The Lady in the Tower: Medieval Courtesy Literature for Women* (Hamden, 1983).

Bornstein, D., 'William Caxton's Chivalric Romances and the Burgundian Renaissance in England', *English Studies* 57 (1976), 1–10.

Bremmer, J., and H. Roodenburg, eds., *A Cultural History of Gesture: From Antiquity to the Present Day* (London, 1991).

Brentano, Sister M. T., *Relationship of the Latin Facetus Literature to the Medieval English Courtesy Poems*, Bulletin of the University of Kansas 36, Humanistic Studies 5 (Kansas, 1935).

Brigden, S., 'Youth and the English Reformation', *Past and Present* 95 (1982), 37–67.

Brunner, I. A., 'On Some of the Vernacular Translations of Cato's *Distichs*', in *Helen Adolf Festschrift*, ed. S. Z. Buehne, J. L. Hodge and L. B. Pinto (New York, 1968), pp. 99–123.

Bryson, A., *From Courtesy to Civility: Changing Codes of Conduct in Early Modern England* (Oxford, 1998).

Budra, P. V., A *Mirror for Magistrates* and the de casibus *Tradition* (Toronto, 2000).

Capp, B., 'Separate Domains? Women and Authority in Early Modern England', in *The Experience of Authority in Early Modern England*, ed. P. Griffiths, A. Fox and S. Hindle (New York, 1996), pp. 117–45.

Carlson, D. R., *English Humanist Books: Writers and Patrons, Manuscripts and Print, 1475–1525* (Toronto, 1993).

Carpenter, C., *Locality and Polity: A Study of Warwickshire Landed Society, 1401–1499* (Cambridge, 1992).

Carruthers, M. J., *The Book of Memory: A Study of Memory in Medieval Culture* (Cambridge, 1990).

Carter, P., 'Polite "Persons": Character, Biography and the Gentleman', *Transactions of the Royal Historical Society* 12 (2002), 333–54.

Castor, H., 'Calle, Richard (*d*. in or after 1503)', *Oxford Dictionary of National Biography* (Oxford, 2006, online edn, 2006).

Chambers, E. K., *The Mediaeval Stage*, 2 vols. (London, 1903), I.

Cherewatuk, K., 'Aural and Written Reception in Sir John Paston, Malory, and Caxton', *Essays in Medieval Studies* 21 (2004), 123–31.

Clifton, N., 'The "Seven Sages of Rome", Children's Literature, and the Auchinleck Manuscript', in *Childhood in the Middle Ages and the Renaissance: The Results of a Paradigm Shift in the History of Mentality*, ed. A. Classen (Berlin, 2005), pp. 185–201.

Cockburn, J. S., H. P. F. King and K. G. T. McDonnell, eds., *A History of the County of Middlesex*, 13 vols. (London, 1969), I.

Coldiron, A. E. B., 'Taking Advice from a Frenchwoman: Caxton, Pynson, and Christine de Pizan's Moral Proverbs', in *Caxton's Trace: Studies in the History of English Printing*, ed. W. Kuskin (Notre Dame, 2006), pp. 127–66.

Coldiron, A. E. B., 'Translation's Challenge to Critical Categories: Verses from French in the Early English Renaissance', *Yale Journal of Criticism* 16 (2003), 315–44.

Coleman, J., *Public Reading and the Reading Public in Late Medieval England and France* (Cambridge, 1996).

Coletti, T., '"Curtesy Doth it Yow Lere": The Sociology of Trangression in the Digby *Mary Magdalene*', *English Literary History* 71 (2004), 1–28.

Collette, C. P., 'Chaucer and the French Tradition Revisited: Philippe de Mézières and the Good Wife', in *Medieval Women: Texts and Contexts in Late Medieval Britain, Essays for Felicity Riddy*, ed. J. Wogan-Browne, R. Voaden, A. Diamond, A. Hutchison, C. M. and L. Johnson (Turnhout, 2000), pp. 151–68.

Collier, H., 'Richard Hill – A London Compiler', in *The Court and Cultural Diversity*, ed. E. Mullally and J. Thompson (Cambridge, 1997), pp. 319–29.

Collinson, P., *Godly People: Essays on English Protestantism and Puritanism* (London, 1983).

Collinson, P., *The Religion of Protestants: The Church in English Society 1559–1625* (Oxford, 1982).

Coudert, A. P., 'Educating Girls in Early Modern Europe and America', in *Childhood in the Middle Ages and the Renaissance: The Results of a Paradigm Shift in the History of Mentality*, ed. A. Classen (Berlin, 2005), pp. 389–413.

Crane, S., 'Social Aspects of Bilingualism in the Thirteenth Century', in *Thirteenth Century England, VI: Proceedings of the Durham Conference 1995*, ed. M. Prestwich, R. H. Britnell and R. Frame (Woodbridge, 1997), pp. 103–15.

Crawford, S., *Childhood in Anglo-Saxon England* (Stroud, 1999).

Cressy, D., 'Educational Opportunity in Tudor and Stuart England', *History of Education Quarterly* 16 (1976), 301–20.

Cressy, D., *Literary and the Social Order: Reading and Writing in Tudor and Stuart England* (Cambridge, 1980).

Crouzet, D., '"A strong desire to be a mother to all your subjects": A Rhetorical Experiment by Catherine de Medici', *Journal of Medieval and Early Modern Studies* 38 (2008), 103–18.

Cunningham, H., 'Histories of Childhood', *American Historical Review* 103 (1998), 1195–1208.

Dane, J. A., *The Myth of Print Culture: Essays on Evidence, Textuality, and Bibliographical Method* (Buffalo, 2003).

Davies, C., 'Vaughan, Sir William (*c*.1575–1641)', *Oxford Dictionary of National Biography* (Oxford, 2004, online edn, 2006).

Davis, K. M., 'The Sacred Condition of Equality – How Original were Puritan Doctrines of Marriage?', *Social History* 5 (1977), 563–80.

Daybell, J., 'Interpreting Letters and Reading Script: Evidence for Female Education and Literacy in Tudor England', *History of Education* 34 (2005), 695–715.

de Gendt, A. M., *L'Art d'eduquer les nobles damoiselles:* Le Livre du Chevalier de la Tour Landry (Paris, 2003).

deMause, L., ed., *The History of Childhood* (New York, 1974).

Bibliography

DeMolen, R. L., *Richard Mulcaster (c.1531–1611) and Educational Reform in the Renaissance* (Nieuwkoop, 1991).

Dixon, S., *The Roman Mother* (London, 1988).

Dronzek, A., 'Gender Roles and the Marriage Market in Fifteenth-Century England: Ideals and Practices', in *Love, Marriage, and Family Ties in the Later Middle Ages,* ed. I. Davis, M. Müller and S. Rees Jones (Turnhout, 2003), pp. 63–76.

Dronzek, A., 'Gendered Theories of Education in Fifteenth-Century Conduct Books', in *Medieval Conduct,* ed. K. Ashley and R. L. A. Clark (Minneapolis, 2001), pp. 135–59.

Duffy, E., *The Stripping of the Altars: Traditional Religion in England, 1400–1580* (New Haven, 1992).

Dunham Jr., W. H., and S. Pargellis, eds., *Complaint and Reform in England, 1436–1714: Fifty Writings of the Time on Politics, Religion, Society, Economics, Architecture, Science and Education* (New York, 1938).

Dunham Jr., W. H., and C. T. Wood, 'The Right to Rule in England: Depositions and the Kingdom's Authority, 1327–1485', *American Historical Review* 81 (1976), 738–61.

Dyer, C., *Standards of Living in the Later Middle Ages: Social Change in England, c.1200–1520,* rev. edn (Cambridge, 1998).

Eco, U., *Experiences in Translation,* trans. A. McEwen (Toronto, 2001).

Edwards, A. S. G., 'Chaucer From Manuscript to Print: The Social Text and the Critical Text', *Mosaic* 28.4 (1995), 1–12.

Edwards, A. S. G., and C. M. Meale, 'The Marketing of Printed Books in Late Medieval England', *The Library* 6th s. 15 (1993), 95–124.

Eisenstein, E. L., *The Printing Press as an Agent of Change: Communications and Cultural Transformations in Early Modern Europe,* 2 vols. (Cambridge, 1979).

Elias, N., *The Civilizing Process: Sociogenetic and Psychogenetic Investigations,* trans. E. Jephcott, rev. edn (Oxford, 2000).

Evans, D. D., 'The Babees Book', in *Medieval Literature for Children,* ed. D. Kline (New York, 2003), pp. 79–92.

Fałkowski, W., 'Carolingian *speculum principis* – The Birth of a Genre', *Acta Poloniae Historica* 98 (2008), 5–27.

Fein, S. G., ed., *Moral Love Songs and Laments* (Kalamazoo, 1998).

Fildes, V., *Wet Nursing: A History from Antiquity to the Present* (Oxford, 1988).

Fleming, P. W., 'Household Servants of the Yorkist and Early Tudor Gentry', in *Early Tudor England,* ed. D. Williams (Woodbridge, 1989), pp. 19–36.

Fletcher, C. D., 'Narrative and Political Strategies at the Deposition of Richard II', *Journal of Medieval History* 30 (2004), 323–41.

Fletcher, C. D., 'Manhood and Politics in the Reign of Richard II', *Past and Present* 189 (2005), 3–39.

Ford, J. A., 'A View from a Village: Popular Political Culture in Sixteenth-Century England', *Journal of Popular Culture* 34 (2000), 1–19.

Freeman, J., 'Sorcery at Court and Manor: Margery Jourdemayne, the Witch of Eye next Westminster', *Journal of Medieval History* 30 (2004), 343–57.

Friedman, A. T., 'The Influence of Humanism on the Education of Girls and Boys in Tudor England', *History of Education Quarterly* 25 (1985), 57–70.

Fumerton, P., *Cultural Aesthetics: Renaissance Literature and the Practice of Social Ornament* (Chicago, 1991).
Gadd, I. A., and P. Wallis, eds., *Guilds, Society and Economy in London 1450–1800* (London, 2002).
Gauci, P., 'Informality and Influence: The Overseas Merchant and the Livery Companies, 1660–1720', in *Guilds, Society and Economy in London 1450–1800*, ed. I. A. Gadd and P. Wallis (London, 2002), pp. 127–39.
Gieben, S., 'Robert Grosseteste and Medieval Courtesy Books', *Vivarium* 5 (1967), 47–74.
Gill, L., 'William Caxton and the Rebellion of 1483', *English Historical Review* 112 (1997), 105–18.
Gillespie, A., 'Balliol MS 354: Histories of the Book at the End of the Middle Ages', *Poetica* 60 (2003), 47–63.
Gillespie, A., '"Folowynge the trace of mayster Caxton": Some Histories of Fifteenth-Century Printed Books', in *Caxton's Trace: Studies in the History of English Printing*, ed. W. Kuskin (Indiana, 2006), pp. 167–195.
Gillespie, A., 'Poets, Printers, and Early English *Sammelbände*', *Huntington Library Quarterly* 67 (2004), 189–214.
Gillespie, A., *Print Culture and the Medieval Author: Chaucer, Lydgate, and their Books, 1473–1557* (Oxford, 2006).
Gillingham, J., 'From *Civilitas* to Civility: Codes of Manners in Medieval and Early Modern England', *Transactions of the Royal Historical Society* 12 (2002), 267–89.
Ginzburg, C., *The Cheese and the Worm: The Cosmos of a Sixteenth Century Miller*, trans. J. and A. Tedeschi (Baltimore, 1980).
Girouard, M., *Robert Smythson and the Elizabethan Country House*, rev. edn (New Haven, 1983).
Goldberg, P. J. P., 'Female Labour, Service and Marriage in the Late Medieval Urban North', *Northern History* 22 (1986), 18–38.
Goldberg, P. J. P., 'Girls Growing Up in Later Medieval England', *History Today* 45 (1995), 25–32.
Goldberg, P. J. P., 'Household and the Organisation of Labour in Late Medieval Towns: Some English Evidence', in *The Household in Late Medieval Cities: Italy and Northwestern Europe Compared*, ed. M. Carlier and T. Soens (Leuven, 2001), pp. 59–70.
Goldberg, P. J. P., 'Masters and Men in Later Medieval England', in *Masculinity in Medieval Europe*, ed. D. M. Hadley (London, 1999), pp. 56–70.
Goldberg, P. J. P., *Medieval England: A Social History 1250–1550* (London, 2004).
Goldberg, P. J. P., 'Urban Identity and the Poll Taxes of 1377, 1379, and 1381', *Economic History Review* n.s. 43 (1990), 194–216.
Goldberg, P. J. P., 'What Was a Servant?', in *Concepts and Patterns of Service in the Later Middle Ages*, ed. A. Curry and E. Matthew (Woodbridge, 2000), pp. 1–20.
Goldberg, P. J. P., *Women, Work and Life Cycle in a Medieval Economy: Women in York and Yorkshire, c.1300–1520* (Oxford, 1992).
Goldberg, P. J. P., 'Women's Work, Women's Role, in the Late Medieval North', in *Profit, Piety and the Professions in Later Medieval England*, ed. M. Hicks (Gloucester, 1990), pp. 34–50.
Goldberg, P. J. P., F. Riddy and M. Tyler, 'Introduction: After Ariès', in *Youth in the Middle Ages*, ed. P. J. P. Goldberg and F. Riddy (York, 2004), pp. 1–10.

Gowing, L., *Domestic Dangers: Women, Words, and Sex in Early Modern London* (Oxford, 1996).

Gowing, L., '"The freedom of the streets": Women and Social Space, 1560–1640', in *Londinopolis: Essays on the Cultural and Social History of Early Modern London*, ed. P. Griffiths and M. S. R. Jenner (Manchester, 2000), pp. 130–53.

Grabes, H., *The Mutable Glass: Mirror-Imagery in Titles and Texts of the Middle Ages and English Renaissance*, trans. G. Collier (Cambridge, 1982).

Green, I., *The Christian's ABC: Catechisms and Catechizing in England c. 1530–1740* (Oxford, 1996).

Green, M. H., 'Salerno on the Thames: The Genesis of Anglo-Norman Medical Literature', in *Language and Culture in Medieval Britain: The French of England c. 1100–c. 1500*, ed. J. Wogan-Browne et al. (York, 2009), pp. 220–31.

Grenville, J., 'Houses and Households in Late Medieval England: An Archaeological Perspective', in *Medieval Women: Texts and Contexts in Late Medieval Britain, Essays for Felicity Riddy*, ed. J. Wogan-Browne, R. Voaden, A. Diamond, A. Hutchison, C. M. Meale and L. Johnson (Turnhout, 2000), pp. 309–28.

Griffiths, P., 'Masterless Young People in Norwich, 1560–1645', in *The Experience of Authority in Early Modern England*, ed. P. Griffiths, A. Fox, and S. Hindle (New York, 1996), pp. 146–86.

Griffiths, P., *Youth and Authority: Formative Experiences in England, 1560–1640* (Oxford, 1996).

Grigsby, J. L., 'A New Source of the *Livre du Chevalier de La Tour Landry*', *Romania* 84 (1963), 171–208.

Hagger, M., 'Kinship and Identity in Eleventh-Century Normandy: The Case of Hugh de Grandmesnil, c. 1040–1098', *Journal of Medieval History* 32 (2006), 212–30.

Hanawalt, B. A., *Growing Up in Medieval London: The Experience of Childhood in History* (New York, 1993).

Hanawalt, B. A., *'Of Good and Ill Repute': Gender and Social Control in Medieval England* (New York, 1998).

Hanawalt, B. A., *The Ties That Bound: Peasant Families in Medieval England* (New York, 1986).

Hardman, P., 'A Medieval "Library *in Parvo*"', *Medium Aevum* 47 (1978), 262–73.

Harriss, G., 'Political Society and the Growth of Government in Late Medieval England', *Past and Present* 138 (1993), 28–57.

Harriss, G., *Shaping the Nation, England, 1360–1461* (Oxford, 2005).

Helgerson, R., *Forms of Nationhood: The Elizabethan Writing of England* (Chicago, 1992).

Hellinga, L., *Catalogue of Books Printed in the XVth Century now in the British Library, Part XI, England*, 12 vols. (London, 2007).

Hellinga, L., *Caxton in Focus: The Beginning of Printing in England* (London, 1982).

Hellinga, L., *Printing in England in the Fifteenth Century: E. Gordon Duff's Bibliography with Supplementary Descriptions, Chronologies and a Census of Copies by Lotte Hellinga* (London, 2009).

Hellinga, L., and J. B. Trapp, eds., *The Cambridge History of the Book in Britain, Vol. III, 1400–1557* (Cambridge, 1999).

Helmholz, R. H., *Marriage Litigation in Medieval England* (London, 1974).

Bibliography

Herlihy, D., 'The Family and Religious Ideologies in Medieval Europe', *Journal of Family History* 12.1–3 (1987), 3–17.
Herlihy, D., 'The Making of the Medieval Family: Symmetry, Structure, and Sentiment', *Journal of Family History* 8 (1983), 116–30.
Heywood, C., *A History of Childhood: Children and Childhood in the West from Medieval to Modern Times* (Cambridge, 2001).
Higonnet, M. R., 'Civility Books, Child Citizens, and Uncivil Antics', *Poetics Today* 13 (1992), 123–40.
Hillier, B., and J. Hanson, *The Social Logic of Space* (Cambridge, 1984).
Hogg, J., 'Richard Whytford, A Forgotten Spiritual Guide', *Studies in Spirituality* 15 (2005), 129–42.
Horn, C. B., and J. W. Martens, *'Let the little children come to me': Childhood and Children in Early Christianity* (Washington, 2009).
Horrox, R., 'Service', in *Fifteenth Century Attitudes: Perceptions of Society in Late Medieval England*, ed. R. Horrox (Cambridge, 1994), pp. 61–78.
Horrox, R., 'The Urban Gentry in the Fifteenth Century', in *Towns and Townspeople in the Fifteenth Century*, ed. J. A. F. Thomson (Gloucester, 1988), pp. 22–44.
Huot, S., *The Romance of the Rose and Its Medieval Readers: Interpretation, Reception, Manuscript Transmission* (Cambridge, 1993).
Hylson-Smith, K., *The Churches in England from Elizabeth I to Elizabeth II, Vol. 1: 1558–1688* (London, 1996).
Ingham R., 'Mixing Languages on the Manor', *Medium Aevum* 78 (2009), 80–97.
Ingham R., ed., *The Anglo-Norman Language and its Contexts* (Woodbridge, 2010).
Jaeger, C. S., *The Envy of Angels: Cathedral Schools and Social Ideas in Medieval Europe, 950–1200* (Philadelphia, 1994).
Jaeger, C. S., *The Origins of Courtliness: Civilising Trends and the Formation of Courtly Ideals, 939–1210* (Philadelphia, 1985).
Jambeck, K. K., 'The *Tretiz* of Walter of Bibbesworth: Cultivating the Vernacular', in *Childhood in the Middle Ages and the Renaissance: The Results of a Paradigm Shift in the History of Mentality*, ed. A. Classen (Berlin, 2005), pp. 159–83.
James, M. E., *Family, Lineage, and Civil Society: A Study of Society, Politics and Mentality in the Durham Region, 1500–1640* (Oxford, 1974).
Jewell, H. M., *Education in Early Modern England* (New York, 1998).
Jewell, H. M., '"The Bringing up of Children in Good Learning and Manners": A Survey of Secular Educational Provision in the North of England, c. 1350–1550', *Northern History* 18 (1982), 1–25.
Jewell, H. M., *Women in Late Medieval and Reformation Europe, 1200–1550* (Basingstoke, 2007).
Jewell, H. M., *Women in Medieval England* (Manchester, 1996).
Johns, A., *The Nature of the Book: Print Culture and Knowledge in the Making* (Chicago, 1998).
Johnson, K. M., 'The Invisible Man: Body and Ritual in a Fifteenth-Century Noble Household', *Journal of Medieval History* 31 (2005), 143–62.
Johnson, M., *Housing Culture: Traditional Architecture in an English Landscape* (London, 1993).
Johnston, M. D., 'The Treatment of Speech in Medieval Ethical and Courtesy Literature', *Rhetorica* 4 (1986), 21–46.

Jones, E. A., and A. Walsham, eds., *Syon Abbey and its Books: Reading, Writing and Religion c. 1400–1700* (Woodbridge, 2010).

Karras, R. M., *From Boys to Men: Formations of Masculinity in Late Medieval Europe* (Philadelphia, 2003).

Kaufman, G., 'Juan Luis Vives on the Education of Women', *Signs* 3 (1978), 891–6.

Kay, M. M., *The History of Rivington and Blackrod Grammar School* (Manchester, 1931).

Keen, M., *Origins of the English Gentleman: Heraldry, Chivalry and Gentility in Medieval England, c.1300–c.1500* (Stroud, 2002).

Kent, S., 'Activity Areas and Architecture: An Interdisciplinary View of the Relationship Between Use of Space and Domestic Built Environments', in *Domestic Architecture and the Use of Space: An Interdisciplinary Cross-Cultural Study*, ed. S. Kent (Cambridge, 1990), pp. 1–8.

Kermode, J., 'Sentiment and Survival: Family and Friends in Late Medieval English Towns', *Journal of Family History* 24 (1999), 5–18.

Kerr, J., 'The Open Door: Hospitality and Honour in Twelfth/Early Thirteenth-Century England', *History* 87 (2002), 322–35.

Kerr, J., '"Welcome the coming and speed the parting guest": Hospitality in Twelfth-Century England', *Journal of Medieval History* 33 (2007), 130–46.

Key, E., 'A Register of Schools and Schoolmasters in the County of Cambridge, 1574–1700', *Proceedings of the Cambridge Antiquarian Society* 70 (1980), 127–89.

King, A., 'Fortresses and Fashion Statements: Gentry Castles in Fourteenth-Century Northumberland', *Journal of Medieval History* 33 (2007), 372–97.

King, J. N., 'Seager, Francis (fl. 1549–1563)', *Oxford Dictionary of National Biography* (Oxford, 2004, online edn, 2006).

Kline, D. T., 'Female Childhoods', in *The Cambridge Companion to Medieval Women's Writing*, ed. C. Dinshaw and D. Wallace (Cambridge, 2003), pp. 13–20.

Kluewer, J., 'The Lambeth Lyrics: A New Edition of Lambeth Palace MS 853' (unpublished doctoral dissertation, State University of New York at Stony Brook, 1975)

Knight, S., 'The Voice of Labour in Fourteenth-Century English Literature', in *The Problem of Labour in Fourteenth-Century England*, ed. J. Bothwell, P. J. P. Goldberg and W. M. Ormrod (York, 2000), pp. 101–22.

Kowaleski, M., *Local Markets and Regional Trade in Medieval Exeter* (Cambridge, 1995).

Krueger, R. L., 'Love, Honor, and the Exchange of Women in Yvain, Some Remarks on the Female Reader', in *Arthurian Women*, ed. T. S. Fenster (London, 1996), pp. 3–18.

Krueger, R. L., '"Nouvelles Choses": Social Instability and the Problem of Fashion in the *Livre du Chevalier de la Tour Landry*, The *Ménagier de Paris*, and Christine de Pizan's *Livre des Trois Vertus*', in *Medieval Conduct*, ed. K. Ashley and R. L. A. Clark (Minneapolis, 2001), pp. 49–85.

Krueger, R. L., *Women Readers and the Ideology of Gender in old French Verse Romance* (Cambridge, 1993).

Krug, R., *Reading Families: Women's Literate Practice in Late Medieval England* (New York, 2002).

Kuskin, W., 'Caxton's Worthies Series: The Production of Literary Culture', *English Literary History* 66 (1999), 511–51.

Kuskin, W., '"Onely Imagined": Vernacular Community and the English Press', in *Caxton's Trace: Studies in the History of English Printing*, ed. W. Kuskin (Notre Dame, 2006), pp. 199–240.

Kuskin, W., ed., *Caxton's Trace: Studies in the History of English Printing* (Notre Dame, 2006).

Lake, P., 'Periodization, Politics and "The Social"', *Journal of British Studies* 37 (1998), 279–90.

Lawrence, C. H., ed., *The Letters of Adam Marsh*, 2 vols, Oxford Medieval Texts (Oxford, 2006–10), I.

Lerer, S., *Chaucer and His Readers: Imagining the Author in Late Medieval England* (Princeton, 1993).

Lerer, S., 'William Caxton', in *The Cambridge History of Medieval English Literature*, ed. D. Wallace (Cambridge, 1999), pp. 720–38.

Linton, M., *The Politics of Virtue in Enlightenment France* (Basingstoke, 2001).

Lucas, S. C., *A Mirror for Magistrates and the Politics of the English Reformation* (Amherst, 2009).

Lyon, J. R., 'Fathers and Sons: Preparing Noble Youths to be Lords in Twelfth-century Germany', *Journal of Medieval History* 34 (2008), 291–310.

Madan, F., 'Supplementary Notes', *Collectanea* 2 (1890), 454–78.

Madan, F., 'The Day-Book of John Dorne, Bookseller in Oxford, A.D. 1520', *Collectanea* 1 (1885), 71–177.

Maddern, P., 'Honour among the Pastons: Gender and Integrity in Fifteenth-Century English Provincial Society', *Journal of Medieval History* 14 (1988), 357–71.

Marotti, A. F., *Manuscript, Print and the English Renaissance Lyric* (Ithaca, 1995).

Martin, R. E., 'Gifts for the Bride: Dowries, Diplomacy, and Marriage Politics in Muscovy', *Journal of Medieval and Early Modern Studies* 38 (2008), 119–45.

Mason, J. E., *Gentlefolk in the Making: Studies in the History of English Courtesy Literature and Related Topics from 1531 to 1774* (Philadelphia, 1935).

McCash, J. H., ed., *The Cultural Patronage of Medieval Women* (Georgia, 1996).

McCracken, G., 'The Exchange of Children in Tudor England: An Anthropological Phenomenon in Historical Context', *Journal of Family History* 8 (1983), 303–13.

McCulloch, D., and E. D. Jones, 'Lancastrian Politics, the French War, and the Rise of the Popular Element', *Speculum* 58 (1983), 95–138.

McIntosh, M., *Controlling Misbehaviour in England, 1370–1600* (Cambridge, 1998).

McIntosh, M., 'Response', *Journal of British Studies* 37 (1998), 291–305.

McKitterick, D., *Print, Manuscript, and the Search for Order, 1450–1830* (New York, 2003).

Meale, C. M., '"... alle the bokes that I haue of latyn, englisch, and frensch": Laywomen and Their Books in Late Medieval England', in *Women and Literature in Britain, 1150–1500*, ed. C. M. Meale (Cambridge, 1993), pp. 128–58.

Meale, C. M., 'Caxton, de Worde, and the Publication of Romance in Late Medieval England', *The Library* 6th s. 14 (1992), 283–98.

Meale, C. M., 'Romance and its Anti-Type? The *Turnament of Totenham*, The Carnivalesque, and Popular Culture', in *Middle English Poetry: Texts and Traditions. Essays in Honour of Derek Pearsall*, ed. A. J. Minnis (York, 2001), pp. 103–28.

Mendelson, S., and P. Crawford, *Women in Early Modern England, 1550–1720* (Oxford, 1998).

Bibliography

Mertes, K., *The English Noble Household 1250–1600: Good Governance and Politic Rule* (Oxford, 1988).

Michalove, S. D., 'The Education of Aristocratic Women in Fifteenth-Century England', in *Estrangement, Enterprise and Education in Fifteenth-Century England*, ed. S. D. Michalove and A. Compton Reeves (Stroud, 1998), pp. 116–39.

Millett, F. B., *English Courtesy Literature Before 1557* (Kingston, 1919).

Mooney, L., 'John Shirley's Heirs', *Yearbook of English Studies* 33 (2003), 182–98.

Mooney, L., 'Professional Scribes?: Identifying English Scribes Who Had a Hand in More Than One Manuscript', in *New Directions in Medieval Manuscript Studies*, ed. D. Pearsall (York, 2000), pp. 131–41.

Mooney, L., with Lister M. Matheson, 'The Beryn Scribe and his Texts: Evidence for Multiple-Copy Production of Manuscripts in Fifteenth-Century England', *The Library* 7th s. 4 (2003), 347–70.

Moran, J. A. H., *The Growth of English Schooling, 1340–1548: Learning, Literacy, and Laicization in Pre-Reformation York Diocese* (Princeton, 1985).

Mustakallio, K., J. Hanska, H-L. Sainio and V. Vuolanto eds., *Hoping for Continuity: Childhood, Education and Death in Antiquity and the Middle Ages* (Rome, 2005).

Mynors, R. A. B., *Catalogue of the Manuscripts of Balliol College Oxford* (Oxford, 1963).

Needham, P., *The Printer and the Pardoner: An Unrecorded Indulgence Printed by William Caxton for the Hospital of St Mary Rounceval* (Washington, 1986).

Nicholls, J., *The Matter of Courtesy: Medieval Courtesy Books and the Gawain-Poet* (Cambridge, 1985).

O'Day, R., *Education and Society 1500–1800: The Social Foundations of Education in Early Modern Britain* (London, 1982).

Orme, N., *Education and Society in Medieval and Renaissance England* (London, 1989).

Orme, N., *English Schools in the Middle Ages* (London, 1973).

Orme, N., 'Horman, William (1447–1535)', *Oxford Dictionary of National Biography* (Oxford Press, 2004, online edn, 2006).

Orme, N., *Medieval Children* (New Haven, 2001).

Orme, N., *Medieval Schools: From Roman Britain to Renaissance England* (New Haven, 2006).

Orme, N., 'Whittington, Robert (c. 1480–1553?)', *Oxford Dictionary of National Biography* (Oxford Press, 2004, online edn, 2006).

Owst, G. R., *Literature and Pulpit in Medieval England: A Neglected Chapter in the History of English Letters and of the English People*, 2nd edn (Oxford, 1961).

Owst, G. R., *Preaching in Mediaeval England: An Introduction to Sermon Manuscripts of the Period c. 1350–1450* (Cambridge, 1926).

Painter, G. D., *William Caxton: A Quincentenary Biography of England's First Printer* (London, 1976).

Parkes, M. B., 'The Literacy of the Laity', in *The Mediaeval World*, ed. D. Daiches and A. Thorlby (London, 1973), pp. 555–77.

Pastoureau, M., 'Emblems of Youth: Young People in Medieval Imagery', in *A History of Young People in the West*, ed. G. Levi and J. Schmitt, trans. C. Naish (Cambridge, MA, 1997), pp. 222–39.

Penninger, F. E., *William Caxton* (Boston, 1979).

Phillips, K. M., *Medieval Maidens: Young Women and Gender in England, 1270–1540* (Manchester, 2003).

Pollard, G., 'The Company of Stationers Before 1557', *The Library* 4th s. 18 (1937), 1–38.
Pollock, L. A., *A Lasting Relationship: Parents and Children Over Three Centuries* (London, 1986).
Pollock, L. A., *Forgotten Children: Parent–Child Relations from 1500–1900* (Cambridge, 1983).
Pollock, L. A., '"Teach her to live under obedience": The Making of Women in the Upper Ranks of Early Modern England', *Continuity and Change* 4 (1989), 231–58.
Potter, U., 'Elizabethan Drama and The Instruction of a Christian Woman by Juan Luis Vives', in *What Nature Does Not Teach: Didactic Literature in the Medieval and Early-Modern Periods*, ed. J. F. Ruys (Turnhout, 2008), pp. 261–85.
Potter, U., 'Pedagogy and Parenting in English Drama, 1560–1610: Flogging Schoolmasters and Cockering Mothers' (unpublished doctoral dissertation, University of Sydney, 2001).
Potter, U., 'Performing Arts in the Tudor Classroom', in *Tudor Drama Before Shakespeare, 1485–1590: New Directions for Research, Criticism and Pedagogy*, ed. L. E. Kermode, J. Scott-Warren, and M. van Elk (New York, 2004), pp. 143–65.
Powell, C., *English Domestic Relations, 1487–1653: A Study of Matrimony and Family Life in Theory and Practice as Revealed by the Literature, Law, and History of the Period* (New York, 1917).
Radulescu, R., *The Gentry Context for Malory's* Morte Darthur (Cambridge, 2003).
Radulescu, R., 'Yorkist Propaganda and *The Chronicle from Rollo to Edward IV*', *Studies in Philology* 100 (2003), 401–24.
Rappaport, A., 'Systems of Activities and Systems of Settings', in *Domestic Architecture and the Use of Space: An Interdisciplinary Cross-Cultural Study*, ed. S. Kent (Cambridge, 1990), pp. 9–20.
Rappaport, S., *Worlds Within Worlds: Structures of Life in Sixteenth Century London* (Cambridge, 1989).
Rawson, B., *Children and Childhood in Roman Italy* (Oxford, 2003).
Rees Jones, S., 'The Household and English Urban Government in the Later Middle Ages', in *The Household in Late Medieval Cities: Italy and Europe Compared*, ed. M. Carlier and T. Soens (Louvain, 2001), pp. 71–87.
Rees Jones, S., 'Women's Influence on the Design of Urban Homes', in *Gendering the Master Narrative: Women and Power in the Middle Ages*, ed. M. C. Erler and M. Kowaleski (Ithaca, 2003), pp. 190–211.
Report of the Commissioners for Inquiring Concerning Charities: Cambridgeshire, 1815–1839 (London, 1837).
Rhodes, J. T., 'Syon Abbey and its Religious Publications in the Sixteenth Century', *Journal of Ecclesiastical History* 44 (1993), 11–25.
Rhodes, J. T., 'Whitford, Richard (d. 1543?)', *Oxford Dictionary of National Biography*, (Oxford, 2004, online edn, 2006).
Riddy, F., 'Mother Knows Best: Reading Social Change in a Courtesy Text', *Speculum* 71 (1996), 66–86.
Riddy, F., '"Women talking about the things of God": A Late Medieval Sub-Culture', in *Women and Literature in Britain, 1150–1500*, ed. C. M. Meale (Cambridge, 1993), pp. 104–27.

Rust, M. D., 'The "ABC of Aristotle"', in *Medieval Literature for Children*, ed. D. Kline (New York, 2003), pp. 63–78.

Rutter, R., 'William Caxton and Literary Patronage', *Studies in Philology* 84 (1987), 440–70.

Ruys, J. F., 'Didactic 'I's and the Voice of Experience in Advice from Medieval and Early-Modern Parents to their Children', in *What Nature Does Not Teach: Didactic Literature in the Medieval and Early-Modern Periods*, ed. J. F. Ruys (Turnhout, 2008), pp. 129–62.

Ruys, J. F., 'Peter Abelard's *Carmen ad Astralabium* and Medieval Parent–Child Didactic Texts: The Evidence for Parent–Child Relationships in the Middle Ages', in *Childhood in the Middle Ages and the Renaissance: The Results of a Paradigm Shift in the History of Mentality*, ed. A. Classen (Berlin, 2005), pp. 203–27.

Scaglione, A., *Knights at Court: Courtliness, Chivalry and Courtesy from Ottonian Germany to the Italian Renaissance* (Berkeley, 1991).

Scattergood, J., 'Fashion and Morality in the Late Middle Ages', in *England in the Fifteenth Century: Proceedings of the 1986 Harlaxton Symposium*, ed. D. Williams (Woodbridge, 1987), pp. 255–72.

Schochet, G. J., *Patriarchalism in Political Thought: The Authoritarian Family and Political Speculation and Attitudes Especially in Seventeenth Century England* (New York, 1975).

Schultz, J. A., *The Knowledge of Childhood in the German Middle Ages, 1100–1350* (Philadelphia, 1995).

Seaborne, M., *The English School: Its Architecture and Organization 1370–1870* (London, 1971).

Shagan, E. H., *Popular Politics and the English Reformation* (Cambridge, 2003).

Shahar, S., *Childhood in the Middle Ages* (London, 1990).

Shaner, M. E., 'Instruction and Delight: Medieval Romances as Children's Literature', *Poetics Today* 13 (1992), 5–15.

Sheingorn, P., '"The Wise Mother": the Image of St Anne Teaching the Virgin Mary', *Gesta* 32 (1993), 69–80.

Shorter, E., *The Making of the Modern Family* (London, 1976).

Shrank, C., *Writing the Nation in Reformation England, 1530–1580* (Oxford, 2004).

Simon, J., *Education and Society in Tudor England* (Cambridge, 1966).

Smith, R. D., 'Lily, William (1468?–1522/3)', *Oxford Dictionary of National Biography* (Oxford, 2004, online edn, 2008).

Spencer, H. L., *English Preaching in the Late Middle Ages* (Oxford, 1993).

Sponsler, C., *Drama and Resistance: Bodies, Goods, and Theatricality in Late Medieval England* (Minneapolis, 1997).

Sponsler, C., 'Eating Lessons: Lydgate's "Dietary" and Consumer Conflict', in *Medieval Conduct*, ed. K. Ashley and R. L. A. Clark (Minneapolis, 2001), pp. 1–22.

Spufford, M., 'Puritanism and Social Control?', in *Order and Disorder in Early Modern England*, ed. A. Fletcher and J. Stevenson (Cambridge, 1985), pp. 41–57.

Stephens, W. B., 'Literacy in England, Scotland, and Wales, 1500–1900', *History of Education Quarterly* 30 (1990), 545–71.

Stock, B., *The Implications of Literacy: Written Language and Models of Interpretation in the Eleventh and Twelfth Centuries* (Princeton, 1983).

Stone, L., *The Crisis of the Aristocracy* (Oxford, 1965).

Stone, L., *The Family, Sex and Marriage in England 1500–1800* (London, 1977).
Stroud, M., 'Chivalric Terminology in Late Medieval Literature', *Journal of the History of Ideas* 37 (1976), 323–34.
Sturley, D. M., *The Royal Grammar School Guildford* (Guildford, 1980).
Summerson, J., *Architecture in Britain, 1530–1830* (Harmondsworth, 1953).
Summit, J., 'William Caxton, Margaret Beaufort and the Romance of Female Patronage', in *Women, the Book and the Worldly: Selected Proceedings of the St Hilda's Conference, 1993*, ed. L. Smith and J. H. M. Taylor, 2 vols. (Cambridge, 1995), II, 151–65.
Sutton, A. F., *The Mercery of London: Trade, Goods and People, 1130–1578* (Aldershot, 2005).
Tadmor, N., 'Friends and Neighbours in Early Modern England', in *Love, Friendship and Faith in Europe, 1300–1800*, ed. L. Gowing, M. Hunter and M. Rubin (Basingstoke, 2005), pp. 150–76.
Tarbin, S., 'Caring for the Poor and Fatherless Children in London, c. 1350–1550', *Journal of the History of Childhood and Youth* 3 (2010), 391–410.
Taylor, A., *Lords of Misrule: Hostility to Aristocracy in Late Nineteenth- and early Twentieth-Century Britain* (Basingstoke, 2004).
Thrupp, S. L., *The Merchant Class of Medieval London, 1300–1500* (Chicago, 1948).
Todd, M., 'Humanists, Puritans and the Spiritualized Household', *Church History* 49 (1980), 18–34.
Trapp, J. B., ed., *Manuscripts in the Fifty Years after the Invention of Printing* (London, 1983).
Trigg, S., 'Learning to Live', in *Oxford Twenty-First Century Approaches to Literature: Middle English*, ed. P. Strohm (Oxford, 2007), pp. 459–75.
Trotter, D., 'Bridging the Gap: The (Socio)linguistic Evidence of Some Medieval English Bridge Accounts', in *The Anglo-Norman Language and its Contexts*, ed. R. Ingham (York, 2010), pp. 52–62.
Tudor, P., 'Religious Instruction for Children and Adolescents in the Early English Reformation', *Journal of Ecclesiastical History* 35 (1984), 391–413.
Turner, D., 'Conduct and Politeness in the Early Modern Period', in *Defining Gender: 1450–1910, Five Centuries of Advice Literature Online* (Adam Matthew Publications, 2003).
Turville-Petre, T., 'Some Medieval English Manuscripts in the North-East Midlands', in *Manuscripts and Readers in Fifteenth-Century England: the Literary Implications of Manuscript Study*, ed. D. Pearsall (Cambridge, 1983), pp. 125–41
Udry, S., 'Robert de Blois and Geoffroy de la Tour Landry on Feminine Beauty: Two Late Medieval French Conduct Books for Women', *Essays in Medieval Studies* 19 (2002), 90–102.
Vaughan, M. F., 'An Unnoted Translation of Erasmus in Ascham's "Schoolmaster"', *Modern Philology* 75 (1977), 184–6.
Volk-Birke, S., *Chaucer and Medieval Preaching: Rhetoric for Listeners in Sermons and Poetry* (Tübingen, 1991).
Voss, P. J., 'Books for Sale: Advertising and Patronage in Late Elizabethan England', *Sixteenth Century Journal* 29 (1998), 733–56.
Wakelin, D., *Humanism, Reading, and English Literature, 1430–1530* (New York, 2007).
Wall, B., *The Narrator's Voice: The Dilemma of Children's Fiction* (New York, 1991).

Walsham, A., '"Domme Preachers"? Post-Reformation English Catholicism and the Culture of Print', *Past and Present* 168 (2000), 72–123.

Wang, Y., 'Caxton's Romances and Their Early Tudor Readers', *Huntington Library Quarterly* 67 (2004), 173–88.

Warner, J., 'Historical Perspectives on the Shifting Boundaries around Youth and Alcohol: The Example of Pre-Industrial England, 1350–1750', *Addiction* 93 (1998), 641–57.

Watson, F., *Vives and the Renascence Education of Women* (London, 1912).

Watts, J., '*De Consulatu Stiliconis*: Texts and Politics in the Reign of Henry VI', *Journal of Medieval History* 16 (1990), 251–66.

Weinberg, S. C., 'Caxton, Anthony Woodville, and the Prologue to the *Morte Darthur*', *Studies in Philology* 102 (2005), 45–65.

Weiss, A., 'Casting Compositors, Foul Cases, and Skeletons: Printing in Middleton's Age', in *Thomas Middleton and Early Modern Textual Culture: A Companion to the Collected Works*, ed. G. Taylor and J. Lavagnino (Oxford, 2007), pp. 195–225.

Weiss, J., 'The Power and Weakness of Women in Anglo-Norman Romance', in *Women and Literature in Britain, 1150–1500*, ed. C. M. Meale (Cambridge, 1993), pp. 7–23.

Wells, S., 'Manners Maketh Man: Living, Dining and Becoming a Man in the Later Middle Ages', in *Rites of Passage: Cultures of Transition in the Fourteenth Century*, ed. N. F. McDonald and W. M. Ormrod (York, 2004), pp. 67–81.

West, W. N., 'Old News, Caxton, de Worde, and the Invention of the Edition', in *Caxton's Trace: Studies in the History of English Printing*, ed. by W. Kuskin (Notre Dame, 2006), pp. 241–74.

Williams, G., 'The Dissolution of the Monasteries', in *The Agrarian History of England and Wales: Volume 4, 1500–1640*, ed. J. Thirsk (Cambridge, 1967), 383–7.

Wilmot, D., *A Short History of the Grammar School, Macclesfield, 1503–1910* (Macclesfield, 1910).

Wilson, A., 'The Infancy of the History of Childhood: An Appraisal of Philippe Ariès', *History and Theory* 19 (1980), 132–53.

Winston, J., '*A Mirror for Magistrates* and Public Political Discourse in Elizabethan England', *Studies in Philology* 101 (2004), 381–400.

Wogan-Browne, J., et al., eds. *Language and Culture in Medieval Britain: The French of England c. 1100–c. 1500* (York, 2009).

Wogan-Browne, J., *Saints' Lives and Women's Literary Culture: Virginity and its Authorizations* (Oxford, 2001).

Wooden, W., *Children's Literature of the English Renaissance, Edited, with an Introduction, by Jeanie Watson* (Lexington, 1986).

Woolgar, C. M., 'Fast and Feast: Conspicuous Consumption and the Diet of the Nobility in the Fifteenth Century', in *Revolution and Consumption in Late Medieval England*, ed. M. A. Hicks (Woodbridge, 2001), pp. 7–26.

Woolgar, C. M., 'Food and the Middle Ages', *Journal of Medieval History* 36 (2010), 1–19.

Woolgar, C. M., *Household Accounts from Medieval England*, 2 vols. (Oxford, 1992–3).

Woolgar, C. M., *The Great Household in Late Medieval England* (New Haven, 1999).

Wrightson, K., and D. Levine, *Poverty and Piety in an English Village: Terling, 1525–1700*, rev. edn (Oxford, 1995).

Youings, J., *The Dissolution of the Monasteries* (London, 1971).

INDEX

Ages   11–12, 16, 36–7, 38, 39, 47–9, 53, 60, 88, 96–7, 124–5, 148, 153, 154, 175–6, 183
  definitions of   2, 48, 96, 132–3
  delaying adolescence   53–4, 118, 143
Alehouses   63–4, 117, 172, 179, *see also* taverns
Apprentices   52–4, 56–7, 63, 112, 119, 144 n.75, 159, 169, 190
Ascham, Roger   168

Book of Curtesye (Caxton, William)   15 n.11, 27 n.58, 56, 64 n.87, 80, 82, 83 n.13, 88, 90, 95–105, 111, 127
Book of Good Manners   19, 80, 85, 120–25, 137, 196
Book of the Knight of the Tower   5, 62, 66, 79, 80, 106–12, 114 n.127, 135, 137, 197
Boy-bishop sermon   167, 170–1, 177, 193
Boys, socialisation of   5, 11–57, 68, 71, 72–8, 89–92, 95–105, 112–26, 127, 142–58, 159–93, 194–99, *see also* Clothing, Boys; Meekness, for boys
  behaviour   32, 68, 99–100, 101–3, 117, 142, 145–7, 164–5, 176, 188
  elite   11–34, 154–7, 168, 194
  independence   17, 115, 118–19, 142, 171
  masculinity   13, 18, 20–1,
  merchant   13, 21, 41, 49–54, 105, 116–18, 165, 175, 195, 197
  misbehaviour   24, 76–7, 124, 163, 166–7, 170–2
  morality   27–34, 64, 65, 76–8, 89–92, 93–105, 114–18, 121–22, 128, 143, 146–8, 155–58, 165, 166, 168, 181, 192, 194, 196–9
  status   32, 48, 71 n.123, 99

Catechism   150 n.92, 153, 173, 185
Catholic books   55, 135, 136–7, 150–54
Caton   80, 85, 92, 112–20, 122, 125, 196
Caxton, William   5, 7–8, 19, 56, 79–126, 129, 141, 195–8, *see also* Merchants, Printing
  audience   79, 81–7, 92, 97, 99, 104–5, 105–7, 123, 125–6, 195
  instructional books   8, 15 n.11, 27 n.58, 64 n.87, 80–126, 127
  patronage   85–7, 105–6, 114, 120–1
  prologues   80, 85–6, 95, 106–8, 112–16, 120–1, 123
  translator   85
Chaucer, Geoffrey   11, 13, 20–1, 41, 42, 100, 199
Chivalry   17, 21, 29, 31, 36, 37, 45, 77, 86, 123, 154, 156–7
Churl   24–5, 42, 77, 91, 98, 156, 195
Clothing   48–9, 63 n.82, 75, 101–4, 188, 192
  boys   74–5, 101–4, 111, 167–9
  girls   62, 68–9, 71, 103, 110–11
  sumptuary legislation   49, 75, 104
Community, attitudes of   62, 65–6, 69–72, 93, 135, 153–4, 177–85
Conduct literature   80, 131
Coote, Edmund   171, 173 n.52, 176, 190
Courtesy   11–42, 46–78, 88–92, 95–105, 112–25, 140–3, 145–9, 154, 156–7, 159, 161, 163, 164–6, 170–4, 176, 187–9, 192, 194–9, *see also* Courtesy poems
  audience   28
  awareness of others   18, 146
  conservative nature of   5, 13, 22, 90–1, 100, 110, 116, 148, 197–8
  definition   4, 13, 27–34, 101
  moderation   26, 27, 90, 117–18, 146, 176
  monastic background   29
  negative connotations   75, 100–4, 146–7, 154–8, 196
  self-serving   18–20, 26, 35–6, 98–9, 101, 156–7
Courtesy poems   2, 3, 6–7, 11–42, 46–78, 79, 84, 86, 87–90, 95–105, 108, 111, 141–9, 159, 165, 194–9, *see also* Courtesy

265

Index

audience 7, 11–13, 34, 35, 39, 42, 46–54, 59–61, 72–4, 78, 87–9, 194–5
  female audience 59–61, 71
definition of 6, 80
first-person narrative 15–17
How the Good Wife Taught her Daughter 5, 7, 14, 31, 46, 58–72, 75, 95, 110, 111, 120, 135, 137, 139–40, 197
How the Wise Man Taught his Son 2, 6, 13, 14, 20, 47–8, 128
Idley, Peter, *Instructions to his Son* 7, 14, 20, 46, 59, 72–7, 115–16, 128, 137
manuscript variations 7, 44–57, 64–9
movement away from elite reading networks 7, 13, 26, 28, 35–6, 39, 41, 43–72, 72–8, 85–7, 99, 104–5, 125, 145, 195
ownership 11, 13, 46, 54, 55, 57, 87, 195
parental metaphor 14, 58–60, 128
Russell, John, *Boke of Nurture* 6, 16, 25, 33, 34–41, 59, 145
Stans puer ad mensam 6–7, 10, 13, 15, 18–19, 21–4, 27 n.58, 31, 38, 41–2, 67, 87–9, 96, 127, 141, 142, 147, 171, 195
  MS Ashmole 61 7, 16, 19 n.24, 46–54, 57, 74, 92
  MS Lambeth 853 18–19, 21, 22 n.45, 24
The Babees Book 6, 13, 24–5, 27 n.58, 33, 41–2
the boke of curtasye 6, 13, 15, 19, 23, 27 n.59, 34–41, 62, 67, 97, 115
The Good Wyfe Wold a Pylgremage 7, 14, 31, 46, 58–72, 75, 95, 110, 111, 120, 135, 137, 139–140, 197
The Lytylle Childrene's Book 6, 7, 13, 25, 27 n.59, 32, 33, 42, 50, 54–7, 115–16
The Thewis of Gud Women 7, 46, 58–72, 95, 110, 111, 120, 135, 137, 139–40, 197
The Young Children's Book 7, 17, 25 n.54, 47, 50–4
themes 6, 14–26, 34, 35, 38, 60, 74, 76–8, 97, 103, 118, 176, 195
Urbanitatis 6, 13, 16–17, 20, 27 n.59, 31, 38, 42, 127

de Worde, Wynken 56, 84, 86 n.22, 88, 101 n.75, 121, 187, 190
Dining *see* Eating
Dress *see* Clothing

Eating 5, 6, 13, 23, 26, 31–2, 36, 51, 54, 57, 90, 159, 165, 176
  elite households 22, 41–2, 51, 117, 122, 156–7
  changes in 22, 39
  manners 21–2, 24–5, 32, 99
  non-elite households 57, 117, 143, 145–6
Education 3, 9, 53–4, 56, 70, 113, 152–3, 159–93, *see also* Schools, Literacy
  arithmetic 56, 169, 190
  books, non-grammar 152, 168, 171, 173, 174, 175–6, 184, 186–7, 190–1
  boys 52–4, 144–5, 159–93, 198–9
  girls 128, 133–5, 139, 164, 183–4, 191, 199
  in households 133, 164, 182–4, 199
  social education 25, 44, 71, 95
Elyot, Thomas, Sir 168, 180
Erasmus, Desiderius 1, 27–28 n.61, 178, 191–2, 199
Etiquette 20, 28, 30 n.71, 101, 148–9

Family 3, 14, 45–6, 70–1, 112, 113, 118–19, 124–5, 128–30, 137–40, 142–4, 149–54, 157–8, 159–60, 174–6, 187–8, 195
  definitions 112
  family coats of arms 104
  family's financial well-being 169
  fathers 12, 20, 73–7, 110, 114, 119, 122–3, 133, 156, 173, 192, 196
    authority of 8, 14–15, 49, 118–20, 125, 129, 142–4, 151–2, 158, 162, 163, 174–6, 188, 192, 198
    father-son relationships 6, 14, 74
  mothers 14, 58–61, 62, 71, 113, 125, 129, 131–3, 142–4, 156, 163–4, 175–6, 183, 188, 198
  reading audience 44, 46–54, 55–7, 59–60, 78, 80, 85–9, 112–26, 127–31, 137, 142, 147–8, 149–54, 157–8, 159–60, 175–6, 190–1, 196, 198
  roles 57, 137–40, 144
Fiston, William *see* Phiston, William
Food *see* Eating
Fostering 2–3, 12, 44, 54, 57, 60, 137–40,

266

Index

142, 194, *see also* Venetian traveller, Households
French language 3–4, 25, 29, 41, 45, 56–7, 106, 110, 114, 120, 121
  French romances 109
  study of French 55–6, 133, 164

Girls, socialisation of 5, 7, 9, 14, 46, 48, 58–72, 78, 95, 105–12, 127–40, 158, 164, 170, 184, 191, 196–9
  misbehaviour 62–3, 135, 139, 171
  morality 58, 61–8, 71–2, 80, 108–12, 127, 128, 131–40, 158, 196–7
    chastity 58, 66, 109–10, 131, 133, 139, 197
  self-control 66, 109, 135
Grammar books 11, 187–91
Grosseteste, Robert, Bishop of Lincoln 31, 195

Hierarchy 3, 13, 18, 26, 42, 49, 69, 91–2, 98, 110, 118–19, 129, 147
  in courtesy poems 23–5, 48, 69, 75, 91–2, 98, 116–17
  in households 23–5, 162
Hill, Richard 47–8, 55–7, 74, 87–8, 89, 98 n.64, 195
Hospitality 34–8, 43, 73, 122, 155–7, 195
Household books *see under* Family, reading audience
Households 1–9, 109, 115, 127, 130–58, 159–60, 161, 164, 169, 170, 171, 172–6, 183, 184, 186, 188, 189, 190, 192, 193, *see also* Fostering
  elite 3, 5, 11–42, 71, 73, 98, 99, 107, 112, 117, 125, 128, 137–8, 141, 155, 162, 180, 194, 195, 196, 199
  employment 34–6, 40–1
  physical spaces 22
  roles in 6, 15, 16, 23, 25, 36, 38, 48
  size of 35 n.81, 39
  structure 11–12, 22, 35, 41, 43–4, 58
  emotions 2, 5, 40, 112
  household estate books 5, 105
  non-elite households 7, 45–6, 51–2, 57–72, 72–8, 112–13, 117, 118–20, 125–6, 128–30, 137–40, 140–5, 147, 163, 198
Household miscellany 46–57, 87–9, 98 n.64

How the Good Wife Taught her Daughter see Courtesy poems
How the Wise Man Taught his Son see Courtesy poems
Humanism 56, 134, 149 n.89, 160, 189, 191
  Erasmus's humanist background 28 n.61
Hyrde, Richard 5, 9, 130, *see also* Vives, Juan Luis

Idley, Peter 72–3, *see also* Courtesy poems, Idley
Individual schools *see also* Schools
  Dame Alice Owen's School (Middlesex) 168–70, 179
  Dame Elizabeth Periam's School (Oxfordshire) 169
  Guildford Grammar School (Surrey) 163, 165–6, 178
  Macclesfield (Cheshire) 159, 164
  Rivington Grammar School (Lancashire) 163, 168, 172–5, 178–9, 185
  Sherborne Grammar School (Dorset) 168, 172, 174–5, 185
  St Albans (Hertfordshire) 159, 164–5, 171–2
  Westminster 167–8, 169
Infancy 2, 19, 96, 124, 131–3, 154, 191–2

Kempe, William 175–6, 190–1

la Tour Landry, Geoffrey de., *see Book of the Knight of the Tower*
Literacy 53, 133–4, 149–50, 152–4, 160, 170, 186, 195
  boys 100
  girls 133–4
London 7, 43, 70, 79, 104, 112–14, 119–20, 155–6, 190
  books 7, 79, 104–5, 112–15, 119–21, 187
  guilds 53, 113, 120
  merchants 45, 85, 92, 104–5, 112–15, 120–1
Lydgate, John 41, 47, 57, 73 n.130, 96, 100

Manners *see* Courtesy
Markets
  behaviour of girls 59, 63, 197

Index

Marriage 14, 48, 61–2, 65, 71, 91–2, 108–10, 132, 136, 197
Meekness 13, 18–21, 31, 124, 194
   for boys 19–21, 42, 67, 75
   for girls 20–1, 67–8, 131
Merchants 3, 7, 12, 28, 76–8, 128, 133, 140–1, 155–6, 159, 161, 165, 190, 196, *see under* London
   audience 12, 13, 26, 28, 41, 44–72, 75, 85–7, 93–5, 99, 104–5, 109–10, 112–26, 129, 145, 195
   behaviour 41, 45, 50, 104, 122, 131, 140, 197
   reputation 45, 50–2, 103–5, 114
   texts associated with 23, 47–58, 86–7, 120–1, 175, 190
   wives 61, 63
Morality 3, 7, 42, 45, 52, 65, 68, 74, 76–8, 79–80, 89–92, 93–4, 95, 97–119, 123, 125–6, 127–8, 131–42, 145, 148–9, 154–5, 158, 159–60, 166, 168, 177–85, 189, 192, 194–9, *see under* Boys, socialisation of; Girls, socialisation of; Virtue
   definitions 27–34
   moral reform 76, 93–4, 146–7, 154–8
Mulcaster, Richard 191

Parvus Cato 80, 82, 83 n.13, 89–92, 98, 101–2, 127
Pastons 67 n.102, 135–6, 140 n.59
Phiston, William 5, 9, 128, 136–40, 174, 198
Politics 2, 17, 26, 36–7, 43, 58, 76–7, 80, 85–6, 92–5, 104, 113–14, 123–4, 126, 127, 137, 141, 150, 181, 194, 195, 197–8
   political networks 14, 185
Poll taxes 5, 60, 63
Printing 79–126, 127–30, 136, 141, 145, 150, 186–91, 195–6, *see also* Caxton, William
   languages 4
   national identity 4, 93–5, 123, 136–7
   price 86, 129, 157, 188
   relationship to manuscripts 8, 81–4, 87–9, 90–2, 95–9, 195–6
   Sammelbände 82–3
   technological advances 7–8, 81, 87–9, 126, 129, 196
   woodcuts 88

Reformation 127, 136–7, 140, 150, 153, 160, 180–5, 193, 198, *see also* Catholic books, Religion
Religion 1–2, 6, 20, 26, 29, 36, 90, 127–8, 136–7, 140, 148, 173, 180–85, 188, 198, *see also* Catholic books, Reformation
   socialisation 8, 9, 19, 20, 31–4, 61–2, 72, 75–6, 87, 97, 115–16, 118–19, 121–2, 124–5, 143, 146–8, 149–54, 158, 160, 166, 172–3, 181, 185, 186–7, 192, 194
Rhodes, Hugh 9, 127, 137, 141–9, 150, 197–8
Russell, John, *Boke of Nurture* 13, 38, 195

Salter, Thomas 5, 9, 128, 136–40, 156, 198,
Schools 1, 9, 52–4, 144–5, 153, 155 n.115, 158, 159–93, 194, 198–9, *see also* Education, Individual schools, Grammar books
   behaviour in 164–76
   courtesy 161–3, 165–7, 170–4
   curriculum 56, 134, 159, 161, 166
   elementary schools 133, 161, 164, 168–70, 173, 183–5, 190–1
   governors 162, 168, 174–5, 179–80
   grammar schools 159–69, 171–76, 177–82, 185, 187, 189, 191
   licences 164, 180–85, 193
   moral lessons 52, 134, 159–60, 166, 174, 179, 181, 184
   physical space 162–3, 169
   scholars 52, 153, 182, 190, 199
      elementary scholars 168–71, 183–5
      grammar scholars 159, 161, 162, 163, 164–8, 170–6, 177–8, 181, 187–9, 191, 192
   schoolmaster 153, 156, 160, 161, 162, 165, 166, 167, 168–9, 171, 173–6, 177–85, 191
      reputation 156, 177–85
   socialising 134, 159–82, 185–93, 198–9
   statutes 9, 56, 135 n.32, 161, 163–74, 177–80, 182, 185, 192
   women teachers 183–4
Scribal authority 7, 41, 45, 46–57, 82, 96
Seager, Francis 9, 141–2, 145, 147–9, 150, 170–1, 197–8

Index

Self-discipline *see also* Girls, socialisation of, self-control
  for adults   18, 118, 151, 177–80
  for young people   15–17, 42, 66, 109, 118–19, 124–5
Servants   6, 54, 57, 112, 115, 117, 118, 119, 122, 129, 130, 139, 148, 152, 157, 159, 162, *see also* Fostering; Households
  boys   11–26, 34–6, 38–41
  child-exchange   11–12, 14
  elite households   11–12, 98–100, 107, 112, 141, 171, 196
    status   12, 20, 23, 35, 43–4, 48, 50, 99
  girls   41, 60–72, 107, 139–40
  non-elite households   60–72, 112, 120, 135, 141–3, 145, 197
Shelford, Robert   9, 143–4, 146–8, 153, 154, 174, 198
Social class   3, 11–12, 25, 30, 35, 45, 70, 72, 73, 78, 86, 91, 92, 94, 98, 101, 110, 127, 145, 156, 191, 194, 197, *see also* Merchants
  bourgeois class   62, 99, 104
  elite class   154, 155, 161, 162
  gentry class   11–14, 17, 26, 28, 41–2, 43–4, 46, 52–4, 72–8, 85–7, 92–4, 104–5, 131, 134, 140–1, 145, 154–6, 161, 167–8
  middling class   17, 59, 71, 125, 146, 164, 168, 184, 198
  mobility   2, 3, 24, 28, 39, 41, 60, 69, 71, 74, 91–2, 99, 104, 116, 140–1, 155–6, 161

Stans puer ad mensam (Caxton, William)   56, 80, 82–3, 87–9
Streets, behaviour in   19, 22–23, 49, 59, 63, 65, 142, 170–2
Sumptuary legislation *see* Clothing

taverns   59, 63, 75, 117, 120, 172
The Good Wife Wold a Pylgremage see Courtesy poems
The Instruction of a Christen Woman see Vives, Juan Luis
The Thewis of Gud Women see Courtesy poems

Vaughan, William   9, 154–7, 159, 198
Venetian traveller   2–3, 138, 194
Virtue   9, 27–34, 36, 45, 52, 57, 74, 78, 79–126, 134, 139, 146–9, 154–8, 159, 160, 161, 164, 168, 174, 177, 181, 184, 188, 191–2, 196–9, *see under* Morality
Vives, Juan Luis   5, 9, 128, 130–6, 138 n.50, 154, 197–8

Wars of the Roses   77, 80, 92, 198
Whitford, Richard   9, 150–4, 198
Women   58–72, 105–12, 130, 131–2, 138–9, 140, 172, 183, 184, 197, *see also* Girls, Family
  young women   5, 46, 80, 133, 134, 135

Youth *see* Ages

www.ingramcontent.com/pod-product-compliance
Lightning Source LLC
Chambersburg PA
CBHW051606230426
43668CB00013B/2003